Your God-Given Task

Your God-Given Task

WHAT DID GOD PUT IN YOU DURING CREATION?

*KNOWING YOUR PURPOSE ON EARTH
AND HOW TO ACCOMPLISH IT SUCCESSFULLY*

Gift Zawadi

© 2016 Gift Zawadi
All rights reserved.

For ministry bookings or testimonies:
E-mail: gzawadi3@gmail.com
Website: gzawadi.wixsite.com/gift
Text or WhatsApp to: 404-510-2512

ISBN: 069262032X
ISBN 13: 9780692620328

All scripture is from the New King James Version (NKJV) unless otherwise noted. Scripture taken from the New King James Version®. Copyright © 1982 by Thomas Nelson. Used by permission. All rights reserved.
Scripture quotations marked (WEB) are from the World English Bible Version of the bible.
Scripture quotations marked (KJV) are from King James Version of the bible.
Scripture quotations marked (NLT) are taken from the Holy Bible, New Living Translation, copyright © 1996, 2004, 2007 by Tyndale House Foundation. Used by permission of Tyndale House Publishers, Inc., Carol Stream, Illinois 60188. All rights reserved.
Scripture quotations marked (AMP) are taken from the Amplified Bible, Copyright © 1954, 1958, 1962, 1964, 1965, 1987 by The Lockman Foundation. Used by permission.
Scripture quotations marked (NIV) are taken from the Holy Bible, New International Version®, NIV®. Copyright © 1973, 1978, 1984, 2011 by Biblica, Inc.™ Used by permission of Zondervan. All rights reserved worldwide.
Scripture quotations marked (WE) are taken from THE JESUS BOOK - The Bible in Worldwide English. Copyright SOON Educational Publications, Derby DE65 6BN, UK. Used by permission.
Scripture taken from The Expanded Bible. Copyright ©2011 by Thomas Nelson. Used by permission. All rights reserved. Scripture taken from *The Message*. Copyright © 1993, 1994, 1995, 1996, 2000, 2001, 2002. Used by permission of NavPress Publishing Group.

Endorsements

"Your God-Given task" is such a delightful read and a call to action. It is a MUST read for all flock including shepherds. This book is a gift from God to all mankind in this generation. It equips us to live a full life as God intended it from the beginning. As Jeremiah 33:3 says, "'Call to Me, and I will answer you, and show you great and mighty things, which you do not know.'"- I believe with all my heart that this scripture is being fulfilled to anyone who will invest their time in reading the wisdom and knowledge that God has poured out through His servant in this book. Indeed, Jeremiah 33:14 continues to say that "'Behold, the days are coming,' says the Lord, 'that I will perform that good thing which I have promised to the house of Israel and to the house of Judah:" This promise is unfolding in this generation through this book. I thank God for authoring this book through His beautiful servant Zawadi whom I am favored and extravagantly blessed to have as my wife. Zawadi's dedication to a life of faith has always challenged me to do more. It is my sincere hope that through this book, many more will be challenged to begin their God-given assignment as I have been. Honey, it is my prayer that God will continue to feed His children through you now and always. I love you.
- Isaac Kiriga

"Your God-Given Task" is a beautiful work of art that enriches the lives of believers. The scripture-based message speaks wisdom and strength

to the heart. Not only are the chapters encouraging, but they are challenging. They offer thought-provoking questions, leaving the reader aware of, equipped for, and ready to embark on the path so wonderfully created for their individual strengths by the Heavenly Father. It reaches every maturity level of believer as it clearly spells out the Gospel message and demonstrates the steps to a full, rich, and healthy relationship with God the Father, Jesus Christ and the Holy Spirit. It is a call to action just like in Romans 12:1b (New International Version (NIV)), "offer your bodies as a living sacrifice, holy and pleasing to God. This is your true and proper worship."
-Kimberly Craig

Gift is a true gift from God and I am blessed to know her. She has given herself to be a vessel for God's Glory and Kingdom. Through her, God has revealed so much in my life. Her testimony and wisdom have strengthened my prayer life, saved my marriage, encouraged my motherhood, and motivated me as a woman to carefully listen and be obedient to the Holy Spirit. It has taught me to nurture the seeds planted by God that I did not even know existed. I had so much of the same head knowledge we all share but was unable to truly live out the plans God had for me. Today I am still growing in God and learning how to live each day with purpose for HIS glory. I pray this book will inspire, encourage and speak to those who are unknowing of the amazing wonderful God we have, to those who are unknowing of what God desires for them, and those seeking to grow in their relationship with God.
-Yvonne V Cabera- Perez

My Sister in Christ, Zawadi is a jewel, very precious in the sight of God. She is adorned by many for her faithful service to God. Her love for Jesus is a bright light that shines in the darkest places. A light that leads the dark to our Lord and Savior. Her life is a living testimony of her obedience to God's kingdom. I will forever be thankful and grateful to call her my sister and my friend. Thank you for beginning the bible

study that has changed many lives. Through Zawadi, I have learned to be a doer of the Word of God and not just a hearer. My relationship with Christ has deepened and my marriage strengthened because of her ministry. "Your God-Given task" will change many lives, lead you to Jesus if you don't know Him, strengthen your relationship with Him if you know Him, and lead you into knowing Him personally if you only know about Him. It will challenge and provoke you to go to the next level of intimacy with God and equip you to live a purposeful life. The life you were created to live. Your life will never be the same again.
-Regina Chapman

Acknowledgements

My deepest appreciation to…
Yahweh, thank you heavenly Father for Your love, for Your Son Jesus Christ and Your Holy Spirit; for all You have done, are doing and will do. To Jesus Christ, the author and finisher of our faith! Thank you for Your great sacrifice, dying for me and rising up again making it possible for me to be called a child of God and Your bride. Thank you Holy Spirit for inspiring, revealing and teaching me God's ways and truths and my God-given task. Continue to help me fulfill it all in Jesus's name. There is none greater than You my Lord, my GOD. Thank you for writing this book through me, You truly use the weak things of this world to confound the strong as in 1 Corinthians 1:27. I am all Yours LORD JESUS! Use me for Your glory.

Isaac, the priest of our home, my best friend, husband and confidant. I not only want to spend my lifetime with you here on earth, I look forward to spending eternity with you. I'm grateful for your abundant love, encouragement and constant cheer along the way. Your constant, powerful prayers for our family have held us together and hidden us in Christ in God. I am so blessed to be married to a God-loving, God-fearing man. I Thank God so much for you my love and pray that you will live to fulfill all your God-given task on earth in Jesus's name!

Trevor, son, your love and sensitivity is so much appreciated. Thanks for keeping me company when I had to write till late in the night. I treasure your encouragement and hugs, you are truly a great joy Son! Thanks for setting a great example for your brothers and friends. Keep loving God and live your life to the fullness of what you were created to be in Jesus's name. There is greatness in you!

Tevin, son, what a sweet and gentle spirit you have. You are big and tall for your age yet so tender and loving. Thank you for always being ready to serve. Your heart of a servant reminds me of Christ. We are proud of you for being the son that you are. You are a great example to others. Keep loving God and live your life to the fullness of what you were created to be in Jesus name. There is greatness in you!

Amani, Son, you are one of a kind! You are peaceful just as your name means, very loving and genuine in all you do. I admire your passion and zeal in what you set your mind to do. You stand up and stand out for God regardless of what people say. Thanks for making Jesus proud! I know that God has placed His greatness in you and I pray that as you grow up you will discover this and live to the fullness of what God created you to be in Jesus's name.

My grand-parents, thanks for teaching my parents and I the ways of God, through you, many generations will be blessed. For those who are still alive, may you live long to fulfill your God-given task successfully in Jesus's name.

My parents, Mr. K.J. Mbugua and Reverend Priscilla K.J. Thanks for teaching me about the one true God and leading me to my heavenly Father. I am so glad God picked you for my parents. There was no better choice. I love you both abundantly and pray that you will fulfill your God-given task successfully in Jesus's name.

My siblings, my brother Godwin and sisters Anne, Pendo and Blessing. I would never have asked for better siblings. You are a great blessing in my life. I love you and pray that you will fulfill all your God-given tasks in Jesus's name.

My enemies, thank you for challenging me and pushing me to the next level of prayer and intimacy with God through your attacks. I love you and I pray for you to know Christ intimately and to fulfill your God-given task successfully in Jesus name. My extended family, friends, acquaintances and strangers who have blessed my life and those that have been blessed through my life; I love you all and I pray that your passion for Christ will be ignited and will increase. I pray that you will fulfill your God-given purpose on earth in Jesus's name!

Special Thanks to…

Mr. Isaac Kiriga, Mrs. Kimberly Craig, Mrs. Andrea Clemens and all professional editors for their assistance with editing. I am forever grateful. Many lives will be changed through your selfless contributions. May God bless you and your families and enlarge your territories. You have invested in eternity and your reward is great.

"…and he who is wise captures *and* wins souls [for God—he gathers them for eternity]." (Proverbs 11:30b Amplified)

Dedication

I dedicate this book to…..

*God the Father, God the Son and God the Holy Spirit.
Because of Your Agape Love for all humanity this book is written.
You created our assignments before you created us,
Yet most of us still wander in confusion as to why we are here on earth.
Thank you for Your love which has called upon the writing of this book.
Your inspiration and Grace has birthed it.
I thank you for this book and many more to come.
May we hunger and thirst after You.
Help us to seek and understand what Your will is.
May we be doers of Your word and not just hearers.
Place a great urgency in our hearts to do Your will.
Use us for Your glory and Help us to number our days,
That we may, like David said in Psalm 90:12, 'gain a heart of wisdom' to do
YOUR PERFECT WILL in Jesus's holy, mighty, magnificent, powerful and
precious name. Amen!*

Foreword

IT IS WITH GREAT PLEASURE that I introduce to you this new author and her premier work entitled "Your God-given Task". Her name is Gift Zawadi, but I know her as "Esther". We share the same church family and God drew me to her one Sunday morning during our time of worship. As we stood together, with hearts full of praise, I sensed the Spirit of God stirring in me; urging me to get to know this beautiful worshipper of Jesus beside me!

Over the course of a few months, we have had many "divine appointments" that have brought us together as friends and spiritual encouragers. I can tell you this . . . The Spirit of God communicates through her. THAT'S WHY I am so excited to have her insight in written form! Esther has been given a gift to illustrate the scriptures. Her writing style reminds me of The Apostle Paul. She relentlessly and sacrificially proclaims the Gospel truth of Christ AND she is passionate about helping us know how God has equipped all of us to do the same! She teaches us from the Word of God that we each have a unique, God-given assignment to accomplish this side of Heaven.

Have you ever asked the question . . . What am I here on this earth for? What is the meaning of life? Philosophers have been asking this question for centuries. The answers to all of life's "big questions" can be found in God's Word and Esther brings the Word to light through her teaching in this book. She gives us a Biblical view of our role in God's plan . . . His "Big Picture" . . . His "Portrait". We learn that AGAPE love is the driving force behind all that God has done, is doing and will do and we must follow His example to love Him and love others in the same way!

She also shares her own spiritual triumphs and failures with great humility. Being a native of Kenya, and now living in the United States, Esther has a world-view that is very broad, which allows her to share truth in an un-biased and direct way. I guarantee that God will directly challenge you through His Word (and hers) to seek His truth for yourself as she shares her journey of faith and deep spiritual awakening.

Occasionally, throughout the book, Esther includes prayers. As I would pray her prayers to God, it gave me a sense that she and I, together, were going before the Lord. I appreciated that greatly as I remembered a verse that encourages me, "For where two or three are gathered together in My name, I am there in the midst of them." Matthew 18:20.

No doubt, whether you already know your God-Given Task or not, you will take away a new and fresh perspective on who we are and Who's we are!

Andrea Clemens, B.S. in Music Education & Bible.
Wife of Pastor Dan Clemens, Discovery Christian Church,
Moreno Valley CA.

Contents

Endorsements ·v
Acknowledgements · ix
Dedication · xiii
Foreword ·xv
Introduction · xix

Chapter 1	The God-Given Task · · · · · · · · · · · · · · · · · ·	1
Chapter 2	Who Are We? ·	9
Chapter 3	Carry Your Cross and Follow Jesus · · · · · · · · · · · · · · · · ·	·29
Chapter 4	The Wilderness and the appointed time · · · · · · · · · · ·	·39
Chapter 5	Message ·	·52
Chapter 6	Salvation ·	·75
Chapter 7	The Helper, the Holy Spirit · · · · · · · · · · · · · · ·	87
Chapter 8	Sins against the Holy Spirit · · · · · · · · · · · · · · ·	·126
Chapter 9	Relationship or Religion? · · · · · · · · · · · · · · · · ·	·142
Chapter 10	The Prayer ·	·160
Chapter 11	Obedience and the Fear of God · · · · · · · · · · · · ·	·172
Chapter 12	Faith ·	·196
Chapter 13	Your Script ·	·218
Chapter 14	Whom Do You Live For? · · · · · · · · · · · · · · · · ·	246
Chapter 15	The Enemy ·	·258

Chapter 16	How to Stay on Task	284
Chapter 17	Challenges	329
Chapter 18	True Worship and Final Prayer	372
	Final Prayer	393

Introduction

THIS BOOK WAS BIRTHED FROM my brokenness; when I got tired of "church as usual" and a deep desire of knowing God for who He really was burned within me. I used to know about God, I read about Him, I told others stories of Him, I sang to Him, lead others into praise and worship of Him, but I was still empty.

I knew about the God of Abraham, Isaac and Jacob, but I did not know the God of Zawadi. What about my God! People want to hear about what God is doing right now in my life and your life; His signs and wonders. Hebrews 13:8 tells me that 'Jesus Christ is the same yesterday, today and forever'. What is He doing in your life to change the world today? Can you perceive it? Can others see it?

I knew there was much more to God than religion. Jesus never endorsed religion when He walked on Earth and He still does not. Instead, He came to bring back RELATIONSHIP between us and God. This is what I lacked, RELATIONSHIP. I had religion, I had works of service in the church, I had a God whom I prayed to but never had any intimate relationship with Him. My prayer, I call it 'the prayer' shared in this book, in my brokenness started me on a journey and route I should have been travelling on since birth.

Beloved, we are all on a journey back to God, eternity where we came from, but the end point, eternal life or eternal death, is determined by which route you take. Have you ever driven for miles in the wrong direction and had to turn around? The feeling of not being sure where you are going and feeling lost is very frustrating. But when you find the right direction, and are sure that you are travelling on the right course, what a great and confident feeling you experience; a feeling of purpose and hope of a successful end.

Following Christ is a journey where many of us get lost from following traditions, habit, religion, our own understanding and the understanding of others. There is a right direction that we must follow to get to God. We must receive Jesus Christ as our LORD and Savior, and be totally and continually led by His Holy Spirit.

"Trust in Yahweh with all your heart, and don't lean on your own understanding. In all your ways acknowledge him, and he will make your paths straight." Proverbs 3:5-6 (World English Bible (WEB))

King Solomon said… "I have seen the God-given task with which the sons of men are to be occupied." (Ecclesiastes 3:10)

King Solomon, the wisest man who ever lived, was shown by God that people are supposed to be occupied with their God-given assignments. Are you occupied with your God-given assignment? Do you know what your God-given assignment is? If you do, then this book will help you learn how to carry it out successfully according to God's standards. If you don't, this book will help reveal how to know what your God-given assignment is and what you will need to accomplish it by God's standards; being successful like Christ.

CHAPTER 1
The God-Given Task

What profit has the worker from that in which he labors? *I have seen the God-given task with which the sons of men are to be occupied.* He has made everything beautiful in its time. Also He has put eternity in their hearts, except that no one can find out the work that God does from beginning to end. I know that nothing is better for them than to rejoice, and to do good in their lives, and also that every man should eat and drink and enjoy the good of all his labor—it is the gift of God. I know that whatever God does, it shall be forever. Nothing can be added to it, And nothing taken from it. God does it, that men should fear before Him. That which is has already been, and what is to be has already been; And God requires an account of what is past.

(ECCLES. 3:9–15; ITALICS ADDED)

"JESUS SAID TO THEM, "My food is to do the will of him who sent me, and to accomplish his work."" (John 4:34 WEB).

"Then the Lord answered me and said: "Write the vision and make it plain on tablets, that he may run who reads it. For the vision is yet for an appointed time; But at the end it will speak, and it will not lie. Though it tarries, wait for it; because it will surely come, it will not tarry. Behold the proud, His soul is not upright in him; but the just shall live by his faith" (Hab. 2:2–4).

Are you tired of being taken advantage of? Are people using your gifts, talents, skills, and potential to progress their agendas and business in order to make them successful and give you a little change while they make a fortune off you? At the end of the day, do you feel tired, used, and abused with no peace, joy, or satisfaction but only more pressure to please people who expect you to make them look good and increase their success? This pressure could be in what major to take in school, what career pays more, or what position has more prestige or more pay at work; or you could feel pressure even within your calling when you are in the wrong place or direction.

Are you just making a living instead of living the making? That is, living the life God made and created you to live? How do you rid yourself of all these pressures? How do you perform your God-given task successfully like Jesus did instead of the human-given task? Many are called, but few are chosen. They are "chosen" because they completed their tasks successfully and according to the given rules and instructions— in this case, according to God's commandments. Just like in drafting of sports players in athletics, *many are called to do it, but only the successful and hard workers, those who excel in the sport, are chosen.*

In this life of salvation, Christ came to call all sinners unto repentance, to save all, that WHOSOEVER believes in Him shall not perish but have everlasting life (John 3:16). By saying whosoever, God means everyone. Regardless of race, creed, color, or gender—any human being. No discrimination or partiality exists in Christ whatsoever. So many people come to Christ and receive Him in their hearts, but few live the life they were called to live. These few are the ones who will be chosen in the last day to spend eternity with Christ. These are the good and faithful servants. Jesus Himself taught this when He said;

""Enter in by the narrow gate; for wide is the gate and broad is the way that leads to destruction, and many are those who enter in by it. How narrow is the gate, and restricted is the way that leads to life! Few are those who find it." (Matt. 7:13–14 WEB).

For many are called, but few are chosen. Matthew 22:14

> Don't you realize that in a race everyone runs, but only one person gets the prize? So run to win! All athletes are disciplined in their training. They do it to win a prize that will fade away, but we do it for an eternal prize. So I run with purpose in every step. I am not just shadowboxing. I discipline my body like an athlete, training it to do what it should. Otherwise, I fear that after preaching to others I myself might be disqualified. (1 Cor. 9:24–27 New Living Translation (NLT))

All of us were created to do a specific, God-given task. When God created us, He did so with our assignment in mind. What do I mean? When you want to write, you use a pen or a pencil, not a cup; when you want to drink, you get a cup and not a pen, and both tools are not interchangeable. The pen and the cup can never and will never take the place of the other because each was made and equipped to work differently and satisfy different desires of the user. This means that if the cup broke or leaked, the pen cannot step in and be a cup, and if the pen broke, the cup would never be able to write as a pen. What does this tell us? There is no one competing with you in your God-given task. We were all created and equipped differently for the fellowship and service of our Creator.

Long before we were created, God had a desire and a plan to do something on earth. He could fulfill this task all by Himself, but He desired to partner and fellowship with people in His great plan. God created humans and equipped them for the specific tasks He wanted to accomplish through them, to satisfy His desires on earth for His Kingdom and His glory.

Just as a cup is not a cup for its own fulfillment but for the owner's fulfillment, and a pen is not a pen for its own fulfillment but for the writer's fulfillment and profit, we also were created to do our God-given task for God's fulfillment and not our own. Our God-given task is for the profit of the Kingdom of God. Just as writers will sharpen their pencils or ink their pens to equip them to properly work for their benefit, we are all fully equipped to accomplish our God-given task successfully, with ease and joy, by the grace of God and by His Holy Spirit.

Our God-given assignment is meant to please God the Father and bring Him glory. People cannot please God without being in Christ and without being led by His Holy Spirit. The God-given task is only fulfilled through God's power, not human power. For people to be successful, God has to be leading them and providing for them so that the "bigger than human," supernatural, God-given task can be performed.

A pen or pencil cannot be useful unless it is in a writer's hand and is controlled by the writer. It writes only when being used and it does not take any credit for the words written or the story given. Why? Because it did not have to think of the story line, the vocabulary, or the grammar. The only thing required of it was to yield to the writer. The pen moves as the writer moves, and it stops when the writer stops. The ink pen needs to be refilled often, but as long as it remains yielded to the writer's hand, it will continue to be useful to its master.

We too, just like the pen, have no business trying to alter the story or the plot that God has written for us. We should not try to correct it to suit our desires. We shouldn't worry about how the story will play out because it has already been perfectly written. The script that God has already written for you is meant to make Him great, and in turn He will honor you in the end for a job well done. You will be protected and cared for by the Master as long as you are in His will and plan. A writer gets glory from many people for a great story written. The people who read and enjoy the story never glorify the pen or the device used to write it down. Only the writer gets all the glory, and in his or her own way, glorifies the equipment he used. The God-given task, as you might have already figured out by now, is a task that only God can do through people and not one that people can do through God. People are tools in God's hands. The pen cannot use the writer to write the story, but the opposite is true.

Many people want to turn the tables around and use God to work out their agendas instead of letting God work out His agenda through them. Let us take an example. You buy a car to help you accomplish what you want to do. When you start the car, it starts OK, but when you want to back it up, it refuses and instead moves forward. When you step on the gas, it stops instead of moving. When you steer it right, it goes left. How successful will you be in accomplishing your tasks? You, the owner of this car, will get frustrated and stop trying to use it. You will definitely get another car that will do what it was created to do, obey your every command. Likewise, God is our owner and He works best with yielded vessels.

However, most of us receive Christ in our hearts, become born again, and instead of reporting to God and inquiring of Him as to what His desires are for us each day and each moment in time, we just show up in prayer to tell Him what we require of Him each day. We give Him assignments instead of going to receive assignments from Him. We tell Him what we plan on doing and tell Him to come along with our plan. We use Him to accomplish our agendas instead of the other way around. Just like a student giving the teacher an assignment instead of the student receiving an assignment from the teacher. We need to learn from Joshua in this text:

> And it came to pass, when Joshua was by Jericho, that he lifted his eyes and looked, and behold, a Man stood opposite him with His sword drawn in His hand. And Joshua went to Him and said to Him, "Are You for us or for our adversaries?" So He said, "No, but as Commander of the army of the Lord I have now come." And Joshua fell on his face to the earth and worshiped, and said to Him, "What does my Lord say to His servant?" Then the Commander of the Lord's army said to Joshua, "Take your sandal off your foot, for the place where you stand is holy." And Joshua did so. (Josh. 5:13–15)

Joshua asked the commander of God's army if He was for them or for their enemy, and his reply was neither; for God doesn't take sides. It is, therefore, entirely up to us to pick a side whether we are for God or against Him. As soon as Joshua realized this, look at how he reacted: He fell down and worshiped and asked God what He required of him. Joshua reported to duty, as we all should.

Many of us act as if we own God; as if we created Him for our use. We forget that we are not sovereign. Only God is sovereign. God can accomplish His task without us and can get someone else to take our place; just as the owner of the unyielding car will get another car that will yield to his commands and desire. Remember King Saul? He was rejected by God because of his rebellion and disobedience. And David, the shepherd boy, was chosen to take his place. God described David as "a man after His own heart". What does this mean? Being "a man or woman after God's own heart" means valuing what God values and desiring what He desires. It simply means living a life fully yielded to God through Jesus Christ, His Son. It means total submission and obedience to God.

What profit has the worker from that in which he labors? Ecclesiastes 3:9

For every labor to be successful, it must bring some profit. It must profit the laborer and the one he or she labors for. For example, I work as an RN in a hospital and get paid for the work I do, therefore I profit in that way from my labor. On the other hand, my employer profits from my services because he or she gets paid for the services I provide. The same is true in the spiritual realm. If you accept Jesus Christ as your Lord and Savior, and yield to Him; He rescues you from the bondage of slavery of Satan.

On the other hand, Satan makes you work for his profit only because sin has temporary pleasures, and the devil disguises himself in 2 Corinthians 11:14 as "the angel of light" so he can get you on his team. In the end, he will kill you. The Bible says, "The wages of sin is death, but the gift of God is eternal life through Jesus Christ our Lord" (Rom. 6:23). It also says, "The thief's purpose is to steal and kill and destroy. My purpose [God's purpose] is to give them a rich and satisfying life" (John 10:10 NLT).

According to the scriptures above, when we yield our lives to God, we have eternal life as our inheritance. In turn, God's Kingdom continues to expand.

We Have Victory in Christ Jesus!

Ecclesiastes 3:9 asks, "What profit do you have from your labor?" Are you working for the Kingdom of eternal life, or are you working for the kingdom of eternal death? Coming to Jesus does not mean freedom from having a master or lord. When the children of Israel were rescued from the Egyptians and their slavery, they accepted being led by God and following His commandments. God became their Master.

"Then Jesus said, 'Come to me, all of you who are *weary and carry heavy burdens*, and I will give you rest. *Take my yoke upon you. Let me teach you*, because I am *humble and gentle* at heart, and *you will find rest for your souls. For my yoke is easy to bear, and the burden I give you is light*'" (Matt. 11:28–30 NLT; italics added).

Christ has a yoke... His yoke will give you rest, not overload you. He says in the scripture above that His yoke is easy to bear, and the load, or burden, He will give you is light. Oxen are usually yoked together and when one pulls on one side, they all go to that side. When you are yoked to the devil, where he goes, you will go. When you are yoked to Christ, you will go where He leads.

Satan is unfair, and because he hates God, he hates you too no matter who you are because we were all created in the image of God. You remind the devil of God, and he will never warm up to you. It doesn't matter if you sell your soul to him and work for him, he will never like you. If you are using your talent for the devil's kingdom, you are helping him destroy you and many others who follow you (your fans). Satan was the most beautiful angel, made by God with very costly material, and was very gifted and talented. God never took this gift from him because His word says, "For God's gifts and his call can never be withdrawn" (Rom. 11:29). The devil was, and still is, powerful compared to humans, as he was a strong archangel. He wonders why God values humans who were made from the cheapest material—dust—and why He put His glory in humans and called them "gods". Just as a baby snake is a snake, a baby God is a god. We are children of God if we are in Christ Jesus. Let's examine a few scriptures on this.

"When I consider your heavens, the work of your fingers, the moon and the stars, which you have ordained; what is man, that you think of him? What is the son of man, that you care for him? For you have made him a little lower than God, and crowned him with glory and honor. You make him ruler over the works of your hands. You have put all things under his feet:" (Ps. 8:3–6 WEB)

"Jesus answered them, "Isn't it written in your law, 'I said, you are gods? 'If he called them gods, to whom the word of God came (and the Scripture can't be broken), do you say of him whom the Father sanctified and sent into the world, 'You blaspheme,' because I said, 'I am the Son of God?'" (John 10:34–36 WEB).

"See how great a love the Father has given to us, that we should be called children of God! For this cause the world doesn't know us, because it didn't know him. Beloved, now we are children of God, and it is not yet revealed what we will be. But we know that, when he is revealed, we will be like him; for we will see him just as he is." (1 John 3:1–2 WEB).

"But we have this treasure in clay vessels, that the exceeding greatness of the power may be of God, and not from ourselves." (2 Cor. 4:7 WEB).

CHAPTER 2

Who Are We?

§

SINCE WE WERE CREATED AS gods, when sin came we were condemned to die as mere men.

"I said, "You are gods, all of you are sons of the Most High. Nevertheless you shall die like men, and fall like one of the rulers." (Ps. 82:6–7 WEB).

But thanks be to God for Christ who came to restore us back to the glory we had before sin. According to the scripture in Rom. 3:23, *"For all have sinned and fall short of the glory of God"* (Italics added).

> Jesus said these things, and lifting up his eyes to heaven, he said, "Father, the time has come. Glorify your Son, that your Son may also glorify you; even as you gave him authority over all flesh, he will give eternal life to all whom you have given him. This is eternal life, that they should know you, the only true God, and him whom you sent, Jesus Christ. I glorified you on the earth. I have accomplished the work which you have given me to do. Now, *Father, glorify me with your own self with the glory which I had with you before the world existed."* (John 17:1–5 WEB; italics added)

Jesus prayed to God for restoration of His glory, since He had become a man and died in sin. He had taken up our sinful nature and had fallen short of the glory of God. He did not come in His glory when He came on earth, but when He returns to earth in the last day, He shall return in His glory. We once had the glory of God because we were created as gods in the beginning. Sin took away that glory because God never sins. That is why only God could come and pay the penalty for the sin that we "gods" made.

We are so high ranking in heaven and on earth in Christ Jesus we do not even know it! We have been created in God's image and likeness to have fellowship with God. Take for example, someone owes you a billion dollars and wants to satisfy the debt with a twenty-dollar asset, would you accept that? Absolutely not! That is why the blood of animals could never satisfy our debt of sin—only the blood of God Himself.

Fellowship is done by people who are at the same level. You cannot fellowship with someone at a level that is too low or too high from you. We were created to fellowship with God. We were given the power of life and of death. Our tongue has creating power just like God's tongue. He spoke the world into being, and He commanded us to do the same. He created the animals and brought them to Adam for naming.

> Yahweh God said, "It is not good for the man to be alone. I will make him a helper comparable to him." Out of the ground Yahweh God formed every animal of the field, and every bird of the sky, and brought them to the man to see what he would call them. Whatever the man called every living creature became its name. The man gave names to all livestock, and to the birds of the sky, and to every animal of the field; but for man there was not found a helper comparable to him." (Gen. 2:18–20 WEB)

Humans were involved in creation and were given dominion over all that God had created. One entrusts his or her property to someone who is at the same level. You cannot give a poor person your Bentley and ask them to watch it for you. You look for someone who has a similar rank and give it to that person to watch it for you, because that person knows its value and knows how to care for it.

The enemy comes to make us doubt our identity because he is unhappy about the glory that God bestowed on us, humans. The devil wanted that same glory which caused his downfall. In Genesis, we see this evident, when he was tempting Eve. He made her doubt her identity by saying that she would be like God:

"The serpent said to the woman, "You won't surely die, for God knows that in the day you eat it, your eyes will be opened, and you will be like God, knowing good and evil."" (Genesis 3:4-5 WEB)

Eve believed this lie in verse 6 (WEB), "When the woman saw that the tree was good for food, and that it was a delight to the eyes, and that the tree was to be desired to make one wise, she took some of its fruit, and ate; and she gave some to her husband with her, and he ate it, too."

Let us look closely at the real truth. Was Eve going to be like God or was she already like God?

"God said, "Let us make man *in our image, after our likeness*: and let them have dominion over the fish of the sea, and over the birds of the sky, and over the livestock, and over all the earth, and over every creeping thing that creeps on the earth." God *created man in his own image. In God's image he created him; male and female he created them*." (Gen.1:26–27 WEB; italics added).

Image is a visual representation, while likeness means being similar. We not only have the visual representation of God, but we are similar to Him.

Hold on…can someone please help Eve here and remind her that she is already like God! She was created as God. The devil just promised her what she already had and was. He made her believe that she was not like God and that she would be like God if she disobeyed God. What a LIE! That is how NOT to be like God. Disobedience is not God-like. That is how to be a mere human. If you do not know what you have and who you are in Christ, you will be cheated out of your inheritance. Jesus told us that the devil is a father of lies, and when he lies, he is speaking his native language in John 8:44.

"You belong to your father, the devil, and you want to carry out your father's desires. He was a murderer from the beginning, not holding to the truth, for there is no truth in him. *When he lies, he speaks his native language, for he is a liar and the father of lies*" (John 8:44 New International Version (NIV); italics added).

The devil will strip you of your identity if you are not confident of who you are. He tried this with Jesus after Jesus's baptism and a public declaration of Him being the Son of God by God Himself. Then in the first temptation in the wilderness, the devil tells Jesus; "*The tempter came and said to him, "If you are the Son of God, command that these stones become bread.""* (Matt. 4:3 WEB; Italics added).

To fulfill our purpose on earth, we must know who we are in Christ! Get your identity right. Many Christians suffer an identity crisis, which makes them live as slaves even when they are kings. What does God call us? Let us review who we are in Christ. The image and likeness of God was, and still is, God's ultimate will for all people. We have the gift of choice—to be conformed to this world or to be transformed into the image and likeness of God:

"Don't be conformed to this world, but be transformed by the renewing of your mind, so that you may prove what is the good, well-pleasing, and perfect will of God." (Rom. 12:2 WEB).

Who Are We in Christ?

<u>I am seated with Christ in the heavenly places.</u>

"But God, being rich in mercy, for his great love with which he loved us, even when we were dead through our trespasses, made us alive together with Christ (by grace you have been saved), *and raised us up with him, and made us to sit with him in the heavenly places in Christ Jesus,*" (Eph. 2:4–6 WEB; italics added).

"If then you were raised together with Christ, seek the things that are above, where Christ is, seated on the right hand of God. Set your mind on the things that are above, not on the things that are on the earth. For you died, and your life is hidden with Christ in God. When Christ, our life, is revealed, then you will also be revealed with him in glory." (Col. 3:1–4 WEB).

<u>I am chosen, king and priest, and holy, and I belong to God.</u>

"But you are a chosen race, a royal priesthood, a holy nation, a people for God's own possession, that you may proclaim the excellence of him who called you out of darkness into his marvelous light: who in time past were no people, but now are God's people, who had not obtained mercy, but now have obtained mercy." (1 Pet. 2:9–10 WEB).

In Christ…

The Devil Cannot Touch Me

"We know that whoever is born of God doesn't sin, but he who was born of God keeps himself, and the evil one doesn't touch him." (1 John 5:18 WEB).

I Am Blessed with Every Spiritual Blessing

"Blessed be the God and Father of our Lord Jesus Christ, who has blessed us with every spiritual blessing in the heavenly places in Christ;" (Eph. 1:3 WEB).

I Am the Righteousness of God in Christ

"But now apart from the law, a righteousness of God has been revealed, being testified by the law and the prophets; even the righteousness of God through faith in Jesus Christ to all and on all those who believe. For there is no distinction," (Rom. 3:21–22 WEB).

"For him who knew no sin he made to be sin on our behalf; so that in him we might become the righteousness of God." (2 Cor. 5:21WEB).

I Am a Child of God

"But as many as received him, to them he gave the right to become God's children, to those who believe in his name:" (John 1:12 WEB).

I Am a Friend of God

"No longer do I call you servants, for the servant doesn't know what his lord does. But I have called you friends, for everything that I heard from my Father, I have made known to you." (John 15:15 WEB).

I Am God's Property; I Belong to God

"for you were bought with a price. Therefore glorify God in your body and in your spirit, which are God's." (1 Cor. 6:20 WEB).

I Am One with Christ

"Now you are the body of Christ, and members individually." (1 Cor. 12:27 WEB).

I Am Anointed, Established in Christ, and Sealed with the Holy Spirit

"Now he who establishes us with you in Christ, and anointed us, is God; who also sealed us, and gave us the down payment of the Spirit in our hearts." (2 Cor. 1:21–22 WEB).

I Am Heaven's Citizen

"For our citizenship is in heaven, from where we also wait for a Savior, the Lord Jesus Christ;" (Phil. 3:20 WEB).

I Am a Joint Heir with Christ

"and if children, then heirs; heirs of God, and joint heirs with Christ; if indeed we suffer with him, that we may also be glorified with him." (Rom. 8:17 WEB).

I Am Loved and Chosen by God

"We know, dear brothers and sisters, that God loves you and has chosen you to be his own people" (1 Thess. 1:4).

I Am God's Choice, Holy, and Greatly Loved

"Therefore, as the elect of God, holy and beloved, put on tender mercies, kindness, humility, meekness, longsuffering" (Col. 3:12).

I Am God's Idea, Masterpiece in Christ with a Great Assignment from the Beginning

"For we are God's masterpiece. He has created us anew in Christ Jesus, so we can do the good things he planned for us long ago" (Eph. 2:10 NLT).

I Am a Stranger in This Earth; Heaven Is My Home

"Dear friends, I warn you as 'temporary residents and foreigners' to keep away from worldly desires that wage war against your very souls" (1 Pet. 2:11).

"I *am* a stranger in the earth; do not hide Your commandments from me." (Psalm 119:19)

I Am Loved and Valued

God gave His ONLY begotten Son to die a sinner's death though He never sinned, just for me.

"For God so loved the world that He gave His only begotten Son, that whoever believes in Him should not perish but have everlasting life" (John 3:16).

God gave His all to me, He is for me, He protects me, justifies me, prays for me, fights my battles and He makes me more than a conqueror. God loves me infinitely, and nothing or no one can ever separate me from His love.

> Who shall separate us from the love of Christ? Could oppression, or anguish, or persecution, or famine, or nakedness, or peril, or sword? Even as it is written, "For your sake we are killed all day long. We were accounted as sheep for the slaughter." No, in all these things, we are more than conquerors through him who loved us. *For I am persuaded, that neither death, nor life, nor angels, nor principalities, nor things present, nor things to come, nor powers, nor height, nor depth, nor any other created thing, will be able to separate us from the love of God, which is in Christ Jesus our Lord."* (Rom. 8:35–39 WEB; italics added)

I Am Valuable

"Again, the Kingdom of Heaven is like a man who is a merchant seeking fine pearls, who having found one pearl of great price, he went and sold all that he had, and bought it." (Matt. 13:45–46 WEB).

Christ Will Never Leave Me Or Forsake Me

"Be strong and of good courage, do not fear nor be afraid of them; for the Lord your God, He is the One who goes with you. He will not leave you nor forsake you" (Deut. 31:6).

"No man shall be able to stand before you all the days of your life; as I was with Moses, so I will be with you. I will not leave you nor forsake you" (Josh. 1:5).

"Teaching them to observe all things that I have commanded you; and lo, I am with you always, even to the end of the age. Amen" (Matt. 28:20).

I Am Protected

"Oh, how great is Your goodness, which You have laid up for those who fear You, Which You have prepared for those who trust in You In the presence of the sons of men! You shall *hide them in the secret place of Your presence from the plots of man*; *You shall keep them secretly in a pavilion from the strife of tongues*" (Ps. 31:19–20; italics added).

"After these things the word of the Lord came to Abram in a vision, saying, 'Do not be afraid, Abram. *I am your shield, your exceedingly great reward*'" (Gen. 15:1; italics added).

"No harm comes to the godly, but the wicked have their fill of trouble" (Prov.12:21).

Because you have made Yahweh your refuge, and the Most High your dwelling place, no evil shall happen to you, neither shall any plague come near your dwelling. For he will put his angels in charge of you, to guard you in all your ways. They will bear you up in their hands, so that you won't dash your foot against a stone. You will tread on the lion and cobra. You will trample the young lion and the serpent underfoot. "Because he has set his love on me, therefore I will deliver him. I will set him on high, because he has known my name. He will call on me, and I will answer him. I will be with him in trouble. I will deliver him, and honor him. I will satisfy him with long life, and show him my salvation." (Ps. 91:9–16 WEB)

Christ Wants Me to Rule and Reign with Him

"If we endure, we shall also reign with Him. If we deny Him, He also will deny us" (2 Tim. 2:12).

There are endless descriptions and identities of who we are in Christ Jesus. When we grasp this, then and only then, shall we be able to live the lives we were created to live. We will take our God-given task seriously, without wasting time, because we know that at any time we may be needed back home, and we'll go and give an account of what we have been doing in regard to our assignment. With this knowledge, we should not be distracted by the pleasures of this world. Instead, we should be like the servant who did the right thing and kept watch for His master's return.

If you are still living in sin and unbelief, then you are yoked to the devil, and his end point, as we now know, is eternal death in hell. Hell was created for him and his angels, as it says in Matthew 25:41. The devil's yoke is not only very heavy, but very hard. You will get weary and you will never find rest for your soul. It will lead you to eternal death. You will suffer the same punishment with him because he has already been condemned. That is why many people are committing suicide and doing drugs to try to ease up this heavy burden and to try to find rest for their souls.

The devil is full of pride and is very harsh. Unlike Jesus, who is humble and gentle. The best solution is to be yoked to the giver of joy, peace, life, and the giver of love, to find rest in the already finished work of the cross. If you become yoked to Jesus Christ, you will be walking in the same victory as He. You will be seated with Him, ruling at the right hand of God. Where He is you will be also, because you will be yoked with Him.

You see, the difference is that Jesus, *our Creator*, humbled Himself and died to pay for all our sins. He took our burden and yoke of sin and death upon Him and satisfied the payment we owed that the devil held against us. Eternal death is God's punishment for sin, and the devil knows it because he got sentenced himself. The enemy entices people to sin so that people can get the same sentence as he. Jesus paid the wages we owed for sin by dying for us. He has fulfilled the sentence for all who will accept His payment for them, by allowing Him to be Lord over their lives.

The devil wanted Jesus to remain dead, but thanks be to God for the POWER OF RESURRECTION, because Jesus is the Resurrection and the Life! He created all things and gave us life. He could do it all over again, and so He did. Jesus Christ rose from the dead and made it possible for us to start all over again, with a clean slate and without the inherited sin from Adam and Eve. We who receive Christ now inherit righteousness from Christ because we are born again. Many religions and cults portray Jesus as still being on the cross, because the devil wants to show the defeated Christ. If Christ died and never rose again, death would have won. But our victory is complete because of the power of Resurrection. That is why Paul said in Philippians 3:7–11, WEB:

> "However, I consider those things that were gain to me as a loss for Christ. Yes most certainly, and I count all things to be a loss

for the excellency of the knowledge of Christ Jesus, my Lord, for whom I suffered the loss of all things, and count them nothing but refuse, that I may gain Christ and be found in him, not having a righteousness of my own, that which is of the law, but that which is through faith in Christ, the righteousness which is from God by faith; *that I may know him, and the power of his resurrection, and the fellowship of his sufferings, becoming conformed to his death; if by any means I may attain to the resurrection from the dead.*" (Italics added)

"Jesus told her, 'I am the resurrection and the life anyone who believes in me will live, even after dying. Everyone who lives in me and believes in me will never ever die. Do you believe this, Martha?'" (John 11:25–26 NLT).

Let us therefore embrace the fullness of who we are and what we have in Christ Jesus and live victorious lives in Jesus's name. Jesus also spoke of receiving a profit in God's Kingdom. What does God profit from the workers in the Kingdom? What is your profit as a worker in God's Kingdom? Let us look at a few scriptures.

> He called the multitude to himself with his disciples, and said to them, "Whoever wants to come after me, let him deny himself, and take up his cross, and follow me. For whoever wants to save his life will lose it; and whoever will lose his life for my sake and the sake of the Good News will save it. For what does it profit a man, to gain the whole world, and forfeit his life? For what will a man give in exchange for his life? For whoever will be ashamed of me and of my words in this adulterous and sinful generation, the Son of Man also will be ashamed of him, when he comes in his Father's glory, with the holy angels." (Mark 8:34–38 WEB)

We must follow Jesus confidently, relentlessly, wholeheartedly, and without fear or shame. We must accept being ridiculed and mocked for the sake of Christ and the Gospel of Jesus Christ and being enemies of the world and friends with God.

"You adulterers! Don't you realize that friendship with the world makes you an enemy of God? I say it again: If you want to be a friend of the world, you make yourself an enemy of God" (James 4:4 New Living Translation, NLT).

"So letting your sinful nature control your mind leads to death. But letting the Spirit control your mind leads to life and peace. For the sinful nature is always hostile to God. It never did obey God's laws, and it never will" (Rom. 8:6–7).

The profit here is for God, so that His Kingdom will grow. Sinners will hear the good news, be turned from death to life, and the enemy will lose in his plan to destroy God's beloved people. God will have His beloved people back in everlasting fellowship with Him as He originally intended.

God will reward those who work for and are yielded to Him, without being ashamed of saying who they are: those who shine the light of Christ in this sinful generation where it is not cool to say "I am blessed" or to share the good news of Christ in public, those who are not afraid to bless or to pray in public and do this without fear of offending others. The children of the world do not care if they offend you, or God, so why should you be afraid of offending them . . . rather than offending God?

Clearly, doing away with the laws of God and making human laws to accommodate people's sinful desires leads to destruction. The bold men and women who will stand and not fear to declare the laws of God to all people and show it in their lives even unto death will get rewarded and honored just as Jesus said. He will acknowledge them before His Father, God, and the angels. You will be recognized in heaven just as you made Christ recognized here on earth. Your honor in heaven will go hand in hand with the honor you showed Christ here on earth. The apostle Paul said to Timothy;

> Preach the word [as an official messenger]; be ready when the time is right and *even* when it is not [keep your sense of urgency,

whether the opportunity seems favorable or unfavorable, whether convenient or inconvenient, whether welcome or unwelcome]; correct [those who err in doctrine or behavior], warn [those who sin], exhort *and* encourage [those who are growing toward spiritual maturity], with inexhaustible patience and [faithful] teaching. For the time will come when people will not tolerate sound doctrine *and* accurate instruction [that challenges them with God's truth]; but *wanting* to have their ears tickled [with something pleasing], they will accumulate for themselves [many] teachers [one after another, chosen] to satisfy their own desires *and* to support the errors they hold, and will turn their ears away from the truth and will wander off into myths *and* man-made fictions [and will accept the unacceptable]. (2 Timothy 4:3-4 Amplified (AMP)

"For this reason I also suffer these things; *nevertheless I am not ashamed, for I know whom I have believed and am persuaded that He is able to keep what I have committed to Him until that Day.*" (2 Timothy 1:12; italics added)

Beloved, let us not be ashamed to declare the gospel of Jesus Christ and to speak the truth in love to all people.

Different Kinds of Servants

"For it is like a man, going into another country, who called his own servants, and entrusted his goods to them. To one he gave five talents, to another two, to another one; to each according to his own ability. Then he went on his journey. Immediately he who received the five talents went and traded with them, and made another five talents. In the same way, he also who got the two gained another two. But he who received the one talent went away and dug in the earth, and hid his lord's money. "Now after a long time the lord of those servants came, and reconciled accounts with them. He who received the five talents came and brought another five talents, saying, 'Lord, you delivered to me five talents. Behold, I have gained another five talents besides them.' "His lord said to him, 'Well done, good and faithful servant. You have been faithful over a few things, I will set you over many things. Enter into the joy of your lord.' "He also who got the two talents came and said, 'Lord, you delivered to me two talents. Behold, I have gained another two talents besides them.' "His lord said to him, 'Well done, good and faithful servant. You have been faithful over a few things, I will set you over many things. Enter into the joy of your lord.' "He also who had received the one talent came and said, 'Lord, I knew you that you are a hard man, reaping where you did not sow, and gathering where you did not scatter. *I was afraid*, and went away and hid your talent in the earth. Behold, you have what is yours.' "But his lord answered him, *'You wicked and slothful servant.* You knew that I reap where I didn't sow, and gather where I didn't scatter. You ought therefore to have deposited my money with the bankers, and at my coming I should have received back my own with interest. *Take away therefore the talent from him, and give it to him who has the ten talents. For to everyone who has will be given, and he will have abundance, but from him who doesn't have, even that which he has will be taken away. Throw out the unprofitable servant into the outer darkness, where there will be weeping and gnashing of teeth.'"* (Matt. 25:14–30 WEB; italics added)

As we read from the scripture above, there are different kinds of servants—profitable and unprofitable. The parable of the talents speaks of what God requires of His Kingdom workers. We are to profit the Kingdom and bring increase. The servants who worked and multiplied the talents and gave them back to their master with profit were considered good and faithful servants. The servant who made more profit was given authority over more wealth so he could make even more profit for his master. The servant who returned the talent in the same way he received it was called "a wicked servant" and was kicked out of the Kingdom. The talent that "the lazy and unprofitable servant" had was taken away from him and was given to the one who had more.

It is worth noting that the unprofitable servant expressed fear. That is why he buried his talent instead of investing it for his master. Fear is a spirit from the devil that will keep you from using your gifts and talents to profit God's Kingdom. Paul, the apostle, wrote a letter to Timothy and addresses this same issue in 2 Timothy 1:6-7. He made it clear that Timothy was not using his gifts or talents at the time. He said, "Therefore I remind you to *stir up the gift of God which is in you* through the laying on of my hands. *For God has not given us a spirit of fear, but of power and of love and of a sound mind.*" (Italics added)

The evil spirit of fear works against your God given task. It causes loss in God's Kingdom. Unprofitability is wickedness (or sin) in God's Kingdom. God does not equally distribute talents; He gives according to the profitability of His servants. God is a great businessman who does not run His Kingdom at a loss. He sacrificed His ONLY Son so He could have many more sons and daughters in return. He planted a seed of a Son, and it was multiplied to many sons of God.

> But who is there among you, having a servant plowing or keeping sheep, that will say, when he comes in from the field, 'Come immediately and sit down at the table,' and will not rather tell him, 'Prepare my supper, clothe yourself properly, and serve me, while I eat and drink. Afterward you shall eat and drink'? *Does he thank that servant because he did the things that were commanded? I think not. Even so you also, when you have done all the things that are commanded you, say, 'We are unworthy servants. We have done our duty.'*"(Luke 17:7–10; italics added)

When we only do what is required of us, we should not expect to be recognized, but if we go way beyond our call of duty, then we will be rewarded and recognized by God. This is done here on earth, too. Your employer does not reward you for doing your job; you were hired to do your job. You don't go thanking your employer for your paycheck; you earned your paycheck. But if you go beyond your call of duty and profit the employer beyond his or her expectation, the employer will recognize you and reward you. You, in turn, will be grateful for that recognition.

The Kingdom of God should be full of the profitable servants. Unfortunately, we have more unprofitable servants than profitable servants. We like to do the bare minimum to get by as Christians. We believe in false humility and we try to be at peace with all people, which leads to us conforming to this world. We should be peacemakers and not peace-keepers. Jesus taught in His Sermon on the Mount, Matt. 5:9 NLT; "God blesses those who work for peace, for they will be called the children of God."

Peace-keepers are not called sons of God. Many people have been deceived and settle on being peacekeepers. Keeping the peace means not doing anything to confront the problem, but letting the problem persist and ignoring it so as to not offend others. Peace-keepers are passive; they make up about ninety nine percent of Christians. On the other hand, peacemakers are bold and confrontational. They face the problem head on and call a spade a spade and not a big spoon. They call things as they are and work toward changing them for the better. They suffer ridicule, criticism, rejection and they lose many friends. That is why God specifically has a blessing for these people. Peacemakers do not keep peace; they make peace.

Keeping peace and making peace are two very different things. According to the *Merriam-Webster Dictionary*, *keep* means "to cause (someone or something) *to continue* in a specified state, condition, or position" and *make* means "to cause to exist, occur, or appear: *to create*. To bring into being. *"Peace-keepers continue* with the present situation while *peacemakers destroy* the bad *and create* a new right thing. It is hard work to create something and to build it from scratch, but it is easy to keep something in the same condition, because nothing needs to be done for it; it can be left like it is. Peace-keepers are called "the lazy and wicked servants"; they do not profit God's Kingdom. But peacemakers are "the good and faithful servants" because they profit God's Kingdom.

Jesus said He did not come to bring peace. He brought change, which people dislike. The process of making peace is not peaceful. It is very hard and chaotic and will make many enemies instead of friends. Martin Luther King and many people who fought for their independence and freedom were not peacekeepers; they were peacemakers. They worked to make peace even unto death. Which of these are you? A peace-keeper or a peacemaker?

Jesus said it clearly;

"Don't think that I came to send peace on the earth. I didn't come to send peace, but a sword. For I came to set a man at odds against his father, and a daughter against her mother, and a daughter-in-law against her mother-in-law. A man's foes will be those of his own household. *He who loves father or mother more than me is not worthy of me; and he who loves son or daughter more than me isn't worthy of me."* (Matt. 10:34–37 WEB; Italics added).

The Lord said, "Who then is the faithful and wise steward, whom his lord will set over his household, to give them their portion of food at the right times? Blessed is that servant whom his lord will find doing so when he comes. Truly I tell you, that he will set him over all that he has. But if that servant says in his heart, 'My lord delays his coming,' and begins to beat the menservants and the maidservants, and to eat and drink, and to be drunken, then the lord of that servant will come in a day when he isn't expecting him, and in an hour that he doesn't know, and will cut him in two, and place his portion with the unfaithful. *That servant, who knew his lord's will, and didn't prepare, nor do what he wanted, will be beaten with many stripes, but he who didn't know, and did things worthy of stripes, will be beaten with few stripes. To whomever much is given, of him will much be required; and to whom much was entrusted, of him more will be asked."* (Luke 12:42–48 WEB; italics added)

He spoke this parable. "A certain man had a fig tree planted in his vineyard, and he came seeking fruit on it, and found none. He said to the vine dresser, 'Behold, these three years I have come looking for fruit on this fig tree, and found none. Cut it down. Why does it waste the soil?' He answered, 'Lord, leave it alone this year also, until I dig around it, and fertilize it. If it bears fruit, fine; but if not, after that, you can cut it down.'" (Luke 13:6–9 WEB)

"Every tree that does not bear good fruit is cut down and thrown into the fire" (Matt. 7:19).

"I am the true vine, and my Father is the farmer. Every branch in me that doesn't bear fruit, he takes away. Every branch that bears fruit, he prunes, that it may bear more fruit. You are already pruned clean because of the word which I have spoken to you. Remain in me, and I in you. As the branch can't bear fruit by itself, unless it remains in the vine, so neither can you, unless you remain in me." (John 15:1–4 WEB).

Jesus is very clear about God's character as a businessman. He shows God giving people time to bear fruit as they daily and continually feed from God's Word and are led by God's Spirit. God also does not hesitate to get rid of the unprofitable servants. He compares them to branches that do not bear fruit. You may be connected to Christ but refuse to grow. God will cut you off if you do not repent, turn away from evil, and seek Him on how you can grow in Christ as you pray and read God's Word.

Be a doer of the Word so you can profit the Kingdom of God. Refuse to just settle for the title of 'a Christian', because titles don't count in heaven—only the fruits that we bear will count. Our fruits (actions) dictate our titles in the spiritual realm. Jesus made it clear on how to differentiate between His followers and the non-followers of Christ and between the faithful and wicked servants. They both have the same title of Christian, and they both profess to follow Christ, but the authenticity is in the fruit they produce.

> Beware of false prophets, who come to you in sheep's clothing, but inwardly are ravening wolves. By their fruits you will know them. Do you gather grapes from thorns, or figs from thistles? Even so, every good tree produces good fruit; but the corrupt tree produces evil fruit. *A good tree can't produce evil fruit, neither can a corrupt tree produce good fruit.* Every tree that doesn't grow good fruit is cut down, and thrown into the fire. *Therefore by their fruits you will know them.* (Matt. 7:15–20 WEB; italics added).

There are two different kinds of servants: the servant who knows what he or she should do and does it, and the other who knows what he or she should do but doesn't do it. Which of these are you? Let us all stop and take a look in the mirror to determine which of these servants we are, and urgently make the necessary adjustments to be profitable in God's Kingdom.

"To him therefore who knows to do good, and doesn't do it, to him it is sin." (James 4:17 WEB).

CHAPTER 3

Carry Your Cross and Follow Jesus

§

We must pass through the wilderness to get to the promise.

Now large crowds were going along with Jesus; and He turned and said to them, "If anyone comes to Me, and does not hate his own father and mother and wife and children and brothers and sisters, yes, and even his own life [in the sense of indifference to or relative disregard for them in comparison with his attitude toward God]—he cannot be My disciple. *Whoever does not carry his own cross [expressing a willingness to endure whatever may come] and follow after Me [believing in Me, conforming to My example in living and, if need be, suffering or perhaps dying because of faith in Me] cannot be My disciple.* "For which one of you, when he wants to build a watchtower [for his guards], does not first sit down and *calculate the cost*, to see if he has enough to finish it? "Otherwise, when he has laid a foundation and is unable to finish [the building], all who see it will begin to ridicule him, saying, 'This man began to build and was not able to finish!' "Or what king, when he sets out to meet another king in battle, will not first sit down and consider whether he is strong enough with ten thousand men to encounter the one who is coming against him with twenty thousand? Or else [if he feels he is not powerful enough], while the other [king] is still a far distance away, he sends an envoy and asks for terms of peace. "So then, none of you can be My disciple who does not [carefully consider the cost and then for My sake] give up all his own possessions." (Luke 14:25–33 Amplified (AMP); italics added)

Jesus is simply telling His disciples and the others around Him to count their cost, carry their cross (their God-given assignment), and follow Him wholeheartedly—to follow His plan and not our plans, other people, or the easy way out. In other words, we cannot follow Christ without fully regarding Him over everyone and everything else. We must carry our own cross, our God-given task, with a healthy fear of God only and not a fear of people. This will cost us friendships, relationships, you will give up your will for His will, your pleasures for His, your reputation for His reputation, your ways for His ways and much more.

For Jesus, His "cross" (or God-given assignment) was to literally carry the cross for us, so we can be set free to carry our own "crosses". For John the Baptist, it was to prepare the way for Jesus to come as Savior. For Paul, it was to introduce and preach the good news to the Gentiles and Jews alike. With our God-given assignment comes persecution, trials, and tribulations, but this must not be an excuse for us to bail out.

According to Matt. 11:28–30 when Jesus says, *"My yoke is easy, and my burden is light,"* He means that each of us must be yoked or joined to someone, which means we must also carry that person's burden. Before we belonged to Christ, we were yoked (united or joined) to the devil, and we carried the devil's burdens. We did what he wanted us to do, we went where he led us, and we carried his heavy burden of guilt, shame, and regret. It weighed so heavy on us. Some people were killed, some committed suicide, and some were wounded beyond hope and were left in critical condition to die. This was because we were yoked to a thief, murderer, and destroyer. Jesus says, "The thief does not come except to steal, and to kill, and to destroy. I have come that they may have life, and that they may have it more abundantly" (John 10:10).

Now that we are yoked (united or joined) to Jesus Christ, we follow Christ and obey His Word. We go where He goes, and we carry His burden that is light by living for Him, doing His will, and performing our assignment on earth. The burden is light because He is always ready to help us, forgive us, and cleanse us from all unrighteousness, guilt, and shame. He, in the end, rewards us with abundant life, and He allows us to rule and reign with Him. God the Father says the following about Jesus Christ His Son who regarded His Father's assignment over His life;

"Therefore will I give him a portion with the great, and he will divide the plunder with the strong; because he poured out his soul to death, and was numbered with the transgressors; yet he bore the sin of many, and made intercession for the transgressors." (Is. 53:12 WEB).

David, the shepherd boy who then became the king of Israel, is a great example of someone who carried his cross. He went through the wilderness before he possessed the promise of becoming the King of Israel.

In 1 Samuel 17:24-31, David went and faced Goliath head on because he loved God so much and trusted in God's ability instead of other people's ability. He also had his eyes on the prize set before him. David asked the Israelite soldiers who Goliath thought he was because he defied God and His army. He also inquired about the prize to be given to whoever fought and destroyed Goliath.

Also in 1 Samuel 25:23-39, When David was running from Saul in the wilderness before he was king, he and his men had protected Nabal's men and his sheep while they were with them in the wilderness. When David sent his men to ask Nabal for some food and supplies, Nabal sent them away with insults.

God put Nabal's wife, Abigail, on David's path when David wanted to kill Nabal and all the males in that household. Abigail reminded David who he was and what God had anointed him to be. She kept him from sinning before God and saved his anointing as king so that he does not get rejected by God like King Saul was. Instead, David allowed God to fight for him.

When Nabal was sober, his wife told him what had happened. As a result, he had a stroke, and he lay paralyzed on his bed like a stone. About ten days later, the Lord struck him, and he died.

"When David heard that Nabal was dead, he said, "Blessed be the LORD, who has pleaded the cause of my reproach [suffered] at the hand of Nabal and has kept His servant from [retaliating with] evil. For the Lord has returned the wickedness of Nabal on his own head." Then David sent word to Abigail, proposing to take her as his wife." (1 Sam 25:39 AMP)

It took David fifteen years before he could even become king of Judah; and another seven years before he became king of Israel. Before David's anointing as king, he was a shepherd boy who never had to run from anyone. He had no enemies but the bear and lion who tried to steal his father's sheep. After he was anointed and victorious over Goliath, he became a celebrity with whom everyone wanted to associate and be identified. He even became part of the palace dwellers. What a promotion, from the fields to the palace! He had a taste of living in the palace until Saul became very jealous of his victories and fame. Saul attacked David and wanted to kill him, but David ran away into the wilderness. At this time, David's dream of becoming the king of Israel seemed dead. Read 1st and 2nd Samuel.

While in the wilderness waiting for your promise,
You need to forgive, get delivered, grow, and learn about real love—agape.
Obtain a different spirit that obeys, trusts, has faith, and fears God.

As David waited, he was not sitting down and whining. He did not go back to look after sheep either. Instead, he knew who he was. He was a king in the spirit waiting for the physical manifestation. As he waited, David knew that faith was believing in the things he hoped for, and acting as if he had received those things already even when they were not physically evident or visible. His actions had to align him with God's Word, who God said he was, not who people said he was at the time. David did not need a palace to be a king nor did he need the military troops, the gold, the fame, the glory, the concubines, or the servants to be king. King Saul had all these, yet he was rejected as king.

To God, Saul was no longer the king of Israel, even though he was physically still in the palace and had all the wealth of the kingdom. In reality, King Saul had been dethroned in the spirit by God and David had been anointed in his place as king, which was waiting to be manifested in the physical. Saul was a flesh king, not a faith king, while David was a faith king, the real king.

While David waited to be king, he was not thinking of how he was going to take the kingdom by force. He was not thinking of how he would destroy King Saul or Abner or the others who stood in his way. Instead, David was fighting the enemies of Israel and dividing his spoil with Judah. He never kept it for himself or built his own kingdom. He was genuinely saddened by the death of his enemies, King Saul, and Abner, and never sought revenge for himself. Instead, David destroyed anyone who rose against King Saul and anyone who threatened to kill the "anointed of God". He knew that God had the power to promote and demote; to destroy a kingdom or to build and prosper a kingdom.

"It is He who changes the times and the seasons; He removes kings and establishes kings. He gives wisdom to the wise and [greater] knowledge to those who have understanding!" (Dan. 2:21 AMP).

David was wise and had understanding from God. David knew and believed that the God who saved him from the bear, the lion, and Goliath was the same God who would save him from King Saul and all his enemies. God would give David the kingdom He promised. King David was not only loyal to God but he trusted God and believed that no matter how long it would take, as long as he remained faithful, God's Word would never fail. He did what Galatians 6:9 says, that we should not grow tired of doing good, for we shall reap a harvest of blessings if we do not give up.

The "cross" is not easy to carry, and the wilderness is not easy to walk through. Think of it this way, the process of preparing and cooking food takes longer than the eating time. If the preparation is rushed and some ingredients are missed then no one will enjoy the food. The period between receiving the Word of promise to its fulfillment is the wilderness time.

Jesus endured the cross in obedience to His Father and for the joy set before Him (Heb. 12:2). God tells us the end from the beginning for this very reason; that we may endure the cross. In Genesis 37 to Chapter 44, the story of Joseph, Joseph was told by God (in a dream) that he would be a great ruler. But when he shared his dream with his family all hell broke loose.

There is wisdom in keeping things that God tells you to yourself, and pondering them in your heart like Mary, the mother of Jesus did. She is a great role model. As young as Mary was, she did not go around telling all her friends that she saw an angel and that she was the favored one… and not just favored, but highly favored, to bear God's Son, Jesus Christ. If that would have happened today, it would have been shared across all social media. Because in this day and age people STILL do not know how to discern the things of God and how to keep those things to themselves and pray. Many people are very hungry for the temporary pleasures and glory of this world.

Joseph, like David, got his dream, shared it, and created enemies from his own household. His brothers sought to kill him, but instead, after throwing him into a ditch, they saw trades people and decided to sell him as a slave. He was sold as a slave in Egypt, where he rose up again in rank and was placed in charge of his master's property. Because Joseph feared God, God favored him, and he prospered in all he did. Everything was great and he must have thought that the dream was finally becoming a reality, until his master's wife desired him. When he refused to sin against God and his master, Potiphar, all hell broke loose again! In spite of his faithfulness to God and his master, he was demoted and thrown in prison.

He went lower than he began. The dungeon was a dream-killer place, but Joseph did not allow his dream to die. Joseph knew that he did not give himself the dream. And the One who gave him the dream (His assignment) cannot lie or be stopped by anyone or any circumstance. Joseph knew that only his faith in the dream giver would keep his dream alive in the place where dreams die. He went even lower than the pit his brothers threw him in. The people to whom he was faithful betrayed him yet a second time.

One day the Holy Spirit showed me the importance of the dungeon and these situations in our lives. He said, "To jump high we must bend our knees and go down and then we can jump high. If we don't bend our knees, we cannot jump as high, because it is the going down that gives us the momentum and power to jump really high". Just as well, for an arrow to go far the bow must be pulled and bent back more.

Joseph kept a great attitude, and he took what was handed to him and used it to serve others. His light shone so much that it rescued others from the dungeon. Some people you help to succeed will not remember you in their success, but God will always remember you. Therefore when you work or help anyone, do it as unto the LORD there is great reward. The king's cupbearer had been locked up with Joseph, and he, together with another servant of the king, told Joseph about a dream they had. Joseph, by God's grace, revealed to them the meanings of their dreams and it came to pass exactly as he told them. One was restored to his work and the other was killed. Joseph asked the one who was restored back to his position in the palace to remember him and put in a good word for him. The man left the dungeon and forgot about Joseph.

People will forget you and your good deeds, but do not grow tired of doing good unto all people because God sees, and He shall reward you at the right time if you continue doing good without giving up. God will make them remember you. Don't worry. In Joseph's case, God caused a problem in the palace that no one could solve but Joseph, and this brought Joseph into the memory of the king's servant. God will cause a book of remembrance to be opened up so that your good deeds will be remembered and rewarded (just like Mordecai in the book of Esther). That is why we are commanded to keep doing good. The king had a dream that no one could reveal to him, but his servant remembered Joseph and told the king all about him and how he interpreted the servants' dreams accurately.

Because of Joseph's faithfulness and maturity, he was promoted to second-in-command after the king, and finally the dream came true. Even when he met his brothers, who came to Egypt where they had sold him into slavery, he was mature and God-fearing enough not to take revenge, but to forgive them and make peace. Through him the children of Israel came to Egypt and lived there and did not die of famine.

The lesson here is that the process, though painful, prepares us for the glory. We cannot have the glory without the wilderness. The process to get to our promise is our "cross". Our assignments are given to us before creation and then revealed to us. But we must trust God through the process, take up our cross, and follow Him. God will cause people to remember and favor you. He will create problems that only you can solve. Can God trust you with leadership after so much pain? Being in authority over those who caused you the pain and grief? Or will you seek revenge when God promotes you? David and Joseph were faithful in doing this, Jesus Himself was and is still faithful in doing this, He loves all His enemies and calls all to repentance.

Abraham got his promise of a son and being the father of a great nation when he and his wife were still barren. They waited for this promise for about twenty-five years. They went through the wilderness of barrenness, and when they got tired of waiting, they decided to help God fulfill His promise. They looked at their ages and the biological clock instead of gazing at God, the promise-giver. Abraham had been asked by God, when He gave him the promise, to look up and count the stars in the sky; this was how many descendants he would have.

When Abraham faced doubt in the wilderness of barrenness, all he had to do was LOOK UP to God and His Word, count the stars and remind himself of the promise and the great God who created the stars and know that if He did that, nothing is impossible with Him. He was not supposed to look at his wife or other people. We MUST realize that God is not limited by any laws of nature or of people. When they trusted God and stopped helping Him, the promise came. Baby Isaac was born, and then Israel was born from Isaac, and now we have the nation of Israel scattered all over the world, making Abraham the father of many nations!

God does this so people will fear Him. We must carry our cross and follow Jesus, enduring trials and tribulations, because this is a "God-allowed" process to make us ready to rule and reign in God's Kingdom and to shine His light in this dark world. Like James said,

> Count it all joy, my brothers, when you fall into various temptations, knowing that the testing of your faith produces endurance. Let endurance have its perfect work, that you may be perfect and complete, lacking in nothing. But if any of you lacks wisdom, let him ask of God, who gives to all liberally and without reproach; and it will be given to him. But let him ask in faith, without any doubting, for he who doubts is like a wave of the sea, driven by the wind and tossed. For let that man not think that he will receive anything from the Lord. He is a double-minded man, unstable in all his ways. Blessed is the man who endures temptation, for when he has been approved, he will receive the crown of life, which the Lord promised to those who love him. (James 1:2–8, 12 WEB)

Our cross is worth carrying; let us set our eyes on the prize. There are many stories in the Bible of men and women who waited and held on to God's promises and allowed the wilderness process to make them and mold them and change their spirits and hearts like Caleb and Joshua, so they could inherit their promised land.

You have a "promised land." Are you making the best use of the wilderness or are you still stuck in Egypt? Did you leave Egypt but did not let Egypt leave you? Are you still a slave of your past? Angry, bitter, resentful, unforgiving, complaining, selfish, being too competitive, or looking for the worst in people rather than the best in them?

Remember, God will never use these attitudes. He will keep you out there in the wilderness because the wilderness experience is supposed to get Egypt out of you. Egypt is a slave mentality, which is a great destruction to the mind of a king. God cannot entrust His Kingdom to slaves, and for this reason He sent His only begotten Son, Jesus Christ, to come and get us out of slavery and make us His sons and daughters and then mature us for kingship.

The King is always ruling with His Family—His wife and sons and daughters. The Kingdom is ruled by the family, not by election. If we are in God's family, then we rule and reign with Christ. It is only for those in the nuclear family, not the extended family. This means you cannot inherit the Kingdom if you are related to someone who is born again and you are not. You cannot be a distant cousin, uncle, aunt, nephew, or niece in God's Kingdom. God is the King of kings, and only His bride and His sons and daughters will rule with Him.

> He (Christ) was in the world, and though the world was made through Him, the world did not recognize Him. He came to that which was His own [that which belonged to Him—His world, His creation, His possession], and those who were His own [people—the Jewish nation] did not receive and welcome Him. But to as many as did receive and welcome Him, He gave the right [the authority, the privilege] to become children of God, that is, to those who believe in (adhere to, trust in, and rely on) His name—who were born, not of blood [natural conception], nor of the will of the flesh [physical impulse], nor of the will of man [that of a natural father], but of God [that is, a divine and supernatural birth—they are born of God—spiritually transformed, renewed, sanctified]. (John 1:10–13 AMP)

CHAPTER 4

The Wilderness and the appointed time

§

The wilderness is where we have a personal encounter with God.

MOSES WAS USED BY GOD to get the children of Israel out of slavery, across the Red Sea, through the wilderness, and into the Promised Land. Before his assignment could be carried out he had to have a wilderness experience. This was not easy, but it prepared him for the great task ahead. He met with God, "I AM," in the wilderness where he realized his assignment. The children of Israel had a wilderness experience which they did not use to their benefit. Instead, they used it to destroy themselves. Only Caleb and Joshua made it into the Promised Land because they used the wilderness experience in the right way. They viewed it in the right perspective. They saw it as God's "pressure washer".

One time I asked God why I was going through so much in my life, and I felt like Paul; it seemed like it was never ending. Like Paul said he had a thorn in his flesh and prayed for God to take it out in 2 Corinthians 12:6-9. I prayed for God to take this thorn out. However, God revealed that my wilderness experience was acting as His pressure washer to clean me up really well. In other words, His grace was sufficient for me in the wilderness, because in my weakness, He is strong. In the wilderness, He is my strength. His grace and power are revealed and made perfect in my weakness.

The wilderness is a cleansing place; it is like a shower. Some people go through the wilderness but come out unchanged. Others become worse than before while others come out totally transformed. This is the place of meeting with God and receiving deliverance. Many Christians will never get to their promised land because they have refused the fact that they need deliverance. Deliverance is for those adopted by God through His Son Jesus Christ. Without deliverance, you will never enter your promised land, the rest of God. This is because without deliverance, evil still dwells in you. The Israelites from Egypt went through the Red Sea, but they never got to their destination, the Promised Land. The wilderness is meant to cleanse you from the evil in you and transform you into the likeness of God.

Many people think that being born again into Christ means living a smooth and easy lifestyle. This is a lie from the devil. That is why many people backslide because they have been deceived by the enemy in this way. It is the devil's tactic to get you to hate God and blame Him for your troubles and struggles in life just like the Israelites did often. They complained and wished they were back in Egypt, where they had been in slavery. Likewise, you desire the days you were living in sin because you think life was better then.

Let us look at it this way. You are a civilian, you have no gun, and you are not a threat to anyone. You also have nothing to protect yourself in case of an attack. Most likely, your life will be nice and simple with nothing to fear, and you will intimidate no one. But when the enemy comes all of a sudden, because you are not protected and you have no weapon (not ready for war), you will be easily subdued. On the other hand, let's say you have just been recruited in the US Navy SEAL Program, which has the toughest military training. Does it mean that they will give you a gun and other weapons before they train you so you can go along and shoot some bad guys? Absolutely not! This means that you will go through the MOST EXTREME, TOUGH, BRUTAL, and CHALLENGING training that only a handful survive.

You will be tempted to quit, but when you look at the end result, you will want to fight to the end. This is your wilderness time. When you are done you will receive great honors like no other; you will basically rule in honor. People will highly respect you and your enemies will fear you. You will be fully armed and ready for battle to protect the country you serve. When the enemy comes, he will be defeated miserably because of the wilderness (training) you went through and because you allowed it to transform you into a ruler, a victor and great man or woman of war.

So it is being in Christ. We enroll in the Navy SEALs of the Kingdom of God to wage war against the kingdom of darkness. We go through the wilderness for training and transformation so we can live a victorious life in God, defeating all powers of darkness. A Navy SEAL is always prepared and ready for battle, as he or she can be called upon anytime. As children of God, like Ephesians 6 says, we must "put on the full armor of God" so we can defeat the enemy at all times. We must, as James said...

"My brethren, count it all joy when you fall into various trials, knowing that the testing of your faith produces patience. But let patience have its perfect work, that you may be perfect and complete, lacking nothing" (James 1:2–4).

"In every situation [no matter what the circumstances], be thankful and continually give thanks to God; for this is the will of God for you in Christ Jesus" (1 Thess. 5:18 AMP).

How many times do you celebrate trials? Or give thanks at all times? When we know and appreciate the value of trials and realize that they raise us to the next level, the rocks thrown at us will be assets to us because we will use them for our good to build a staircase to rise to the next level. There is no promotion without a test. There is no victory without a battle, and there is no graduation without tests. We should long for these trials and thank God for them, because they precede promotion. In the trials, we have all our answers in the Bible. It is an open-book test with our Helper, the Holy Spirit, instructing us. We must be on our knees and not talking, except to God and His faithful followers. .

I have learned to smile at the storm, knowing that I have authority over it. Just as a horse smiles at the sound of battle and is not afraid, I smile at trials because in Christ Jesus I am fully armed. I have my Helper, God the Holy Spirit, revealing to me all the plans and secrets of the enemy and how to destroy and fight him while hidden in Christ in God.

Many people struggle with righteous living because there is wickedness still living in them. Salvation does not take away evil from inside you. It gives you the legal right and power to evict all evil spirits indwelling you from your previous lifestyle of sin. It gives you a head start to the promised land. It points you toward that direction.

It is up to us to yield to God and learn what He wants to teach us, and then execute that which we have learned in the wilderness. As you learn God's way by daily reading and practicing the Bible, by listening to and obeying God, then the Word of God will cleanse you. It acts as a mirror; it shows you where you need to fix something in your life. Jesus told His disciples that the Word of God (which He had taught them) had cleaned them. You will do away with the old ways, evicting all evil from within you, in Jesus's name, and embracing the fullness of God in you by His Spirit.

"For husbands, this means love your wives, just as Christ loved the church. He gave up his life for her to make her holy and clean, *washed by the cleansing of God's word. He did this to present her to himself as a glorious church without a spot or wrinkle or any other blemish. Instead, she will be holy and without fault*" (Eph. 5:25–27 NLT; italics added).

When you adopt a grown child they do not automatically know and do your will. You must train them. Before you train them it is important to understand their past in order to help them to get through any trauma, abuse, and pain they may have gone through before coming to you. Otherwise, you will not be successful in having a healthy bond or relationship with them. If they were abused, and you fail to help them through it, they will see you in the same way they saw their abuser and will live in fear of being abused by you, no matter how kind you are to them.

Many marriages in which people had been abused by their spouses in their previous marriages or relationships, suffer divorce because the abused left their abuser physically, by relocating and re-marrying, but they did not get the abuser out of them mentally and emotionally. They therefore treat their new spouse as the abuser because they did not heal from the situation. They are usually insecure and bring a lot of baggage into their new relationship which makes them start on defeated ground. Moving physically from one place to another does not mean the place or person you moved from is out of you. In the same way, you can be a Christian, born again, but not delivered.

However, you can ask for deliverance now that you are safe in your adopted home. Open up to God and tell Him all you feel. He knows everything but He wants you to expose these bad feelings and spirits and in Jesus's name cast them out of your life and be delivered. It is very simple. We, as children of God, are entitled to deliverance through Jesus Christ our Lord. The Bible says that they who call on the name of the Lord shall be delivered. Then we can have a different spirit from God, like Caleb and Joshua.

"And it shall come to pass, that *whosoever shall call on the name of the Lord shall be delivered*: for in mount Zion and in Jerusalem shall be deliverance, as the Lord hath said, and in the remnant whom the Lord shall call" (Joel 2:32 King James Version (KJV); italics added).

Getting saved and not delivered is like going into the shower and standing under the water without using soap or scrubbing your body. The person comes out of the shower soaking wet, showing evidence of being cleansed by water, but in reality he or she is still dirty and smelly. The Christians who acknowledge that Jesus came to deliver them are like those who decide to get into the shower, use soap and a scrubber, and allow the power of the water, soap, and scrubber to make them clean; removing all the dirt and odor.

The devil does not like it if you get saved. However, if you get saved he will work hard so that you remain ignorant of all that Jesus paid for at Calvary; your deliverance, healing, peace, prosperity, blessed marriages, etc. The devil is afraid of your deliverance and he knows that salvation without deliverance, life is a disaster for you. Remember, the devil needs a body to operate on earth and since he is not God, he cannot create a body. He relies on the bodies already created by God to fulfill his mission.

Many people suffered slavery in the colonial days and have been free now for a long time. However, to some, this freedom is only in the physical sense because they still have the slave mentality. If they suffer persecution from the tribe or race that enslaved them before, even if the people did not mean it in a discriminative way, they interpret it as taking them back to slavery. Sometimes this is true, but most of the time it is not. Everyone suffers persecution, but because of insecurity people fight foolishly. A person may molest someone once, but the molested person, through their un-forgiveness and lack of healing from the molestation, will re-live the molestation over and over again, giving the molester power to molest them in their absence over and over again.

God will allow trials and tests to come upon us, but God never tempts anyone. He will allow tests to come our way for our growth. These come from people and situations in our own families, strangers, and with those closest to you. He uses these trials as His pressure washer to wash the slave mentality out of us. It is never a pleasant experience, but the pressure washer gets all the dirt out of us, (God's house) and makes "the house" look as good as new. God can only work with new wineskins, not old wineskins. He has new wine for you and me, like Jesus said:

"But no one puts a piece of unshrunk (new) cloth on an old garment; for the patch pulls away from the garment, and a worse tear results. Nor is new wine put into old wineskins [that have lost their elasticity]; otherwise the wineskins burst, and the [fermenting] wine spills and the wineskins are ruined. But new wine is put into fresh wineskins, so both are preserved" (Matt. 9:16–17 AMP).

"The temptations in your life are no different from what others experience. And God is faithful. He will not allow the temptation to be more than you can stand. When you are tempted, he will show you a way out so that you can endure" (1 Cor. 10:13 NLT).

God will only entrust His Kingdom and His wealth to mature sons and daughters. No father or mother would entrust his or her wealth to an immature child, because the child will squander all the wealth and bring poverty to the family. A father or mother will entrust his or her wealth to the mature child who will use it wisely to increase and multiply the wealth so that the family will become wealthier than before.

The same is true with God. He is concerned about us and wants to mold us into who He created us to be, like Christ, so that we can take up our Father's business, like Jesus did, and follow Him. In Luke 2:41-52, Jesus, as a twelve-year-old, got left behind by His parents. They looked for Him and eventually found Him in the temple discussing God's Word. When His mother questioned Him and expressed her concern about why He was left behind, He said He was about His Father's business. Like Christ, we, too, must always be about our Father's business.

Christ's wounds, bruises, chastisement, and beatings (stripes) brought us grace, forgiveness, deliverance, peace, and healing. Who would ever think that such pain inflicted on someone would bring about freedom to another? This is why Jesus tells us we must deny ourselves, carry our cross, and follow Him. The cross is not pleasant or easy to carry. Denying ourselves is not pleasant or easy, but we should follow the example of Jesus Christ, our Savior, so that we may build God's Kingdom. Our reward awaits us if we do not give up.

"But He was wounded for our transgressions, He was bruised for our iniquities; the chastisement for our peace was upon Him, and by His stripes we are healed" (Isa. 53:5).

"We know what real love is because Jesus gave up his life for us. So we also ought to give up our lives for our brothers and sisters" (1 John 3:16 NLT).

We must give up fear, pride and anything that keeps us from spreading the gospel of Jesus Christ. We must do it at all costs like Jesus did. This is the real love. Agape love.

> But I'll tell you whom to fear. Fear God, who has the power to kill you and then throw you into hell. Yes, he's the one to fear. "What is the price of five sparrows—two copper coins? Yet God does not forget a single one of them. And the very hairs on your head are all numbered. So don't be afraid; you are more valuable to God than a whole flock of sparrows. "I tell you the truth, everyone who acknowledges me publicly here on earth, the Son of Man will also acknowledge in the presence of God's angels. But anyone who denies me here on earth will be denied before God's angels. (Luke 12:5–9 NLT)

The Appointed Time

He has made everything beautiful in its time. (Eccl 3:11a)

"Yahweh answered me, "Write the vision, and make it plain on tablets, that he who runs may read it. For the vision is yet for the appointed time, and it hurries toward the end, and won't prove false. Though it takes time, wait for it; because it will surely come. It won't delay." (Hab. 2:2–3 WEB).

The appointed time is usually not revealed to people in advance, and it is not dependent on the person. The appointed time is God's time. That is why some people think God has taken too long, and the prophecies take a long time to come to pass. Even those prophecies received by the Israelites took many years to be fulfilled, but remember, God's math is not humans' math. It cannot even be close to human understanding. He counts a day as a thousand years and a thousand years like one day. How can the human mind fathom that? He multiplied the sound of four lepers into the sound of three great armies—the Egyptian, Hittite, and Israelite Armies (2 Kings 7:6-7). Who can fathom that, either? God spoke to King David and the prophets of old about the coming of the Messiah. Look at how long it took for that to happen and how accurate God's Word was.

"So when the apostles were with Jesus, they kept asking him, 'Lord, has the time come for you to free Israel and restore our kingdom?' He replied, '*The Father alone has the authority to set those dates and times, and they are not for you to know.* But you will receive power when the Holy Spirit comes upon you. And you will be my witnesses, telling people about me everywhere—in Jerusalem, throughout Judea, in Samaria, and to the ends of the earth'" (Acts 1:6–9 NLT; italics added).

There is an appointed time for your God-given task (GGT). God makes all things beautiful in its time. We must have patience and trust God to accomplish our GGT in His perfect time, each step of the way. There is a time for everything. For David to be king, it took several years from the time he was anointed as king. David learned obedience from the things he suffered. The wilderness prepared him for the kingdom. Joseph had a GGT before he was created. In a dream, God revealed to Joseph the end result of his assignment, but the process he was going to go through to get to the end was not revealed. It took several years in the wilderness as a part of his journey for Joseph to see his dream come true. What about Jesus? For Jesus to start His work on earth and step into His role as Savior, it took Him thirty years. He had to endure the wilderness and then the glory.

"Jesus therefore said to them, "My time has not yet come, but your time is always ready. The world can't hate you, but it hates me, because I testify about it, that its works are evil. You go up to the feast. I am not yet going up to this feast, *because my time is not yet fulfilled.*" Having said these things to them, he stayed in Galilee." (John 7:6–9 WEB; italics added).

The God-given task speaks of the end. Write your vision; make it plain.

God always tell us of the end from the beginning. He tells us of the end so that we may trust Him no matter what we go through before we get to the victorious end. It is like watching a movie without knowing the middle but knowing the end. For example, in an action movie, there are good guys and the bad guys. In the beginning of the movie, the bad guys always seem to be winning. They may kill the family members of the good guys, destroy their properties, and make the town a desolation.

They seem to have won, and there is no hope for the good guys, but just when we think all is lost, the good guys somehow rise above all odds and destroy all the bad guys and their strongholds. The victory is great because the bad guys are destroyed beyond comeback, but the pain the good guys went through was great too. They have wounds to heal and scars to show. Any good action movie always has the bad guys looking as if they are winning, which gets the viewers anxious and on edge; but later on there is victory for the good guys, and the audience go home relieved that good has overcome evil.

This plot was God's idea; people just copied it. God created the earth and made humans, and it was all beautiful. Then the bad guys (Satan and his demons) showed up and destroyed the beautiful family God had made. They killed, stole, and destroyed, making what God had created look bad and through sin, separated humans from God. Then God thought of a plan to get back His creation and destroy the bad guy. He did this, but it costs Him His only family, His only Son, Jesus Christ. He sent His Son to rescue man-kind from the kingdom of darkness, however, the enemy thought he would destroy Him through crucifixion.

It seemed like the bad guys won again until that Easter Sunday morning, on the third day, when Jesus Christ, the Son of the ONLY living God rose up from the grave! He destroyed sin and DEATH; He rose in victory over all principalities and powers of evil. The Bible says that Jesus went down and came up with the gifts of humans. He took back from the devil all the dominion and authority he had stolen from people in the Garden of Eden and gave it all back to them. In Jesus's name, we have authority over all powers of darkness. Jesus went through a lot of pain to get to the victorious part. He even has scars to prove this, just in case we have a "doubting Thomas" in our midst (John 20:24–29).

"And all the people who belong to this world worshiped the beast. They are the ones whose names were not written in the Book of Life that belongs *to the Lamb who was slaughtered before the world was made"* (Rev. 13:8 NLT; italics added).

In God, nothing just happens; at the appointed time it will come to pass. The appointed time was made before the foundations of the world. Even the devil has an appointed time for His destruction. The apostle Paul in his letter to Timothy also revealed that God gave us purpose and grace way before time began and it was finalized in the physical with the finished work of the cross. Paul also reveals his God-given task in;

2 Timothy 1:9-11 *"who has saved us and called us with a holy calling, not according to our works, but according to His own purpose and grace which was*

given to us in Christ Jesus before time began, but has now been revealed by the appearing of our Savior Jesus Christ, *who* has abolished death and brought life and immortality to light through the gospel, to which I was appointed *a preacher, an apostle, and a teacher of the Gentiles*" (italics added)

There is a time for everything. King Solomon makes this very clear, when He spoke of a time for everything.

> For everything there is a season, and a time for every purpose under heaven: a time to be born, and a time to die; a time to plant, and a time to pluck up that which is planted; a time to kill, and a time to heal; a time to break down, and a time to build up; a time to weep, and a time to laugh; a time to mourn, and a time to dance; a time to cast away stones, and a time to gather stones together; a time to embrace, and a time to refrain from embracing; a time to seek, and a time to lose; a time to keep, and a time to cast away; a time to tear, and a time to sew; a time to keep silence, and a time to speak; a time to love, and a time to hate; a time for war, and a time for peace." (Eccles. 3:1–8 WEB)

One time a friend asked me when I would record my next music album, and my response to her was, "at the appointed time." Do not compare your life with others or conform to the timings of this world. We must align ourselves with God, His standards and timing. For Gideon, who was called a mighty man of war while he was hiding from his enemies, it was not the right time to tell him to go fight his enemies because he was terrified of them. But according to God, it was the right time because His strength is made perfect in weakness.

Do not judge according to what you see or feel or what the "norm" is or what people say about you. Let God guide the appointed time. Many times in my life, God has done things greater than me because I trusted in His ability and not mine, in His timing and not mine. He spoke, and I spoke what He spoke, and it came to pass. Did I sound crazy? Yes! Many times my family and friends thought I had lost it, but it came to pass, and that is why I love this God!

It is critical to wait upon the appointed time. For example, if you are expecting a baby, at the appointment time you will give birth to the baby. But if you get impatient and decide to get the baby out before the appointed time, you will be aborting the baby and you will never enjoy being a mother or a father. To enjoy the fullness of the promise, we must trust God and wait patiently for the appointed time no matter how long, how painful, uncomfortable or tiresome the process is. We must keep our minds on the promise, not the problems we face.

CHAPTER 5
Message

ACCORDING TO *MERRIAM WEBSTER* DICTIONARY, a message is "a communication in writing, in speech, or by signals"

To have a message, one must be sent. To be sent, one must have an encounter with the sender of the message. Jesus sent His disciples to all the world to preach the good news. They had an encounter with the message giver. Paul too had an encounter with Jesus and he was given a message to give to the Gentiles. I too and many others have had encounters with God and have a message to the world from God. Many times these encounters are experienced in the most difficult times of our lives. God uses these times to reveal Himself to us in a special way and we in turn reveal Him to others. In this, we become His messengers. He relays a message to the world through us. Some people however take the trials they face negatively, and at the end they have bitterness and rage instead of a message of hope and redemption to others who would be facing similar trials.

I will break this down into three different categories of people, and three different stages in life that bring about a message, making one a messenger of Christ.

THREE TYPES OF PEOPLE; THREE DIFFERENT STAGES

1. MESS – AGE = MESS (Mess without Age, which means maturity is just a MESS)

These people have nothing to be admired or to offer the world. They are not profitable in God's Kingdom. This is because they do not mature from their mistakes and messes in life. They stay in the mess and some even die in the mess. This may have been a stage some of us have gone through and hopefully matured from it.

2. – Mess + Age = Age (without any Mess with Age only = Maturity)
These people are usually prideful, lack grace, and are unable to relate to others or to help them in their failures to rise up again. They don't understand why people make mistakes or messes, they are very judgmental; these people are not profitable in God's Kingdom. They are too self-righteous to profit others. We may have been in this stage before, at least I know I have and yes, I was very judgmental, now I thank God for the messes I had to go through in my life to humble me and give me humility and grace for others.

3. Mess + Age (Maturity) = Message

These people have everything to offer the world. They have been there, done that, learned from it, and now are ready to be of service to others to help them through their struggles. They have pearls to share and grace to give. They have patience to teach and are an extension of God's hand to His children. These people are very profitable to God's Kingdom. They snatch people out of darkness and preach hope through their experiences. God uses these people greatly; they are His messengers because they have a MESSAGE. They are a living testimony of God's grace, power and restoration.

Who Is a Messenger?

A messenger is one who brings messages. If you want to be a messenger, you must have a Mess plus Age. You cannot be used by God or profit the Kingdom of God if you lack this combination. That is why, instead of Jesus praying for Peter's victory in temptation, He valued Peter's faith and his lesson from the failure (MESS+AGE) so he would strengthen others and be useful to God's Kingdom. I am so grateful to God for all the things I have been through and lessons learned from my mess through the years. I am excited to help and strengthen others through their trials. God is amazing; no wonder James 1:2–4 tells us to count it all joy when we go through various trials and temptations.

> *When you fall and you get up and you are restored,*
> *Strengthen your brothers.*

Remember when Aaron led the children of Israel into idol worship? His brother, Moses, was up on the mountain with God getting the Ten Commandments. God was angry, they repented, and God chose the same priest who led people into idol worship to be His priest and lead people into worship of Yahweh. Why would God do this instead of using a blameless person? This is because Aaron would be the best priest, having received grace from God for himself; he would extend the same grace and intercede for others with sympathy and a genuine, nonjudgmental heart. Remember why Jesus is the great High Priest for us?

"For we do not have a High Priest who is unable to sympathize and understand our weaknesses and temptations, but One who has been tempted [knowing exactly how it feels to be human] in every respect as we are, yet without [committing any] sin" (Heb. 4:15 AMP).

"And the Lord said, 'Simon, Simon! Indeed, Satan has asked for you, that he may sift you as wheat. *But I have prayed for you, that your faith should not fail; and when you have returned to Me, strengthen your brethren.*' But he said to Him, 'Lord, I am ready to go with You, both to prison and to death.' Then He said, 'I tell you, Peter, the rooster shall not crow this day before you will deny three times that you know Me'" (Luke 22:31–34; italics added).

A Righteous Man Falls Seven Times

"For a righteous man falls seven times and rises again, but the wicked stumble in time of disaster and collapse" (Prov. 24:16 AMP).

Mess – Age (maturity) = Hebrews 6:8

"For soil that drinks the rain, which often falls on it and produces crops useful to those for whose benefit it is cultivated, receives a blessing from God; [8] *but if it persistently produces thorns and thistles, it is worthless and close to being cursed, and it ends up being burned.*" (Hebrews 6:7-8 AMP; italics added)

Stumbling and falling create a mess in our lives. No one likes to have these messes, but when we learn from our mistakes, we are able to avoid repeating them and can help others not to make the same mistakes we made. Instead of all of us making the same mistakes, God will allow a handful of people to make the mistake and learn from it. He then restores them for the sake of millions behind them, who would otherwise make the same mistake. They in turn teach others to avoid the same error so that the mistake will only be made a few times instead of "a million" times.

Let us take, for example, people who are walking on a path. In this path there is a hole covered with grass so that it is not visible to them. The first few people walking through the path will fall into the hole, and they will be rescued by others. They in turn will put a sign to detour others so they do not fall into the same hole. They may even put up a barrier or someone there to lead others away from the dangerous hole. As much as it was a painful experience, these people who fell into the hole learned from that unpleasant experience. It cost them their time, it was painful and scary. Therefore, they are set on a mission to make sure no one experiences the pain of falling into that particular hole. Some of them may have a scar from the fall to show others in order to convince those doubting of the danger ahead.

On the other hand, if they encounter someone who has fallen into the same hole or a similar predicament along the way, they will be gracious to the person and take their time to help rescue them because they can relate with the person. They will not laugh or ridicule the person who fell into the hole; rather, they will be remorseful and more than willing to take their time to help restore the person to safe grounds.

Planned Failures

This is the same with us in the spirit. Some failures have been scheduled for our sake and the sake of others. When I went into nursing school, it was very tough with the late nights of study, the training after school, and all that I had to do to be successful. Now as a registered nurse, I realize it was all for the patients that I will treat. I went through all these things to serve others; even though I get paid doing it, my patients benefit from the pain I went through.

In the same way, Jesus went through pain, suffering, and death for the sake of humanity. He did not die for Himself. When He rose again, He kept His scars so others would see and know where He had been and would believe. The wounds and pain were felt by Him, but the scars were and are for others, not Him. One of His disciples was the doubting Thomas, who said unless he saw the scars on Jesus's hands and touched His side, where He was pierced by the spear, he would not believe in the Resurrection of Christ. How much more doubt will those who did not walk with Him side by side, listening to His teaching daily, have? The disciples of Jesus and many others saw Jesus die, and they believed and buried Him, but the power was never in His death. If Christ remained in the grave, there would be no salvation. But because of His power over death, we now live in victory. As a result, all who receive Him as Lord and Savior now live as a new creation in Christ Jesus.

My message comes from my messes in life and from my maturity after the mess. Without my mess, I would only have age to show for, and my life would not be of much use to anyone. On the other hand, without the maturity from my mess, I would only have the mess to show for myself. We all know that person in our family or in our relationships in the past who is old enough to know better but never seems to grow in maturity. He or she is very immature in his or her actions or choice of words. Age without maturity is just a number. Age is only useful with maturity. This means learning obedience from our mistakes and not living a life of practicing sin. We must be able to go through something to help someone else who is going through a similar situation. Message is helping someone by sharing what you have learned over the years from the mistakes you have made. Only mature people have a message because they have been restored and have learned from their mistakes.

We all know not to seek advice on raising children from someone who has never raised a child or marriage counseling from someone who has never been or is not married. Jesus learned obedience from the things He suffered.

"Though He was a Son, yet He learned obedience by the things which He suffered. And having been perfected, He became the author of eternal salvation to all who *obey Him*" (Heb. 5:8–9; italics added).

"When I was a child, I spoke as a child, I understood as a child, I thought as a child; but when I became a man, *I put away childish things*" (1 Cor. 13:11; italics added).

I always say the wounds are mine, but the scars are yours. We ought to learn from our experiences in life and be ready to strengthen others. Jesus said to Peter that Peter would deny that he knew Jesus three times. This was the temptation Peter was going to face. We, too, face it today. We confess we are Christians only in the congregation of Christians or when it is convenient or politically correct. But in the midst of all the cursing and gossip and worldly lusts and sin around us, we act as if we do not know who Jesus is. We are ashamed to confess Christ in fear of persecution. Jesus Christ was never ashamed to confess us in the presence of people even unto death. Why should we be afraid to confess Him even if it means losing all we have, including our lives? How many of us are ready to die confessing Jesus Christ as Lord?

"Simon, Simon! Indeed, Satan has asked for you, that he may sift you as wheat." (Luke 22:31; italics added)

What Does It Mean to Sift As Wheat?

Jesus was saying to Peter that Satan asked for permission from God to tempt him, and God allowed it. The temptation was going to bring unrest in Peter's life, and it was going to disorganize his plans and move him from his comfort zone. The temptation was going to challenge Peter and break him down. It was going to reveal what was in Peter, so that he would know and deal with it.

Jesus went on to reassure Peter that He had already prayed for him. The next thing Jesus said surprised me and taught me to trust in Jesus as our great High Priest forever. Jesus went on to explain what He had prayed for and why He had made that prayer as we shall see later. The purpose of sifting wheat is to separate it from chaff. God loves us so much that He will allow us to be sifted so that the chaff can be separated from the wheat. We go through temptation to remove the bad things that dwell within us so we can be useful in God's hands.

Heads up!

Jesus told Peter what the enemy was planning to do. He gave Him a sneak preview of what would happen. But why Peter? The answer is in the verse below.

> Now when Jesus came into the parts of Caesarea Philippi, he asked his disciples, saying, "Who do men say that I, the Son of Man, am?" They said, "Some say John the Baptizer, some, Elijah, and others, Jeremiah, or one of the prophets."

He said to them, "But who do you say that I am?" Simon Peter answered, "You are the Christ, the Son of the living God." Jesus answered him, "Blessed are you, Simon Bar Jonah, for flesh and blood has not revealed this to you, but my Father who is in heaven. I also tell you that you are Peter, and on this rock I will build my assembly, and the gates of Hades will not prevail against it. I will give to you the keys of the Kingdom of Heaven, and whatever you bind on earth will have been bound in heaven; and whatever you release on earth will have been released in heaven." (Matt. 16:13–19 WEB)

Peter was the rock. He was the one to whom it was revealed who Jesus was. He was also the one who desired to be like Jesus when he asked Jesus to call him to walk on water (Matt. 14:22–33). When others turned away saying that the teaching of Christ was hard, after Jesus had taught about eating His body and drinking His blood in John 6:53–65, Peter stayed and supported Jesus. Jesus asked His disciples if they too wanted to turn away from Him, but Simon Peter replied, "Lord, to whom would we go? You have the words that give eternal life. We believe, and we know you are the Holy One of God…Where can we go knowing you are the messiah?" (John 6:68–69)

Peter was eager to learn the things of God; he wanted to please and protect Jesus. He cut off the soldier's ear when they came to arrest Jesus. Peter was sold out for Jesus, but there was a little part that he was still holding on to. Although he said he was willing to die with Jesus, he did not know how afraid he was to lose his life until he faced that threat the night that Jesus was arrested. Jesus and God knew Peter had this fear, but Peter did not know it until he denied Jesus three different times! Jesus knew this sifting had to take place so that Peter may see the chaff that was in him, deal with it and be purified, ready for God's use. This sifting worked because after Jesus went back to heaven, Peter preached fearlessly on the day of Pentecost by the power of the Holy Spirit, and about three thousand people received Jesus in one meeting!

Assurance

"But I have prayed for you, that your faith should not fail." (Luke 22:32a italics added)

Jesus gave Peter the assurance that He had prayed for him. Jesus did not pray for the temptation not to come, nor did He pray for Peter to overcome the temptation. This is because God is not interested in people getting an A in the test; He is interested in people learning from their F's and then tutoring others so as not to get F's. God's school is not like regular human made school. Your spiritual GPA is not increased by how many A's you get; rather it increases from the learned F's and how much you strengthen others.

God calls people and then qualifies them for the task. He does not look for qualified people to give them the task. He does not need a flawless résumé to qualify you for work. He gives you the work and then qualifies you. He trains you, regardless of your past history or background. Some people despise themselves because they think they are too messed up for God to accept them. The filthier you are, the better, because the person who is forgiven much, loves much. Jesus prayed that Peter's faith would not fail him. Without faith in God we cannot please God, and the enemy will destroy us. In Ephesians 6:16 our shield is faith which quenches the fiery darts of the evil one.

The prayer that Jesus prayed for Peter was for the greater good of the church of Jesus Christ, and for Peter's growth, not for Peter's comfort. Through it all, Peter was assured of support in prayer from the great High Priest, Jesus Christ, and so are we. Jesus prays for our FAITH, not our COMFORT.

End Result

And <u>when</u> you have returned to Me (Luke 22:32b)

Jesus told Peter the end result. He told him of the outcome of the temptation; that he was going to be restored back to Christ. Notice that Jesus said, "WHEN you have returned to Me" not IF. This meant that Peter would fall short of God's glory, but his comeback was guaranteed. Peter had denied Jesus and by this he had dis-enrolled himself from being Christ's disciple. He then felt sorry and wanted to be reinstated. Jesus never leaves us nor forsakes us, but we can leave Him and forsake Him just like Peter did. Peter left Jesus but Jesus never left Peter.

"But go, tell His disciples—and Peter—that He is going before you into Galilee; there you will see Him, as He said to you" (Mark 16:7; italics added).

Assignment

Strengthen your brethren. (Luke 22:32b)

The wounds are yours to learn from, but your scars are for others to know God's grace and power. You are to strengthen others by your testimony and sharing your experiences to encourage others who are being sifted or who will be sifted soon. Jesus allows us to go through some lessons for others. Just as He laid His life down for us (John 3:16), we also ought to lay down our lives for our brothers and sisters (1 John 3:16). The wheat goes through sifting and purification, and it is then ready for use. If the wheat is not used, it will expire, making the purification process a waste. Just as wheat is purified for the farmer's use, we are purified for God's use.

If we keep our message to ourselves instead of helping others by revealing the scars we got from the mess we have been through, we are of no use to the Kingdom of God. If I became a nurse or a doctor and never used my license, then I am no use to the medical field. For me to renew my RN license, I must show proof of using it actively and currently. We go through life and learn from our mistakes for the sake of others. We therefore must use our experiences to strengthen each other. We must let the devil suffer loss for the pain he caused us, by strengthening our brothers and sisters. We must not act as if we have never messed up. This is great deception from the enemy that prevents us from helping each other grow. It doesn't matter what others think of you, it matters what God thinks of you. Just because you can run, doesn't mean you never crawled. Sympathize and help the crawling Christians and those who are learning to walk as they fall because you were once there. It is disgusting to see how many people despise others because they are not as spiritually strong as they are. Be careful lest you fall. God is the God of all; babes in Christ and mature Christians. He judges all according to their level. Be faithful in your calling and help (strengthen) others in humility and grace.

Manifestation of the Script Jesus Told Peter

Peter Sins (Sifted as Wheat)

They seized him, and led him away, and brought him into the high priest's house. But Peter followed *from* a *distance*. When they had kindled a fire in the middle of the courtyard, and had sat down together, Peter sat among them. A certain servant girl saw him as he sat in the light, and looking intently at him, said, "This man also was with him." He denied Jesus, saying, *"Woman, I don't know him."* After a little while someone else saw him, and said, "You also are one of them!" But Peter answered, *"Man, I am not!"* After about one hour passed, another confidently affirmed, saying, "Truly this man also was with him, for he is a Galilean!" But Peter said, *"Man, I don't know what you are talking about!"* Immediately, while he was still speaking, a rooster crowed." (Luke 22:54–60 WEB; italics added)

Peter said he loved Jesus, but he had not counted the cost of following Him even though Jesus had taught on this. His other disciples also ran away, but none of them were put in Peter's shoes of sifting. Earlier, God had chosen Peter to reveal Jesus to the other disciples when Jesus asked them who they thought He was. Peter was also used by Satan to try and talk Jesus out of His mission on earth. Peter was the only one willing to step out of the boat, his comfort zone, and walk on the stormy sea with Jesus. He was willing to obey Jesus having fished all night but couldn't catch any fish, however when Jesus asked them to cast their nets one more time, Peter responded,

"… "Master, we have toiled all night and caught nothing; nevertheless at Your word I will let down the net."" (Luke 5:5).

Peter was like a roller coaster, but God knew that he really wanted to follow Jesus against all odds. Peter was now following Jesus Christ FROM A DISTANCE. Peter had said that he would never leave Christ but now he had distanced himself from Him. Peter loved his life more than He did Christ, and this "chaff" had to be separated from him, the "wheat." This was necessary, not for God to hurt Peter, but to mold him and make him into a true disciple of Christ. Peter's end result was to be a rock that God spoke of. Someone once said, God is not interested in our comfort but in our growth. Going to the gym is not fun, but the results of working out are awesome!

Peter Regrets His Sin

"The Lord turned and looked at Peter. And Peter remembered the word of the Lord, how He had told him, 'Before a rooster crows today, you will deny Me three times.' And he went out and wept bitterly [deeply grieved and distressed]" (Luke 22:61–62).

Peter was very grieved by his sin, which showed regret. The first step toward repentance is to acknowledge the sin and to be deeply grieved by it. If you sin and are not deeply grieved, then you are more likely to repeat the same sin. Peter was assured of Christ's love even in his mess. The difference between Peter and Judas was only one thing. Peter's faith did not fail him, while Judas's faith failed him, and he committed suicide. Faith in Jesus is the difference between everlasting life and eternal death.

Peter Restored

> After breakfast Jesus asked Simon Peter, "Simon, son of John, do you love me more than these?" "Yes, Lord," Peter replied, "you know I love you." *"Then feed my lambs,"* Jesus told him. Jesus repeated the question: "Simon son of John, do you love me?" "Yes, Lord," Peter said, "you know I love you." *"Then take care of my sheep,"* Jesus said. A third time he asked him, "Simon son of John, do you love me?" Peter was hurt that Jesus asked the question a third time. He said, "Lord, you know everything. You know that I love you." Jesus said, *"Then feed my sheep."* (John 21:10–17 NLT; italics added)

Peter had fallen short of the glory of God, and that was why he needed restoration. Jesus did not count Peter as one of His disciples until He restored him. When you leave Jesus, He does not force you back, but if you come back to Him, He will restore you. For each time Peter denied Jesus, Jesus restored him. Peter denied Jesus three times; Jesus restored Peter three times. The pain Peter went through when he denied Jesus was for him, but the scar was for others. For us! Each betrayal was a wound that now had turned into a scar, and for each scar, there was an assignment. Jesus told Peter that he would deny Him three times—not once, not twice, but three times, but after restoration, he was to strengthen other followers of Christ.

God's grace is amazing. Imagine your best friend denying you when you need him or her the most. Not once, not twice, but three times. Would you restore that person back as your friend? Maybe once or twice—but three times? Christ expects us to give the same grace to others as we receive from Him. Peter's three denials formed three wounds and three scars which produced three assignments: to care for our brethren's spirit, soul, and body.

THREE SCARS, THREE ASSIGNMENTS

From Peter's sifting, he was wounded three times and when he healed, he had three scars to show for, that symbolized his assignments after restoration.

THE FIRST SCAR'S ASSIGNMENT WAS TO:

"THEN FEED MY LAMBS"

Growing up in Africa, we had cows, sheep and goats that I saw being taken care of. A lamb is a young sheep, less than one year old, that needs to be fed and nurtured to grow well. Lambs can die from starvation, or from low body temperature; they need warmth. They can also die from diarrhea, if you change the feeds rapidly or feed them too much. Lambs need a lot of work and attention for them to survive.

Likewise, newborn believers are likened to lambs by Christ. He is the great shepherd, and He has entrusted the mature sheep with His lambs. The Word of God will protect them and give them warmth, fill them, and help them mature. We must not give them the meat of the

Word before they learn to drink the milk. This was the first restoration assignment that Christ gave to Peter.

Peter in turn taught believers saying, "Putting away therefore all wickedness, all deceit, hypocrisies, envies, and all evil speaking, as *newborn babies*, long for the *pure milk* of the Word, that with it you may grow, if indeed you have tasted that the Lord is gracious:"

(1 Pet. 2:1–3 WEB; italics added).

THE SECOND SCAR'S ASSIGNMENT WAS TO:

"THEN TAKE CARE OF MY SHEEP"

A sheep is an adult lamb. The care of a sheep is different from the care of a lamb. The sheep needs shelter and care like shearing and hoof trimming. They also need vaccinations and deworming. Sheep need to be led and guided in the right direction at all times, or they may wander away. They follow each other even into danger. They are defenseless against predators, because they cannot fight, so they run from predators but often lose because they have no speed. They need a leader and protector, a lot of guidance, and supervision. They need enough space to graze and shelter from harsh weather. They definitely need a shepherd.

When Jesus speaks of sheep here, He is referring to maturing Christians. These Christians still need to be cared for so that they can continue to grow and mature into strong Christians. They will learn how to lead others into the ways of God. Some Christians get mistreated by others, and they despair along the way because they expect the preachers or the "leaders" to be more like Christ. This is a good expectation but a deadly one, because not all "leaders" follow Christ and obey Him fully. There are those who act like the Pharisees. They make up religious laws and hold it against others but do not follow it themselves. We must know that leaders will make mistakes sometimes because they too are sheep.

They need to be constantly led by the great shepherd, Jesus Christ. They need to obey Christ fully and teach others to do the same.

THE THIRD SCAR'S ASSIGNMENT WAS TO:

"THEN FEED MY SHEEP"

Sheep feed on a full vegetarian diet and water. Likewise, Jesus here speaks of mature Christians who need to be continually fed by the pure Word of God, in order to grow into the knowledge of God. We must monitor where and from whom we feed constantly for sound doctrine and the uncompromised Word of God. We must not attend church for the mere reason of membership. Christ never introduced membership—people did. You must test the spirit of your preacher and not be ignorant, because some preachers started in the spirit but end in the flesh. Likewise preachers and teachers of the Word need to continually feed from Christ so as to feed His sheep. Read Ezekiel 34 to see the prophecy against the shepherds of Israel who mistreated the lambs and sheep of God...

PETER USED BY GOD AFTER RESTORATION

Peter was used by God in Acts chapter 2 on the day of Pentecost, the glorious day in which the promise of the Holy Spirit was sent to earth in the hearts of men and women who received Christ. The Holy Spirit is a witness of Christ unto the world through the lives of believers. Peter, who was once ashamed of Christ was now transformed to the rock that Christ had named him. (Matt. 16:13-20)

On this day, Peter boldly faced the accusers of the brethren: "But Peter, standing with the eleven, raised his voice and addressed them: 'Men of Judea and all you who live in Jerusalem, let this be explained to you; listen closely and pay attention to what I have to say. These people are not drunk, as you assume, since it is [only] the third hour of the day (9:00 a.m.); but this is [the beginning of] what was spoken of through the prophet Joel'" (Acts 2:14–16 AMP).

Peter did this out of his love for God. When Jesus restored Peter, He asked Peter if he loved Him, and Peter responded that he loved Jesus. Peter showed his love for Christ by being His witness. Peter was not afraid of the consequences of his witness for Christ; he no longer feared people as he had done before. Rather, he feared God and kept his word to Christ.

Are we willing and ready to put our love for Christ into action, regardless of the consequences involved? Are we more afraid of people's punishment than God's? Remember, people can kill only the body, but God can kill both body and soul. Peter acted as the rock when he and John were arrested for being witnesses for Christ in Acts 4:13–20

> Now when they saw the *boldness* of Peter and John, and had perceived that they were *unlearned* and *ignorant* men, they *marveled*. They recognized that they had been with Jesus. Seeing the man who was healed standing with them, they could say nothing against it. But when they had commanded them to go aside out of the council, they conferred among themselves, saying, "What shall we do to these men? Because indeed a notable miracle has been done through them, as can be plainly seen by all who dwell in Jerusalem, and we can't deny it. But so that this spreads no further among the people, *let's threaten them*, that from now on they don't speak to anyone in this name." They called them, and commanded them not to speak at all nor teach in the name of Jesus. But Peter and John answered them, "Whether it is right in the sight of God to listen to you rather than to God, judge for yourselves, for we can't help telling the things which we saw and heard." (Acts 4:13–20 WEB; italics added)

Just like people saw and could not dispute God's work through Peter and John, they cannot dispute the power of God working in and through your life. However, they can threaten you and make you afraid to fulfill your God-given task. God hates fear. Fear is the opposite of faith and without faith it's impossible to please God. Fear stops God from working through us because God is a FAITH God not a God of the FEARFUL or the COWARDLY. Before God used Peter, He dealt with Peter's fear of being a witness for Christ which was Peter's GGT. Another great example is found in Judges 6:12. The first thing God did before using Gideon was to deal with his fear. God changed Gideon's name from a coward to a mighty man of war, Gideon believed it, received it and God defeated the enemy through the mighty man of war, not through the coward. The fate of cowards is clearly spoken of in the book of Revelation.

"He who overcomes shall inherit all things, and I will be his God and he shall be My son. But the *cowardly*, unbelieving, abominable, murderers, sexually immoral, sorcerers, idolaters, and all liars shall have their part in the lake which burns with fire and brimstone, which is the second death." (Revelation 21:7-8; italics added)

Jesus started the category of people who will inherit hell with the "Cowardly". I believe He did this because this category consists of the largest group of people today, that is why Jesus is warning us. Are you in this group? Are you afraid to live your GGT because of people or lack of security or stability in finances or family. Give it all to God and follow Him. Don't be like the rich young ruler who valued financial security more than eternal security. God will never take you where His grace is not. Trust Him and in His ability to keep you and all that concerns you. He is God, remember? He created you and the whole universe, nothing is too difficult for Him.

"Jesus answered him, "If you wish to be perfect [that is, have the spiritual maturity that accompanies godly character with no moral or ethical deficiencies], go and sell what you have and give [the money] to the poor, and you will have treasure in heaven; and come, follow Me [becoming My disciple, believing and trusting in Me and walking the same path of life that I walk]." But when the young man heard this, he left grieving and distressed, for he owned much property and had many possessions [which he treasured more than his relationship with God]. Jesus said to His disciples, "I assure you and most solemnly say to you, it is difficult for a rich man [who clings to possessions and status as security] to enter the kingdom of heaven. Again I tell you, it is easier for a camel to go through the eye of a needle, than for a rich man [who places his faith in wealth and status] to enter the kingdom of God.'" (Matthew 19:21-24 AMP)

The following scripture should be our prayer especially now, when people are intimidated to spread God's Word, yet the world is not afraid to do evil. Children of God, we need to wake up and be restored, and out of our love for Christ, we must be bold witnesses for Christ. The disciples prayed for boldness in the following prayer and so must we.

"Now, Lord, look at their threats, and grant to your servants to speak your word with all *boldness*, while you stretch out your hand to heal; and that signs and wonders may be done through the name of your holy Servant Jesus." *When they had prayed, the place was shaken where they were gathered together. They were all filled with the Holy Spirit, and they spoke the word of God with boldness."* (Acts 4:29–31 WEB; italics added).

Equipped for the Work

God works in us and transforms us so that we can be fully equipped for the work He created us to do. The higher the building is, the deeper the foundation must be. As soon as the builder decides that he or she wants to build a magnificent building, he finds the land and plans it all out. The building does not start from the ground level. The builders must dig down below, deep enough for a foundation of a very tall and strong building. During this stage, the site is a mess, dirty, unattractive and hard to tell if any progress is being made. All that people see here is dirt and darkness in the hole. It takes a long time to lay the foundation of a big building, and people who pass by and see signs of an upcoming building may ridicule the owner. They may think that the owner ran out of funding for his or her building or that it was a big mistake to begin with.

On the other hand, both the owner and the builder have the finished project in mind. The deeper, muddier, and the uglier the scene looks to the general public, the more beautiful it is to the owner and the builder. This is because the deeper the foundation, the stronger the building will be in the end, and this is a great sight for the owner to behold.

This is so with our God-given assignments. From God's point of view, the deeper the foundation, the greater the ministry. God must dig out the dirt in our lives and expose it. This is a very painful process and one that isolates us and exposes our weakness and filth, not our beauty. The people who were at one point comfortable in our lives before the exposure are now nowhere to be seen; they ridicule us and point a finger, showing how ugly and dirty we look. They speak of how defeated and low we are and perhaps how we will never get back up again. They laugh at us, and if you have been here, it is a very lonely place. This is where your so-called friends, your family, and even your spouse may leave and forsake you. It is a place no one understands, a process we must go through alone, because we were created as individuals. We came to earth as individuals with individual assignments, and we will go back to God as individuals with a report from our assignments. In this place, only the builder and master planner of your life, God, understands you. He never leaves you or forsakes you. Someone once said that we should not be discouraged when we see someone succeeding faster than we are, especially if we are on the right track, living in obedience to God, because a palace takes longer to build than an ordinary house.

Jesus could have died as a baby for the world and shed His blood for our salvation, but God waited for Him to grow and start His ministry after He was thirty years old, and He completed it after three years. This is a ratio of 10:1. Ten years of life lesson for every 1 year of ministry. The foundation had to be built, which takes longer than the building itself. This was no ordinary child but the Son of God and yet He had to wait that long. How much more must we wait and go through the process for our ministry or assignment? Patience is a great virtue and extremely rare but of great importance in fulfilling our God-given assignments.

God has put in us eternity; we just do not know it. We were created with eternity in mind. Rom. 8:28–30 says that we were predestined. God created us in His image and likeness. Image is the outward appearance or frame. Likeness is the resemblance in actions and behavior. We were created to live forever, just as God lives forever. We live forever because our spirits never die. We either live life with God in heaven forever after life on earth is done, or eternal death in hell with the devil and his angels for those who disobey God's Word.

When we obey God and teach others to obey Him, we are living with eternity in mind. We save souls from eternal death by praying for them, living like Christ; letting our lives to be a living testimony of who He is and by telling them about the life given freely to us in Christ Jesus.

We all like to know the whole plan and sequence of our lives because we like to plan ahead and get things ready and in order. However, God's ways are too complex for us. We are not in a position to take in everything that God has planned for us all at once as the scripture says,

> "For my thoughts are not your thoughts, and your ways are not my ways," says Yahweh. "For as the heavens are higher than the earth, so are my ways higher than your ways, and my thoughts than your thoughts." (Isa. 55:8–9 WEB)

We were created and assigned for eternity. This is how you test and see whether you are doing your God-given task or a human-given task. Does your assignment affect eternity? Are you growing God's Kingdom, are you destroying it or are you doing nothing about it? We must be about our Father's business like Christ and grow His Kingdom.

If we obey and do our GGT, we will rejoice for what God will do through us. Our assignments will make way for us and will prosper our lives. The assignment gives provision and prosperity which we enjoy because this is God's gift to us as we obey Him.

"Do you see a man skillful and experienced in his work? He will stand [in honor] before kings; He will not stand before obscure men" (Prov. 22:29 AMP).

"A man's gift makes room for him and brings him before great men" (Prov. 18:16).

Our God is an awesome God. His Word is established in the heavens and earth, and His love endures forever. His plans cannot be altered, and no one can contend with Him. When God has decided to bless, no person can curse. If God curses you, no one can bless you. Look at what God did with Christ; He made His work of salvation for eternity, and no one can add or take away from it. That is why no one can correct God or teach Him. He is the God of all flesh, and He has the final Word in every situation. His Word stands forever.

"Forever, O Lord, thy word is settled in heaven" (Ps. 119:89 KJV).

"I have seen that all [human] perfection has its limits [no matter how grand and perfect and noble]; Your commandment is exceedingly broad *and* extends without limits [into eternity]." (Ps. 119:96 AMP)

"Heaven and earth will pass away, but My words will by no means pass away" (Matt. 24:35).

Everything that has been on earth and that will be has already been there in the spirit. There is nothing we see now or we shall see on earth that has not been seen in the spirit first. Everything has to exist in the spirit first before it manifests in the physical. That is why it says in Revelation that Jesus was the Lamb of God, who was slain before the foundations of the world. Jesus died in the spirit and rose again, and then it was made manifest in the physical. That is why, when God gives you a

Word, it has already happened in the spirit. It is up to us to believe it and call it into existence in the physical.

Many of our promises are still waiting to be called forth into manifestation. So often we get discouraged, our minds and intellect get in the way, and we do not believe God's Word, which hinders it from coming to pass. We must believe and speak out in Faith what God has said to us.

The key to calling the things in the spirit into manifestation in the natural is FAITH. Find out what God says about a specific situation, what His will is, and then call it into the physical by faith, without any doubt. When we repeat His Word and say what He says, it must come to pass. Hold God accountable to His Word; He wants us to.

"So will My word be which goes out of My mouth; It will not return to Me void (useless, without result), without accomplishing what I desire, And without succeeding in the matter for which I sent it" (Isa. 55:11 AMP).

God has given us a blank check to withdraw from heaven's treasures, but we must believe that the funds are available and then write the check and wait for the manifestation with expectation. According to Proverbs 23:18, the expectations of the righteous shall not be cut off.

We were created to prosper. Just as a fish excels in swimming and a bird in flying, we were created to excel in our God-given assignment. Words are spirit; we must speak what God says about the situation we face, and it must obey. If we acknowledge the situation instead of God's Word on the situation, we will always be miserable and remain in the defeated situation.

CHAPTER 6
Salvation

You Must Be Born Again

BELOVED, WITHOUT GOD, WE ARE nothing. We cannot live independent of Him. Even nonbelievers, knowingly or unknowingly, rely on God for their next breath, for the sunrise and rain. Even though they are ignorant of the true source of life, it does not negate the fact that they are dependent on God. To be able to know and be successful in our God-given tasks, we need to be born again. For you to be entrusted with the things of the kingdom, any kingdom, you must be a citizen of that kingdom. You cannot be president of a country you are not a citizen of, but you can work in a country you are not a citizen of. You can be in the church and serve and do everything to serve God's kingdom, but if you are not born again, you will not enter the Kingdom of God. Your good works can never save you.

"Jesus answered him, "I assure you *and* most solemnly say to you, *unless a person is born again [reborn from above—spiritually transformed, renewed, sanctified], he cannot [ever] see and experience the kingdom of God.*"" (John 3:3 AMP; italics added)

People pledge allegiance to their country, to be faithful and loyal, and to serve for the good of their country without pushing their selfish agendas. In the same way, if you want to be great in God's Kingdom, you must learn to be a servant of all. To be a citizen of God's Kingdom, you MUST be born again. You must believe in the greatest sacrifice of love given to all humanity by God, His only begotten Son, Jesus Christ. You must confess with your mouth that Jesus is Lord and believe in your heart that God raised Him from the dead.

> "But what does it say? "The word is near you, in your mouth, and in your heart"; that is, the word of faith, which we preach: *that if you will confess with your mouth that Jesus is Lord, and believe in your heart that God raised him from the dead, you will be saved. For with the heart, one believes unto righteousness; and with the mouth confession is made unto salvation.* For the Scripture says, "Whoever believes in him will not be disappointed." For there is no distinction between Jew and Greek; for the same Lord is Lord of all, and is rich to all who call on him. For, *"Whoever will call on the name of the Lord will be saved.""* (Rom. 10:8–13 WEB; italics added)

Christ Became Sin Who Knew No Sin

"For He made Him who knew no sin to be sin for us, that we might become the righteousness of God in Him" (2 Cor. 5:21).

Sin came in when Adam and Eve disobeyed God in the Garden of Eden, however, in the Garden of Gethsemane Christ took up all our sins to the cross. Sin brought nakedness, shame, and death that is why Jesus was stripped naked, suffered shame and died on the cross once He took up all our sin.

"For the wages of sin is death; but the gift of God is eternal life through Jesus Christ our Lord" (Rom. 6:23 KJV).

Adam and Eve were hiding from God after they sinned, because they were naked. (Gen. 3:6–8)

They tried to cover up their sin (nakedness) by using leaves. This was very temporary, because leaves dry up and fall off. Leaves have no life in them when disconnected from the branches, which are connected to the tree. God had to kill an animal for Adam and Eve's atonement for sin for them to have temporary covering that would last a few months, before another animal had to die to cover their sin, nakedness, again. To save their life, a life had to be given. In this case, the lamb that God sacrificed, because life is in the blood.

"For the life of the body is in its blood. I have given you the blood on the altar to purify you, making you right with the Lord. It is the blood, given in exchange for a life, that makes purification possible" (Lev. 17:11).

The animal God sacrificed had to take on the sin of Adam and Eve so that it would be condemned to die. Otherwise, they would have had to die to pay for their sin, because Rom. 6:23 says that the punishment for sin is death but the gift of God is eternal life through Jesus Christ our LORD.

"Also for Adam and his wife the Lord God made tunics of skin, and clothed them" (Gen. 3:21).

After this, animals had to die to cover people's sin and nakedness. Then God had to look for a permanent solution to cover humans' nakedness forever.

"He saw that there was no man, and wondered that there was no intercessor; Therefore His own arm brought salvation for Him; and His own righteousness, it sustained Him" (Isa. 59:16).

God Himself had to die for humans to be righteous forever because only He is righteous. But how could He die? God is God, and God never dies, but humans do. People were made in God's image. Therefore, God had to come to earth in the form of a human being to die a sinner's death so that humans can live forever. For Jesus to be legal on earth so He can to die for us, He had to take up the perishable in humans. This is why His mother had to be human, but His Father remained fully God. He had to have the righteousness of God to save the unrighteous and had to have a vessel to destroy sin in.

To conquer death, Jesus Christ had to be God, because death cannot beat God. For Him to fight for our freedom, He had to be stronger than the enemy. He had to be God because the devil, Lucifer, was an angel and angels are stronger than humans. The devil was not just any angel but an archangel who had been given a lot of power. God never took the power from him when he sinned, because God's gifts are without repentance. Only God could rescue us from this great terrorist of our spirit, souls, and body.

"Mary asked the angel, 'but how can this happen? I am a virgin.' The angel replied, 'The Holy Spirit will come upon you, and the power of the Most High will overshadow you. *So the baby to be born will be holy, and he will be called the Son of God*'" (Luke 1:34–35 NLT; italics added).

He could now pay for all of humanity's sin and cover people's nakedness forever with His garment of righteousness. Jesus Christ was therefore fully God, righteous, and fully human, sinful nature. He was tempted as humans are, and He never sinned. He was able to take up sin and save us forever in His righteousness. He took our sin and nakedness to the cross, was stripped naked, and His garment of righteousness was given to us so we no longer have to rely on a temporary sin regimen.

The blood of animals only covered up sin awhile but could not take away the sin. The blood of animals was just like using the bathroom, having a bowel movement, not flushing the toilet just spraying the bathroom to take away the stench, but the mess is still there, visible to all. The blood of Jesus, on the other hand, is like when one does have a bowel movement, flushes the toilet, and sprays the bathroom leaving no evidence of any mess or stench. It cleanses us and justifies us leaving no evidence of sin or guilt. Once sin is confessed and washed by the blood of Jesus, you are justified, just as if you had never sinned.

Jesus could not be crucified with His robe of righteousness. In the Garden of Gethsemane, He was in a lot of distress because He had to drink the cup of sin and suffering. He had never experienced this before because He lived a sinless life on earth and He prayed for God the Father to take His cup of suffering away. We do the same when we face unfamiliar tests and trials. Sin always leads to separation from God which leads to suffering. Jesus, taking up all our sin in that garden, was drinking the cup of sin that would lead to His suffering. No one was able to stone or hurt Him before this time, when He went into the garden. This is because He was hidden in God and was under divine protection in His sinless life. He was blameless, and God protects the righteous. His angels encamp around those who fear Him (Ps. 34:7).

God the Father is a consuming fire and does not dwell in sin, so from the time Jesus took up our sin in Gethsemane, He was no longer hidden in God. God the Father had to separate Himself from His Son, and for the first time ever, Jesus was all alone and in such agony that He sweat blood (Luke 22: 41–44).

God the Father could no longer cover Him from sin's consequences, and so He was open to sin's punishment. The devil was in full control at this point against the sinful nature of man, for the wages of sin is death. That is why Jesus felt forsaken at the cross, and He cried to God: "And about the ninth hour Jesus cried with a loud voice, saying, 'Eli, Eli, lama sabachthani?' That is to say, *'My God, my God, why hast thou forsaken me?'"* (Matt. 27:46 KJV; italics added).

Let's examine a few supportive scriptures...

"For as the heavens are high above the earth, So great is His mercy toward those who fear Him; As far as the east is from the west, So far has He removed our transgressions from us. As a father pities his children, so the Lord pities those who fear Him" (Ps. 103:11–13).

"Therefore if the Son makes you free, you shall be free indeed" (John 8:36).

> There is therefore now no condemnation to those who are in Christ Jesus, *who don't walk according to the flesh, but according to the Spirit.* For the law of the Spirit of life in Christ Jesus made me free from the law of sin and of death. For what the law couldn't do, in that it was weak through the flesh, God did, sending his own Son in the likeness of sinful flesh and for sin, he condemned sin in the flesh; that the ordinance of the law might be fulfilled in us, who walk not after the flesh, but after the Spirit. (Rom. 8:1–4 WEB; italics added)

Note: *The words in italics are the* KEY *to no condemnation, but the NIV version of the Bible omits this. Be careful of deception; compare Bible versions,* make sure they are saying the same thing as the original KJV *as some are known to omit God's* WORD, leading many astray.

It is not enough to be in Christ, you must live righteously, led by the Spirit of God.

"Not everyone who calls out to me, 'Lord! Lord!' will enter the Kingdom of Heaven. Only those who actually do the will of my Father in heaven will enter" (Matt. 7:21 NLT; italics added).

> And as Moses lifted up the serpent in the wilderness, even so must the Son of Man be lifted up, that whoever believes in Him should not perish but have eternal life. *For God so loved*

the world that He gave His only begotten Son, that whoever believes in Him should not perish but have everlasting life. For God did not send His Son into the world to condemn the world, but that the world through Him might be saved. "He who believes in Him is not condemned; but he who does not believe is condemned already, because he has not believed in the name of the only begotten Son of God. And this is the condemnation, that the light has come into the world, and men loved darkness rather than light, because their deeds were evil. For everyone practicing evil hates the light and does not come to the light, lest his deeds should be exposed. But he who does the truth comes to the light, that his deeds may be clearly seen, that they have been done in God." (John 3:14–21; italics added)

How Can I Be Born Again?

To be born again, you MUST accept Jesus Christ as your Lord and Savior. God the Father sent His Son Jesus Christ to pay the full price for our sins through His death. We receive forgiveness of sin and His eternal life through Christ's death and Resurrection. By doing this, we cross over from the kingdom of darkness into the Kingdom of light, from the burden of sin to the freedom of righteousness.

"Nor is there salvation in any other, for there is no other name under heaven given among men by which we must be saved" (Acts 4:12).

"Jesus said to him, 'I am the way, the truth, and the life. No one comes to the Father except through Me'" (John 14:6).

Then Jesus promised that He would not leave us alone but would give us a Helper, who will teach us all things and remind us what we have learned. The Holy Spirit is only given to the sons of the Kingdom. You do not have to clean up or have your act together to come into the Kingdom of God. You may be a murderer, adulterer, fornicator, liar, thief, or any sin you may think of—you qualify to be born again. All you need to do is to accept the sacrifice already paid for you. Remember this scripture...

"*If you openly declare that Jesus is Lord and believe in your heart that God raised him from the dead, you will be saved.* For it is by *believing in your heart* that you are *made right with God*, and it is by *openly declaring your faith* that you are *saved*" (Rom. 10:9–10 NLT; italics added).

When you become born again, you enroll into God's Kingdom. After enrolment, you need to be trained on Kingdom living and Kingdom business. This is when you ask for the Helper, the Counselor, the Holy Spirit, the gift from God, who is given to believers in Christ who are born again (sons and daughters) and who ask.

"If a son asks for bread from any father among you, will he give him a stone? Or if he asks for a fish, will he give him a serpent instead of a fish? Or if he asks for an egg, will he offer him a scorpion? If you then, being evil, know how to give good gifts to your children, *how much more will your heavenly Father give the Holy Spirit to those who ask Him*!" (Luke 11:11–13; italics added).

Note that Jesus said if a *son* asks from a father, not a stranger asking from God. The Father only gives His Spirit to His sons and daughters, not to strangers. When you become born again, you cease to be a stranger, you become a child of the kingdom.

"*For as many as are led by the Spirit of God, these are sons of God.* For you did not receive the spirit of bondage again to fear, *but you received the Spirit of adoption by whom we cry out, 'Abba, Father.'* The Spirit Himself bears witness with our spirit that we are children of God, and if children, then heirs—heirs of God and joint heirs with Christ, if indeed we suffer with Him, that we may also be glorified together" (Rom. 8:14–17; italics added).

"But to all who believed Him and accepted Him, *He gave the right to become children of God*" (John 1:12 NLT; italics added).

When someone goes to adopt a child from the streets, they do not tell the child that they need to be well groomed before they can be accepted for adoption. The person takes the child just as they are. They clean, groom, and teach the child how to live as a member of the family. God does the same thing.

When you accept Jesus Christ to be the LORD of your life, LORD means owner, one you have given full control to, you must do away with all the idols in your life and other gods you used to worship. Just like you cannot be married to someone and keep dating your boyfriends or girlfriends, when you come to Christ, you MUST not continue with idol worship.

If you have any images of Buddha or other idols, saints or pictures of them, you must repent and destroy them, don't give them to anyone! Just like you will not let your husband or fiancée see someone else, Christ will not have you worship or bow to or pray through any other name but His name.

It is a sin to pray to God through the saints, Mary or any other name because only Jesus Christ, the Son of God died for us and is omnipresent, the saints have no ability to hear or even know that you are praying to them or asking them to pray for you. They are not God. We are not even allowed to pray to angels, how much more a mere human being? Jesus Christ is perfect and He made the sacrifice for all humanity. He knows you and hears you. He knows your thoughts and what is in your heart. God the father does not listen to anyone who comes to Him in any other name but the name of Jesus Christ His Son. Yahweh, hates idols and He commands this in Exodus 20:2-6 NLT; italics added

> "I am the Lord your God, who rescued you from the land of Egypt, the place of your slavery. *"You must not have any other god but me. "You must not make for yourself an idol of any kind or an image of anything in the heavens or on the earth or in the sea. You must not bow down to them or worship them, for I, the Lord your God, am a jealous God who will not tolerate your affection for any other gods.* I lay the sins of the parents upon their children; the entire family is affected—even children in the third and fourth

generations of those who reject me. But I lavish unfailing love for a thousand generations on those who love me and obey my commands."

God is passionate about loving you and you loving Him and recognizing Him as the only one true God. He does this not to restrict you, but to protect you from the enemy and from being cursed because He can never go back on His Word. The wages of sin is death. He wants us to live eternally with Him, not to die in sin.

Prayer to Accept Christ in Your life (to Be Born Again)

Father, in Jesus's name, I thank You for Your love. Thank You for Your Son, Jesus Christ. Thank You for the greatest sacrifice for me at Calvary. I acknowledge that I am a sinner. I confess and repent all my sins. Please forgive me. Cleanse me by the blood of Jesus from all unrighteousness. Create in me Your heart and renew a right spirit within me. I believe that Jesus Christ is Lord *and that You raised Him from the dead. Write my name in the Lamb's book of life, and make me Your child now. I now receive Your forgiveness and salvation with thanksgiving. Father, now as Your child, please fill me with Your Holy Spirit. Teach me all Your ways and show me Your truths. I evict every evil spirit in me in Jesus's name. May Your Holy Spirit take full control over my life. Thank You, Lord, for saving me. Thank you for making me Your child. Thank You for the gift of Your Holy Spirit. Grant me the spirit of wisdom and understanding, the spirit of counsel and might, the spirit of knowledge, and the fear of the* Lord. *May I, like Christ, delight in the spirit of the fear of the* Lord *in Jesus's name, that I may live in total obedience to Your will and in humility walk with You. In Jesus's name I pray, believe, and receive with thanksgiving,* Amen*!*

Now praise God with song and dance for the greatest miracle of Salvation! Buy a New King James Version of the Bible as it is easier to understand without omitting some words, and fill your spirit and mind with the Word of God. Ask God to teach you His ways and give you the understanding of His Word in Jesus's name. Pray for a good bible teaching church, ask God to lead you to the church of His choice because not all churches preach the uncompromised gospel of Jesus Christ.

If you are born again but you have gone astray and do not live fully for God, here is a prayer for you to rededicate your life to Jesus. He is waiting for you with open arms like the prodigal son story in the bible. He will restore you like He did Peter.

PRAYER TO REDEDICATE YOUR LIFE TO CHRIST

Father, in Jesus's name, I exalt and lift You on High, for there is none other than You. No one compares to You, LORD. Your love and power no one can fathom. I thank You so much for Jesus and for the finished work of the cross. I thank You for Your Holy Spirit. I confess all my sins, LORD. I have turned away from You and leaned on my own wisdom and understanding. Please forgive me. Cleanse me from all unrighteousness. Create in me a clean heart, oh LORD, and renew a right spirit within me. Cast me not away from Your presence; take not Your Holy Spirit from me. Restore unto me the joy of Your salvation. I evict every evil spirit that came in me while I strayed from You in Jesus's name! I rebuke the spirit of rebellion from my life in Jesus name! Fill me with Your Holy Spirit; teach me all Your ways and paths. Grant me the spirit of wisdom and understanding, the spirit of counsel and might, the spirit of knowledge, and the fear of the LORD. May I, like Christ, delight in the spirit of the fear of the LORD in Jesus's name. May I live in total obedience to Your will and in humility walk with You. I thank you, Father, for receiving me back into Your Kingdom and restoring my position as Your child. In Jesus's name, I pray, believe, and receive with thanksgiving. Amen!

Prayer for blessings:

Father in Jesus name, thank You for making me Your child. I now repent all the sins of my ancestors and denounce every generational curse that has come to me and my family because of their sins. I denounce their blood line and cross over to the blood line of Jesus Christ because Christ took up all curses on the cross so I may be blessed. I receive all the gifts and blessings that my ancestors were meant to have that lay wasted in their graves, I take it all back in Jesus name for me and my children. Just like you gave the promise to the Israelites to see the Promised Land but because of sin the promise was given to their children instead. I receive all the blessings of Abraham and of being in Christ in Jesus's name. I embrace perfect health in spirit, soul and body. I uproot, tear down and destroy every curse and satanic programs against me and my family in Jesus's name. I receive every blessing and promise you have spoken of in Your Word as Your child now in Jesus's name. Thank You Father for blessing me and my family, thank you for You have promised salvation for me and my family. I receive all these blessings with thanksgiving in Jesus's name, Amen!

CHAPTER 7

The Helper, the Holy Spirit

THE HOLY SPIRIT IS PART of the Holy Trinity. He is God; He is not an 'it'. He is God in the Godhead which consists of; God the Father, God the Son, and God the Holy Spirit—three in one. Just as we were created in God's image, three in one, we operate as three in one: spirit, soul, and body.

"In the beginning, God created the heavens and the earth. The earth was formless and empty. Darkness was on the surface of the deep and God's *Spirit was hovering over the surface of the waters*. God said, "Let there be light," and there was light." (Gen. 1:1–3 WEB; italics added).

The earth was not created without the Holy Spirit; He was there during creation and knows ALL things. In Genesis 1, the Holy Spirit brings the Word of God to pass. He was hovering over the chaos of the earth, when God spoke and said, "Let there be light," and God the Holy Spirit brought the Word to pass.

It is amazing to note that the Holy Spirit of God was hovering on the chaos, not on the perfect earth. He however perfected it at God's Word. The 1st lesson is that God the Holy Spirit comes to purify, cleanse and bring order at God's Word according to the Father's desire and standards. Without Him, Order would not have been accomplished in the Chaos. The Holy Spirit raised Jesus from the dead and changed the chaos of death into victory over death, eternal life! He knows God's perfect will so He exists to reveal and perfect it in us who believe and receive Him. So when chaos abound in your life, it doesn't mean that the

Holy Spirit is not around, all you need is the Word of God for the Holy Spirit to put things in order.

The Holy Spirit specializes in bringing chaos into order using God's Word. He did not bring order until God spoke the Word, who was Christ. The Word of God is Christ. All things were created through Christ (The Word)

"In the beginning was the Word, and the Word was with God, and the Word was God. The same was in the beginning with God. All things were made through him. Without him was not anything made that has been made. In him was life, and the life was the light of men." (John 1:1-4 WEB; italics added)

The Holy Spirit does not do anything out of His own will apart from God the Father through God the Son. Otherwise, if He worked alone, He would have brought order before God spoke His Son, the Word, but He didn't. This was symbolic of the order that was going to come through Christ in a dark chaotic world of sin. The light of Christ's salvation was going to shine into the darkness with God the Holy Spirit's help. That is why the Holy Trinity is structured as:

1. God the Father
2. God the Son
3. God the Holy Spirit

God the Father, speaks God the Son, and God the Holy Spirit manifests God's will through God the Son. The same as we were created in God's image, three in one, spirit, soul and body. The spirit gives life, the soul feeds from the spirit and the body manifests what the soul and spirit have agreed on. The body is the action part of the spirit and soul. It is the manifestation of them. Your spirit may be bubbling with praise, your soul takes it and feels it and the body lifts up your hands and dances and cries all in manifestation of what your spirit and soul are doing within you.

If someone is paralyzed and mute, there is no way of knowing how they truly feel. They are locked in and are powerless. In the same way, being a Christian without the Holy Spirit is being a paralytic Christian. No one can hear or know you or even desire to be in your situation. They actually feel sorry for you. You can never win anyone to Christ without the Holy Spirit. You can never be a witness for Christ because the Holy Spirit is His witness.

Now I know why Jesus never performed a single miracle before He was baptized with God the Holy Spirit. Jesus, the Word, was already sent by God the Father. He needed someone to manifest Him and so the Holy Spirit had to be present or the ministry of Christ would be a paralyzed ministry. Jesus knew this and that is why He told His disciples not to leave to go preach until the Holy Spirit came in them. Then the Holy Spirit would confirm His Word, Jesus, with signs and wonders following.

The Holy Spirit will not move before the Word, and the Word will not act without the Holy Spirit. The Word will not come forth without the Father, and that was why God sent His Word, Jesus Christ, who never returned to Him void, but accomplished all that He was sent to do through God the Holy Spirit.

Genesis and John speak the same thing. John explains how the creation in Genesis took place through the Word.

The reason God the Holy Spirit is on Earth now, in this last testament, is to bring chaos into order through Jesus Christ whom God spoke (sacrificed). The Holy Spirit is the power of God! That is why no one can ever know God or Jesus Christ without Him because He illuminates them. He shows or displays them. You don't see Him but you see His works; what God the Father has released to us through His Son (The Word). The Holy Spirit is now on Earth because it is the most chaotic since the beginning of creation, to bring back order from the Father's sacrifice through Christ. God the Holy Spirit responds to God's command through the Word (Christ).

When the Word became flesh, and was given the name Jesus, the Holy Spirit did what He did in the beginning but now in the Spirit. He brought Light into darkness and made man a new in His own likeness -like Christ- which is the destiny of all created a new in Christ Jesus; the new creation, new birth. There is no Holy Spirit without Christ because as we saw, He never does anything apart from Him. That being said, He is given to only those who receive Christ in their hearts. Those who are born again. He serves the Kingdom of God by being a personal trainer of kingdom living.

For instance, if you go to a country you have never been to before, you will need a map and someone to advise you on the laws of the land. You will need to know what is required of you to live successfully and to prosper in that land. To be a citizen of the country, you will need to know what is expected of you and about your benefits in the country. But if you go to the country and have no one to guide you, you will find yourself in trouble most of the time. You will get frustrated living there in your own wisdom because you cannot live using the same laws you used in your former country. If you do, you will struggle, fail and get in trouble with the law. You will find yourself going back to your former country instead of staying and succeeding in the country where you could be very successful. You may even lose your life there, perishing for lack of knowledge because you have rejected knowledge.

Likewise, if you become born again and come into God's kingdom with the world's wisdom, you will be frustrated because you will fail. You will walk under a curse, never blessings. You will not know how to live in God's kingdom and succeed like Christ did. You will perish for lack of knowledge because you have rejected the guidance of the Holy Spirit.

This is the mistake many of us make. We become born again but we do not ask to receive our tour guide, Kingdom mentor, God the Holy Spirit. We go about God's kingdom in our worldly wisdom and wonder why we are not blessed. We end up envying sinners because of their success forgetting that their success is short lived and their wealth will be soon transferred to the righteous. However, you will never get the wealth transfer without the Holy Spirit because without Him you can never be righteous. Our righteousness is like filthy rags to God, but the righteousness of Christ is only found in Him through His blood and His Holy Spirit. Jesus explained this perfectly clear to NICODEMUS the night he came to see Jesus. Jesus told Him that we must be born again by Water (repentance) and Spirit (righteousness). Water which cleanses and Spirit which anoints and teaches us kingdom living. Jesus was cleansed and anointed during His baptism.

1 John 2:27

"But the anointing which you have received from Him abides in you, and you do not need that anyone teach you; but as the same anointing teaches you concerning all things, and is true, and is not a lie, and just as it has taught you, you will abide in Him."

> Now there was a man of the Pharisees named Nicodemus, a ruler of the Jews. The same came to him by night, and said to him, "Rabbi, we know that you are a teacher come from God, for no one can do these signs that you do, unless God is with him." Jesus answered him, "Most certainly, I tell you, unless one is born anew, he can't see God's Kingdom." Nicodemus said to him, "How can a man be born when he is old? Can he enter a second time into his mother's womb, and be born?" Jesus answered, "Most certainly I tell you, unless one is born of water and spirit, he can't enter into God's Kingdom! That which is born of the flesh is flesh. That which is born of the Spirit is spirit. Don't marvel that I said to you, 'You must be born anew.' The wind blows where it wants to, and you hear its sound, but don't know where it comes from and where it is going. So is everyone who is born of the Spirit." (John 3:1-8 WEB)

By seeing the Kingdom of God, Jesus meant seeing signs and wonders of God. It means seeing God at work in us, partnering with Him. It meant His Kingdom coming and His will being done on earth as it is in heaven through us. We must be born of WATER (cleansing of the Word) and SPIRIT (Anointing of the Holy Spirit) to do God's will successfully.

I cannot emphasize it enough that God the Holy Spirit will not come apart from Jesus. John the Baptist made this clear. He said...

"Therefore produce fruit worthy of repentance! Don't think to yourselves, 'We have Abraham for our father,' for I tell you that God is able to raise up children to Abraham from these stones. "Even now the ax lies at the root of the trees. Therefore every tree that doesn't produce good fruit is cut down, and cast into the fire. I indeed baptize you in water for repentance, but he who comes after me is mightier than I, whose shoes I am not worthy to carry. He will baptize you in the Holy Spirit." Matthew 3:8-11 (WEB)

"Jesus, when he was baptized, went up directly from the water: and behold, the heavens were opened to him. He saw the Spirit of God descending as a dove, and coming on him. Behold, a voice out of the heavens said, "This is my beloved Son, with whom I am well pleased."" Matthew 3:16-17 (WEB)

John the Baptist baptized men unto repentance. Repentance not of the mouth only but he said they must change their actions too. We must turn from our evil ways and bear fruit that show repentance. But there is one who baptizes with the Holy Spirit and Fire, Jesus Christ. The Holy Spirit does not come apart from Jesus. Jesus was baptized by John the Baptist and then with the Holy Spirit by His Father God. Only God can fill you with Himself, not man. Baptism of the Holy Spirit is God immersing you in Himself that all we eventually see and hear is Him living through you. He transforms you into the likeness of Christ. If Christ needed to be baptized by the Holy Spirit, and after that His ministry began with great power and was successful to complete it with signs and wonders, how much more do we need Him? The Holy Spirit is God, given to man only through Christ, the Son of God. No Christ, no Holy Spirit.

John the Baptist said that God the Father who sent him to prepare the way of Jesus told him how he will know who Jesus Christ was. Jesus looked ordinary, nothing could tell Him apart but The Holy Spirit of God being in Him and staying with Him. If Jesus Christ, God's only begotten Son could not be told apart by looking at Him but by the signs and wonders done by the Father through Him by the Holy Spirit, how much more must we have the Holy Spirit to distinguish us from the world as ones who belong to God? As children of God, brides of Christ?

"John testified, saying, "I have seen the Spirit descending like a dove out of heaven, and it remained on him. I didn't recognize him, but he who sent me to baptize in water, he said to me, 'On whomever you will see the Spirit descending, and remaining on him, the same is he who baptizes in the Holy Spirit.'" (John 1:32-33 WEB)

The Holy Spirit remained on Jesus Christ. He remains in those who are in Christ. In the Old Testament and before Christ came, the Holy Spirit never remained on anyone. He came and empowered and did the supernatural and then left, like when Samson would fight against the enemies.

"Then went Samson down with his father and his mother to Timnah, and came to the vineyards of Timnah; and behold, a young lion roared against him. Yahweh's Spirit came mightily on him, and he tore him as he would have torn a young goat; and he had nothing in his hand, but he didn't tell his father or his mother what he had done." (Judges 14:5-6 WEB)

This is because of man resisting God's Spirit as we see God say in Genesis 6:3 (WEB) "Yahweh said, "My Spirit will not strive with man forever, because he also is flesh; so his days will be one hundred twenty years.""

Jesus said that the Holy Spirit will confirm the Word of God with signs and wonders following those who believe.

The plan of redemption was not possible without God the Holy Spirit. He made the conception of Jesus possible through Mary. He took Jesus through His ministry on earth doing the work of God the Father. He took Him through the wilderness and through suffering and raised Him from the dead. The Holy Spirit made the God-given task of Jesus possible and successful because Jesus relied on Him to guide Him, for He knew the heart of God and the will of the Father.

When Mary received the news that she was going to have a baby, she was shocked and wondered how she would conceive without knowing a man. The Holy Spirit stepped in because it was not by the might or power of a human to carry out God's will on earth but by the Holy Spirit of God. Even now, we must have God the Holy Spirit to fulfill God's will on earth.

"Mary said to the angel, "How can this be, seeing I am a virgin?" The angel answered her, "The Holy Spirit will come on you, and the power of the Most High will overshadow you. Therefore also the holy one who is born from you will be called the Son of God."" (Luke 1:34–35 WEB).

The Spirit that raised Christ from the dead lives in us!

"But you are not in the flesh but in the Spirit, if it is so that the Spirit of God dwells in you. But if any man doesn't have the Spirit of Christ, he is not his. If Christ is in you, the body is dead because of sin, but the spirit is alive because of righteousness. But if the Spirit of him who raised up Jesus from the dead dwells in you, he who raised up Christ Jesus from the dead will also give life to your mortal bodies through his Spirit who dwells in you." (Rom. 8:9–11 WEB).

We cannot live a successful Christian life without God the Holy Spirit.

The Bible confirms that all have sinned and fallen short of the glory of God in Romans 3:23. But looking at it all after redemption and living in Christ, the glory of God has been bestowed back to us through Christ for those who are hidden in Christ in God. The latter glory is greater than the former glory.

Like the children of Israel who had built God a temple that had so much glory, when they began sinning, the enemy came and took them captive, destroyed the temple, and took all the precious things from the temple. In Haggai 2:1–9, God encourages them to continue working on rebuilding the temple and promised them that His Spirit would never leave them and that the glory of the latter temple will be much greater than the former. This would be made possible only *by His Spirit*. God the Father said in Zachariah 4:6b, "'Not by might nor by power, but by My Spirit,' Says the Lord of hosts."

The Fruit of the Holy Spirit

But I say, walk by the Spirit, and you won't fulfill the lust of the flesh. For the flesh lusts against the Spirit, and the Spirit against the flesh; and these are contrary to one another, that you may not do the things that you desire. But if you are led by the Spirit, you are not under the law. Now the deeds of the flesh are obvious, which are: adultery, sexual immorality, uncleanness, lustfulness, idolatry, sorcery, hatred, strife, jealousies, outbursts of anger, rivalries, divisions, heresies, envy, murders, drunkenness, orgies, and things like these; of which I forewarn you, even as I also forewarned you, that those who practice such things will not inherit God's Kingdom. *But the fruit of the Spirit is love, joy, peace, patience, kindness, goodness, faith, gentleness, and self-control. Against such things there is no law.* Those who belong to Christ have crucified the flesh with its passions and lusts. If we live by the Spirit, let's also walk by the Spirit. Let's not become conceited, provoking one another, and envying one another. (Gal. 5:16–26 WEB; italics added)

The Holy Spirit has fruits. Just like a tree produces fruits, we produce fruits. An orange tree produces oranges, not lemons or bananas. If the Holy Spirit lives in you, you will produce His fruits, which the flesh or the sinful nature, cannot produce: unconditional love, joy, peace, patience, kindness, goodness, humility (gentleness), and self-control. Is this what others see in us and feel through us? An orange tree consistently produces oranges—nothing else! A mango tree produces mangoes, not lemons.

Love must be in action and not just in words. John 3:16 is love in action, *"For God so loved the world that He gave* His only begotten son..." He loved and then followed it with the action of giving that which cost Him all He had. His BEST. Challenge yourself and instead of telling someone you love them, show them. God never said "I love you world!" and then stop at that; rather, He showed the world His love by sacrificing His only begotten Son. We too must follow His example. Love is a doing word.

The Holy Spirit has fruits of joy and peace in the midst of the storm and not only when things are good. Patience, in the most trying times. Sometimes we get so impatient and unkind to people that if we had an opportunity to minister Christ to them, we would fail miserably because they will not receive it from us. This is because our actions toward them did not display us as Christ-like. We lacked the fruit of patience which is followed by kindness. It is hard to be kind to mean people, but once the fruit grows in you, it is very rewarding. Your kindness despite their mean attitude, will lead them to repentance, otherwise if you are mean back to them you are no different than they are. We must have Goodness and faithfulness in all we do and say that the goodness and faithfulness of Christ may be evident through us. We must possess humility and self-control regardless of the situations we face. These fruits represent what is in Christ and if we have all these, it is easy to win souls for Christ because they will desire what we have.

Jesus gave us the best way to know what spirit is in a person. He said we shall know them by their fruits.

Beware of false prophets, who come to you in sheep's clothing, but inwardly are ravening wolves. By their fruits you will know them. Do you gather grapes from thorns, or figs from thistles? Even so, every good tree produces good fruit; but the corrupt tree produces evil fruit. A good tree can't produce evil fruit, neither can a corrupt tree produce good fruit. Every tree that doesn't grow good fruit is cut down, and thrown into the fire. Therefore by their fruits you will know them." (Matt. 7:15–20 WEB).

This is so with those led by the Spirit of God. The oranges in an orange tree appear when the tree is mature enough to produce fruit. As we spend time with God the Holy Spirit, we grow and mature in Christ, and we produce these fruits. May we constantly allow God the Holy Spirit to lead us continually so we can be like Christ whom we were predestined to be like.

"For whom He foreknew, He also predestined to be conformed to the image of His Son, that He might be the firstborn among many brethren" (Rom. 8:29).

"But we all, with unveiled face, beholding as in a mirror the glory of the Lord, are being transformed into the same image from glory to glory, just as *by the Spirit of the Lord*" (2 Cor. 3:18; italics added).

"And do not be conformed to this world, but be transformed by the renewing of your mind, that you may prove what is that good and acceptable and perfect will of God" (Rom. 12:2).

We renew our mind daily by the Word of God, replacing the ungodly thoughts with God's Word and doing, obeying, God's Word. We must be led by the Holy Spirit continually because without Him we cannot have the revelation of God's Word, which has the transforming power. Reading the Bible or hearing the Word of God without divine revelation is like reading or listening to just another novel or book. The Word of God is the power of God.

"*By the word of the Lord* were the heavens made; and all the host of them by the breath of his mouth" (Ps. 33:6 KJV; italics added).

How Do We Bear Lasting Fruit Successfully?

As we read earlier…

"Blessed is the man who doesn't walk in the counsel of the wicked, nor stand on the path of sinners, nor sit in the seat of scoffers; but his delight is in Yahweh's law. On his law he meditates day and night. *He will be like a tree planted by the streams of water, that produces its fruit in its season, whose leaf also does not wither. Whatever he does shall prosper.*" (Ps. 1:1–3 WEB; italics added).

We bear lasting fruit successfully by choosing to live consciously according to God's Word by the grace of God through His Holy Spirit. The scripture above requires a conscious decision and choice not to do evil or associate with evil company. We must delight in God's Word, not just reading and going through the motions. What you delight in you will enjoy doing.

My Story…

One day in Kennesaw State University's parking lot in Georgia U.S.A., I sat in my car with a friend before or after class, and we were talking excitedly on the goodness of Jesus. As we spoke, I felt as if Jesus was there listening in, enjoying the conversation of His praises, when suddenly I was caught up in heaven. I was standing on the left side of God the Father, and He shone so brightly I could not look into the light at Him, as it was too strong for my natural eyes.

In front of us stood many thin, beige-colored beings, some so small and tiny, some medium sized, and some so tall that there was no end to them.

I said to God, "Father, what are we looking at?"

He responded, "This is what I see when I look at people. These are the spirits of people. Do you see these that are tiny and malnourished? These are the spirits of men and women who don't read the Word of God, or pray, obey, and grow in bearing fruits. You see these tall ones without any end? These are the obedient children who pray, seek God, read the Word of God, hear God's voice, and respond promptly. You don't see their end because there is no limit to the Spirit!"

Then immediately, as fast as I left earth, I returned back in my car. This happened so fast that my friend did not notice that I had been caught up in heaven in the spirit. It was so fast that our conversation was not interrupted at all.

"Wow! God has just given me His eyes to wear!" I said to my friend and went on to tell her of my experience.

This is a great revelation and challenge to all people. It is very true, when God told the prophet Samuel in 1 Samuel 16:7, "But the Lord said to Samuel, 'Do not look at his appearance or at his physical stature, because I have refused him. *For the Lord does not see as man sees; for man looks at the outward appearance, but the Lord looks at the heart*'" (italics added).

What does God see in you? Are you malnourished or growing beyond limits? If God gave us His eyes to see your spirit, what would we see? Let's seek God and invest in eternity. The body will soon die, but the spirit will live forever. We can, therefore, invest in the flesh, which leads to eternal death, or invest in the spirit, which leads to eternal life. We have a free will. God already did His part by giving us life through His Son Jesus Christ. It is up to us to accept Him and live our lives in total obedience to Him. This should be our first and serious investment, not on temporary pleasures of sin. Like Jesus said, what would it profit you if you gained the whole world and lost your soul? Let us always be led by the Holy Spirit of God, and we shall be victorious!

Remember, we are spirits in a body, not a body in the spirit. We were spirits first, and then God prepared a body for us to do His will. When you look at yourself in the mirror, what you see is your outfit; the person wearing your body is the real you, just as you are not the clothes you wear. When people speak with you, they don't speak to your clothes; they speak to the person wearing the clothes. Likewise, God does not speak to our body. He speaks to the one wearing the body. Jesus said in John 4:24 that God is Spirit, and they who worship Him MUST worship Him in spirit and in truth. When you remove your clothes, they cannot move or function; your clothes only move and go places when you wear them.

Likewise, our body can never function without the spirit. When the spirit of a person leaves him or her, the body dies. It falls down and cannot function. Unfortunately, this truth has been hidden to people by the enemy, and we see many people taking care of their outward appearance and neglecting their spirits. They feed the desires of their body and flesh and ignore what keeps them alive. That is why Jesus said;

"Woe to you, scribes and Pharisees, hypocrites! For you cleanse the outside of the cup and dish, but inside they are full of extortion and self-indulgence. Blind Pharisee, first cleanse the inside of the cup and dish, that the outside of them may be clean also. Woe to you, scribes and Pharisees, hypocrites! For you are like whitewashed tombs, which indeed appear beautiful outwardly, but inside are full of dead men's bones and all uncleanness. Even so you also outwardly appear righteous to men, but inside you are full of hypocrisy and lawlessness" (Matt. 23:25–29).

It is like wearing clean clothes with dirt and sweat on your body. People see the clean clothes, but the smell is bad because you did not clean your body. But if you clean your body and wear dirty clothes, you don't smell, but people may judge you because they like to see cleanliness on the outside. People would rather associate with the clean outside and dirty inside than the clean inside and dirty outside. That is the opposite of people and God. God looks on the inside; people look on the outside.

You can be a construction worker who is wealthy; clean on the inside wearing a nice cologne or perfume but dirty on the outside because of the nature of your work, yet people will judge you by your appearance. On the other hand a homeless person can wear nice clothes on the outside but is smelly on the inside, and people will view him or her as clean. The person who is dirty on the inside may have infectious diseases due to improper hygiene, but the one dirty on the outside doesn't have infectious diseases. The person who is filthy minded and is full of sin but clean on the outside is infectious. The Bible says bad company corrupts good morals. A person who has godly thoughts but is dirty on the outside is viewed as clean in God's eyes. Whose eyes do you have? Yes, we live in a blind world, because as Jesus said, Satan, the prince of this world, has blinded people.

"Even if our Good News is veiled, it is veiled in those who perish; in whom the god of this world has blinded the minds of the unbelieving, that the light of the Good News of the glory of Christ, who is the image of God, should not dawn on them." (2 Cor. 4:3–4 WEB).

We bear lasting fruits by relying on God the Holy Spirit to lead us into all truths; by trusting in the Word of God, memorizing scripture, obeying God's Word, and being doers of the Word and not just hearers because the fruits come in doing, not hearing. Our actions are our fruits. Like David said;

"How can a young man keep his way pure? By living according to your word. With my whole heart, I have sought you. Don't let me wander from your commandments. I have hidden your word in my heart, that I might not sin against you." (Ps. 119:9–11 WEB).

The Gifts of the Holy Spirit

The Holy Spirit of God has gifts that Jesus paid for and He now distributes to children of God as He sees fit.

Now concerning spiritual things, brothers, I don't want you to be ignorant. You know that when you were heathen, you were led away to those mute idols, however you might be led. Therefore I make known to you that no man speaking by God's Spirit says, "Jesus is accursed." No one can say, "Jesus is Lord," but by the Holy Spirit. Now there are various kinds of gifts, but the same Spirit. There are various kinds of service, and the same Lord. There are various kinds of workings, but the same God, who works all things in all. But to each one is given the manifestation of the Spirit for the profit of all. For to one is given through the Spirit the word of wisdom, and to another the word of knowledge, according to the same Spirit; to another faith, by the same Spirit; and to another gifts of healings, by the same Spirit; and to another workings of miracles; and to another prophecy; and to another discerning of spirits; to another different kinds of languages; and to another the interpretation of languages. But the one and the same Spirit produces all of these, distributing to each one separately as he desires. God has set some in the assembly: first apostles, second prophets, third teachers, then miracle workers, then gifts of healings, helps, governments, and various kinds of languages. Are all apostles? Are all prophets? Are all teachers? Are all miracle workers? Do all have gifts of healings? Do all speak with various languages? Do all interpret? But earnestly desire the best gifts. Moreover, I show a most excellent way to you." (1 Cor. 12: 1–11, 28–31 WEB; italics added)

To read more on the gifts see Eph. 4:7–16

The Holy Spirit has gifts which He gives as He wills for the edification of the church of Jesus Christ. You can never buy or earn these gifts. Rather, the Holy Spirit distributes them at His discretion. These gifts came forth through Jesus Christ's victory over the enemy when He gave us back our dominion. We can desire and pray for these gifts, but that's it—just like people place gifts under a Christmas tree with no obligation or work required on the receiver of the gift. The gift giver does not have to give the gifts, but he or she chooses to do it and chooses whom to give the gifts to. Likewise, gifts are given by the Holy Spirit to whomever He chooses, and the receiver does not have to do any work or perform any rituals to receive the gift.

> Now when the apostles who were at Jerusalem heard that Samaria had received the word of God, they sent Peter and John to them, who, when they had come down, prayed for them, that they might receive the Holy Spirit; for as yet he had fallen on none of them. They had only been baptized in the name of Christ Jesus. Then they laid their hands on them, and they received the Holy Spirit. Now when Simon saw that the Holy Spirit was given through the laying on of the apostles' hands, he offered them money, saying, "Give me also this power, that whomever I lay my hands on may receive the Holy Spirit." But Peter said to him, "May your silver perish with you, because you thought you could obtain the gift of God with money! You have neither part nor lot in this matter, for your heart isn't right before God. Repent therefore of this, your wickedness, and ask God if perhaps the thought of your heart may be forgiven you. For I see that you are in the gall of bitterness and in the bondage of iniquity." Simon answered, "Pray for me to the Lord, that none of the things which you have spoken happen to me." (Acts 8:14–24 WEB; italics added)

Many of us admire the gifts but are not willing to pay the price needed to successfully use these gifts. Unlike gifts that are given freely, fruits of the Spirit need work to produce them. Without the fruits of the Holy Spirit, which produce in us the character of Jesus Christ, the gifts will be perverted. We need character to successfully carry out the gifts of God in our lives for the benefit of the Kingdom. It is the Holy Spirit who works in us to make us willing to do and carry out God's will. Only by the Holy Spirit can we put to death the deeds of the flesh so we can live in the fear of the Lord.

"Therefore, my beloved, as you have always obeyed, not as in my presence only, but now much more in my absence, work out your own salvation with fear and trembling; for it is God who works in you both to will and to do for His good pleasure" (Phil. 2:12–13).

"For if you live according to the flesh you will die; but if by the Spirit you put to death the deeds of the body, you will live" (Rom. 8:13).

Just as a farmer has to work hard at cultivating the land and taking care of the crops so that they bear healthy fruits, we too must work out our salvation with fear and trembling. We must continually rely on the Holy Spirit, crucify our flesh and offer our bodies daily as a living sacrifice, holy and pleasing to God, which is the true act of worship (Rom. 12:1). Fruits take time to grow into you, but gifts are instant. Gifts do not depend on works like fruits do, (cultivating, watering, weeding, and pruning); rather, they are dependent on the gift giver and his timing.

Having gifts without the fruit is very destructive. It is like giving an eight-year-old child a car to drive assuming the child can drive the car safely. The child will drive it like he or she plays video games—recklessly! The car would be a danger to the child others.

That is why the Holy Spirit, in every believer, wants everyone to have all His fruits. He distributes gifts according to our maturity level. The Holy Spirit sees the heart and what fruits you have in reality and gives gifts at His discretion. Just as parents will withhold some of their property from their children until they are mature enough to safely handle it, God also knows what His children can handle. He will not give you something that will destroy you and others. To succeed, you must be continually led by the Holy Spirit!

"Now I say that the heir, as long as he is a child, does not differ at all from a slave, though he is master of all, but is under guardians and stewards until the time appointed by the father" (Gal. 4:1–2).

The Work of the Holy Spirit

<u>The Holy Spirit is a seal and deposit God gave us, guaranteeing our inheritance.</u>

"For as many as are led by the Spirit of God, these are sons of God." (Rom. 8:14).

"In Him you also trusted, after you heard the word of truth, the gospel of your salvation; in whom also, having believed, you were sealed with the Holy Spirit of promise, who is the guarantee of our inheritance until the redemption of the purchased possession, to the praise of His glory" (Eph. 1:13–14).

<u>The Holy Spirit Is the Witness of Christ</u>

No one knows you more than your spirit. Likewise, no one knows God more than His Spirit. The Holy Spirit teaches us about Christ and confirms His Word with signs and wonders being a great witness of Christ and the finished work of the cross.

"For what man knows the things of a man except the spirit of the man which is in him? Even so no one knows the things of God except the Spirit of God" (1Cor. 2:11).

<u>The Holy Spirit Gives Boldness</u>

The Holy Spirit gives boldness to witness to others about Christ in our actions and our words. If the world sees Christ in us by our agape love for one another, they will hunger for Him. But if they don't see a difference, they will not desire Him. The Holy Spirit is God in us; He displays God to the world through obedient sons and daughters of God. When we are sealed, we belong to God and no one can touch us without touching God because only God, the owner, can break the seal. Without the seal, we are exposed to defeat by the evil one, because the Holy Spirit is not there to reveal to us what our spiritual enemies are up to. God the Holy Spirit sees and knows all in the Spirit, and we are undefeated as long as He lives in us and we obey Him.

The Holy Spirit Completes God the Father's Work on Earth

He did it in Christ and that is why Christ said it was better that He goes so that we could get the Helper, the Holy Spirit. Jesus wanted us to have the same exact Teacher, Counselor, Life Coach, and Guide that He had. So no one has an excuse of not living the same as Christ did—victoriously! We are more than conquerors because Christ has already conquered.

Christ came and lived the tough life, where the dominion God gave to Adam and Eve was still with the devil. Christ, by the Holy Spirit, made it unto death and went to hell to take back our stolen dominion and gave it back to us. He descended and ascended and brought the gifts to us (Eph. 4:7–12). Jesus disarmed the principalities and powers; they have no authority over us. We now have authority over them in His name.

"Having wiped out the handwriting of requirements that was against us, which was contrary to us. And He has taken it out of the way, having nailed it to the cross. Having disarmed principalities and powers, He made a public spectacle of them, triumphing over them in it" (Col. 2:14–15).

"But very truly I tell you, it is for your good that I am going away. Unless I go away, the Advocate will not come to you; but if I go, I will send him to you" (John 16:7 NIV).

Jesus tells His disciples in Luke 24:49 NIV, "I am going to send you what my Father has promised; but stay in the city until you have been clothed with power from on high."

Jesus also commanded the disciples to baptize in the name of the Father, the Son, and the Holy Spirit. This also shows the importance of baptism after receiving salvation.

"Then Jesus came to them and said, 'All authority in heaven and on earth has been given to me. Therefore go and make disciples of all nations, baptizing them in the name of the Father and of the Son and of the Holy Spirit, and teaching them to obey everything I have commanded you. And surely I am with you always, to the very end of the age'" (Matt. 28:18–20 NIV).

The Holy Spirit Is the POWER of God

Jesus was spoken of by John the Baptist as One who baptizes with the Holy Spirit and fire.

"I baptize with water those who repent of their sins and turn to God. But someone is coming soon who is greater than I am— so much greater that I'm not worthy even to be his slave and carry his sandals. He will baptize you with the Holy Spirit and with fire" (Matt. 3:11 NLT).

"Being assembled together with them, he commanded them, "Don't depart from Jerusalem, but wait for the promise of the Father, which you heard from me. For John indeed baptized in water, but you will be baptized in the Holy Spirit not many days from now."" (Acts 1:4–5 WEB).

"But you will *receive power when the Holy Spirit comes upon you. And you will be my witnesses, telling people about me everywhere*—in Jerusalem, throughout Judea, in Samaria, and to the ends of the earth" (Acts 1:8 NLT; italics added).

Jesus Himself never started His ministry until He was baptized with the Holy Spirit. He would not even have been conceived were it not for the Holy Spirit. The Holy Spirit led Jesus through His God-given task even when it was very hard, led Him through temptations, strengthened Him, reminded Him what to say and when to say it, made Him wiser than His teachers, and gave Him boldness so that others marveled at His teaching. They said Jesus taught as one with authority. Therefore Jesus warned His disciples against preaching and being His witness before they were baptized with the Holy Spirit, because the Holy Spirit is His witness. See Luke 24:49

The Holy Spirit Reveals Jesus Christ

Without the Holy Spirit, we cannot know Jesus intimately and without the intimate knowledge and relationship with Christ, we cannot know the Father. Jesus said to His disciples in Luke 10:21–23, after He had sent the seventy followers and they had performed miracles and were glad that the demons obeyed them in Jesus's name, that they should not be happy that demons obey them, but rather that their name is written in the book of life. This shows that demons can obey you in Jesus's name, but still you can go to hell. Remember, He said not all who call Him Lord will enter the kingdom of heaven but only those who do the will of His Father in heaven (Matt. 7:21).

Just like a son does not take every girlfriend he has to his parents and introduce the girl as his bride, Jesus will only introduce His intimate friends, His brides, to His dad. I pray to be one of them. Why do I say this? Jesus said it in Matthew 22, when He gave the parable of the wedding feast. He said the Kingdom of God is like this parable. When the wedding was ready, the servants were sent to call in the invited guests but the guests were unwilling, so strangers and all others were invited. However, one of the guests refused to wear the wedding garment (salvation). He was thrown out in the outer darkness. So if the wedding supper is prepared and there are guests and friends of the bridegroom, then there must be a bride. John the Baptist said that he must decrease as Christ increases because Christ Jesus was the bridegroom, and the friend of the bridegroom, John the Baptist, was happy for the bridegroom to be joined with his bride (John 3:29–36).

> In that same hour Jesus rejoiced in the Holy Spirit, and said, "I thank you, O Father, Lord of heaven and earth, that you have hidden these things from the wise and understanding, and

revealed them to little children. Yes, Father, for so it was well-pleasing in your sight." Turning to the disciples, he said, "All things have been delivered to me by my Father. *No one knows who the Son is, except the Father, and who the Father is, except the Son, and he to whomever the Son desires to reveal him.*" Turning to the disciples, he said privately, "Blessed are the eyes which see the things that you see," (Luke 10:21–23 WEB; italics added)

The Holy Spirit purifies us (God's Temple) for God to Dwell In

A new homeowner requires the house to be cleaned and will desire new furniture and a new beginning, according to his or her preference.

"When an unclean spirit has gone out of a man, he passes through waterless places, seeking rest, and doesn't find it. Then he says, 'I will return into my house from which I came out,' and when he has come back, he finds it empty, swept, and put in order. Then he goes, and takes with himself seven other spirits more evil than he is, and they enter in and dwell there. The last state of that man becomes worse than the first. Even so will it be also to this evil generation." (Matt. 12:43–45 WEB).

When God the Holy Spirit helps you to clean your house, you must fill it with the Word of God by reading, meditating, memorizing, and living according to His Word. If the Word of God does not occupy your heart (the house), demons worse than the ones you had before will come in easily. You will be tempted, and you will fall into temptation if you do not have the Word of God in you. The Word of God is the sword of the Spirit that destroys the enemy.

"And they overcame him by the blood of the Lamb and by the word of their testimony, and they did not love their lives to the death" (Rev. 12:11).

We need the blood of the Lamb to cleanse us as we allow Christ into our hearts. We need the Word of God to wash and fill us and renew our minds as we follow Christ.

The Holy Spirit Will Teach You All Things

"But the Helper, the Holy Spirit, whom the Father will send in My name, *He will teach you all things, and bring to your remembrance all things* that I said to you" (John 14:26; italics added).

"You gave also your good Spirit to instruct them, and didn't withhold your manna from their mouth, and gave them water for their thirst." Nehemiah 9:20 (WEB)

"Teach me to do your will, for you are my God. Your Spirit is good. Lead me in the land of uprightness." Psalm 143:10 (WEB)

"But there is a spirit in man, and the breath of the Almighty gives them understanding.'" Job 32:8 (WEB)

The Holy Spirit will teach you ALL things—I mean ALL. He is much more than amazing. He will reveal Jesus so vividly to you. He will teach you about the Father. He will reveal your assignment, and not only that, but He will also help you to fulfill it to perfection beyond your comprehension. He is doing the same to me.

The Holy Spirit teaches us all things. He is all knowing, which makes Him the greatest instructor in heaven and on earth. He knows your language, and He knows how you understand things, and so His lessons are customized for you. He not only does that, but He opens your mind to understand His teaching. He also reminds you of the information you learned when you need to remember it so that you may put it into action. He teaches you at that particular time what you need to do and say, in any situation. He is always speaking, and has a great, I mean GREAT, sense of humor.

He has taught me how to cook dishes I had tried over and over to cook but to no avail. He has taught me subjects in school that I needed to understand more and how to relate to people—my husband, my children, friends, and enemies. He has taught me how to know who is talking to me in discerning of spirits. He has taught me and teaches me everything. Whatever subject you can think of, He knows it.

The Holy Spirit Helps Us through Temptation Like He Did Christ

"Then Jesus, being filled with the Holy Spirit, returned from the Jordan and was led by the Spirit into the wilderness, being tempted for forty days by the devil. And in those days He ate nothing, and afterward, when they had ended, He was hungry" (Luke 4:1–2).

"Now when the devil had ended every temptation, he departed from Him until an opportune time" (Luke 4:13).

Needless to say, Jesus was victorious over the enemy. Hallelujah! Thank God for the Holy Spirit, who teaches us and leads us to triumph in Christ Jesus!

The Holy Spirit Helps Us to Pray Effective Prayers

"Likewise the Spirit also helps in our weaknesses. For we don't know what we should pray for as we ought, but the Spirit Himself makes intercession for us with groanings which cannot be uttered. Now He who searches the hearts knows what the mind of the Spirit is, because He makes intercession for the saints according to the will of God" (Rom. 8:26–27).

My Story: Headache Prayer

One day I woke up with a throbbing headache. I was scheduled to work that day but the headache was so bad that my husband asked me to call off work. I had faith in God that He would heal me and besides, it was too late to call off work. So I prayed as I got ready for work, "Father, in Jesus' name, heal this headache. It hurts so badly, please…"

Before I could finish, God the Holy Spirit stopped me and said to me, "What are you saying?"

I asked Him, "What do you mean?"

He said, "God knows about your headache, but the headache doesn't know about your God! Did David, while facing Goliath, pray and tell

God about Goliath, or did he tell Goliath about his God? Did Shadrach, Meshach, and Abednego tell God about the king who wanted to throw them into the fiery furnace that was heated seven times higher than normal, or did they tell the King Nebuchadnezzar about their God? Jesus said if you speak to the mountain and tell it to move, by faith, it shall move! He never said you shall speak to Him about the mountain."

There you go, prayer lesson learned! Immediately my prayer changed to a prayer of faith from a prayer of sympathy because God doesn't respond to anything but faith. I told the headache about my God, who is a healer, about the finished work of the cross and my victory in Christ Jesus. I reminded the headache that by the stripes of Jesus Christ, I was healed over two thousand years ago and my healing was not negotiable. By the time I got to work, the headache was gone and never returned! I shared this with my patient and his family, who needed the same Word. You see, without the Helper, the Holy Spirit, the headache would have succeeded in stealing my joy, peace, money, and patient care. My patient would have missed this Word from God when he needed it. With God we are more than conquerors because we have His Spirit, who helps us fight these battles. Let us embrace the Holy Spirit in us to teach us all things and remind us of things God has taught us. Hallelujah!

The Holy Spirit teaches us all things and reminds us of what Jesus said to us. After Jesus was baptized, the Holy Spirit led Him into the wilderness to be tempted by the devil. Just as someone works out in the gym to have stronger muscles, our spiritual muscles must be trained through temptations, but God walks us through it. You can't graduate if you don't get tested on what you have been taught; this is true in the physical and spiritual world.

The Holy Spirit led Jesus in the wilderness to be tempted but did not leave Him. He was there, and He reminded Jesus what scripture to quote back to defeat the devil. The Word of God is the sword of the Spirit. Without the Word of God, we can never be victorious over the enemy. Read the temptation of Jesus in Matthew 4:1–11.

My Story: The Holy Spirit Reminds Us in Temptation

It was about 3:00 a.m. when the Holy Spirit woke me up to pray. As I prayed for a friend's mother who was a minister of the Gospel but was suffering from ESRD (End Stage Renal Disease) and was on dialysis, I heard demons threatening me, saying, "You better stop praying, because if you don't, we will do to you what we did to your mother."

I knew they had caused my dad's stroke because my mother is a minister of the Gospel, and she does deliverance ministry. She expels demons from their victims by the power of God through the Holy Spirit, and the demons hate it, so they attacked my dad to distract her from her ministry. They were threatening to attack my husband in the same way they did my father. I ignored them, finished praying, and went to bed. I used to sleep with my baby, who was about two years old at the time, because my husband traveled a lot as a businessman.

About thirty minutes into my sleep, the Holy Spirit said to me, "Turn around."

I had been lying on my abdomen, so I turned around and lay on my back. As soon as I turned, I looked up at the white ceiling in the dark room. It was as clear as day. There were formless black demonic spirits hovering from side to side that filled my ceiling. My first thought was that these demons had come to get me, but my baby was there and I wished they had found me alone.

Immediately, God, the Holy Spirit reminded me of a scripture I had read a few weeks before, He asked me to proclaim that I am hidden in Christ in God!

This scripture amazed me with the fact that in Christ I am protected in layers and I am untouchable. If anyone was to come and get me, they would have to go through God the Father to get to God the Son to get to me, which is impossible to go through. It is like being the yolk of an egg inside a chicken. For anyone to get to you, they must catch the chicken, kill it, take the egg, break it, and then get the yolk. How hidden we truly are!

"If then you have been raised with Christ, seek the things that are above, where Christ is, seated at the right hand of God. Set your minds on things that are above, not on things that are on earth. For you have died, and *your life is hidden with Christ in God*" (Col. 3:1–3: italics added).

I shouted from the scripture, "I AM HIDDEN IN CHRIST, IN GOD!" and immediately the demons vanished! I felt the protection and boldness come over me. I commanded the demons never to come back or even interrupt my sleep anymore. I slept so well after that.

When I woke up in the morning, the Holy Spirit asked me, "Do you know why they came?"

I replied, "No. Why did they come?"

He said, "Because when they threatened you, you did not speak back the Word of God like Jesus did in the wilderness when He was tempted by the devil. When you kept quiet, it showed that you accepted their threat and by so doing you opened a door for them to attack you. You gave them the legal right to attack you. Remember in every test in the wilderness, Jesus responded by quoting God's Word and He won! The Word of God is the Sword that destroys the enemy."

From that day, I learned my lesson. Whenever evil thoughts come—and by evil I mean thoughts not of God or thoughts contrary to what God has said or promised—I fight back with God's Word. For example, when I feel fearful or I get thoughts of fear, I know fear is not from God, so I do what the Word of God says, in 2 Corinthians 10:4–6 (Italics added): "For the weapons of our warfare are not carnal but mighty in God for pulling down strongholds, casting down arguments and every high thing that exalts itself against the knowledge of God, *bringing every thought into captivity to the obedience of Christ*, and being ready to punish all disobedience when your obedience is fulfilled."

I know that these thoughts of fear are not just thoughts, but strongholds, arguments, and high things that exalt themselves against the knowledge of God. I therefore get the weapon of our warfare, which is the Word of God, to counter the attacks of the enemy.

Ephesians 6:17 (Italics added) says, "And take the helmet of salvation, *and the sword of the Spirit, which is the word of God.*"

For the spirit of fear, I quote the scripture in 2 Timothy 1:7 and personalize it. I speak it to the spirit of fear that is trying to come in me and I declare that, *"God has not given me a spirit of fear but He has given me a spirit of power, a spirit of love, and a spirit of a sound mind.* So I rebuke the spirit of fear now and expel it from me in Jesus's name!"

This scripture tells me what stronghold I am dealing with; it is a spirit called fear. It is a stronghold of fear. It also comes with the spirit of anxiety. In the medical profession, we have names for these spirits. We call it anxiety disorder. The fear of being in a small space or closed spaces is called claustrophobia. This and any other phobia or fears are all the evil spirit's stronghold. The Word of God says that fear is not from God. Fear is of the devil.

The weapon against this spirit is not medication to help you relax. These medications will work only for a few hours before you need to take and buy more, continuing with this cycle for the rest of your life. You will not only live a dysfunctional life, but you will lose your money to these medications and to doctors, who will have to keep your medications regulated to accommodate this spirit in you. Why do we allow the enemy to steal what is ours? Why don't we trust God enough to receive what God has given us in Christ Jesus? Remember, the weapons of our warfare are not carnal but are mighty through God. Through the Word of God, I immediately get the victory over the spirit of fear. If you are suffering from this spirit, read the Word of God, give your life to Jesus, pray against this stronghold with the Word of God in Jesus's name, and be set free.

If you are on medication, pray as you work with your doctor. I believe God can set you free from these spirits.

Notice that power is a spirit, love is a spirit and a sound mind is a spirit. Ask God to replace the evil spirit that causes mental instability with the spirit of power, love and sound mind. Physical, mental and spiritual health is a promise from God, Jesus paid for it. By His stripes we were healed, it says in Isaiah 53:5 (AMP; italics added)

"But He was wounded for our transgressions, He was crushed for our wickedness [our sin, our injustice, our wrongdoing]; *the punishment [required] for our well-being fell on Him, and by His stripes (wounds) we are healed.*"

Jesus paid for our well-being and healing! Sound mind is paid for! Claim it, believe it and receive it in His name!

I have a friend who had the fear of flying. She shared this with me, and I told her about fear being a spirit from the enemy. I explained to her that we defeat the enemy by the sword of the Spirit, which is the Word of God. I gave her the assignment of looking up in the Bible what God says about fear, which she did. She came back after a mini-vacation, where she took a flight with her family and she said she took God at His Word and declared it. The scripture that worked for her was Isaiah 41:10 NLT:

"Don't be afraid, for I am with you. Don't be discouraged, for I am your God. I will strengthen you and help you. I will hold you up with my victorious right hand."

The battlefield is in the mind. If you win it in the mind, then it is easier to win it in the physical because it has not entered your heart. Scripture says we must guard our hearts, for the heart is the wellspring of life. Just like you wouldn't sign for a package that is not yours. Likewise, we must cast down arguments and every high thing that exalts itself against the knowledge of God as it comes. Refuse to take anything that the enemy delivers to you. Jesus did not suffer for nothing. He paid all the debt we owed because of sin. Christ came that we may have life and have life more abundantly.

Another example would be the spirit of depression. What does God say about depression?

"To console those who mourn in Zion, To give them beauty for ashes, The oil of joy for mourning, *The garment of praise for the spirit of heaviness*; That they may be called trees of righteousness, The planting of the Lord, that He may be glorified" (Isa. 61:3; italics added).

God calls depression, which is heaviness in the soul, spirit and body as it weighs one down, *A SPIRIT* of heaviness. *Depression is a spirit* that is broken only by the weapon of praise. Are you depressed? If so, put on praise like a garment so that all we see in you and hear from you is praise, and the spirit of depression will have no place in you. It can never stand praise because God dwells in the praises of His people. Declare this in Jesus's name: "I put on the garment of praise in exchange for this spirit of depression or heaviness in me, in Jesus's name! Lord Jesus, deliver me from this spirit of heaviness. I thank you for deliverance. I receive it with thanksgiving in Jesus's name, amen!"

This spirit of depression cannot stand praise. It is destroyed by praising Jesus. We have given these spirits medical names like bipolar, schizophrenia, psychosis – (hallucination, delusion), etc. including suicidal ideations. These spirits cause people to harm or kill themselves or others around them.

The weapons of our warfare are not carnal. They are mighty through God! Jesus paid the price for all our freedom of the spirit, soul, and body! Do not accept bondage anymore! King David said in Psalm 34:1, regardless of the situation he found himself in, "I will bless the Lord at all times; *His praise shall continually be in my mouth*" (italics added). Our situations must never dictate our praise rather our praise should dictate our situations instead.

Saul had an evil spirit of depression tormenting him and David the shepherd boy played the harp under the anointing of God and the evil spirit left King Saul. Just playing praise and worship music in your house and car instead of ungodly music, the evil spirit will flee because God dwells in the praises of His people. When God comes, evil flees! Look at the power of anointed praise over evil in the scripture below.

> Now Yahweh's Spirit departed from Saul, and an evil spirit from Yahweh troubled him. *Saul's servants said to him, "See now, an evil spirit from God troubles you. Let our lord now command your*

servants who are in front of you to seek out a man who is a skillful player on the harp. Then when the evil spirit from God is on you, he will play with his hand, and you will be well." Saul said to his servants, "Provide me now a man who can play well, and bring him to me." Then one of the young men answered, and said, *"Behold, I have seen a son of Jesse the Bethlehemite who is skillful in playing, a mighty man of valor, a man of war, prudent in speech, and a handsome person;* **and Yahweh is with him***."* Therefore Saul sent messengers to Jesse, and said, "Send me David your son, who is with the sheep." Jesse took a donkey loaded with bread, and a bottle of wine, and a young goat, and sent them by David his son to Saul. David came to Saul, and stood before him. He loved him greatly; and he became his armor bearer. Saul sent to Jesse, saying, "Please let David stand before me; for he has found favor in my sight." When the spirit from God was on Saul, David took the harp, and played with his hand; so Saul was refreshed, and was well, and the evil spirit departed from him." (1 Samuel 16:14-23 WEB; italics and bold emphasis added)

Derek Prince, a minister of the Gospel who went to be with the Lord, tells his story about this spirit of depression and how this scripture worked against this spirit! His book is a must read for everyone. Christians, especially, need to be delivered and set free to fulfill their God-given task. We must be delivered! Salvation is not deliverance, so please invest in this book as it helped me through deliverance, and my life has never been the same.

I thought that since I was born again and serving God, I was delivered but I was wrong. People of God perish for lack of knowledge. Many people who are born again and serve God have anger issues, greed, pride, lust, gossip, and many other issues. These are evil spirits at work in you that you need to expel. Inherited illnesses are also from iniquities of our forefathers—we need to be delivered from all generational curses.

I have shared this book with many Christians, and they in turn have shared it with their families and friends. It is more than amazing; it is heavenly revelation! Please read it. The title is *They Shall Expel Demons* by Derek Prince.

Assuming that once you are a Christian you are automatically delivered is a great deception from the devil. He wants you to believe this so that he can control you from the inside like he did the children of Israel. They were saved by the blood of the sacrificed lamb on the doorpost. They all came from slavery in Egypt and went through the Red Sea on their way to the Promised Land. We see in their journey that they complained and wished they were back in slavery many times. This caused them to die in the wilderness because they left Egypt, but Egypt was still in them. They left their masters behind, but they were still controlled in their minds by their previous masters. What their masters wanted for them, which was to die in poverty, came to pass. They refused to be delivered from their slave mentality and realize who they were in God. They didn't learn God's ways and obey Him, which would have led to their freedom of spirit, soul, mind and body. Only two people from the group that had been slaves in Egypt got to enter the rest promised by God because they had a different spirit.

Do you have a different spirit, or are you still a slave to sin and to your past? Is it hard for you to let go and forgive yourself and the people who hurt you in the past? Do you blame God for things that happened to you or to others? Remember, God does not cause bad things to happen to people; the enemy and sin cause bad things to come to pass.

> Let no man say when he is tempted, "I am tempted by God," for God can't be tempted by evil, and he himself tempts no one. But each one is tempted when he is drawn away by his own lust, and enticed. Then the lust, when it has conceived, bears sin; and the sin, when it is full grown, produces death. Don't be deceived, my beloved brothers. Every good gift and every perfect gift is from above, coming down from the Father of lights, with whom can

be no variation, nor turning shadow. Of his own will he gave birth to us by the word of truth, that we should be a kind of first fruits of his creatures. (James 1:13–18 WEB)

Did you repent and expel the spirits that got access into your life through your past sins and un-forgiveness? Do you struggle with sin or evil thoughts? If you are struggling to obey God, you must be delivered. Then, like Caleb and Joshua, you can see God clearly. Caleb and Joshua saw their God as being greater than their enemies, while the others saw their enemies as being greater than their God.

No matter what battle you are in, I cannot stress how important it is to be a doer of the Word of God, not to just being a hearer and reader of the Word. You are well equipped to overcome by using the Word of God as the powerful sword of the spirit that it is.

If you are breaking the stronghold of a spirit already in you, believe and quote this promise from God, in Joel 2:32: "And it shall come to pass that *whoever calls on the name of the Lord Shall be saved*. For in Mount Zion and in Jerusalem there shall be *deliverance*, As the Lord has said, among the remnant whom the Lord calls" (italics added).

Prayer for Deliverance

Praise God and worship Him and then repent each sin by name. For example, the sin of abortion is murder, hatred is murder according to 1 John 3:15. Lust after any man or woman is adultery; other sins include offense, fear, fornication, stealing, laziness, and gossip, etc. Call the sin what God calls it, and do not sugarcoat it. As the saying goes, call a spade a spade, not a big spoon. Expose each sin bearing in mind that sin is not a weakness, it is sin! Don't hide the evil in you. Remember, you cannot be delivered from your friend, only from your enemy. Just like a doctor cannot heal what you do not reveal, God will not deliver you if you do not want to let go and expose your sin. He already knows it. You are the one in need of help, not God. Expose the sin! Then pray:

Father, in the name of Jesus, You promise in Your Word that whoever calls on Your name shall be delivered. I call on Your name, Lord Jesus. Deliver me from this spirit of _____ (if abortion, call it murder; hatred is murder. Other spirits are offense, fear, lust, adultery, fornication, pornography, anger, gossip, suicide, fear, depression, lying, manipulation—call it what God calls it) in Jesus's name! I now expel these spirits from me in Jesus's name never to return again! I ask for Your Holy Spirit to fill me and cleanse me with the blood of Jesus. May Your Holy Spirit occupy every place that the enemy had occupied in me in Jesus name. I thank You for Your deliverance and for setting me free, I believe it, and receive it with thanksgiving in Jesus's name Amen.

Thank God for Your deliverance and praise Him, and like Jesus told those He healed and delivered, I say to you, 'go and sin no more'.

"*Therefore if the Son makes you free, you shall be free indeed*" (John 8:36).

You must fight to keep your deliverance because the enemy wants to keep you enslaved. He will try to make you believe that you did not get delivered. When he brings doubt, quote back to him the scripture above: "Jesus has made me free; therefore, I am free indeed." Now protect your mind in this way: confess God's Word. Fight the enemy from without; don't allow him back in. When he suggests an idea contrary to God, rebuke it and replace it with the Word of God.

Jesus gave us a glimpse in the spirit realm of how the demons operate. Remember what He said in Matthew 12:43–46. When the evil spirit finds your house or your heart EMPTY, it is because the Word of God does not dwell richly in you. You are not meditating on it day and night and obeying it. Remember, out of the abundance of the heart, the mouth speaks. When you are empty, you cannot encourage or teach someone the Word of God because it is not in you. The evil spirit comes back with more demons ten times stronger than it was, so that it will be harder to expel them, and the condition of the person becomes worse than before they were delivered.

After deliverance from sickness and evil spirits of insanity, Jesus told the people to go and sin no more, or worse things would happen. When the evil spirit comes and finds your heart SWEPT and IN ORDER, because you have been born again and delivered from the evil spirit, but you do not work out your salvation with fear and trembling, the evil spirits will go and get stronger demons than the ones you had before to come and occupy your heart. Your condition then will be worse than before. You must put on the full armor of God constantly and crucify your flesh daily. Don't think that because you are born again, it ends there. If you are a lukewarm Christian and you do not feed your spirit with the Word of God, you are in danger of destruction. Jesus warns about this lifestyle. He calls these kinds of Christians a wicked generation, Christians whom the devil will destroy, and the last state of these Christians will be worse than their first state.

My Story:

One day I was asleep, when I had a dream that was so real in the spirit. In this dream, my Helper, the Holy Spirit, was disclosing to me what the enemy was doing in the spirit. This was a leakage in the spirit. I dreamt that I was asleep and suddenly woke up. I went out of the bedroom and to the hallway, only to find an extremely tall lady carrying a small basket with some flyers in it. She was heading straight to my bedroom, where my husband lay. I stopped her and asked her who she was and what she was doing in my house. She said she was going to give my husband something, and that she had entered my house because "I found your door closed but not LOCKED." As tall as she was, I fought her, not with my knowledge or strength, but by the Holy Spirit. He fought her through me. I twisted her arm behind her, hit the back of her knee with my knee which forced her to kneel, brought her to submission, and threw her down the stairs and out the door. She tried to resist but was defeated miserably! I learned that it was the door of my marriage. I had closed it, but I had not locked it.

This time I closed my door, locked it, and gave the key to Jesus! When I woke up that morning, I was sore all over as if I had worked out! My muscles hurt! I was led in prayer by the Holy Spirit on my marriage. I lifted my marriage up in my hands and prayed for God to take it. With my hands lifted up high I admitted that I was tired of working out my marriage in my own wisdom and strength. As I prayed this prayer, submitting my marriage to God, my hands fell down suddenly as if a heavy load was taken from my hands without my knowledge. I stopped in the middle of my prayer and in awe kept saying to God, "You took it, LORD. You have taken my marriage! Thank you LORD JESUS for taking my marriage."

My marriage door is now closed and locked, and the keys are with Christ. My marriage is hidden in Christ in God, where no weapon formed against it shall prosper, and every tongue that rises against my marriage is condemned in Jesus's name! You can have your marriage delivered from the enemy's manipulation. Release it to God, close all doors, and lock your marriage from all evil by living righteous and holy. Remember, we open doors to the enemy through sin. I love this God! I love my Helper! There is no losing when you have God the Holy Spirit as your Counselor.

Beloved, read the Word of God and store up treasures in you, that God the Holy Spirit may remind you what you should say at the right time.

My Story:

My husband worked as a businessman, driving our truck from state to state, while I went to nursing school and took care of our three precious boys. He was not comfortable on the road with someone else watching our children and we both agreed it was best for our family that I stop working and raise our children. I was a director in an assisted living at the time, so I stopped working when our third baby was born. I was home alone most of the time all week, and he would come home on the weekends. Sometimes he came home for a few days in the middle of the week, depending on his workload and the distance.

One morning as I was doing dishes right before I went to school, I heard a voice.

It was a still, calm voice that said;

"Your husband is going to die today."

If I did not have the Holy Spirit of God in me and His gift of discernment, I would have thought it was God telling me this before it happened to prepare me. However, with the help of the Holy Spirit, I knew it was Lucifer himself, not just his demons, and definitely not God, because God is not an author of confusion. He does not contradict His Word or promises. I knew what God said about me and my husband and our future and destinies. He has promised us long lives, and I knew that my husband was God's voice to me as the head of our home. God spoke and still speaks to me through my husband, and I was not about to let it go. My husband was not going to die prematurely!

I immediately remembered what the Holy Spirit taught me, to speak back the Word of God to the enemy. I had nothing to fear with the Word of God and my Helper with me. I said to Lucifer out loud and sternly, "No! My husband will not die today, because he is God's voice to me, and God has promised us long lives. My husband has a great future ahead therefore NO! My husband will not die, but he will live to tell the goodness of the Lord in the land of the living!"

I finished doing the dishes and left for school. That day I tried reaching my husband on the phone severally but to no avail. Then at about 3:30 p.m., my phone rang. It was a call from a number I did not recognize. I picked it up and it was my husband! I asked him what was going on, and he went on to explain that he had been walking for about five miles to get to a place where he could borrow a phone because his phone did not have network. His truck had lost control and was now hanging over a cliff in the Tennessee Mountains. He had called a tow truck company and upon arrival, the crew had a difficult time trying to recover the truck. They could not get to it easily without compromising their safety and that of their truck. They suggested that the best option to recover the truck was to flip it on its side and pull it out. This would cause great loss on our part. My husband prayed for God's wisdom to get his truck out, and he told them to look for other ways to do it besides flipping it. Finally, after a long struggle, they recovered the truck safely. My husband was alive and safe, glory to God! I told him about my conversation with the devil earlier that morning. He was shocked and grateful that I did not agree with the enemy's plan.

You see, when you trust in God and are led by His Holy Spirit, the enemy cannot do anything to you unless you give him permission to. The enemy wanted to kill my husband and was in a sly way asking for my permission. But because God, the Holy Spirit, is my Helper and I read and hear the spoken Word of God through spending time with God, I did not fall for the trick. Jesus said that His sheep hears His voice, and a stranger they will not follow.

> Most certainly, I tell you, one who doesn't enter by the door into the sheep fold, but climbs up some other way, the same is a thief and a robber. But one who enters in by the door is the shepherd of the sheep. The gatekeeper opens the gate for him, and the sheep listen to his voice. He calls his own sheep by name, and leads them out. Whenever he brings out his own sheep, he goes before them, and the sheep follow him, for they know his voice. They will by no means follow a stranger, but will flee from him; for they don't know the voice of strangers. (John 10:1–5 WEB)

CHAPTER 8
Sins against the Holy Spirit

THE HOLY SPIRIT IS THE most protected Godhead. The Bible warns us from sinning against God the Holy Spirit. Let us look at some of the sins against the Holy Spirit mentioned in God's Word.

THE HOLY SPIRIT CAN BE BLASPHEMED

> Then one possessed by a demon, blind and mute, was brought to him and he healed him, so that the blind and mute man both spoke and saw. All the multitudes were amazed, and said, "Can this be the son of David?" But when the Pharisees heard it, they said, "This man does not cast out demons, except by Beelzebul, the prince of the demons." Knowing their thoughts, Jesus said to them, "Every kingdom divided against itself is brought to desolation, and every city or house divided against itself will not stand. If Satan casts out Satan, he is divided against himself. How then will his kingdom stand? If I by Beelzebul cast out demons, by whom do your children cast them out? Therefore they will be your judges. But if I by the Spirit of God cast out demons, then God's Kingdom has come upon you. Or how can one enter into the house of the strong man, and plunder his goods, unless he first bind the strong man? Then he will plunder his house. "He who is not with me is against me, and he who doesn't gather with me, scatters. Therefore I tell you, every sin

and blasphemy will be forgiven men, but the blasphemy against the Spirit will not be forgiven men. Whoever speaks a word against the Son of Man, it will be forgiven him; but whoever speaks against the Holy Spirit, it will not be forgiven him, neither in this age, nor in that which is to come." (Matt. 12:22–32 WEB)

"Most certainly I tell you, all sins of the descendants of man will be forgiven, including their blasphemies with which they may blaspheme; but whoever may blaspheme against the Holy Spirit never has forgiveness, but is subject to eternal condemnation."—because they said, "He has an unclean spirit.'" (Mark 3:28–30 WEB).

Many people blaspheme the Holy Spirit when they condemn His work in men and women and say that they are workings of the evil spirit. If you are not certain, it is better to pray for the spirit of discernment. God will give it to you graciously rather than let you sin against the Holy Spirit. Do not credit God's work to the devil.

The Holy Spirit Can Be Grieved

"And do not grieve the Holy Spirit of God, by whom you were sealed for the day of redemption" (Eph. 4:30).

The Holy Spirit is grieved by rebellion and disobedience when we continue to practice sin even after He has warned us. The Holy Spirit is very patient. He can also be taken away from us.

I grieved the Holy Spirit once in my very close walk with Him. He was very patient and warned me several times about something I was doing that would lead to my downfall, but I had more confidence in my flesh than I needed to have. As surely as the Holy Spirit had warned me, I fell and grieved Him, and He was taken away from me.

"But they rebelled and grieved His Holy Spirit; So He turned Himself against them as an enemy, And He fought against them" (Isa. 63:10).

God became their enemy when they grieved the Holy Spirit. It is a dangerous thing to have God as your enemy. This is described by the Israelites in the wilderness, who had a habit of disobedience and rebellion. The Holy Spirit is very patient and will help you through your mistakes. If you learn and turn away from them, He will use your mistakes to make you a better person, but if you practice sin, He will be taken away from you.

"Create in me a clean heart, O God. Renew a right spirit within me. Don't throw me from your presence, and don't take your Holy Spirit from me. Restore to me the joy of your salvation. Uphold me with a willing spirit." (Ps. 51:10–12 WEB).

This scripture was King David's prayer after he murdered one of his faithful soldiers, Uriah the Hittite, to cover up his sin of adultery against him. David took Uriah's wife, Bathsheba, when Uriah was in battle and made her pregnant. He then sent for Uriah from battle so he could come home to sleep with his wife, but Uriah refused to be comfortable with his wife while his fellow soldiers were still in battle. David got him drunk, but Uriah slept outside the palace, not in his house. David, seeing that he would be found out, sent Uriah back to the battlefield with his own death note, instructing the commander of the army to assign Uriah a position in the heat of battle so he would be killed. After this was done, David was so grieved by this sin. He repented and prayed for forgiveness and for God not to take His Holy Spirit from him. He asked God to restore the joy of his salvation that he had lost by sinning.

Many times we get into the same predicament, but if we confess our sins, God is faithful and just to forgive us and cleanse us from all unrighteousness. David knew this and had faith in God's grace.

The Holy Spirit Can Be Taken Away: This Is Spiritual Death
My Story:

One time, years ago, the Holy Spirit warned me several times of the danger of falling into sin while I was busy helping someone else. He said,

"If the person you are trying to rescue from drowning was pulling you down into the water and fighting the rescue, you must leave them alone, or both of you will drown." He again said, "It is easier to be pulled down by someone who's in a low position than for you to pull them up." We are not God; only God changes people.

"But others save with fear, pulling them out of the fire, hating even the garment defiled by the flesh" (Jude 1:23).

I had confidence in myself and flesh instead of taking precaution as the Holy Spirit had warned. I fell into sin against His temple and my life was stained because I did it by my might and wisdom. When I grieved the Holy Spirit and He was taken away from me, I was the most miserable person ever. This is because He was my best friend, my Teacher, Counselor, Comforter, and source of wisdom. He was everything to me. He told me of things before they happened, helped me through the things I faced at that specific time, gave me words to speak when I had none, encouraged me, and revealed my destiny to me. I lost everything when I lost Him.

I learned my lesson really fast and very painfully, because I used to and still do write songs only by the Holy Spirit. But when He left, I did not have any song. I prayed and confessed my sin, repented, turned back to God, and asked God to give me back His Spirit. I came to realize that no person or thing is worth me losing God the Holy Spirit for. My God the Holy Spirit was and is worth more than life itself.

For almost a whole year, from January to November, I never got any song. Then in November, a song came, and that was how I knew that God had mercy on me and had given me back His Holy Spirit. The song was in Swahili language saying, "Touch me once more, touch me once more, fill me with Your Holy Spirit, Lord, touch me once more, touch me once more." I was so excited and from then on, I learned NEVER to grieve the Holy Spirit of God. Life is empty and unbearable without Him.

No one is greater; nothing is better. I had rather lose it all than lose the Holy Spirit. Thank God for a very tough but unforgettable lesson. Living without hearing from God through His Spirit is like going deaf and blind all of a sudden after enjoying great eyesight and hearing.

I plead with you, don't grieve the Holy Spirit. He has feelings, He is sensitive and passionate. He transforms us into the image of Christ. That's why Jesus said you can blaspheme Jesus (the Son of God) all you want, but never do it to the Holy Spirit. Even the blood of Jesus cannot cleanse you from this unforgivable sin. I hope and pray that you enjoy and cherish God the Holy Spirit and don't wait to lose Him to know His value. Many people know the value of someone or something after they lose it. Learn from my mistake, because it is was the worst feeling one would ever have. I tremble at the remembrance of that hopeless and helpless feeling I had.

David was a witness of King Saul not having the Spirit of God. King Saul's rebellion cost him the Holy Spirit and as a result, an evil spirit would torture him from time to time. David the shepherd boy would play music for King Soul so that the evil spirit would stop tormenting him. David knew what it was like to have the Holy Spirit, and after he sinned, he could not imagine living without God the Holy Spirit in His life.

"Then Samuel took the horn of oil, and anointed him in the middle of his brothers. Then Yahweh's Spirit came mightily on David from that day forward. So Samuel rose up and went to Ramah. *Now Yahweh's Spirit departed from Saul, and an evil spirit from Yahweh troubled him.*" (1 Sam. 16:13–14 WEB; italics added)

Samson, the strongest man, lost the Holy Spirit through disobedience.

> When Delilah saw that he had told her all his heart, she sent and called for the lords of the Philistines, saying, "Come up this once, for he has told me all his heart." Then the lords of the Philistines came up to her, and brought the money in their hand. She made him sleep on her knees; and she called for a man, and shaved off the seven locks of his head; and she began to afflict him, and his strength went from him. She said, "The Philistines are upon you, Samson!"

He awoke out of his sleep, and said, "I will go out as at other times, and shake myself free." *But he didn't know that Yahweh had departed from him.* (Judg. 16:18–20 WEB; italics added)

Samson was destroyed for disobedience. He grieved the Holy Spirit, who was in him, by disclosing the secret of his strength to his enemies and having his hair cut off, which God had commanded him not to do.

If you have grieved the Holy Spirit and He has been taken away, know that God is gracious and merciful. You must confess it as sin, repent, and turn away from your sin and seek God again with passion until God gives Him back to you. Only God the Father can give you back His Spirit. He gave us His Son and He never stopped there. He gave us His Holy Spirit as well. What a great God we serve! He sets us up to be fully equipped to succeed and live as children of God on earth. The same power and strength Christ had while on earth that helped Him through His God-given task is the same power you and I have to fulfill our God-given assignment. Glory to God!

Some people may argue and say; Jesus said that the Holy Spirit will be with us forever in John 14:16. Yes but Christ put a condition to this promise.

John 14:15-17 WEB says:
"If you love me, keep my commandments. I will pray to the Father, and he will give you another Counselor, that he may be with you forever,— the Spirit of truth, whom the world can't receive; for it doesn't see him, neither knows him. You know him, for he lives with you, and will be in you."

We must love Christ through OBEDIENCE for the Holy Spirit to come and remain in us forever. But for those who rebel, the Holy Spirit cannot dwell in you and go with you to Hell. He cannot strive with you as God said in Genesis 6:1-3 when sin abounded and men wanted to lead themselves into their own lusts. The Holy Spirit is a guarantee for those who are in Christ Jesus alone. Remember, He will not operate apart from the Word, and the Word will not operate unless the Father speaks or sends the Word. If you insist on disobedience like I did, the Holy Spirit will be taken away from you. Realize that even in the Old Testament, the Holy Spirit did not remove Himself from the people, He did not leave them, He was taken away by the Father at His Word (the Son). The Holy Spirit did not Speak, the Father Spoke and said;

""When men began to multiply on the surface of the ground, and daughters were born to them, God's sons saw that men's daughters were beautiful, and they took any that they wanted for themselves as wives. *Yahweh said, "My Spirit will not strive with man forever, because he also is flesh; so his days will be one hundred twenty years."*" (Genesis 6:1-3 WEB; italics added)

Notice that when the Spirit of God was taken away, the life span of man was decreased significantly, where as humans used to live very long. Methuselah lived the longest at 969 years, almost 1000. God cut down 849 years to only 120 years for man. See what disobedience yields? Death!
Genesis 5:27 (WEB)
"All the days of Methuselah were *nine hundred sixty-nine years*, then he died."

The Holy Spirit Cannot Be Deceived or Lied To

But a certain man named Ananias, with Sapphira, his wife, sold a possession, and kept back part of the price, his wife also being aware of it, and brought a certain part, and laid it at the apostles' feet. But Peter said, "Ananias, why has Satan filled your heart to lie to the Holy Spirit, and to keep back part of the price of the land? While you kept it, didn't it remain your own? After it was sold, wasn't it in your power? How is it that you have conceived this thing in your heart? You haven't lied to men, but to God." Ananias, hearing these words, fell down and died. Great fear came on all who heard these things. The young men arose and wrapped him up, and they carried him out and buried him. About three hours later, his wife, not knowing what had happened, came in. Peter answered her, "Tell me whether you sold the land for so much." She said, "Yes, for so much." But Peter asked her, *"How is it that you have agreed together to tempt the Spirit of the Lord?* Behold, the feet of those who have buried your husband are at the door, and they will carry you out." She fell down immediately at his feet, and died. The young men came in and found her dead, and they carried her out and buried her by her husband. Great fear came on the whole assembly, and on all who heard these things. (Acts 5:1–11 WEB; italics added)

The Holy Spirit is God. No one can ever lie to God. God is all knowing, omnipotent, omnipresent, and omniscient. He is the discerner of the hearts of people. He knows the intentions of our hearts; He created humans.

"Do not be deceived, God is not mocked; for whatever a man sows, that he will also reap" (Gal. 6:7)

It is great deception to think that we can lie to God.

The Holy Spirit Can Be Quenched

"Do not quench the Spirit" (1 Thess. 5:19).

My Story: Consequences of Quenching the Holy Spirit

I was in a situation where the pastor in the church I attended quenched God the Holy Spirit during worship *on a Resurrection Sunday*. It all began when God gave me a new song, and the Holy Spirit had been teaching me on worship. I recorded the music with my producer and asked the pastor's wife if I could share the song and worship in church. I told her that I was willing to wait until they had a chance for me to worship God. I said this because they usually gave people a chance to sing to the congregation, but I was not a performer; rather, I was a worshiper and wanted to lead the people into worship with the new song, and allow the Holy Spirit to move in the congregation.

She was excited and asked me to go and speak to the praise and worship team at their Saturday meeting and share what the Holy Spirit had taught me on worship, and then sing the song on Sunday, just before the pastor came to preach. I was excited since I had rivers of living waters bubbling in my belly ready to flow. On the Wednesday of the same week, before Resurrection Sunday, I was doing my devotions and Bible study in my dining room, when God the Holy Spirit spoke to me as clearly as He always did. He said, "I don't want you to lead worship just before the pastor comes. I want you to lead the worship in the main worship service."

I was shocked! I was not part of the praise and worship team, how could I take over and lead worship? But I knew so well not to argue with Him, so I said to Him, "You know that it is such an honor for me to get a chance to worship at all this soon, not counting it is even harder and very special to get a chance just before the preacher preaches. Nevertheless, I will do whatever you want me to do, but please, You tell this to the pastor's wife."

As soon as we finished this conversation with the Holy Spirit, I heard my phone vibrating on the couch in my living room and I went to see who was texting me.

It was the pastor's wife saying, "Hi, I am sorry I forgot that I had put someone else to sing just before the pastor preached, but I would like you to lead the main worship service on Sunday. It will be very powerful if the other person sings and you lead the worship." You can imagine what my reaction was. Yes, you are absolutely right! My jaw dropped, and I was amazed at how God worked so fast. God knew what my answer would be because He created me, and so He had already dealt with the pastor's wife.

I told the pastor's wife of the conversation I had a few minutes ago with the Holy Spirit, she was shocked and excited.

I went and spoke to the worship team on Saturday and taught them the worship song. The worship team and I were amazed and marveled at the Holy Spirit and how He revealed God to us that day.

Now on the Resurrection Sunday, as God had instructed me to lead worship, I started to lead worship, and the Holy Spirit took over totally. I was in the service, being led by God the Holy Spirit. But before I knew it, the pastor came out of his seat and started talking on the microphone over me. He signaled the sound team to cut my sound off and sent his wife up on the stage to stop me. Before I knew what was going on, the pastor's wife touched my shoulder, and when I looked at her, she snatched her hand so fast from my shoulder and moved back and looked down and could not look at me anymore. She acted as if she had seen a ghost. She was trembling. I knew that God had revealed something to her and she realized what they had just done. Immediately the Holy Spirit reminded me of a dream He had shown me a few weeks earlier concerning the church, and all that was happening in the dream just replayed at that moment.

In the dream, we were in church sitting in the congregation. As we sat there, the pastor and his wife were standing at the pulpit and were busy looking at some paperwork. Up on the altar, I saw that the dark red curtains were falling off completely on one side. I rushed from my chair up to the altar and climbed up a chair so I could reach and fix the curtains. My husband helped me on the other side to hold up the curtain rod as I fixed the curtain. The pastor and his wife were still busy looking at some paperwork, and the fallen curtains at the altar did not bother them. As I was busy putting the curtains back, God warned the pastor and his wife through my husband, who shouted out to them repeatedly, trying to get their attention, saying, "You cannot ignore this (pointing at the curtains and what I was doing) for the next level! You cannot ignore this for the next level! You cannot ignore this for the next level!" Then I woke up.

In reality at the service that day, the pastor attempted to stop the service, but the Holy Spirit made Him repeat all the songs we had sang. The pastor later called the worship team leaders in a meeting and told them that I was demon possessed.

My husband and I were so discouraged that Sunday when we went home that we went and took a nap. I asked God the Holy Spirit to encourage me. He asked me why I was discouraged. He said that the pastor and his wife never attacked me; they attacked Him.

He asked me a simple question. "If someone comes to fight you, do they fight you or the clothes you are wearing? You are my outfit." He said. "They attacked Me, not you. The pastor called Me a demon, for I was in you. If you need encouragement, you know the principle: give, and it shall come back to you, in good measure, pressed down, shaken together, and running over. If you need encouragement, encourage someone else."

I went and got scripture from the Bible and sent it to all my phone contacts. In a few minutes, I received many encouraging texts back, and the text-messaging ministry was birthed out of the pain and need of encouragement. A ministry was birthed out of my misery. That ministry exists to this day, reaching many around the world.

From this, I had been called over spiritual by people in the church and by my "friends." Others thought I was demon possessed. My husband did not understand my friendship with God the Holy Spirit and the boldness in me to share God's message and to prophecy to the pastor and others I was sent to. He had felt bad for me and also felt embarrassed by the incident in church. My husband had said to me that day as we drove home;

"That is why I told you not to stand in front of people."

I responded to him that I was willing to be ridiculed and persecuted for Christ's sake, and that I was going to obey God even unto death.

Few months later, the pastor called my husband and I to the side one Sunday after service. He apologized to us for his behavior that Resurrection Sunday. He confessed and said that he realized he had quenched the Holy Spirit because he was a respecter of people. He went on to say that these same people whom he had feared and respected had now turned against him. He explained that on that Resurrection Sunday, he feared that his unsaved church members would get bored, so he came in and cut off the worship. Thinking he was attacking me, he attacked God Himself.

Needless to say, he ignored what God wanted to do, and he never got to the next level. He later lost his new church building, which was worth over a million dollars, and more than half of his church members. He lost his influence to many because he did not value what God valued. He feared people and not God. Because he was not sensitive to God the Holy Spirit, he kicked God out of His own house but embraced people who did not care anything about God.

"No one can serve two masters. Either you will hate the one and love the other, or you will be devoted to the one and despise the other. You cannot serve both God and money" (Matt. 6:24 NIV).

We must all know that God is not a respecter of persons. He values worship. Let us love Him enough to value what He values and not fall into the sin of quenching, grieving, or blaspheming God the Holy Spirit.

The Seven Spirits of God

"There shall come forth a Rod from the stem of Jesse, and a Branch shall grow out of his roots. The Spirit of the Lord shall rest upon Him, The Spirit of wisdom and understanding, The Spirit of counsel and might, The Spirit of knowledge and of the fear of the Lord. His delight is in the fear of the Lord, And He shall not judge by the sight of His eyes, nor decide by the hearing of His ears" (Isa. 11:1–3).

The seven Spirits of God are:

1. Spirit of God
2. Spirit of wisdom
3. Spirit of understanding
4. Spirit of counsel
5. Spirit of might
6. Spirit of knowledge
7. Spirit of the fear of the Lord

Without these Spirits from God, it is difficult to succeed in your God-given task. Jesus Himself, when He came to do His assignment, was empowered by these Spirits from God. One thing truly stands out—the Spirit that Jesus delighted in was the Spirit of the fear of the Lord. My life turned around, and God started using me profoundly, when I prayed for and received this Spirit. I did not know that the fear of God is a spirit.

Why Delight in the Spirit of the Fear of the Lord?

- "Fear of the Lord is the foundation of true wisdom. All who obey his commandments will grow in wisdom" (Ps. 111:10 NLT).
- "The fear of the Lord is the beginning of *wisdom*, and the *knowledge* of the Holy One is *understanding*" (Prov. 9:10; italics added).

- "And this is what he says to all humanity: 'The *fear of the Lord* is true *wisdom*; to forsake evil is real *understanding*'" (Job 28:28 NLT; italics added).
- "The *wise* are *mightier* than the strong, and those with *knowledge* grow stronger and stronger" (Prov. 24:5 NLT; italics added).

When we live and delight in the fear of God, we get wisdom, which leads to knowledge and understanding, giving us might and counsel for daily work that we were created to do.

When we delight in the spirit of the fear of God like Jesus Christ did, we will attract all these other spirits of God in our lives and be fully equipped to fulfill our God-given assignments. Jesus was successful because He had the seven spirits of God.

"And to the angel of the church in Sardis write, 'these things says *He who has the seven Spirits of God* and the seven stars: "I know your works, that you have a name that you are alive, but you are dead"'" (Rev. 3:1; italics added).

"From the throne came flashes of lightning and the rumble of thunder. And in front of the throne were *seven torches with burning flames. This is the sevenfold Spirit of God*" (Rev. 4:5 NLT; italics added).

"But **the Helper, the Holy Spirit**, whom **the Father will send in My name**, He will teach you *all things*, and bring to your remembrance all things that I said to you." (John 14:26 ; italics and bold added)

The Holy Spirit of God has the seven fold Spirit of God in Him that is why Jesus was given the Holy Spirit WITHOUT measure. We too must pray for the Holy Spirit without measure.

John 3:34 (WEB)

'For he whom God has sent speaks the words of God; for God gives the Spirit without measure."

To Receive the Holy Spirit, you MUST be Born Again.

This is because God the Holy Spirit is sent to us by God the Father *only in the name of Jesus Christ (God the Son)*. If you do not have the power to use the name of Jesus Christ you cannot ask for or receive the Holy Spirit. Only those who have made Jesus Christ their LORD and Savior have the right to be called by His name. They can ask and receive God's gift, the Holy Spirit.

It is similar to someone asking for the right to receive direct connection and information to all intelligence information from the U.S.A. military while he or she belongs to the enemy's military. This information is usually kept confidential for the protection and benefit of the country. It is only accessible to the U.S.A military. In the same way, the Holy Spirit of God knows the secret things of God and so He is only given to those in the kingdom of God for the benefit of His Kingdom. He is the KIA (Kingdom Intelligence Agent)

If you are born again, ask God to fill you with His Holy Spirit without measure, and then ask the Holy Spirit to come in and clean you and rid you of all that is not of God in you. Ask Him to fill you with His fruits and gifts. Ask Him to give you the gift of speaking in tongues. Believe you receive, open your mouth, and start speaking in the language He gives. The devil and your mind will try to work against your spirit, saying that the language is fake or made up. But keep speaking; don't give up, because you are allowing God to use your tongue to speak mysteries that your mind can't comprehend and neither can the devil. You are speaking directly to God; it is the perfect prayer by the Holy Spirit through you to the Father. You must open your mouth and make a sound! Just like talking, you can't learn to talk with your mouth closed.

Prayer to Receive the Holy Spirit

Father, in Jesus's name, You say that every perfect gift comes from You. You also said that if I ask for the Holy Spirit, You will not withhold Him from me. Father, I ask that You forgive me, cleanse me and purify me for Your sake. Fill me with Your Holy Spirit without measure, teach me all Your ways and truths, and give me the gift of speaking in tongues and the interpretation of tongues as in Your Word. I receive the Holy Spirit and His power now in Jesus's name. I ask that You fill me with the fullness of Your Spirit, the seven Spirits of God, in Jesus's name. I pray this, trusting, believing and receiving Your gift with thanksgiving in Jesus's name, amen!

Now open your mouth and allow the Holy Spirit to speak through you in Jesus's name!

CHAPTER 9
Relationship or Religion?

§

What's your relationship with Christ?

SOME PEOPLE HAVE A RELATIONSHIP with God where they only pray when in need; otherwise, they live for themselves, and once in a while, when it is "politically correct," they reveal that they are followers of Christ. I call these long-distance-relationship Christians, just as in your phonebook you have people you only text when you need something or you need their service, or on holidays to wish them well. These are the people you remember when you scroll down the contacts on your phone or a when need arises. Some of Christ's followers have chosen to be acquaintances, coworkers, friends, or brides of Christ.

ACQUAINTANCE

Acquaintance Christians know God casually. They *know about Christ* but do not *know Christ*. No one cares to invest in a casual relationship, because it is of minimal importance. These types of Christians will go to church on occasion or holidays or watch Christian TV only when they are down. They may even go to church religiously for social purposes, but their relationship with Christ is only on an as needed basis. They say they are born again but do not care to work out their salvation with fear and trembling as we ought to. They still love their lives and their reputation more than they love God.

"So then, my beloved, even as you have always obeyed, not only in my presence, but now much more in my absence, *work out your own salvation with fear and trembling. For it is God who works in you both to will and to work, for his good pleasure.*" (Phil. 2:12–13 WEB; italics added).

"He who loves father or mother more than me is not worthy of me; and he who loves son or daughter more than me isn't worthy of me. He who doesn't take his cross and follow after me, isn't worthy of me. He who seeks his life will lose it; and he who loses his life for my sake will find it." (Matt. 10:37–39 WEB)

> He called the multitude to himself with his disciples, and said to them, "Whoever wants to come after me, let him deny himself, and take up his cross, and follow me. For whoever wants to save his life will lose it; and whoever will lose his life for my sake and the sake of the Good News will save it. For what does it profit a man, to gain the whole world, and forfeit his life? For what will a man give in exchange for his life? For whoever will be ashamed of me and of my words in this adulterous and sinful generation, the Son of Man also will be ashamed of him, when he comes in his Father's glory, with the holy angels." (Mark 8:34–38 WEB)

"Remember Lot's wife! Whoever seeks to save his life loses it, but whoever loses his life preserves it. I tell you, in that night there will be two people in one bed. The one will be taken, and the other will be left. There will be two grinding grain together. One will be taken, and the other will be left" (Luke 17:32–35 WEB).

"He who loves his life will lose it. He who hates his life in this world will keep it to eternal life. If anyone serves me, let him follow me. Where I am, there will my servant also be. If anyone serves me, the Father will honor him." (John 12:25–26 WEB).

These are the Christians spoken of in Revelation 2 as the loveless, compromising, and corrupt Christians. In Chapter 3 they are the dead and lukewarm Christians. These may be Christians who may have gone through some trauma in life. They got angry at God for allowing things to happen to them because they do not know God. They blame God for the work of the enemy and the consequences of sin. They still know God is God and use Him only when in need. They may be ones who value the temporary things of this world and are preoccupied with them rather than investing in the eternal relationship with Christ. We do not allow acquaintances to come into our homes like we would our friends, and we should not expect God to do so either.

Coworkers

Coworkers are just like the name suggests. They work in the work of God but have no other relationship outside work. I know there are coworkers who are best friends, but here I am talking about coworkers ONLY. We all have worked with people whom we can put up with only for the hours we are at work as long as we don't go home with them. Other coworkers we cannot even see eye to eye with. There are, sadly, pastors and other Kingdom workers who cannot see eye to eye! I worked at a place where some nurses could not work the same shift or unit; they would not see eye to eye. What a bad spirit!

These Christians are regular churchgoers and may even be serving as apostles, bishops, pastors, deacons, ushers, praise and worship leaders and their teams, and everyone else who works for the Kingdom of God. These people only do their jobs and wear their invisible name badges in the service of the Kingdom when they go to work just like any other job, and take it off when the shift is over.

At my workplace, I wear my badge and have access to areas I need to be in, whereas an ordinary person has no access. Other employees respect my title as long as I have my badge on. When I go home, I take my badge off and no one can tell what profession I am in unless something happens requiring me to step in as a nurse.

One time I was at the park with my sons when a child fell off his bike and scraped one of his knees really bad. His mother was home; he had some friends with him who went and got his mother. Without giving it much thought, I stepped in, took care of his wound and stopped the bleeding. His mother arrived on foot and I offered to drive them home. While at their house I asked for a first-aid kit, disinfected and dressed the young boy's wound and offered to pray with them. They were very grateful and they knew that I was a nurse and a Christian, not by my badge or by me telling them, but by my ACTIONS.

I could have easily ignored them and walked away just like the story of the Good Samaritan, where the priest walked away. I was not obligated to help at all. I could have been shy about my Jesus even in the simplest act of prayer, but it was what was in me that came out. A good tree bears good fruit, and a bad tree bears bad fruit. Jesus said you will know them by their fruits. This is the easiest way to know someone for who they really are—not by their title or physical appearance or by who they say they are, but by what they do.

Jesus knew that many people would preach and imitate the truth while serving the kingdom of darkness, so He gave us a way of knowing whose kingdom they are in and who they are connected to. Jesus Christ is the vine and we are the branches. The branches cannot bear fruit by themselves unless they are connected to the vine. Followers of Christ will bear fruit from Christ. They will act like Jesus would in every situation because they are drawing from Him. The opposite is true. Those from the kingdom of darkness will act like the one they are connected to, Satan, in every situation, because they draw from him. You will know them by their fruits (Matt. 7:15–20).

Some of my coworkers only see me at work and do not have my phone number. If it is work related, they can call me from work. I will work with them but after work is over, I invest my time in God's Kingdom and in my family. We mostly think of our coworkers when we see them at work, but when we go home we forget about them. That is how some coworkers are in Christ. They treat Christianity as a job and once out of the workplace (church) they are mean, rude, and abusive to their spouses, children and others. They are angry people, adulterers, fornicators, liars, con men and con women, lovers of money etc. They abuse the people who trust them. These are the kind of workers that God spoke about in Ezekiel 34:2-15. Run to Jesus and trust Him alone.

"Thus says the Lord: 'Cursed is the man who trusts in man and makes flesh his strength, whose heart departs from the Lord'" (Jer. 17:5).

When I was younger, I went through abuse from a bishop, and as traumatizing as the experience was, I did not get angry at God, because He did not cause the traumatizing experience; rather, my sin of disobedience by putting my trust in people brought me under the curse mentioned in the scripture above. The minute I put my trust in the title that he carried (Bishop), I immediately started to walk under a curse because the Word of God warns against it. When I grew up in Africa, we were taught to be a respecter of men because of their title and what they said was right and it was rude to question them. I remember I tried to question this bishop once and he almost slapped me, his hand stopped in the air.

From my abuse experience, I learned not to trust or be a respecter of people and their titles, but to bring all my cares to God for He cares for me. My trust is in Christ, in Him alone. He is the One who created me and the whole universe and nothing is impossible with Him.

"Behold, I am the Lord, the God of all flesh. Is there anything too hard for Me?" (Jer. 32:27)

"Casting all your care upon Him, for He cares for you" (1 Pet. 5:7).

The Word of God is never a request, but a command. Many people suffer because they do not know the Word of God.

"My people are *destroyed for lack of knowledge*. Because you have *rejected knowledge*, I also will reject you from being priest for Me; because you *have forgotten the law of your God*, I also will forget your children" (Hosea 4:6; italics added).

God is not talking about nonbelievers; rather, He is talking about believers who are His priests. These Christians once knew the Word of God, but they have forgotten it. They have rejected God's Word; they do not practice it. God says they will no longer be heard when they pray (priests go to God in prayer for themselves and others), and He will not bless their children. God always insisted on meditating on His Word and being careful to do as He commands for all His blessings to follow and overtake us.

"Now it shall come to pass, if you diligently obey the voice of the Lord your God, to observe carefully all His commandments which I command you today, that the Lord your God will set you high above all nations of the earth. And all these blessings shall come upon you and overtake you, because you obey the voice of the Lord your God" (Deut. 28:1–2). See blessings and curses in Deuteronomy 28.

"But it shall come to pass, if you do not obey the voice of the Lord your God, to observe carefully all His commandments and His statutes which I command you today that all these curses will come upon you and overtake you" (Deut. 28:15).

The only way to live under God's blessings is to always read His Word, meditate on it day and night, do His Word and teach others to obey Him.

"Whoever therefore breaks one of the least of these commandments, and teaches men so, shall be called least in the kingdom of heaven; *but whoever does and teaches them, he shall be called great in the kingdom of heaven*" (Matt. 5:19; italics added).

"This Book of the Law shall not depart from your mouth, but you shall meditate in it day and night, that you may observe to do according to all that is written in it. For then you will make your way prosperous, and then you will have good success" (Josh. 1:8).

Many Christians are walking under a curse, yet they do not know it. They end up getting wounded and living in fear and a lot of heartache.

They even go to the extent of blaming God for their troubles. This is a scheme of the enemy because the enemy knows the Word of God in its entirety while most Christians do not know the Word of God. Satan will therefore cause people to be too busy to study and meditate on God's Word so that they constantly sin without their knowledge. This causes them to be cursed, and they wonder why their life is the devil's playing ground. The devil then deceives them by having them blame God for their trouble, while God has given people His Word to help them live in victory. People of God PERISH (die, get destroyed, are annihilated) for lack of knowledge.

I have heard many times people ask, 'if God is such a loving God as we say, why is there suffering in the world? Why does He throw people in hell if God is so loving?' These questions are ignorant questions; questions that the devil wants people to ask and turn them away from their God. If you turn from God, then you turn to the devil. If you are not for God, you are against God.

The answers to the questions they ask above are very simple. In every country, there are laws and courts that enforce these laws. If someone decides to break the law and is sentenced to death or life in prison or receives any sentencing, does that person blame the president for the sentence? Do the consequences of his or her lawlessness prove that the president of the country is uncaring and unloving or not loyal to his or her country and the citizens he or she serves? If you are a parent or caregiver and you warn a child against playing near the fire in the kitchen or against doing drugs or being in a gang, stealing, or killing, and yet the child rejects your wisdom and does what you warned him or her against and he or she gets hurt or even dies, does that make you a bad and unloving parent? Are you the cause of the child's trouble, or are the child's choice of actions and disobedience the root cause of all his or her problems? In the same way, why are we so harsh on God while He has given us all things to help us live a victorious life?

"Grace to you and peace be multiplied in the knowledge of God and of Jesus our Lord, seeing that *his divine power has granted to us all things that pertain to life and godliness, through the knowledge of him who called us by his own glory and virtue*; by which he has granted to us his precious and exceedingly great promises; that through these you may become partakers of the divine nature, having escaped from the corruption that is in the world by lust." (2 Pet. 1:2–4 WEB; italics added).

God is love and will never love us any less. He is not responsible for the curses we get ourselves into when we disobey because He has instructed us in the way we should go. It is up to us to obey. We should blame ourselves for the consequences we face from disobedience. Just as a parent has rules in the home and punishment follows disobedience, God created hell for the devil and his angels, and provided a ransom for us through Jesus Christ His Son. If you choose death, hell, God is not to blame, but if you choose life, you will benefit. God has already provided all we need to succeed, it is up to us to accept and obey Him fully.

"Who shall separate us from the love of Christ? Could oppression, or anguish, or persecution, or famine, or nakedness, or peril, or sword? For I am persuaded, that neither death, nor life, nor angels, nor principalities, nor things present, nor things to come, nor powers, nor height, nor depth, nor any other created thing, will be able to separate us from the love of God, which is in Christ Jesus our Lord." (Rom. 8:35, 38–39 WEB).

Never be deceived to doubt God's love for you. It is more than enough that God gave His only Son as a ransom for sinful humanity, not counting that He did this great sacrificial love act while we were still sinners. He gave Jesus to us and gave us the righteousness of Christ in exchange for our sins.

"For while we were yet weak, at the right time Christ died for the ungodly. For one will hardly die for a righteous man. Yet perhaps for a righteous person someone would even dare to die. *But God commends his own love toward us, in that while we were yet sinners, Christ died for us.*" (Rom. 5:6–8; italics added).

God's love for us is so much that He sacrificed His only Son for sinners, not the righteous!

Remember, in this world Jesus said we would have trials and tribulations, but to be of good cheer, for He has overcome the world. Trials and temptations are inevitable in this fallen world, but there is a perfect world after this world where we shall live in complete holiness and light of God forever. The devil will not be in the picture in heaven. He has been sentenced already and is on death row now awaiting his destruction; he will be serving eternal life in the lake of fire. But because the enemy still exists here on earth evil will always be here, but evil is never caused by God. Satan doesn't want to die alone eternally and that is why he wants to grieve God by causing us to sin, so that we may die with him even after God has sacrificed it all for us. Let us not fall for his plan.

Friends of Christ

The Friends of Christ are those who do His will, those who obey His commands.

"You are my friends if you do what I command" (John 15:14 NLT).

"If you love me, obey my commandments" (John 14:15).
Abraham was called a friend of God.

"Are You not our God, who drove out the inhabitants of this land before Your people Israel, and gave it to the descendants of *Abraham Your friend* forever?" (2 Chron. 20:7; italics added).
 "But you, Israel, are My servant, Jacob whom I have chosen, the descendants of *Abraham my friend*" (Isa. 41:8; italics added).
 "And the Scripture was fulfilled which says, 'Abraham believed God, and it was accounted to him for righteousness.' And *he was called the friend of God*" (James 2:23; italics added).
 "And the Lord said, 'Shall I hide from Abraham what I am doing, since Abraham shall surely become a great and mighty nation, and all

the nations of the earth shall be blessed in him? For I have known him, in order that he may command his children and his household after him, that they keep the way of the Lord, to do righteousness and justice, that the Lord may bring to Abraham what He has spoken to him'" (Gen. 18:17–19).

What God the Father said about Abraham revealed Abraham's obedience to God and love for God—that Abraham did not love anyone or anything more than he loved God. Therefore God did not keep from Abraham what He was planning to do. God revealed His business to Abraham, His friend.

A friend of God is the one who loves God by obeying His commands; one who loves God more than anything and anyone in his or her life; one who lives to please God and to do His will; one who follows God with no reservations and is relentless in following His will; and one who does WHATEVER God tells him or her to do without questioning God's intelligence and wisdom, without the fear of people. Are you a friend of God?

THE BRIDE OF CHRIST

Who is the bride of Christ? This is the MOST INTIMATE and highest rank a believer in Christ can ever have here on earth and in the life to come in the spirit. It is not the working of miracles or the raising of the dead. It is not being a bishop or apostle or holding the highest title on earth. It is not being a pastor of the largest congregation on earth. It is none of these and more—it is being the bride of Christ. Intimacy with Christ.

The bride of Christ is the one whom the bridegroom is coming for and the wedding supper is being prepared for; it is the bride who completes Christ and the joy of the Father. When a man on earth gets married to his bride, he feels complete. There is celebration, her status changes from Miss to Mrs. He becomes a husband and leader of the home. They get to another level of intimacy that only a husband and wife can get to. So it is with the bride of Christ. There is life and greater intimacy with Christ after this life, after the wedding. Just as life begins all over again the moment one is married, life begins all over again in greater heights when the bridegroom comes for His bride for the wedding supper and when the wedding is done.

The bride of Christ is one who keeps herself pure without blemish and looks forward to each moment in preparation, anticipation and readiness for her bridegroom. She will not compromise or let anyone take the place of her beloved; she will not allow her wedding garment to be soiled. She does not entertain anyone who destructs her from her vision. A bride is one who is led totally and fully by the Holy Spirit of God. That is why the Word of God concludes the bridegroom's coming in Revelation 22:17, "And *the Spirit and the bride say*, '*Come!*' And let him who hears say, 'Come!' And let him who thirsts come. Whoever desires, let him take the water of life freely" (italics added).

The Holy Spirit gets the bride ready for her bridegroom, and they together invite the bridegroom back to come and get His bride.

The bride is a mature son or daughter of God, and once you are married into a family, you become one of the children in that family. You are not just a friend; whatever inheritance the Father gives to the Son, belongs to Him and His bride. There is no marriage in heaven but the marriage of the Son and His church.

The bride of Christ is one who does not only know about Christ but goes deeper into knowing Christ. One can only know Christ by revelation from the Holy Spirit. Looking at the story of the ten virgins, the wise ones knew their bridegroom. They were wise because they realized that even if He took a long time to come, He would surely come at the right time. They did not rely on their timing of Him, but on His timing. They therefore carried extra oil just in case they needed it. They had the Word (lamp) in them and the Holy Spirit's revelation of the Word (Oil), revealing to them who their bridegroom, Jesus Christ, was.

The foolish ones were also virgins, but they did not know their bridegroom—they knew about him. They knew that he was coming, but they were not sensitive for His timing. They got ready according to their timing. They had the Word (lamp) but no revelation (oil). They ignored the Holy Spirit, who is the revealer of their bridegroom, Jesus Christ. Remember, the Psalmist in Psalm 119:105 says, "Thy Word is a lamp unto my feet and a light unto my path."

John said, in John 1:1, "In the beginning was the WORD and the WORD was with God and the WORD was GOD."

The wise ones fully relied on the Spirit of God and therefore had more of the oil to keep their lamps burning. The foolish ones had the Word but lacked enough oil, and without the oil, the lamp goes out. Without the Holy Spirit, the Word of God cannot be effective in your life.

Jesus did not begin His ministry without the baptism of the Holy Spirit. He then instructed His disciples not to go preaching until they were baptized with the Holy Spirit and power. The Holy Spirit illuminates Christ and God the Father to the church. Without Him, God's Word is just like any other book. The devil knows the whole Bible, some non-believers also know the Bible; however, they do not have the revelation of the Word. This is because it is only revealed by the Holy Spirit.

The devil does not know the things of God either, that is why he made the mistake of crucifying Jesus. Had he known the victory in the death and Resurrection of Christ, he would not have played a part in the torture and crucifixion of Jesus. The devil knew all along the scriptures from the prophet Isaiah in chapter 53 on the suffering of the Savior and the victory behind it but did not have the revelation of this scripture. There is no way anyone can know God but by His Spirit. The Holy Spirit of God is God, and only God can reveal God to you. We saw earlier that the only two people who inherited the Promised Land from the people who originally came from Egypt were Joshua and Caleb. God said that the reason they inherited this promise was because they had a "different spirit." They knew God.

"Because all these men who have seen My glory and the signs which I did in Egypt and in the wilderness, and have put Me to the test now these ten times, and have not heeded My voice, they certainly shall not see the land of which I swore to their fathers, nor shall any of those who rejected Me see it. But My servant Caleb, *because he has a different spirit in him and has followed Me fully*, I will bring into the land where he went, and his descendants shall inherit it" (Num. 14:22–24; italics added).

They not only knew about God, but they knew their God. God is never satisfied with people knowing about Him or just believing that He exists. Even the devil and his demons know about Him and believe He exists, and they even tremble. But God delights in those who have the Holy Spirit in them who transforms them daily into the image of Christ. This is how we get to have a different spirit.

"You believe that there is one God. You do well. Even the demons believe—and tremble!" (James 2:19)

Knowing about someone is the initial stage of any relationship. No one in his right mind and judgment would want to get married to someone they only know about; rather, they would like to get married to someone they personally know. Christ is coming back to marry a bride who knows Him. Jesus values relationship, not religion. Religion is man-made not Christ made. Christ did not teach us religion, rather He taught us how to be in relationship and fellowship with God. He never came to establish religion, because many religions existed at the time, He came to establish relationship.

"Thus says the Lord: 'Let not the wise man glory in his wisdom, Let not the mighty man glory in his might, Nor let the rich man glory in his riches; *But let him who glories glory in this, That he understands and knows Me*, that I am the Lord, exercising lovingkindness, judgement, and righteousness in the earth. For in these I delight,' Says the Lord" (Jer. 9:23–24; italics added).

Christian or "Christorian?"

Some people have studied and learned history extensively that they are experts. History is studied in many areas. I have studied Kenyan history and American history. Many of us have studied history at one point or another, such as the history of a country, town, the family, etc. History tells of past events, and sometimes these events are used to predict the future.

Most historians have one thing in common—they talk about what they have studied about in history. They hardly talk about their personal relationship with the people way back in history. This is because most history goes way back in time, most historians never experienced or had a relationship with the people in history. They only talk about what others wrote on the people in history. They tell of the story already told with no emotional ties involved or feelings attached.

For example when most of us studied about the first presidents of different countries, we had no desire to know more than we were taught, yet these men had families, wives, and children who knew them and had an intimate relationship with them. To their families, they were not just historical figures like they are to many of us. These men were; somebody's son, brother, husband, father, uncle, nephew, cousin, friend, etc.

Their families felt the pain and loss of their lives. We appreciate their work but not their person because we had no personal relationship with them. The same is true of many historical independence/freedom fighters around the world. They remain heroes in history, and we thank God for them. We know about them, but we don't know them. If they resurrected, we probably would have a chance to connect with them on a more personal level.

Unfortunately, Jesus Christ, the Son of the one and only living God, the greatest gift of love and sacrifice for all humanity, the undisputed, undefeated champion of love, is just a historical figure to many people. This includes those who call themselves Christians or children of God. Many say they are His disciples but have no personal relationship with Him. They know His history from the Bible. They know about Him but do not know Him. They follow what He did in the past but have no evidence of Him actively working in their lives.

Are you a real sheep who hears His voice? Do you know His voice or His will in every situation? Or do you only quote the Bible verses and preach on what the Word of God says, yet you cannot show it in your life? Does your life tell the story of who Jesus Christ is? Can people know God by looking at your life and how you live? Jesus used to go to gatherings and parties and people would inquire of Him and how He lived. They saw a difference between their lifestyle and His, between His words and theirs, and they wanted to be like Him. He never preached to Zacchaeus, yet his life was changed by being around Christ, and he desired to live like Christ. Does your life draw people unto God like Christ's did?

Many people have used the Gospel of God to make a living only for their benefit that even Paul said that there are those who preach with good intentions and those who are doing it to benefit themselves, but all in all, the Gospel is being preached, and there are people getting saved and knowing Christ (Phil. 1:15–18).

There are many false prophets out there, and that is why we need to be diligent in learning God's Word, to be filled with the Holy Spirit, and to grow intimately with Jesus and in the knowledge of Him to avoid deception. If you know someone intimately, it is very hard for someone else to convince you to turn against that person. But if you only know about the person, it is very easy for someone to turn you against that person because you have no roots to stand on. God specifically warned about this in the Old Testament, stating that people loved Him with their mouths, yet their hearts were far away from Him.

"Therefore the Lord said: 'Inasmuch as these people draw near with their mouths And honor Me with their lips, But have removed their hearts far from Me, And their fear toward Me is taught by the commandment of men, Therefore, behold, I will again do a marvelous work among this people, A marvelous work and a wonder; For the wisdom of their wise men shall perish, And the understanding of their prudent men shall be hidden'" (Isa. 29:13–14).

Jesus Christ repeated this to the people in the New Testament in Matthew 15:7–9, and these Words are being repeated now to this generation.

"Hypocrites! Well did Isaiah prophesy about you, saying: 'These people draw near to Me with their mouth, and honor Me with *their* lips, but their heart is far from Me. And in vain they worship Me, Teaching *as* doctrines the commandments of men.' " (Matt. 15:7–9).

There are many people who call themselves Christians, but in reality they are "Christorians" (know about God but do not know God). They will tell you all about Jesus from the Bible, from what they have studied in the Bible, Bible school, or Bible studies or from many church services. They can teach you all about Jesus from the prophets and the Psalms to the New Testament, but they cannot tell you who Christ is now, at this moment, at this time and what He is doing in their lives. They don't know what He is saying or what His will is for their lives. They do not know why they were created and what part they are to play in the body of Christ. They cannot tell you about their personal experience with Christ.

The devil really likes to capitalize on this ignorance to accomplish his mission which is to kill, to steal, and to destroy. He kills your faith, steals your heart, and destroys your soul! We cannot serve God in ignorance; we must have knowledge to be effective priests in God's Kingdom. Our lack of knowledge not only affects us and those around us but also our children and their children and generations upon generations. This was a message to the Israelites, and it is for this generation today. Remember, God never changes. What He condemned back then, He still condemns now.

"You refuse to understand, so you will be destroyed" (Hosea 4:14 NLT).

The Gospel of the Kingdom of God is alive, and because Jesus Christ died and rose again from the dead on the third day, He ceases to be just a historical figure. He is a present King! The King of kings whose Kingdom is eternal, He is a glorious and mighty God. His Power never ceases and never fails. He now lives through His bride, through people who have intimacy and love that knows no season or boundary. These people are in love with Jesus and want the whole world to know this great King and God. He confirms His Word with signs and wonders following those who believe. The Kingdom of God is not a matter of empty talk, said Paul, but it is power.

"But I will come—and soon—if the Lord lets me, and then I'll find out whether these arrogant people just give pretentious speeches or whether they really have God's power. For the Kingdom of God is not just a lot of talk; it is living by God's power" (1 Cor. 4:19–20 NLT).

"For the Kingdom of God is not eating and drinking, but righteousness and peace and joy in the Holy Spirit" (Rom. 14:17).

Many people today, just like the Israelites, think that the Kingdom of God is a matter of how wealthy you are in material stuff. Remember God overthrew the wisdom of people and had His only begotten Son born in a manger to a humble family. He also chose to reveal His Son's birth through a host of angels to shepherds. Many people missed Jesus because He did not come as they expected Him to, in earthly majesty, power and riches. Even today, we look at some Jews who still await the first coming of Jesus as if they are very strange, while most of us Christians do not know God's voice.

We do not know Him when He comes to us and answers our prayers because we like to tell God how to be God. We give Him the package and wrapping we want Him to use and tell Him to put our gift in it. If God uses a bigger or smaller package and wraps our answers differently with a much greater package than we asked for, we miss it and turn around and complain because we have our own expectations. We MUST allow God to be God and know that we can't teach Him how to be God. God cannot fit into our little plans. I love this God! He is the one and only God whose understanding is unsearchable! This is because if I can figure Him out, then He is not God.

God says to us to seek first His Kingdom, and His righteousness and all these things will be added unto us. What is His Kingdom? Obviously it is not material stuff because He says the material stuff will only be an addition to those who have the Kingdom of God and His righteousness. Do not be deceived and look elsewhere like the children of Israel looked and missed their king's visit on earth. They missed His birth because they had no room for Him when He came. They missed His growing up and His living among them. They did not even know their own King was among them. Some of them are, sadly, still waiting for Him to appear for the first time. Christ will return soon and this time everyone will know it. He will come in all of His majesty and power, authority and dominion. He is coming for those who know Him, not those who only know about Him.

The prince of this world is very materialistic. He tried to get Jesus to sell His Kingdom for food, fame, and material stuff, or wealth, in Matthew 4:1–11. The devil is not a faith devil; he is a sight devil, and many people live by sight and not by faith and that is why they always fall prey to his evil schemes, because without faith it is impossible to please God. "Now when He was asked by the Pharisees when the kingdom of God would come, He answered them and said, *'the kingdom of God does not come with observation*; nor will they say, "See here!" or "See there!" For *indeed, the kingdom of God is within you'*" (Luke 17:20–21; italics added).

CHAPTER 10

The Prayer

Life-changing prayer led by the Holy Spirit

SOME PASTORS WANTED ME TO serve in their church as a praise and worship leader or in the praise and worship team because I led well and they needed to win more people into their church for their benefit. Others tried to talk me out of the church I was going to so as to join their church, saying no other pastor could understand my needs better than a pastor from my country, Kenya, East Africa. But God's Word is universal, no matter where you are from. My mother always said when she came to visit me in the United States that the same Bible she used in Kenya was the same she used in America. No one gives her a different Bible when she lands in the United States. The standards of holiness are the same in all the earth. God never changes!

Some pastors continue to fill up their churches with deception, which becomes just that—"their church"—not the church of Jesus Christ. They preach what people want to hear and they value the opinion of people rather than God's. They have become people pleasers, and that is why there are no longer signs and wonders following them, but people walk in and out of the so-called "church" with the same problems, and they wonder why they do not experience God in the church. They don't know that it is because even God Himself is not invited in these churches.

These leaders invite God in their congregation as one of their members. They tell Him where to sit and when to do what they want according to their programs. They are in control of the service. They forget that God is not a human being and He will not worship people and their programs. These men and women do not revere God anymore. They use Him and the church as a business, a career. They use the word "church" as a franchise. But remember, God is never mocked! Whatever one sows, that person will surely reap. When Paul wrote to Timothy, he was speaking to all teachers and preachers warning of this.

> I command you therefore *before God and the Lord Jesus Christ, who will judge the living and the dead at his appearing and his Kingdom*: preach the word; be urgent in season and out of season; reprove, rebuke, and exhort, with all patience and teaching. For the time will come when they will not listen to the sound doctrine, but, having itching ears, will heap up for themselves teachers after their own lusts; and will turn away their ears from the truth, and turn aside to fables. But you be sober in all things, suffer hardship, do the work of an evangelist, and fulfill your ministry. For I am already being offered, and the time of my departure has come. (2 Tim. 4:1–6 WEB)

Some of the preachers I encountered would lust after me and even contact me anonymously. I got tired of all these and ran to God the Father in Jesus's name. I went on my knees on my living-room floor after a word from God through a praying sister who told me to pray. God told me to pray! Pray about what? He just sent a message for me to pray. I didn't know how to pray long prayers; I did well with short prayers that had a purpose or a trigger like pain or problems. What do I say? I thought, this was like someone telling me to talk without giving a topic of discussion. Surprisingly, I said a prayer, short and to the point that I know was from the Holy Spirit that would change my life forever.

This was my prayer, at my point of brokenness. I was very bold and to the point, blunt, with confidence, and without a doubt. At this point, I had nothing to lose because I had nothing!

After praise, thanksgiving and repentance, I said the following prayer.

The Prayer

"Father, in Jesus's name, I am tired of church as usual and being used and abused by those you have entrusted to teach me Your Word. I want You to personally come and teach me Your Word and reveal Yourself to me. As You say in Isaiah 54:13 "All your children *shall be* taught by the Lord, And great *shall be* the peace of your children."

You also promised to send me a Helper, the Holy Spirit, who would teach me all things. Where is He? I need Him now, in Jesus's name."

Then I said to my Helper, because I believed that I had already received Him;

"Holy Spirit, You were there during creation, when God the Father said, 'Let US make humans in our own image.' You know what was put in me during creation. Reveal that to me and help me accomplish my assignment. Teach me ALL things just as Jesus said you would."

I then prayed; *"And Father, I want to see Jesus. I want to see my Savior, and don't send me any angels. In Jesus's name, amen."*

I had not planned to pray this prayer at all, but this is what came from my Spirit when I prayed, it was from God the Holy Spirit. I had a deep desire to know and see my savior! More than a baby longs for its mother.

When I got up from my knees, I never thought of that prayer again. To me, it was as good as answered. I believed that I had received it and went about my business.

Prophecy of Confirmation

A few days later, my music producer and his wife invited my family to their house for dinner, as it was one of their birthdays. That night it rained cats and dogs. I had four children to take with me to the party. My husband was out of town, and I thought maybe we should not go, but something very strong in me said to go. The roads were really bad with almost zero visibility. We finally got there and had a nice time. In the home, there was a prophet who started prophesying as the anointing of God led him. He prophesied many things confirming what God had said in my life, including being an author of many books, this prophecy is being revealed now. He then said, "You have asked God to reveal Himself to you intimately, and He says that He will do it."

The Prayer Answered

The Vision

About a week after the prophecy, I was directed by the Holy Spirit to go down to the basement of my house to pray. I knelt and prayed and when I was done, I felt a prompting to remain still, on my knees, and listen to God since God had listened to me. The Holy Spirit was teaching me that prayer is supposed to be a dialogue, not a monologue between me and God.

As I waited on my knees with my eyes closed, my answer came! I think we forfeit our answers when we are not willing to be still before God and let Him speak to us.

There in my basement, I saw Jesus come from heaven, walking down graciously from the heavens toward me. He had the most beautiful hair and robe. Half of His face on the left side from the nose down was shaded. The right side of His face was clear to me. He walked down and came to me. My eyes were still shut, but I could see Him very clearly. I believe these were the eyes of the spirit that had been opened. His eye, oh, wow! His right eye that was visible to me was more than breathtaking. I saw the most beautiful blue eye color I have ever seen. But something beyond my comprehension and imagination was happening in that eye. I saw the whole world in His eye! I saw people in different parts of the world doing different tasks, busy with whatever they did. Jesus was there, seeing all things and hearing all. He was in the whole world, everywhere at the same time, yet He took time to come to me in my little basement. This was a revelation of His omnipresence. Amazing! Then as graciously as He had come down, He turned and went back up to heaven.

I had to tell someone about it! I wanted to scream it on the roof top! However, I knew if I told my husband he would think I was now going overboard. I therefore tried as much as I could to hold my peace. Now I understand what the people who were healed by Jesus and then were told not to tell anyone felt. How can you hold your peace when you have had an encounter with Jesus Christ, the God of the universe who humbled Himself and made Himself lower than His creation in order to save us? Only a very strong person can humble himself even unto death, the worst death of all times. Knowing He had the power not to die, He still chose to put Himself under the mercy of His own creation. His creation had no mercy for themselves or their Creator. What kind of love is this!

After experiencing Jesus, my Savior, it was impossible to hold my peace. I had three sons at that time, and the oldest of them was about seven years old. I told him all about the vision, and he was excited too! I told him to keep it to himself. (Yes, I know. I couldn't keep it to myself, yet I expected a seven-year-old to keep it to himself.) After I told him, I felt better for a moment.

The following morning as we were getting ready for church, I felt the urge in me to tell my husband—a grownup—my encounter with my God. I excitedly told him how I asked God to show me Jesus, and God answered my prayer.

My husband replied,

"Why are you so surprised that God answered your prayer? Did you not have faith that He would?"

If you knew my husband then, you would know it was not him speaking, but God speaking to me through him. I was so excited at his response. I LOVE this GOD!

I have and still am growing daily in Christ. I told my mum what I asked God for and how He answered me, and she said,

"You ask for very hard things."

It was hard and impossible with humans and that was why I asked God and not a human being because it was within His scope and ability. My God specializes in impossibilities. What is impossible with us is very possible with God. With God, ALL things are possible if you believe.

God will not do what you do not believe He will do, not because He cannot, but because He will not respond to anything not of faith. Remember, a double-minded person is unstable in ALL his ways, and he will not receive anything from God (James 1:5–8). When you ask, believe that you have received what you asked for, and it shall be yours (Mark 11:24 and Matt. 21:22). When Jesus encountered people who asked Him to heal them or their families, He asked them one question over and over through His healing ministry, and that was, "Do you believe?" Because believing in God's ability is the key to moving God's ability to work on your behalf.

One morning after I had exercised on my treadmill and was going from the garage into the house, God asked me, "Do you do for your seven-year-old son what he can do for himself?"

I replied, "No."

If you know about seven-year-olds, they enjoy their independence and will not allow you to help them do what they can do.

God went on to say, "What about if he asks you to do something for him that you can do but he cannot do, would you do it for him?"

I replied, "Yes, I would, absolutely!"

Then God said to me, "Whatever you cannot do, I can do it. All you have to do is ask."

When I heard that, I was so excited! It was like giving me the whole world. I have no limitations with God. He can do all things; no assignment is impossible. Whatever He gives, I can accomplish with His help. All I have to do is ask.

One day the Holy Spirit led me to ask my husband a question, to see how God feels when we do not trust in His ability. I asked my husband, who is a businessman, what he would do if someone came to him and asked for his help in business, but the person did not believe in my husband's ability to help him or her. My husband said that he would not help the person, even if he could, because of the person's lack of trust in his ability. He was very stern and said that if the person doesn't believe in his ability, he would be very offended by the person, and he said, "Why come to me in the first place?"

I was so excited at his response and told him that is exactly how God feels and even worse, when we underestimate His ability. Jehovah God created all things visible and invisible, yet one little puzzle in our life we think is impossible for Him? We insult God when we go to Him in doubt of His greatness and ability. That is one promise we have been given over and over again in the Bible—when you ask, believe that you have received, and it shall be yours. Without faith, it is impossible to please God.

We must do what God said to the children of Israel. Stand still and see the salvation of the LORD.

"Be still, and know that I am God! I will be honored by every nation. I will be honored throughout the world" (Ps. 46:10).

This means that we must stop all the worrying and running up and down trying to figure things on our own, looking for help and answers in all the wrong places and wrong things. Our trust should d be in God alone. We must be calm and be still. Stop! Turn to Jesus and fully trust that He is God.

One day as I was getting ready for work and I was in front of my mirror, God said to me, "I created the heavens and the earth and the whole universe and all in it. Is there anything I can't do?"

I was so much in awe, tears rolled down my eyes, and I said to Him, "Please, Lord, forgive my unbelief and wrap my whole being, mind, soul, and spirit around this." We are very quick to believe the negative and quick to doubt the positive because our minds have been programmed by the enemy to accept his report faster and easier as the way of life rather than accept the report of our God. This was the same mind-set the Children of Israel had in the wilderness, and it led to their destruction, but Caleb and Joshua had a mind-set that believed what God said was true, and they received God's promise. You will receive what you believe and possess what you confess from your heart. Just as we read earlier…

"But if any of you lacks wisdom, let him ask of God, who gives to all liberally and without reproach; and it will be given to him. But let him ask in faith, without any doubting, for he who doubts is like a wave of the sea, driven by the wind and tossed. For let that man not think that he will receive anything from the Lord. He is a double-minded man, unstable in all his ways." (James 1:5–8 WEB).

"But without faith it is impossible to please Him, for he who comes to God must believe that He is, and that He is a rewarder of those who diligently seek Him" (Heb. 11:6).

I have and will always stand in awe of my God. I know He loves me so much beyond what my mind can comprehend, and that was why He came and died for me, and didn't stop there. He also made provision for me to have a private counselor, advisor and consultant, His Holy Spirit. I am amazed and have no words to describe my awe of Him. I vow to praise Him and live for this God all the days of my life. Not in the history of the world and never in the future will there be such a demonstration of LOVE for me like the Father has done through His Son.

Therefore, I no longer live for myself but for Him alone. Saying that I live for Him alone is not a sacrifice for me. This is because I was created by Him to live for Him; therefore it is my duty and not a sacrifice. I was created to do His will in the first place, and I diverted from it and God. He is the only party here that made the ultimate sacrifice. God was still in His rightful position. His Son Jesus never did any wrong; He was in His rightful place. Jesus did His Father's will from the beginning. God would have easily destroyed all humanity and remained with His angels or created a new set of humans all over again. But He decided to die a sinner's death, for you and for me. He took our rebellion and died in our place. We were the ones destined to die because the penalty of sin is death, but God has given us the gift of eternal life through Jesus Christ our Lord (Rom. 6:23).

Imagine you have a child, a boy who is very obedient and has been from the beginning. He loves and honors you, always walking in obedience to God and to you. He is an honor-roll student; every teacher loves him and wants to clone him. He is always kind and helpful; this child is the image of perfection.

On the other hand, there is your neighbor's son, who is the direct opposite: very rude, arrogant, curses, does not care about school, is a drug addict, always gets in trouble with the law, and is a murderer, fornicator, thief, and destroyer of property. This boy is an exact replica of evil.

One day, the evil child gets in trouble as always, but this time he messed with the wrong people. He is going to get shot and killed by some drug lords, since he owes them more than he could pay physically, emotionally, and financially. As you and your son sit outside your patio talking, you see everything unfolding. This boy is in such big trouble. Your son, who has been perfect, is looking at this commotion. No amount of money can satisfy these killers, only the evil child's life. They came to take life, so life must be given. You then think of eternity…this boy, if he dies, he dies forever. He will die physically and spiritually. But if your son dies, he will die physically but live forever spiritually, eternal life. Your child has a great future on earth through his obedience and sacrifice. The other boy has no future by the way he lived his life. This is your only child, but your neighbor has more children. There is only one option left to save this child's life physically and hopefully, not guaranteed, eternally—your son has to die in his place.

This is very painful and impossible decision, a decision that a human being cannot make by his or her own power; only God could do this. Your son asks you to please let him live because he wants to go to the university and have a family of his own and not to be cut off from earth. All the while this is going on, the evil child is hurling insults at you and your son. But your son goes on to say that he sees the value of his death for life, so he is willing to sacrifice his future on earth for God's Kingdom. He wants to please God, and by the sacrifice, he knows he will please God. Your son freely goes on his own accord. The evil child, in turn, hurls insults, hits and spits at him, calling him every curse name, in ignorance of the serious situation facing him. You see your child being obedient even unto death, an evil child's death for a righteous child. Your only baby is tortured and murdered because they treat him according to the evil done by the other boy.

The evil child now has a chance at life because his evil record has been erased because your son took it all, and now he gets to start a fresh, clean slate. He has a chance of being somebody in life and at eternity if he accepts the sacrifice your son made for him and changes his ways. If this boy gets it and receives the sacrifice and new life your son's death gave him, then the sacrifice was not in vain. What if the evil child saved by your son despises the sacrifice which you and your son made and he continues to live a rebellious lifestyle? Would there be any more salvation for him? What if he does right sometimes and rebels sometimes—would that guarantee his safety from destruction? No! It only takes one slip-up, and he gets destroyed. There would be no more hope for him because your son already died once and will not return to earth to die again.

On the other hand, if the evil child decides to live right, would he be making any sacrifice on his part? Absolutely not! He was supposed to live right in the first place. The only people who made the sacrifice were you and your son. You taught your son right, and he did right, yet you suffered great loss because you gave up the blessing of being called grandma or great grandma, and your child suffered an evil child's death and gave up the chance of being a husband and father, grandfather and great-grandpa.

Likewise, God the Father and His Son Jesus Christ made the ultimate sacrifice for us. We did not and we will never be able to make any sacrifice for God. We are supposed to live our lives in total obedience and submission to God just like Christ did. We cannot live double-standard lives because the enemy roams to and fro like a roaring lion, looking for whomever he may destroy; whoever is living away from God's commands. We must be ready because we never know; the moment we let our guards down might be the moment Christ comes or we go to meet Him. We must always be watchful and ready for Christ's return at all times.

"Be sober and self-controlled. Be watchful. Your adversary, the devil, walks around like a roaring lion, seeking whom he may devour. Withstand him steadfast in your faith, knowing that your brothers who are in the world are undergoing the same sufferings. But may the God of all grace, who called you to his eternal glory by Christ Jesus, after you have suffered a little while, perfect, establish, strengthen, and settle you." (1 Pet. 5:8–10 WEB).

> Much more then, being now justified by his blood, we will be saved from God's wrath through him. For if, while we were enemies, we were reconciled to God through the death of his Son, much more, being reconciled, we will be saved by his life. Not only so, but we also rejoice in God through our Lord Jesus Christ, through whom we have now received the reconciliation. (Rom. 5:9–11 WEB)

There is no way Jesus Christ is coming to earth to die again. You either accept the sacrifice He made and the price He paid by living in obedience to God which leads to eternal life, or you pay the price of sin, which is eternal death. There is no way out for despising the sacrifice God and His Son made.

For if we sin willfully after we have received the knowledge of the truth, there remains no more a sacrifice for sins, but a certain fearful expectation of judgment, and a fierceness of fire which will devour the adversaries. A man who disregards Moses' law dies without compassion on the word of two or three witnesses. How much worse punishment do you think he will be judged worthy of who has trodden under foot the Son of God, and has counted the blood of the covenant with which he was sanctified an unholy thing, and has insulted the Spirit of grace? For we know him who said, "Vengeance belongs to me," says the Lord, "I will repay." Again, "The Lord will judge his people." It is a fearful thing to fall into the hands of the living God. (Heb. 10:26–31 WEB)

CHAPTER 11
Obedience and the Fear of God

WE MUST HAVE THE FEAR of God to obey God. Christ gave us His life, and God's grace to live Holy, we must not take it for granted as many of us do. We must not sin purposefully because the grace of God is sufficient. We must reverence God and obey Him more than we do people.

"For the grace of God has appeared that offers salvation to all people. *It teaches us to say no* to ungodliness and worldly passions and to live self-controlled, upright, and godly lives in this present age, while we wait for the blessed hope—the appearing of the glory of our great God and Savior, Jesus Christ, who gave himself for us to redeem us from all wickedness and to purify for himself a people that are his very own, eager to do what is good" (Titus 2:11–14 NIV; italics added).

"I say this because some ungodly people have wormed their way into your churches, *saying that God's marvelous grace allows us to live immoral lives.* The condemnation of such people was recorded long ago, for they have denied our only Master and Lord, Jesus Christ" (Jude 1:4 NLT; italics added).

"Well then, should we keep on sinning so that God can show us more and more of his wonderful grace? Of course not! Since we have died to sin, how can we continue to live in it?" (Rom. 6:1–2 NLT)

> For he who has died has been freed from sin. But if we died with Christ, we believe that we will also live with him; knowing that Christ, being raised from the dead, dies no more. Death no

more has dominion over him! *For the death that he died, he died to sin one time; but the life that he lives, he lives to God.* Thus consider yourselves also to be dead to sin, but alive to God in Christ Jesus our Lord. *What then? Shall we sin, because we are not under law, but under grace? May it never be! Don't you know that when you present yourselves as servants and obey someone, you are the servants of whomever you obey; whether of sin to death, or of obedience to righteousness?* (Romans 6:7–11, 15–16 WEB; italics added)

The Fear of the Lord Leads to Obedience

"Oh, that they had such a heart in them that they would fear Me and always keep all My commandments, that it might be well with them and with their children forever!" (Deut. 5:29).

It is easy to obey someone whom you hold highly and respect, the person who is the top-most priority in your life, the person you value most. It is very easy to say no to anything or anyone who comes to contradict the ways of the highly exalted one in your life. That is why Jesus, being God, DELIGHTED in the spirit of the FEAR OF THE LORD (Isa.11:3). Jesus Christ regarded no one above His Father. His Father was, on several occasions, pleased with Jesus. He made it known to others, too! Just like a father would praise a son in whom he is delighted in.

"And suddenly a voice came from heaven, saying, 'This is My beloved Son, in whom I am well pleased'" (Matt. 3:17).

"While he was still speaking, behold, a bright cloud overshadowed them; and suddenly a voice came out of the cloud, saying, 'This is My beloved Son, in whom I am well pleased. Hear Him!'" (Matt. 17:5).

"For He received from God the Father honor and glory when such a voice came to Him from the Excellent Glory: 'This is My beloved Son, in whom I am well pleased'" (2 Pet. 1:17).

God used Elisha in place of Elijah when Elijah feared Jezebel instead of God, who was almighty. Elijah was used greatly of God until he accepted the spirit of fear from Jezebel, instead of the spirit of power, love, and a sound mind. His faith was tested but he traded it for fear which displeased God because fear is the opposite of faith, and without faith it is impossible to please God.

God's language is faith; he does not understand any other language. Whining and complaining have no place in God's vocabulary. No one in the Bible or in history has ever received anything from God by complaining and grumbling or by fear and self-pity. But no one who had faith in God's ability and grace, one who believed in God and spoke to the trials or mountains that he or she was facing about God, was ever turned down by God. God is bigger, greater, and stronger than any trials we may face and nothing is impossible with Him.

Joshua was chosen to take the place of Moses when Moses disobeyed God and hit the rock instead of speaking to the rock because he was angry at the Israelites (1 Kings 19:1–18). (See Num. 20:1–12, especially verse 12; Num. 27:12–23; Deut. 31:1–3; and Deut. 3:23–28.)

David, the shepherd boy, was chosen to take Saul's place as king when God rejected Saul because of his disobedience when he made an unlawful sacrifice instead of waiting for the prophet Samuel in 1 Samuel 13:8–14. After this sin, Saul went on to disobey again by refusing to destroy King Agag of the Amalekites and their possessions. Instead, he took the spoil and wanted to make it look like he did it for God, saying that he saved it to sacrifice to God. However, the prophet Samuel rebuked him, and the prophet himself killed the king of the Amalekites as God had commanded in 1 Samuel 15:18 and chapter 16:1–14. From this, Saul was rejected by God as king, the Spirit of the LORD departed from him, and a distressing spirit came in and troubled him. On the other hand, the Spirit of the LORD came upon David from the day he was anointed by the prophet Samuel as King (1 Sam. 16:13). David prophesied about Jesus in Psalm 40:7–8 NLT: "Then I said, 'Look, I have come. As is written about me in the Scriptures: I take joy in doing your will, my God, for your instructions are written on my heart.'"

If Jesus, the Son of God, was yielded to God the Father's will in obedience and humility, how much more must we?

> Have this in your mind, which was also in Christ Jesus, who, existing in the form of God, didn't consider equality with God a thing to be grasped, but emptied himself, taking the form of a servant, being made in the likeness of men. And being found in human form, he humbled himself, becoming obedient to death, yes, the death of the cross. Therefore God also highly exalted him, and gave to him the name which is

above every name; that at the name of Jesus every knee should bow, of those in heaven, those on earth, and those under the earth, and that every tongue should confess that Jesus Christ is Lord, to the glory of God the Father. (Phil. 2:5–11 WEB)

There is great reward in obeying God in this life and in the life to come. David was most afraid of being rejected by God and losing the Holy Spirit when he sinned by killing his faithful servant Uriah and taking the servant's wife Bathsheba for himself. Look at his humble prayer in Psalm 51:9–13.

On the other hand, we do not see Saul humbling before God in prayer; instead he justifies himself.

> Saul said to Samuel, "I have sinned; for I have transgressed the commandment of Yahweh, and your words, because I feared the people, and obeyed their voice. Now therefore, please pardon my sin, and turn again with me, that I may worship Yahweh." Samuel said to Saul, "I will not return with you; for you have rejected Yahweh's word, and Yahweh has rejected you from being king over Israel." As Samuel turned around to go away, Saul grabbed the skirt of his robe, and it tore. Samuel said to him, "Yahweh has torn the kingdom of Israel from you today, and has given it to a neighbor of yours who is better than you. Also the Strength of Israel will not lie nor repent; for he is not a man that he should repent." Then he said, *"I have sinned; yet please honor me now before the elders of my people, and before Israel, and come back with me, that I may worship Yahweh your God."* So Samuel went back with Saul; and Saul worshiped Yahweh. (1 Sam. 15:24–31 WEB; italics added)

King Saul feared people and valued prestige rather than God. He wanted the prophet Samuel to honor him before people and return with him, even though they both knew his kingdom was no more. He was not a man after God's own heart; he had no fear of the Lord, he never took God's commands seriously. He cared about making people angry. He loved the praise of people rather than the praise from God. Partial obedience is disobedience and to seek people's approval is to sign up for God's rejection. This was the direct opposite of David, who had the fear of God and not humans and was a man after God's own heart. David cried and repented to God when He sinned, see Psalm 51. He cared about losing God and His Spirit from his life unlike Saul. His heart's desire was to please God and not people. He was running from Saul instead of killing him when he had the opportunity and peer pressure to do it, even if he was the anointed king. He feared God and would not touch him whom God had once anointed, because God's anointing could not be destroyed by people, only by God.

Another example of disobedience and consequences of it is the prophet Jonah. Jonah was a great prophet of God who was sent to warn the Ninevites of the upcoming doom if they did not repent of their lifestyle and actions, which were an abomination to God. Jonah had been obedient to God many times before, but this time he did not want to obey God. He wanted the people of Nineveh destroyed. He had already judged and given them a death sentence. He was a prophet of God, and I'm sure many would agree with him that those people deserved to be destroyed in the same way they destroyed others.

Thanks be to God because He is not a human being who writes us off when we slip up or fall. He does not give up so easily on us. Jonah knew God so much that he knew God was a God of great mercy and loving kindness (see Jon. 3:10 and 4:1–2). The people were under law, but God's mercy was amazing enough to forgive those who repented and turned from their wicked ways. Even though Jonah knew God was powerful and would destroy the whole nation, he also knew God was merciful enough to forgive and save a nation as wicked as Nineveh if they repented and turned from their wickedness. This is why Jonah decided to go the opposite direction from where God was sending him. Jonah had the task of being the mouth of God to that nation, but he opted out of his calling to please himself rather than God.

"Now Yahweh's word came to Jonah the son of Amittai, saying, "Arise, go to Nineveh, that great city, and preach against it, for their wickedness has come up before me." *But Jonah rose up to flee to Tarshish from the presence of Yahweh.* He went down to Joppa, and found a ship going to Tarshish; *so he paid its fare, and went down into it, to go with them to Tarshish from the presence of Yahweh.*" (Jonah. 1:1–3 WEB italics added).

I am amazed at God's mercy even after we act so foolishly! We can stray from our God-given task out of our own selfish ambitions. On the other hand, we can be on our God-given task and yet allow other people who are running away from their God-given tasks to accompany us on our journey. This is dangerous to both parties—their disobedience will lead to our disobedience because we entertained them without inquiring of God.

The Bible says Jonah was trying to flee from God's presence, so he went to Joppa and found a ship going to Tarshish. He paid the fare and went in the ship. Jonah did not hide to go into the ship without paying; he went into the ship legally. The only requirement was to pay the fare, which Jonah did. Jonah was a prophet of God, yet he was trying to do the impossible, run away from God, which could be interpreted as foolishness. It is no different than when a child plays hide-and-seek and closes their eyes, and because they cannot see you with their eyes closed, they assume that they are truly hiding from you, and you cannot see them. Jonah knew better than that, yet he lacked wisdom like the one King David had when he declared in Psalm 139:7–12 WEB:

Where could I go from your Spirit? Or where could I flee from your presence? If I ascend up into heaven, you are there. If I make my bed in Sheol, behold, you are there! If I take the wings of the dawn, and settle in the uttermost parts of the sea; Even there your hand will lead me, and your right hand will hold me. If I say, "Surely the darkness will overwhelm me; the light around me will be night"; even the darkness doesn't hide from you, but the night shines as the day. The darkness is like light to you.

We are truly wise when we have the fear of the Lord. If Jonah approached this situation with the fear of God, he would not have been so foolish in his approach to God's command.

Solomon, the wisest man who ever lived, made a conclusion of the whole duty of man after all he had experienced in life, and from the wisdom given to him by God.

"This is the end of the matter. All has been heard. *Fear God, and keep his commandments; for this is the whole duty of man.* For God will bring every work into judgment, with every hidden thing, whether it is good, or whether it is evil." (Eccles. 12:13–14 WEB; italics added).

Consequences of Disobedience

Disobedience only hurts us, it does not hurt God. Let us do ourselves a favor and obey God fully. His wisdom is worth following without question. He is too successful in all He has done and does to be challenged or doubted. Let us follow His lead like a child does its parents and it shall be well. May we learn from the children of Israel again and the consequences of their disobedience.

"'Will you steal and murder, commit adultery and perjury, burn incense to Baal and follow other gods you have not known, and then come and stand before me in this house, which bears my Name, and say, "We are safe"—safe to do all these detestable things? Has this house, which bears my Name, become a den of robbers to you? But I have been watching! declares the Lord. "'Go now to the place in Shiloh where I first made a dwelling for my Name, and see what I did to it because of the wickedness of my people Israel. While you were doing all these things, declares the Lord, I spoke to you again and again, but you did not listen; I called you, but you did not answer. Therefore, what I did to Shiloh I will now do to the house that bears my Name, the temple you trust in, the place I gave to you and your ancestors. I will thrust you from my presence, just as I did all your fellow Israelites, the people of Ephraim.' "So do not pray for this people nor offer any plea or petition for them; do not plead with me, for I will not listen to you. Do you not see what they are doing in the towns of Judah and in the streets of Jerusalem? The children gather wood, the fathers light the fire, and the women knead the dough and make cakes to offer to the Queen of Heaven. *They pour out drink offerings to other gods to arouse my anger. But am I the one they are provoking? declares the Lord. Are they not rather harming themselves, to their own shame?* "'Therefore this is what the Sovereign Lord says: My anger and my wrath will be poured out on this place—on man and beast, on the trees of the field and on the crops of your land—and it will burn and not be quenched. "'This is what the Lord Almighty, the God of Israel, says: Go ahead, add your burnt offerings to your other sacrifices and *eat the meat yourselves!* For when I brought your ancestors out of Egypt and spoke to them, *I did not just give them commands about burnt offerings and sacrifices, but I gave them this command: Obey me, and I will be your God and you will be my people. Walk in obedience to all I command you, that it may go well with you.* But they did not listen or pay attention; instead, they followed the stubborn inclinations of their evil hearts. They went backward and not forward. From the time your ancestors left Egypt until now, day after day, again and again I sent you my servants the prophets. But they did not listen to me or pay attention. They were stiff-necked and did more evil than their ancestors.' (Jeremiah 7:9-26 NIV; italics added)

God rejected Saul as king because Saul kept on rebelling in disobedience; (1 Sam. 15:22–26, 1 Sam. 13:13–14). If we keep on sinning, there is nothing left to save us, if we trample the grace of God underfoot and disregard the great sacrifice given to us by our Lord Jesus Christ, we will reap eternal death. Disobedience opens doors for the enemy to attack us.

I had a friend who disobeyed God and as a result she failed her tests, was held back in the university and graduated a semester later than she should have. At the same time, God warned me against associating with her academically because she almost cost me the same loss due to her disobedience.

I was seeking God and praying; I was hungry for God and all of Him, but I associated myself with someone who did the opposite. She was a Christian who was very familiar with God and thought that what God said to her was not a big deal. This is common among many Christians today. Remember, Delayed obedience is disobedience.

Disobedience leads to pain and suffering—not only yours, but of those around you. It exposes you to the enemy, and it causes delay in your assignment and in others who are waiting for you to step into your assignment. Just like the painter of a building must wait for the walls to be built for him or her to paint, if the people building the wall get delayed, the painter cannot paint the wall, which causes a great delay on his or her part. We must stop being selfish and think of all the other people we are holding up as we live a lifestyle of disobedience. We must sober up! Wake up! And live a lifestyle of obedience, growing the Kingdom of God instead of leading many astray by our disobedience.

Disobedience will lead to God rejecting you as His messenger and getting another to take your place. Elisha took Elijah's place when Elijah feared Jezebel and disobeyed God by hiding in 1 kings 19. Joshua was chosen to take the place of Moses when Moses disobeyed God and hit the rock to produce water instead of touching the rock as God had commanded him in Numbers 20. David the shepherd boy took Saul's place due to Saul's disobedience and rebellion. Samson was destroyed by disobedience. He was stripped of his strength when he revealed the secret of his strength to the enemy and his hair was cut off, which cost him the Holy Spirit, and he died in Judges 16. Queen Esther was told if she didn't step up to her assignment of interceding for the Jews to the King due to fear, God would choose another person to take her place (Esther 4:8–17). Esther chose to obey God even if it meant death on her part, rather than trying to save her own life and disobey her calling. The result of her obedience was salvation for the Jews and destruction of their enemies because the king received her and her requests (Esther 5:1–3).

Obedience unlocks your destiny, promise and prosperity.

In the book of Esther, Esther was favored by the king because she desired to find out what pleased the king instead of relying on her own beauty or wisdom. The King gave all the girls who came for the contest a eunuch to consult with and to assist them in their preparation to please the king. The king did this because even though the eunuch was biologically unproductive he was kingdom productive. He knew what pleased the king and what the girls needed to do to win the king's favor and be chosen as the new queen.

Be very careful not to judge as man does because the person whom you despise or look down upon, one who looks "unproductive" in your eyes, might be the same person holding the secret to your breakthrough. They may not seem useful or productive in your eyes but to God they are qualified and productive; and if you're not careful you will miss your blessing because of your judgment. Never despise a eunuch in your life because he has a very special assignment for your destiny.

Esther was the only one among all the girls who made use of her eunuch because she held the king in very high regard and valued his wisdom. She knew that the king doesn't just act without reason, and if the king gave them a eunuch, there was very good reason. The eunuch was a key to their success. She therefore decided to give up her wishes and desires, her likes and wants for what the king desired and found pleasing. She purposed to look at beauty from the Kings perspective rather than her own or the other people's perspective. I can picture Esther asking the eunuch what the king loves and desires and learning keenly what pleases the king. She then would practice it until it became her new normal. With this kind of mindset, Esther had won the contest before she even began.

I also picture the other girls asking for each other's opinion and approval and acting on what they thought to be pleasing in their eyes to entice the king. They totally despised the king's chosen helper. They ignored the eunuch and looked for help from each other, common citizens, instead of the eunuch who was a kingdom dweller. They got too busy with their own desires and likes, they were consumed with what made them look good in their own eyes and in the eyes of the others that they ignored the king's eunuch who was the key to their success. They did not discern the secret behind the eunuch or his purpose. They had no value for the king and took his wisdom for granted. The eunuch looked unproductive in their eyes therefore they despised the key to their destiny. With this mindset, they had already lost the contest before they even began.

They did not want to let go of their traditions and that of other people to embrace the kingdom traditions. They wanted the kingdom life, wealth and benefits but not the kingdom sacrifice. Unlike Esther, they wanted to reign with the king without giving up their own desires for the king's desires. Does that sound like 99.9% of the Christians?

In the end, the girls took a year to prepare to be queen but they were rejected by the king, while Esther was instantly chosen by the king. God's favor is not fair. It is not how long you have been saved, preaching or working in the kingdom that qualifies you to rule and reign with Jesus, it is your constant dying to self and living in obedience, sacrificing your desires for His, your will for His to please Jehovah God and to be continually led by His Holy Spirit, (who would be like the eunuch in the story) that guarantees your selection in God's kingdom. How much do you value and love God?

Our King of Kings, Jehovah our God, has called many people to prepare to live in His Kingdom so as to please Him. He has given us a "eunuch figure", the Holy Spirit, who is there to teach us everything that the King wants and desires. He reveals to us our destiny because He was there during creation and He saw all that the King put in us. He knows all things because He has access to the King twenty four hours a day seven days a week. He is a Kingdom dweller.

He tells us what the King desires and shows us things from the King's perspective. Just like the eunuch, He is available to you if you desire His guidance or expertise, He does not impose on you. Those who listen and obey Him, who seek wisdom from Him on how to please the King, are the only ones who will be chosen as the King's brides. The rest will be rejected in the end. You may be in God's Kingdom, born again, in the palace preparing but doing it in your own wisdom and in the wisdom of men, totally ignoring your "eunuch", the Holy Spirit, who knows the heart of the Father. Just like a eunuch was seen as useless outside the kingdom, the Holy Spirit is despised by the world because they do not see Him.

In the end, because all have been called, if you do not seek for guidance and obey the Holy Spirit on how to please the King, you will be rejected. If we want to be chosen to live in God's Kingdom, we must put God's desires before our own desires. We must seek first the Kingdom of God and his righteousness and all these things shall be added unto us, Matthew 6:33. If we do this, we will be like Esther. We will be favored and chosen as an heir in the Kingdom. But if we decide to change the equation of God from;

Kingdom + Righteousness = all these things added unto us (BONUS) with Eternal life

To

All these things first + kingdom + righteousness = eternal death

If we, like the other girls, choose to seek the temporary pleasures of the flesh and of the world, and then try to seek the king's approval, we will be rejected. It would have been better for us if we had not tasted being in the palace to begin with, because after rejection we will go out to join others who had never entered the palace. It will be a great loss to us because we know and have tasted the goodness of living in the palace and we know what we just missed. It will be more bearable for the non-believer than for the disobedient believer. Remember Matthew 22:14, many are called but few are chosen.

Are you waiting on God? Have you stopped to think that maybe He is waiting on you to fully obey all His commands? He is never late, He is always on time. For example, here in the U.S. we fuel our own cars at the gas station; I say this because in Kenya there are attendants who do the fueling. One gives them the money and tells them which grade of fuel their car takes. If regular, which when I was young is what my father used to say to the attendant, they put regular fuel. Every time we went and parked at the fuel pump for fuel in Kenya, the attendant would come running to us and my father would stick out his hand with the money and say "regular", then the attendant would fuel our car and we would be on our way, sometimes he would get a tip. One day we went and parked at the fuel pump and the attendant took a while to come. My older brother who was young at the time, stuck his head out the car window and shouted; "regular! Come and fuel our car!" He thought the fuel attendant's name was 'regular' because my dad always said to them, "regular". It was very funny.

Here in the U.S.A, when you go to fuel your car, you not only need to swipe your debit or credit card at the fuel pump, you must also follow ALL the commands at the fuel pump for gas to flow into your tank. If you don't follow all the commands you will waste a lot of time waiting in vain. You will get frustrated and frustrate other people who are waiting on you. Even if you have all the money in the world, you still must follow all the commands at the pump like everyone else.

Likewise, God gives us the promise but most of the time we determine our wilderness time by our obedience to Him. The sooner we fully obey and follow all His commands the sooner we get our promise. Remember, time does not and will never change God but time changes us. His promises go from generation to generation and if we don't obey Him, it will be moved from our generation to the next generation that obeys and fears Him. Are you a blessed generation or a cursed generation?

"Therefore know [without any doubt] *and* understand that the Lord your God, *He is God, the faithful God, who is keeping His covenant and His [steadfast] loving kindness to a thousand generations with those who love*

Him and keep His commandments; but repays those who hate Him to their faces, by destroying them; He will not hesitate with him who hates Him, He will repay him to his face." (Deuteronomy 7:9-10 AMP; italics added)

Exodus 20:4-6 NLT (italics added) also says;

""You must not make for yourself an idol of any kind or an image of anything in the heavens or on the earth or in the sea. You must not bow down to them or worship them, for *I, the Lord your God, am a jealous God who will not tolerate your affection for any other gods. I lay the sins of the parents upon their children; the entire family is affected—even children in the third and fourth generations of those who reject me. But I lavish unfailing love for a thousand generations on those who love me and obey my commands.*"

Prayer:

Father in Jesus name, forgive us and cleanse us from all forms of idol worship in form of carved images, pictures, pleasures of this world and all things and people we have idolized (placed before You). We make You our only God and worship You only through our obedience and submission to your will. We now receive all the promises You gave to our ancestors in the past generations which they lost from disobedience and rebellion. We receive it now with thanksgiving in Jesus name in our generation. Teach us and give us the grace to love and obey you, and as we obey you Lord, may we possess the promised land which you promised our ancestors and us now in Jesus name Amen!

Let us live our lives for Christ in total surrender and obedience, trusting that He is able to fulfill all His promises and to keep us from harm and rescue us from all danger. As long as we are doing God's will, though attacks may come, we will always be victorious. God has never lost a battle, and He will not start with us!

Consulting God

Spiritually Legal/Illegal?

Is it possible to be physically legal yet spiritually illegal? Absolutely! It is better to be spiritually legal and physically illegal than the other way around. Jonah was physically legal in the ship to Tarshish (paid his fare) but was spiritually illegal (disobeyed God by boarding it). The laws of people do not supersede the laws of God. Jesus condemned this in the following scripture:

> Then Pharisees and scribes came to Jesus from Jerusalem, saying, "Why do your disciples disobey the tradition of the elders? For they don't wash their hands when they eat bread." He answered them, "Why do you also disobey the commandment of God because of your tradition? For God commanded, 'Honor your father and your mother,' and, 'He who speaks evil of father or mother, let him be put to death. But you say, 'Whoever may tell his father or his mother, "Whatever help you might otherwise have gotten from me is a gift devoted to God," he shall not honor his father or mother.' You have made the commandment of God void because of your tradition. You hypocrites! Well did Isaiah prophesy of you, saying, 'These people draw near to me with their mouth, and honor me with their lips; but their heart is far from me. And in vain do they worship me, teaching as doctrine rules made by men.'" (Matt. 15:1–9 WEB)

People, over the years, have made their own rules that contradict the laws of God due to their rebellion. Jesus was in so many ways spiritually legal but physically illegal while on earth. For example, he was accused of healing on a Sabbath in Luke 13:13–17 WEB:

He laid his hands on her, and immediately she stood up straight, and glorified God. The ruler of the synagogue, being indignant because Jesus had healed on the Sabbath, said to the multitude, "There are six days in which men ought to work. Therefore come on those days and be healed, and not on the Sabbath day!" Therefore the Lord answered him, "You hypocrites! Doesn't each one of you free his ox or his donkey from the stall on the Sabbath, and lead him away to water? Ought not this woman, being a daughter of Abraham, whom Satan had bound eighteen long years, be freed from this bondage on the Sabbath day?" As he said these things, all his adversaries were disappointed, and all the multitude rejoiced for all the glorious things that were done by him.

He was spiritually legal but physically illegal when He dined with sinners:

"The scribes and the Pharisees, when they saw that he was eating with the sinners and tax collectors, said to his disciples, "Why is it that he eats and drinks with tax collectors and sinners?" When Jesus heard it, he said to them, "Those who are healthy have no need for a physician, but those who are sick. I came not to call the righteous, but sinners to repentance."" (Mark 2:16–17 WEB).

He was also spiritually legal but physically illegal when He accepted worship from a prostitute (Luke 7:36–50), or when He cast out demons so that even the people begged him to leave their town (Mark 5:14–17).

The disciples of Jesus followed this same example when they were beaten several times and were commanded by the leaders not to preach the Gospel of Christ, but they said they would rather obey God than people.

"Then they brought the apostles before the high council, where the high priest confronted them. 'We gave you strict orders never again to teach in this man's name!' he said. 'Instead, you have filled all Jerusalem with your teaching about him, and you want to make us responsible for his death!' But Peter and the apostles replied, 'We must obey God rather than any human authority'" (Acts 5:27–29 NLT).

To the disciples, this was not new to them. They had been warned by Jesus Christ way before this happened in Matthew 10:16–20 WEB:

> Behold, I send you out as sheep among wolves. Therefore be wise as serpents, and harmless as doves. But beware of men: for they will deliver you up to councils, and in their synagogues they will scourge you. Yes, and you will be brought before governors and kings for my sake, for a testimony to them and to the nations. But when they deliver you up, don't be anxious how or what you will say, for it will be given you in that hour what you will say. For it is not you who speak, but the Spirit of your Father who speaks in you.

The disciples chose to be spiritually legal rather than physically legal. Jesus said we should not fear people, who can only destroy the body and after that can do nothing else, but we should fear God, who has the power to throw the body into hell after He has killed it (Matt.10:16–20, 24–33).

My Story...My Jonah

I went through nursing school with a Christian friend whom I met there. She lived on campus and we often studied together in her room. Because she was a Christian and a nursing student, she was physically legal to me. However, I made a mistake of not inquiring about her spiritual legality from God. For those who studied nursing, you know many practical exams are done, and you need a partner to practice the physical assessments and patient care on. On one occasion, after we had studied together and did the practical test; to my surprise, we both failed the first try. We had one more try but had to pass 100 percent, or we would be disqualified from going on and would have to repeat the class, which meant graduation would be postponed, and we would be held back a whole semester.

When we went back to her room on campus, out of nowhere, she confessed that she knew why she had failed—it was because she had been told to do something by God, but she was walking in disobedience. I had no reason why I failed because I was living in total obedience to God. I loved Him and had a very intimate relationship with Him. I took my studies very seriously too. When she confessed, my spiritual antennas were raised and immediately the Holy Spirit said to me to separate from her and not to study with her anymore. That was a warning I heeded like nothing before. I did not want to know what she did to disobey or why; all I knew was she knew better than that, and I had to get away from her company just like Psalms 1 says.

The following weekend, my husband and I went to a pastor's meeting that we had been invited to by the head of pastors in the state we lived in, even though we were not pastors, and I was asked to minister in song from my CD. Usually, before I minister anywhere, God the Holy Spirit always confirms to me where He wants me to go and minister in different ways. This time He showed me the meeting in a dream with different pastors and where some would be sitting in the meeting. In the dream, I was leading praise from one of my recorded songs, "Ushindi," meaning "Victory," and that confirmed to me that He wanted me to go and minister there. So I confirmed to them our availability.

The day finally came, and as we sat waiting for the meeting to start, the Holy Spirit took me to the book of Jonah and walked me through it like never before in just a few minutes. He told me to tell all the pastors that they MUST always inquire of the LORD before appointing anyone to any position in their ministry. This was because the person might be physically legal but spiritually illegal and would sink their ministry or cause great loss. He said that the person the pastors might choose could be a Jonah in their ministry.

Just because someone can sing or play instruments perfectly well does not mean they qualify in God's eyes. To people who only see the outside and not the inside, they may qualify but not to God because God looks on the inside, the real you. Remember the disciples in Acts 1:23–26 had to pray for God to reveal to them whom He had chosen to take Judas Iscariot's place. They even trusted God to help them choose people to serve tables in Acts 6. How many pastors or ministers of God pray for God to choose ushers or cleaners in their ministries? We rely on man's wisdom and that is why the Church is not walking in the supernatural like the Church in Acts did. They call it ACTS because of the Acts of God, the supernatural power that they walked and lived in through the Holy Spirit's guidance and council.

The Bible says that Stephen, a man **full of faith and full of the Holy Spirit,** was chosen *to serve tables* among others! Serving tables full of faith and full of the Holy Spirit. Beware of physically legal but spiritually illegal people in your life. Remember, the spirit comes before the body; a battle has to be won in the spirit first before it manifests in the physical. See examples in the Old Testament battles—when they inquired of the Lord, they won the battle even before they began because they were victorious in the spirit, and the physical manifestation followed. When king Jehoshaphat inquired of God before battle, God told him to praise. As he praised, God sent confusion into the enemy's camp, and their armies destroyed each other. Later in his reign, king Jehoshaphat allowed a "Jonah" in his ship and his works were destroyed,

"After this Jehoshaphat king of Judah joined himself with Ahaziah king of Israel. The same did very wickedly: and he joined himself with him to make ships to go to Tarshish; and they made the ships in Ezion Geber. Then Eliezer the son of Dodavahu of Mareshah prophesied against Jehoshaphat, saying, "Because you have joined yourself with Ahaziah, Yahweh has destroyed your works." The ships were broken, so that they were not able to go to Tarshish." (2 Chron. 20:35–37 WEB).

Joshua defeated the Israelites' enemies as long as they followed God's instructions, but the Israelites were defeated when they disobeyed God. An example is when Achan took the accursed things and brought them into the camp (Josh. 7:1–26). Another example is when Joshua and the Israelites did not seek God (inquire of the Lord). They were deceived by the travelers who said they were from a far land because they were afraid of being destroyed, but they were just their neighbors. (Josh. 9)

From the look of things, these people seemed physically legal, and they knew that people only like to see physical evidence, but they lacked spiritual evidence. The mistake that Joshua and his crew made was not consulting God, who looks deeper than the physical evidence of legality. We must be wise enough to ask God to reveal what is in the hearts of those around and among us. In the New Testament, Peter was released from jail by the angel when the saints prayed for his release (Acts 12:5–17). This is because our battle is won first on our knees (in the spirit) and then manifests in the physical.

God told me that my nursing-school friend was physically legal to me because she was in the same nursing program, doing the same subjects, was a Christian, was kind enough to babysit for me on some occasions, and was loved by my family, but she was spiritually illegal due to her disobedience to God, and for me, hanging out with her would cause me great loss or even sink my ship. There is no other remedy for any Jonah in our lives but what is written in the Bible. Throw them into the storm they caused, and let them deal with their own storm. In this way, they learn from the consequences of their disobedience, and maybe they will turn back to God and be saved both in the spirit and in the physical (Jonah. 1:10–16).

God will not calm the sea for you unless you throw Jonah into the sea. If you try to take Jonah back safely to shore, you will be destroyed. This is because Jonah is not a regular person who doesn't know God; he is a person who knows better but is intentionally walking in disobedience. He knows God, yet he chooses to disobey. He should be thrown into the stormy sea so he can get right with God. To avoid all this drama, don't board any Jonahs in your ship. Ask God to reveal to you the Jonahs in your life, and repent for not consulting with God before allowing people into your life. Make sure you always consult God or you will suffer great loss.

Some people you entertain will cause you great loss or sink your marriage, family, career, ministry, finances, your spirit, soul, body and your destiny. The only remedy is to throw them out of your ship. You must repent for the sin of not inquiring from God. Pray and ask God to take care of these Jonahs because it is not in your place but God's to discipline His children. Then, fear God and never repeat the same mistake.

The people did not throw Jonah back into the sea maliciously; it was Jonah's idea. They wanted to resolve it without Jonah experiencing any danger or pain, but God knew how to get Jonah's attention. Trust God. He loves Jonahs and cares for them more than you ever will know. He sent a whale to give Jonah another chance to see and repent of his wrong. Jonah was not evil, but his actions were.

Was this experience pleasant for Jonah? Absolutely not! But this gave him time-out to think about and correct his wrongdoing, while protecting him from the harm of the sea. God must have made the whale full, so that it would not eat any other deadly animal while Jonah was in its belly. What if the whale swallowed a shark whole, and the shark came and met Jonah and destroyed him? God was gracious enough to use the very thing that would have destroyed him to protect him. The whale provided him shelter and silence from the storm that was bound to destroy him, while giving him a free ride to the shore of the city where he was supposed to go to in the first place. God made provision for Jonah to amend his ways and walk in obedience, and I believe Jonah got a new summon that he was and is preaching even today through me and others. Paul also wrote this clearly, in 1 Corinthians 5:11–13, how to deal with sexual immorality among Christians, not among the people of the world.

"I meant that you are not to associate with anyone who claims to be a believer yet indulges in sexual sin, or is greedy, or worships idols, or is abusive, or is a drunkard, or cheats people. Don't even eat with such people. It isn't my responsibility to judge outsiders, but it certainly is your responsibility to judge those inside the church who are sinning. God will judge those on the outside; but as the Scriptures say, "You must remove the evil person from among you" (1 Cor. 5:11–13 NLT).

Here, Paul says that the person who practices (keeps doing it without changing his ways) sexual immorality must be put away to pay for his sin so that the flesh of immorality may die and the spirit of obedience and morality may live and rule in him. This is just like Jonah who had to be put out so that his flesh of disobedience might die and he would live in obedience. What must we do then? We must have the fear of God in us and obey Him, knowing that we can never run away from the presence of God.

In my case, I obeyed God and separated myself from my nursing-school friend and never studied with her again. Needless to say, I passed my practical exam the second time, and she failed. She was held back a semester and I graduated successfully as scheduled. All glory to the most high God!

During this time, I had a dream and in the dream some people had come to steal from me in my house. I found that they had stolen and gone and I started looking around to see what they had stolen and found that they had stolen some of my nursing books. Shortly after, there was a knock on my door and when I opened, I saw a small boy standing there with all the books that had been stolen from me, and he said, *"Take these books. Those men* (Pointing to where they stood about 1 mile away) *told me to bring them back. They said that they could not steal from you because you are a very prayerful woman."* Hallelujah! My education could not be taken away from me because when we pray and live in obedience to God, we release God to fight on our behalf.

When we pray, we are in relationship and communication with God and He reveals to us what we cannot see or know otherwise. When we are obedient to Him, He protects us just as a father protects his son who is obedient to him. Listen to God, let His Spirit lead you, and you will never go wrong or not know His will. God's will is for us to live in the fullness of Him, only successful by His Spirit. They who are led by the Spirit of God are the sons of God (Rom. 8:14). Beloved, ask God to reveal to you the hearts of those whom you associate or hang out with. Let us live in obedience to God through the fear of the LORD and depart from practicing sin. Let us heed what the apostle Paul said to Timothy in 2 Timothy 2:19, "But the truth of God stands strong. It cannot change. These words are sure: 'The Lord knows the people who belong to him' and, *'Let all those who use the name of the Lord stop their wrong ways.'*" (Worldwide English (WE); italics added)

Obedience is not always fun, but the rewards of obedience are worth it! When we obey, we have; victory over the enemies, protection, tremendous success and abundant provision, favor, supernatural life full of God, freedom and great influence. See Leviticus 26:3-13 NIV

> "'If you follow my decrees and are careful to obey my commands, I will send you rain in its season, and the ground will yield its crops and the trees their fruit. Your threshing will continue until grape harvest and the grape harvest will continue until planting, and you will eat all the food you want and live in safety in your land. "'I will grant peace in the land, and you will lie down and no one will make you afraid. I will remove wild beasts from the land, and the sword will not pass through your country. You will pursue your enemies, and they will fall by the sword before you. Five of you will chase a hundred, and a hundred of you will chase ten thousand, and your enemies will fall by the sword before you. "'I will look on you with favor and make you fruitful and increase your numbers, and I will keep my covenant with you. You will still be eating last year's harvest when you will have to move it out to make room for the new. I will put my dwelling place among you, and I will not abhor you. I will walk among you and be your God, and you will be my people. I am the Lord your God, who brought you out of Egypt so that you would no longer be slaves to the Egyptians; I broke the bars of your yoke and enabled you to walk with heads held high.

CHAPTER 12
Faith

We must have faith in God

DANIEL WAS PHYSICALLY ILLEGAL WHEN he disobeyed the law of the land which commanded everyone to worship the king alone and no other God, but was spiritually legal for obeying God and worshiping Him alone. The king was incited by Daniel's haters to command worship of the king alone and no other God for a specified period because they were envious of Daniel's favor and wisdom. But Daniel also delighted in the fear of God and had FAITH in God, for he knew that God was the God of the heaven and earth, and because of this fear, obedience followed. Did Daniel get in trouble? Absolutely! But he chose to get in trouble with people who had limited ability and did not control eternity, rather than get in trouble with God, who controls this life and eternity.

It is like having to choose between being on the same team as the US Army, which is equipped for every tough battle, or the same team as a village army that only has sticks as weapons that can hurt you but not kill you. The choice is obvious—it is better to choose the US Army. But because the devil is not a faith devil, he has taught people not to believe in what they do not see so as to get them away from God.

If the US Army monitored your location using special tracking devices and only showed up when the battle is on, but did not show up or hang around that place any other time, while on the other hand the village army is there constantly intimidating you, would it be easier for you to join them because they can be seen? Even if the US Army is watching over you constantly and are not limited as to how fast they can come to your rescue? When the US Army shows up, they only need a few troops to wipe the existence of the village army off the face of the earth. On the other hand, the village army is barefoot and inefficient, but is there constantly. Having learned from the wisdom of the world to believe only what we see, many people would rather join the village army, and be on the defeated side because they feel secure with an army they can see constantly more than one they cannot physically see. We like to have security we can see and feel; this is false security.

Remember the story of David, the little shepherd boy? The boy was physically illegal from his looks—a dirty shepherd boy, the errand runner of the home, the servant to his brothers, the shortest and youngest, the most insignificant in the family, and unqualified by people to be chosen as king—but God saw David as spiritually legal because God knew David's heart. God saw David as a man after His own heart. God reminded His prophet Samuel that He looks on the inside, not on the outside like people do.

Later we see that, according to David's brothers, David was seen as prideful, but to God, he was full of faith and humility in God's power, and he knew he could not do anything in his own power but by God's grace and power. The world will many times mistake faith and humility for pride, while God sees lack of faith as pride. Do you see the difference between God's wisdom and the world's wisdom? To Saul, David was not physically legal in his battlefield armor, but to God, David was spiritually legal in his armor. He had the full armor of God (Eph. 6:10–18). David knew we do not wage war according to the flesh and blood but according to principalities and powers of darkness in the heavenly places. To win, we MUST involve God. Have faith in God. The weapons of our warfare are not carnal but mighty *through God* (2 Cor. 10:3–6).

David did exactly that when he confronted Goliath. The Philistines' army would be, in this case, like the village army. They intimidated the children of God and placed fear in them so that they lacked faith. In those days, the fear of the Lord was not in them, especially not in their King Saul. That is why God picked David, so He could work deliverance and salvation through him.

David's brothers saw his faith as pride.

"But when David's oldest brother, Eliab, heard David talking to the men, he was angry. 'What are you doing around here anyway?' he demanded. 'What about those few sheep you're supposed to be taking care of? I know about your pride and deceit. You just want to see the battle!'" (1 Samuel. 17:28 NLT):

However, David did not let his brothers put him down.

"And since we have the same spirit of faith, according to what is written, 'I believed and therefore I spoke.'" (2 Cor. 4:13)

David spoke to Goliath what he believed—faith. According to King Saul, who walked and waged war according to the flesh, he was supposed to inquire of God but didn't. David was not fit for battle legally because he was just a youth, and Goliath was a man of war from his youth.

"And Saul said to David, 'You are not able to go against this Philistine to fight with him; for you are a youth, and he a man of war from his youth'" (1 Samuel. 17:33).

Your experience and qualifications are what qualifies you according to the world. These are the questions everyone asks before they hire you or trust that you are able. They ask to see your résumé, and they will hire someone with earthly qualifications rather than with heavenly qualifications. What a different world this would be if we hired people according to their God-given task? According to their spiritual legality? People would work joyfully and without stress because they have the grace needed for their GGT. How many of us *have* to go to work instead of *get* to go to work?

This is where many people fall short. The God-given task is never done according to earthly qualifications but on spiritual qualifications.

Your God-Given Task

Who knows the spirit of people but God? So it takes inquiry from God to get the right people for the task. Jesus, being God, had to pray and inquire of God before He chose His disciples. David looked at Goliath as one who defiled the army of the living God; he portrayed Goliath as one who was against God himself and not people. David shared the same vision and passion God had. He felt the same anger God felt, and he felt God's pain.

God planned for David's dad to send him to the battlefield to check on his brothers on this day at this time, which was the fortieth day since the Philistines defied God and His army. Forty is a number that marks the end of one thing and the beginning of another—the end of the children of Israel living in the wilderness and the beginning of them possessing the promises of God. Jesus started His ministry after forty days and forty nights in the wilderness. Moses got the Ten Commandments after forty days and forty nights. David (little in the physical and gigantic in the spirit) was in God's plan. He gained interest in the reward and confessed victory in his response to Saul:

> David said to Saul, "Your servant was keeping his father's sheep; and when a lion or a bear came, and took a lamb out of the flock, I went out after him, and struck him, and rescued it out of his mouth. When he arose against me, I caught him by his beard, and struck him, and killed him. Your servant struck both the lion and the bear. This uncircumcised Philistine shall be as one of them, since he has defied the armies of the living God." David said, "Yahweh who delivered me out of the paw of the lion, and out of the paw of the bear, he will deliver me out of the hand of this Philistine." Saul said to David, "Go! Yahweh will be with you." (1 Samuel. 17:34–37 WEB)

David made it crystal clear to Saul that his strength was only from one source, God Himself. David knew that the battle was not his; it was the Lord's.

"Then all this assembly shall know that the Lord does not save with sword and spear; for the battle is the Lord's, and He will give you into our hands" (1 Samuel. 17:47).

David refused to war according to the flesh when Saul clothed David in his armor. David was not able to walk or operate in Saul's armor. Saul's armor represents walking by sight and not by faith and trusting in one's own strength and not in God's, just like Saul did. To David, faith was much clearer to him than sight, but according to Saul, David was blind. To Saul, the armor was his sight, but to David, faith was his sight. When Saul gave David his armor, David was blinded by what Saul saw through. When David took off Saul's armor and put on God's armor of faith, Saul was blind to it.

We see David explaining this faith armor to Saul in 1 Samuel 17:33–37. As we saw earlier, and now in verses 38–39, David rejects physical sight for faith. "So Saul clothed David with his armor, and he put a bronze helmet on his head; he also clothed him with a coat of mail. David fastened his sword to his armor and tried to walk, for he had not tested them. And David said to Saul, 'I cannot walk with these, for I have not tested them.' So David took them off."

David also spoke truth and faith to Goliath so he can know who killed him when he dies, in verses 45–47:

> Then David said to the Philistine, 'You come to me with a sword, with a spear, and with a javelin. But I come to you in the name of the Lord of hosts, the God of the armies of Israel, whom you have defied. This day the Lord will deliver you into my hand, and I will strike you and take your head from you. And this day I will give the carcasses of the camp of the Philistines to the birds of the air and the wild beasts of the earth, that all the earth may know that there is a God in Israel. Then all this assembly shall know that the Lord does not save with sword and spear; for the battle is the Lord's, and He will give you into our hands.

David was hidden in God when he fought, therefore God did the fighting in the body of this youth who had believed God was enough. For this belief, he was considered a fool before the eyes of the world.

"For the message of the cross is foolishness to those who are perishing, but to us who are being saved it is the power of God" (1 Cor. 1:18).

"But the natural man does not receive the things of the Spirit of God, for they are foolishness to him; nor can he know them, because they are spiritually discerned" (1 Cor. 2:14).

Look at the contrast of those who walk by sight and those who walk by faith. Goliath said to David in 1 Sam 17 verse 43, *"I'm a dog? You come to me with sticks"* (italics added). Goliath was disgusted by David's simplicity and thought David was very proud and arrogant, immature and a fool, ignorant and lacking discretion. Moreover, he thought David was disrespectful because little David was not intimidated by his sight or by his mighty armor, strength, experience, height, big and deep voice, and all that was sensed by the human senses of sight, smell, hearing, and touch.

The devil is angered by faith, while God is pleased by faith. What Goliath failed to see was the great God in David, whom he was fighting. The first failure in any battle is the inability to recognize who your enemy really is. Goliath thought that the Israelites were his enemies but in the actual sense, it was their God who was his real enemy. Yahweh just wore little David as an outfit so that He could make the strong men of the earth see themselves as nothing. God humbles the proud. He brings them to nothing! He opposes the proud, but He gives grace or power to the humble (Prov. 3:34, James 4:6, 1 Pet. 5:5).

"Everyone proud in heart is an abomination to the Lord; though they join forces, none will go unpunished." (Prov.16:5)

"Pride goes before destruction, and a haughty spirit before a fall. Better to be of a humble spirit with the lowly, than to divide the spoil with the proud" (Prov. 16:18–19).

"A man's pride will bring him low, but the humble in spirit will retain honor. The fear of man brings a snare, But whoever trusts in the Lord shall be safe" (Prov. 29:23, 25).

Because the foolishness of God is wiser than men, and the weakness of God is stronger than men. For you see your calling, brothers, that not many are wise according to the flesh, not many mighty, and not many noble; but God chose the foolish things of the world that he might put to shame those who are wise. God chose the weak things of the world, that he might put to shame the things that are strong; and God chose the lowly things of the world, and the things that are despised, and the things that are not, that he might bring to nothing the things that are: that no flesh should boast before God. (Cor. 1: 25–29 WEB)

David saw the challenge from God's point of view. He knew His God, therefore he was strong and did exploits! The Bible says that those who know their God shall be strong, and they shall do exploits (Dan. 11:32). The army of the Israelites also had to hear David's confession because they were faithless. As we all know, faith comes by hearing the Word of God (Rom. 10:17). Their leader, Saul, had turned from God and was not being led by the Spirit of God, therefore the spirit of fear and intimidation was upon him, and it trickled down to his followers and army.

If one is fearful, that person has no faith. Fear is the opposite of faith, and it comes before defeat. You lack agape love when you have fear. People who are fearful cannot exercise love because the Bible says there is no fear in love, but perfect love casts out fear.

"There is no fear in love; but perfect love casts out fear, because fear involves *torment*. But he who fears has not been made perfect in love" (1 John 4:18).

We can never please God as long as we have the spirit of fear, because without faith it is impossible to please God (Heb. 11:6.)

What is Faith?

Calling those things that are not as though they are.

Faith transitions our promises from the spiritual realm into the physical realm.

"Now faith is the substance of things hoped for, the evidence of things not seen" (Heb. 11:1).

"If any of you lacks wisdom, let him ask of God, who gives to all liberally and without reproach, and it will be given to him. But let him ask in faith, without doubting, for he who doubts is like a wave of the sea driven and tossed by the wind. For let not that man suppose that he will receive anything from the Lord; he is a double-minded man, unstable in all his ways" (James 1:5–8).

David had the Spirit of God in him. He trusted fully in God's ability to deliver the Israelites from the Philistines through FAITH in God; therefore, he had the spirit of power, love, and a sound mind. The Israelite army had let fear paralyze them, and they had given up, and the Bible says they were at war facing their enemy, but they were *sitting down on the ground.* They were not brave or ready for victory in battle because they were clothed in fear; they were ready for defeat. They had no one willing to volunteer to fight the giant, and they saw themselves in the same way their enemies saw them. They had the enemy's eyesight—the devil's viewpoint—and they even saw David in the same light, as a little boy committing suicide by Goliath.

God was not pleased with either army because they both believed in a lie. The Philistines never believed in God, and the Israelites believed more in the Philistines' (the enemy's) ability to destroy them than in God's ability to save them. They all had faith but in the wrong thing. Only little David had a different spirit. He had faith in God's ability to destroy His enemies and those of His people. But when David killed Goliath, the Israelite army saw the GREAT VICTORY and then AROSE! SHOUTED, and PURSUED their enemies, the Philistines

(1 Samuel. 17:52). The Israelites had been sitting down literally—a sign of defeat throughout the battle between David and Goliath—until the boy with the weapon of faith in God, pleased God, and God used him to destroy the great enemy.

People will arise from a low position into their rightful place when you exercise your FAITH in God and take your place. When you are faithful in doing your God-given task, you will cause people around you who have been intimidated by the enemy to arise because of what they see God doing through you. They will desire to be used by God, and stand in their appointed place, to bring glory and honor to God. We need more people like David and not Saul more than ever today, who will stand in boldness and in the power of the finished work of the cross and the power of the Resurrection of Jesus Christ, with the revelation knowledge that the same Spirit that raised Christ from the dead lives in us! Men and women are needed who live boldly without fear or intimidation from the enemy because they believe God's Word that says we are more than conquerors in Christ Jesus, who has forever defeated the Goliath of our souls! Men and women who are continually and totally led by the Holy Spirit of God.

If you are like the Israelite army, you have given up and are sitting down in defeat, not seeing how what God has promised you in your life would ever come to pass; I encourage you to take heart and have faith in God's ability to keep His Word which He promised you, because God honors His WORD over His name (Ps. 138:2). Heaven and earth will pass away, but His Word will NEVER pass away (Matt. 24:35, Mark 13:31, Luke 21:33). God's Word never fails; it endures forever. Do not have faith in your situation's ability. If you have been intimidated for a long time, I encourage you now to ARISE! SHOUT! And PURSUE! Your enemy. Dispossess and destroy the enemy and possess your rightful territory which the enemy has stolen from you.

Lack of faith is caused by poor spiritual eyesight.
Poor spiritual vision causes fear.

Which Lenses Are You looking through— the Spirit's or the Flesh's?

Remember my vision about what God looks at? He allowed me to see through His point of view. God the Father said to me that there is no limit to how much your spirit can grow. The body has a limit to how tall it can grow. The height of the body is determined by the human genes, but the height of the spirit determined by God's spiritual genes, how big and tall is God's Spirit? Unlimited! No end to His Spirit. Your spiritual growth is determined by how much you learn from God and do His will and grow in Him. We all have a chance to control how tall we grow in the spirit. God is limitless, and so is the spirit. David must have been given the eyes of God to see through; he must have seen what God saw, a tiny, malnourished spirit in Goliath. It was so small and malnourished, almost dead in the spirit, fighting with David's gigantic spirit. David had God's eyesight, not people's eyesight. In the spirit, where our battles are fought first before they manifest in the physical, Goliath was a little infant and David was a great giant.

Deception Comes When You Look Through the Eyes of Man

According to 1 Samuel 17:4-7, Goliath was a man of war from his youth, a great giant over nine feet tall; he had a helmet of bronze, a bronze breastplate weighing 125 pounds, bronze leg armor, and a bronze javelin. The shaft of his spear was as heavy and thick as a weaver's beam, tipped with an iron spearhead that weighed fifteen pounds. His armor bearer walked ahead of him, carrying a shield. The Philistine army was stronger and supportive of Goliath their champion; they were courageous and ready for battle. David had no experience of war and no armor of war; he was only a shepherd boy, who had no weapon except for a sling and the five smooth stones he picked up on his way to fight Goliath.

David had no one to encourage him; his brothers ridiculed him, and the king had no faith in him.

The Israelite army was sitting down in defeat. David was all alone, without shield or protection or armor bearer. He was going to face his death, and not only that, the Israelites had given up, and they knew they were already defeated before they even began. If they lost the battle, they were going to be slaves to these merciless Philistines. At this point, they didn't care about being slaves; they figured they already were, but the dilemma was who would volunteer to fight and be killed by this giant? Who was willing to sacrifice his life for them to be slaves? They were ready to get it over with, because it had been forty very long days and nights of fear and intimidation, and someone had to fight this giant already! They figured this little boy had nothing to lose, he had no wife or children, was not even a soldier that the kingdom would lose an asset; to King Saul and the Israelite army, he was not of worth anyway, so he was a good sacrifice.

Do you have faith in God's ability—or the enemy's ability? Many people have more faith in the enemy's ability to destroy them than in God's ability to deliver them.

The disciples believed in the ability of the storm to destroy them when Jesus was in the boat sleeping, they cried out to Him, He woke up and calmed the storm, then He asked them this question in Mark 4:40 "Why are you *so fearful*? How is it that *you have no faith*?" (Italics added)

This is the same question each of us needs to answer. You can have faith but when you doubt, this makes you one of little faith. But if you have fear, you have no faith because fear is the opposite of faith...

The Israelites from Egypt had more faith in the ability of the giants in the land of Canaan to destroy them. In Numbers 13:31-33, they saw themselves as the enemies saw them, grasshoppers, instead of having faith in the ability of their God to destroy their enemies, and give them the huge cities and vine yards. Cities built by giants and vineyards planted by giants are very rich because everything is very huge. Because of this, in Numbers 14:23 God withdrew His promise from them and they died in the wilderness. They only saw the Promised Land but did not possess it. Only the two that believed in God's ability and His promise, Caleb and Joshua, got to possess the Promised Land Numbers 14:24.

The promises of God are not for the fearful and cowards, but for those full of faith and courage in God's ability.

Truth Comes When You Look Through the Eyes of God

In reality we fight our battles in the spirit which is the real battlefield. In this battle field, David was a man of war in the spirit from his youth! Goliath was a baby in the spirit and never fought a single war. David was a giant, who was way taller, bigger, and stronger than Goliath; Goliath was a weak, malnourished baby. David was armed for battle with the full spiritual armor as in Ephesians 6, but Goliath was not armed for battle at all. David also had a greater sword, sharper than a double-edged sword (the Word of God); Goliath had no sword.

David knew that we are spirits with a body to live in to do God's will and if we are fully armed in the spirit, we shall win the battle not only in the spirit but in the physical. The battle is won first in the spirit and then the victory is made manifest in the physical. Our body, Paul said, is a tent.

"For we know that if our earthly house, this tent, is destroyed, we have a building from God, a house not made with hands, eternal in the heavens" (2 Cor. 5:1).

The Holy Spirit showed me that our body is like clothing. When we wear clothes, the clothes get to go where we go; when we take them off, we still exist, but the clothes cannot move unless we wear them. When someone wants to go to the moon, he or she wears a spacesuit. In the same way, for us to come to earth and do our assignment, we needed a bodysuit. Jesus said to God the Father, that 'a body You created for me to do Your will' (see Heb. 10:5–7).

Jesus also said that before Abraham was even born, He existed (John 8:58). This means He was a Spirit just like God is a Spirit, and a body was created for Him to do the will of His Father God. God said to me through His Holy Spirit as He was teaching me this concept, that I am His outfit, and as long as I live in Him, anyone who comes to fight me will be fighting Him.

He asked me, "Does anyone fight with the clothes of the one he is fighting with or does he fight the one wearing the clothes?" The latter is true—people don't fight clothes; they fight the people wearing the clothes. The Holy Spirit said to me that as long as I remain in Him and walk in obedience to God, anyone who comes against me, comes against Him; anyone who insults me, insults Him. This is just like the promise God made to Abraham. God told Abraham, "I will bless those who bless you and curse those who curse you." (Gen 12:3)

David knew that he was anointed by God. He was now God's outfit. David knew God was wearing him and fighting the battle. That was why he was not afraid; he spoke as if God spoke because he was about God's business. On the other hand, the Israelite army saw themselves outside of God. They saw Goliath as coming against them and insulting them; they were all fleshy, and it was all about them. That is why God did not give them victory, lest they take the glory that belonged to God.

David knew that defeating this enemy was going to be by the grace of God and the power of God, for it was not by David's might nor by his power but by the Spirit of God. Clothes cannot receive compliments on their own because they cannot look good hung on a hunger. They look complete and beautiful worn on a body. That is why clothing stores invest in mannequins to model their outfits, and magazines take pictures of people modeling their clothes to get good sales. Likewise, we are supposed to be God's outfit. He wears us, works through us, and He receives the glory, because we are like clothes; we cannot move or do anything or prosper apart from Him.

"For in him we live and move and exist. As some of your own poets have said, 'we are his offspring'" (Acts 17:28 NLT).

Jesus reminded us this in John 15:4–8 WEB: (Italics added)

Remain in me, and I in you. As the branch can't bear fruit by itself, unless it remains in the vine, so neither can you, unless you remain in me. I am the vine. You are the branches. He who remains in me, and I in him, the same bears much fruit, for apart from me you can do nothing. If a man doesn't remain in me, he is thrown out as a branch, and is withered; and they gather them, throw them into the fire, and they are burned. If you remain in me, and my words remain in you, you will ask whatever you desire, and it will be done for you "In this is my Father glorified, that you bear much fruit; and so you will be my disciples.

MY STORY:

When going through nursing school, I had a great hunger for God and wanted to know Him more. He was teaching me so much that I did not want to be distracted by anything or anyone. I therefore made this deal with God.

I said, "God, I want to spend more time with You than I spend studying. If You help me understand nursing and show me what I should study for before my tests, then all my extra time will be yours."

Sometimes we want extra time in our lives for our own selfish ambitions and pleasures which will destroy us. God will not grant that to us. When we ask God to do something for us, let it be to the glory and honor of His name or for the growth of His Kingdom.

Let us not forget who we are. We are Christ's ambassadors here on earth to perform our God-given tasks as representatives of heaven. He created a body for your spirit to live in to do His will.

One time I was taking a chemistry test for my nursing prerequisites and I got to a question I couldn't figure out. Just then I heard God the Holy Spirit shout the answer to me so loudly that I looked up to see who had spoken. Everyone in the class was silent, busy doing their work and the professor was walking around the class. I wrote down what He had shouted out to me and in awe I got the answer right. I got an A in that class, and spent more time with God, learning His ways. The chemistry professor said that I was great in chemistry and asked if there was any way he could talk me out of my nursing major to become a chemistry major.

Ironically, chemistry was my worst subject in high school. I couldn't understand it because the teacher was too soft spoken, barely moved from where he stood it was impossible to enjoy or understand it.

As I drove home that day, I worshiped God and cried like a baby in awe of Him and of His love saying, "You love me so much that You even shouted the answer to me!"

Then He immediately answered, "As long as you put Me first in your life, I REFUSE! To let you struggle."

What an answer. What a God. I thank God the Father, God the Son, and God the Holy Spirit for such love and grace and faithfulness. God always keeps His end of the deal.

Look at how David pointed out to Goliath what Goliath could not see. He said to him in 1 Samuel 17: 45 NLT, "You come to me with sword, spear, and javelin, but I come to you in the name of the Lord of heaven's armies—the God of the armies of Israel, whom you have defied."

Look at the contrast between the reactions of David, who relied on God in verse 48 to that of the Israelite army, who relied on their own strength in verse 24

> "As Goliath moved closer to attack, David quickly ran out to meet him" (1 Sam 17:48 NLT)

"As soon as the Israelite army saw him, they began to run away in fright." (1 Sam 17:24 NLT)

David ran toward his enemy, while the Israelite army ran away from their enemy.

The number five is the number of grace, and grace is God's power at work in us. David knew this, so he took five smooth stones and used God's grace to defeat Goliath who wanted to enslave them. David hit Goliath on his forehead with one stone on a sling and cut the head off because without the head, the body is dead. The head is the life of the body. Unfortunately, when the brain is dead, it does not matter if the heart is beating, the person is automatically declared dead medically. Did you ever wonder why there is no brain transplant, but we have heart transplants? In a brain attack or stroke, the part of the brain that died cannot be repaired. David hit Goliath with one stone, one try the only part of Goliath's head that was left unprotected. Goliath did not have a head covering or protection. He had no spiritual covering while David had spiritual covering from God. We have Christ as our head, our covering and that is why we can defeat the enemy in Christ.

Without the head (leader) of the enemies, the enemies are as good as dead. That is why the Philistines were bold and intimidating as long as their head, Goliath, was alive, but when he died they all ran away. God said to the devil in Genesis 3:15 that the woman's offspring, Jesus Christ, would crush his head. God revealed the birth of Jesus and the victory of Jesus over the devil in Genesis and the devil didn't even get it! Jesus destroyed the devil's kingdom. That is why the devil is so afraid of women rising up to their rightful places in Christ and taking charge of their God-given tasks. Women have been discriminated against from the time God cursed the devil in Genesis until today.

No wonder the devil wanted to kill Jesus so badly because without the head of the church, the LORD Jesus Christ, the church is dead. Jesus defeated Lucifer forever, the Goliath of our souls, when He died and rose again. What a glorious God we serve! How awesome is His name forever!

The God-given task has God as the adviser and master planner. He has already set people in place to accomplish the task, so if we accept someone in our GGT that has not been called to do that assignment at that time and in that place, we will be working against God in disobedience. That is why we MUST inquire of the Lord at all times. If we don't inquire, we will be displacing or delaying someone else on their GGT. This was the case with Jonah until he got back into his rightful place. Before God created you, he had your assignment set out for you to do already.

He has it all planned out and most importantly, TIMED.

If I want to drink some water, I will get a glass or cup to drink with. If I get a knife or a fork I would not be able to fetch any water. The assignment for the cup came before the cup was made. Thirst came before the cup was invented, likewise, the assignment always comes before the worker.

"For we are His workmanship [His own master work, a work of art], created in Christ Jesus [reborn from above—spiritually transformed, renewed, ready to be used] for good works, which God prepared [for us] beforehand [taking paths which He set], so that we would walk in them [living the good life which He prearranged and made ready for us]" (Eph. 2:10 AMP).

We can learn from the disciples in Acts, who numbered eleven at the time because Judas Iscariot was no longer there. They knew that the Word of God speaks of the twelve foundations of the New Jerusalem and that it was God's will to have twelve disciples and not eleven. To select another disciple, they could have cast lots or played rock-paper-scissors, or even choose the most popular one or the most outspoken person. However, these disciples knew one important thing that Jesus taught them, PRAYER. Jesus Himself prayed before picking His twelve disciples. As a follower of Christ, we MUST follow His example of prayer and pray before we allow anyone to work with us in our GGT.

"Now it came to pass in those days that He went out to the mountain to pray, and *continued all night in prayer to God*. And when it was day, He called His disciples to Himself; and from them He chose twelve whom He also named apostles: Simon, whom He also named Peter, and Andrew his brother; James and John; Philip and Bartholomew; Matthew and Thomas; James the son of Alphaeus, and Simon called the Zealot; Judas the son of James, and Judas Iscariot, who also became a traitor" (Luke 6:12–16; italics added).

Jesus Christ was the Son of God, yet He inquired of His Father, to give Him wisdom to choose whom God wanted for His God-given task. He prayed all night long. To this day, Jesus is still praying for us which makes us secure in our assignments on earth.

> And inasmuch as He was not made priest without an oath (for they have become priests without an oath, but He with an oath by Him who said to Him: "The Lord has sworn And will not relent, '*You are a priest forever* According to the order of Melchizedek'"), by so much more Jesus has become a surety of a better covenant. Also there were many priests, because they were prevented by death from continuing. *But He, because He continues forever, has an unchangeable priesthood*. Therefore He is also able to save to the uttermost those who come to God through Him, since *He always lives to make intercession for them*. (Heb. 7:20–25; italics added)

"Who is he who condemns? It is Christ who died, and furthermore is also risen, who is even at the right hand of God, *who also makes intercession for us*" (Rom. 8:34; italics added).

Jesus never sent Himself to earth; He was sent to earth by His Father and had a God-given task to fulfill.

"Sacrifice and offering You did not desire; My ears You have opened. Burnt offering and sin offering You did not require. Then I said, 'Behold, I come; in the scroll of the book it is written of me. *I delight to do Your will, O my God, and Your law is within my heart*'" (Ps. 40:6–8; italics added).

Jesus knew how His Father worked and did not want to mess up. He said He does what He sees His Father do and He says what He hears His Father say. God revealed this to Isaiah, when he said in Isaiah 59:16,

"He saw that there was no man, and wondered that there was no intercessor; Therefore His own arm brought salvation for Him; and His own righteousness, it sustained Him."

God found no one fit enough to intercede for us. Even the priests themselves could not because they had to intercede for themselves first, and then for others. We could not save ourselves even with good works because we were weak and sin dwelt in us. God was the only answer for our salvation.

There is no way a created being can save a created being, just as a broken chair cannot be fixed by another chair. Only the one greater than the chair, who made the chair, can perfect the broken chair that needs fixing. Let's say, for example, the chair in this case is wooden and broken beyond repair, the one who bought it can easily get rid of it and buy another chair, but the one who curved it and took time to make the chair with the wood that was specially made by him or her with special engraving would gladly buy the chair again from the person who wants to totally destroy it, so he or she can restore it to its original condition.

Let's say for instance that initially this chair had been specially made by the ancestor of a family years ago and had been in the family for generations, but down the line, it was stolen and sold for next to nothing. This family would be the only ones who would know the value and cost of the chair and would opt to buy the chair at any cost to have it back into the family possession again. This family would pay a lot of money for this wooden chair that is broken beyond repair and that is being sold as firewood because they know its true value. Just like the saying goes, 'one man's trash is another man's treasure'.

Anyone witnessing this would laugh at this family buying the piece of junk. They would ridicule them and in modern times even take pictures and post it on every social media and news outlets that the family was willing to pay whatever the cost to get a piece of junk back into their possession. This family would not get offended by any amount of ridicule that they would face; rather, there would be feasting and rejoicing because they have recovered their stolen treasure, and they have their priceless piece back into their possession. You see, other people may not know the value of the chair, but this family does.

God knew the cost of His beloved people, and He was willing to give up everything so He can get them back into His possession. God is a consuming fire, He consumes sin, and He knew that humanity would fall into sin in the garden in Eden. Before that happened, God had a plan already figured out to save humanity from the enemy because He is God.

"Just as He chose us in Him before the foundation of the world, that we should be holy and without blame before Him in love, having predestined us to adoption as sons by Jesus Christ to Himself, according to the good pleasure of His will, to the praise of the glory of His grace, by which He made us accepted in the Beloved" (Eph. 1:4–6).

God consumes sin, but His Son JESUS, who perfected His dad's plan, came to save us and we can now live forever in God the Father through Christ Jesus. God created us in His image, to live with him forever. God is a God who works.

"Jesus said to them, 'My food is to do the will of Him who sent Me, and to finish His work." (John 4:34).

Jesus was sustained by doing God's Work and finishing it. What about you?

"But Jesus answered them, 'My Father has been working until now, and I have been working'" (John 5:17).

"For the Father loves the Son, and shows Him all things that He Himself does; and He will show Him greater works than these, that you may marvel" (John 5:20).

"But I have a greater witness than John's; for the works which the Father has given Me to finish—the very works that I do—bear witness of Me, that the Father has sent Me" (John 5:36).

"Jesus answered and said to them, 'This is the work of God, that you believe in Him whom He sent'" (John 6:29).

"I must work the works of Him who sent Me while it is day; the night is coming when no one can work" (John 9:4).

"Jesus answered them, 'I told you, and you do not believe. The works that I do in My Father's name, they bear witness of Me'" (John 10:25).

"Jesus answered them, 'Many good works I have shown you from My Father. For which of those works do you stone Me?'" (John 10:32).

"If I do not do the works of My Father, do not believe Me" (John 10:37).

"But if I do, though you do not believe Me, believe the works, that you may know and believe that the Father is in Me, and I in Him" (John 10:38).

"Do you not believe that I am in the Father, and the Father in Me? The words that I speak to you I do not speak on My own authority; but the Father who dwells in Me does the works. Most assuredly, I say to you, he who believes in Me, the works that I do he will do also; and greater works than these he will do, because I go to My Father" (John 14:10, 12).

"If I had not done among them the works which no one else did, they would have no sin; but now they have seen and also hated both Me and My Father" (John 15:24).

Glorifying God on earth is to finish the WORK (God-given task) He has given us to do just like Jesus did and said in John 17:4: "I have glorified You on the earth. I have finished the work which You have given Me to do."

"And they went out and preached everywhere, the Lord working with them and confirming the word through the accompanying signs. Amen" (Mark 16:20).

Jesus worked with His disciples even after He went to heaven. He is still working, confirming His Word with signs following to those who believe. Do you believe?

CHAPTER 13
Your Script

§

It was written out before the world was created.

DO YOU KNOW YOUR SCRIPT? Every God-given task was written out before the foundations of the world. The Bible says that Jesus Christ is the Lamb of God who was slain before the foundations of the world: "All who dwell on the earth will worship him, whose names have not been written in *the Book of Life of the Lamb slain from the foundation of the world*" (Rev. 13:8; italics added).

Before God created anything, He had already planned it out. He laid it all out, and it actually happened in the Spirit before the physical ever came into being. Jesus had already suffered and was slain in the Spirit way before the world came into being.

Before you build a house, a plan and layout is drawn and the actual rooms and what the house should look like is all put on paper. The building is complete in the plan and all that is left is the physical manifestation. The same is true with our GGT (God-given task). God planned out our GGT, the plan was written out and fulfilled in the Spirit, and the manifestation of the plan in the physical is now taking place.

Jesus said, in Psalm 40:6–8, that God the Father did not desire or delight in sacrifices and offerings, but requires obedience from us. "My ears you have opened" means that Jesus was able to hear clearly and obey His Father's instructions. He goes on to say that His Father does not require burnt offering and sin offering. He clarifies that God the Father did not intend for the plan of sacrificing animals to last forever because it was not pleasing to Him. It was a way out of condemnation for Adam and Eve, but it was not God's perfect plan.

Jesus said in Matthew 5:17, "Do not think that I came to destroy the Law or the Prophets. I did not come to destroy but to fulfill."

Jesus never came to undo the law, which was a shadow of the real thing; He only came to perfect it, just as the Father likes it. Jesus in Psalm 40 reveals two things that God did not desire or require—burnt sacrifices and offerings. If He desired them, He would not have sent Jesus Christ to die on the cross and rise up on the third day to do away with the burnt offerings and sacrifices. God's love worked this plan of salvation. God did not want to stay away from us because He created us in His image and likeness to have fellowship with Him forever. The burnt sacrifices and offerings worked to keep us in a long-distance relationship with God through a mediator (earthly priest) and a veil. With this type of relationship, we could not call Him Father, even the priests, because we would never have received adoption as sons and daughters of God. But glory to God for Christ! Romans 8:15 says, "For you did not receive the spirit of bondage again to fear, but you received the Spirit of adoption by whom we cry out, 'Abba, Father.'"

Just as Jesus calls His Father Abba Father, as long as we are in Christ, we have the power to become children of God, and we call God Abba Father!

What a homecoming! What a reunion! How beyond any comprehension the Father's heart must have felt being reconciled to His children once more. Oh what joy, after thousands of years!

Imagine a father who has been estranged from his son for many years finds out how to get to his son in a distant land. The only way to reach his son is to sell everything he owns and lose everything he has including all his savings and retirement, in order to seek for and find his son. What joy indescribable would that reunion be! What if the son refuses to be reunited with the father and does not want anything to do with him? This would break his father's heart and might kill his father because the father gave up all he had for his son. God the Father feels such great joy every time someone accepts His Son Jesus Christ as their LORD and savior. What sadness He feels when we reject His great sacrifice! God is very saddened by a sinner's death because it is a great loss of sacrifice and relationship.

"As surely as I live, says the Sovereign Lord, I take no pleasure in the death of wicked people. I only want them to turn from their wicked ways so they can live. Turn! Turn from your wickedness, O people of Israel! Why should you die?" (Ezekiel 33:11 NLT)

"Do you think that I like to see wicked people die? Says the Sovereign Lord. Of course not! I want them to turn from their wicked ways and live." (Ezekiel 18:23 NLT)

Because Jesus Christ, His Son, was and is perfect, therefore we are perfected in Christ. We are made righteous in Christ. There is no other name under heaven given to men by which we must be saved (Acts 4:12).

Life Is in the Blood

"For the life of the flesh is in the blood, and I have given it to you upon the altar to make atonement for your souls; for it is the blood that makes atonement for the soul" (Lev. 17:11).

Animal sacrifice was not enough because it was not able to take away sin; it only covered sin. Also, the sprinkled blood of animals spoke and interceded for us, but it only had the power to speak on our behalf for a short period of time, and it cried for God to have MERCY on us.

Mercy is given to someone in lower ranking than the one he or she is begging from, like a master shows mercy to a servant. Mercy is begged for from someone who is in a position to punish another. Animal sacrifice was started when people sinned and fell short of the glory of GOD (when people stopped becoming like God, because God does not sin). We were created in God's image and likeness, clothed with glory and given dominion over all creation, but when we sinned, we fell short of God's glory and became merely human.

Just like the scripture says in Romans 3:23, "for all have sinned and fall short of the glory of God," sin makes us fall short of God's glory. As a result of sin people became servants. That was why the first thing God asked Adam after he and Eve sinned at the Garden of Eden, was "Where are you?" This was a question addressing the *position*, not the *location* of Adam. God is all knowing, but Adam was hiding from God because his wisdom was stripped from him, and he did not remember that it was impossible to hide from God. God revealed that Adam had lost his position in God and had been dethroned from the glory and dominion he once had. He was out of position, and God found that Adam and Eve and all humanity had been stripped naked of all the glory and dominion He had given them by the devil. Sin enslaves us both spiritually and physically.

Animal sacrifice started in the Garden of Eden when God made the first sacrifice for humanity. It symbolized a slave-master relationship between God and humans. God only spoke to a handful of certain people who were set apart as prophets for Him—His servants. All other people were not worthy to be in His presence; only a priest was allowed to intercede on their behalf. The animal to be sacrificed took on the sin of the owner and was killed because the payment for sin was and still is death. When sin came, death came. Before sin, there was only life. The animal's blood was very limited and short lived because it only covered sin; it did not take away sin. The Bible says that John the Baptist declared in John 1:29, "Behold the Lamb of God who TAKES AWAY the sins of the world." Only the blood of Jesus takes away sin.

Look at the insufficiency of animal sacrifices in Hebrews 10:1–23.

> The old system under the Law of Moses was only a shadow, a dim preview of the good things to come, not the good things

themselves. The sacrifices under that system were repeated again and again, year after year, but they were never able to provide perfect cleansing for those who came to worship. If they could have provided perfect cleansing, the sacrifices would have stopped, for the worshipers would have been purified once for a lifetime, and their feelings of guilt would have disappeared. But instead, those sacrifices actually reminded them of their sins year after year. *For it is not possible for the blood of bulls and goats to take away sins.* That is why, when Christ came into the world, he said to God, "You did not want animal sacrifices or sin offerings. But you have given me a body to offer. You were not pleased with burnt offerings or other offerings for sin. Then I said, 'Look, I have come to do your will, O God— as is written about me in the Scriptures.'" *First, Christ said, "You did not want animal sacrifices or sin offerings or burnt offerings or other offerings for sin, nor were you pleased with them"* (though they are required by the law of Moses). *Then he said, "Look, I have come to do your will." He cancels the first covenant in order to put the second into effect.* For God's will was for us to be made holy by the sacrifice of the body of Jesus Christ, once and for all. Under the old covenant, the priest would stand and minister before the altar day after day, offering the same sacrifices again and again, which could never take away the sins. But our High Priest offered himself to God as a single sacrifice for sins, good for all time. Then he sat down in the place of honor at God's right hand. There he waits until his enemies are humbled and made a footstool under his feet. *For by that one offering he forever made perfect those who are being made holy.* And the Holy Spirit also testifies that this is so. For he says, "This is the new covenant I will make with my people on that day, says the Lord: I will put my laws in their hearts, and I will write them on their minds." Then he says, "I will never again remember their sins and lawless deeds." *And when sins have been forgiven, there is no need to offer any more sacrifices*. And so, dear brothers and sisters, we can boldly enter heaven's Most Holy Place because of the blood of Jesus. By his death, Jesus opened a new and life-giving way through the curtain into the Most Holy Place. And since we have a great High Priest who rules over God's house, let us go right into the presence of God with sincere hearts fully trusting him. For our guilty consciences have been sprinkled with Christ's blood to make us clean, and our bodies have been washed with pure water. Let us hold tightly without wavering to the hope we affirm, for God can be trusted to keep his promise. (Hebrews 10:1–23 NLT; italics added)

"To Jesus the mediator of the new covenant, and to the blood of sprinkling that speaks better things than that of Abel" (Heb. 12:24).

The blood of Jesus speaks better things than the blood of Abel. Remember Cain and Abel? Cain killed Abel, and God said to Cain that Abel's blood was crying out to God from the ground (Gen. 4:10). Do you now see the difference? One sacrifice covered sin, and the other took away sin and guilt. One sacrifice cried MERCY, and the other cried GRACE! The blood of Jesus Christ intercedes for us continually. I do not know what the blood of Abel spoke to God about, but I know this much: it was neither mercy nor grace, because Cain didn't receive either. Abel was ambushed for obeying God; he never gave his life willingly, and so his blood must have cried for help or vengeance! Abel's blood was not sacrificed; it was stolen from him. People fight with thieves; they don't let them get away easily, and we see here Cain never got away easily either, even though he thought he had. There is life in the blood and every blood speaks to God. We see God getting angry in response to Abel's blood, and He started cursing.

"So now you are cursed from the earth, which has opened its mouth to receive your brother's blood from your hand. When you till the ground, it shall no longer yield its strength to you. A fugitive and a vagabond you shall be on the earth" (Gen. 4:11–12).

On the contrary, Jesus gave His life as a willing and pleasing sacrifice. No one ambushed Him.

He says in John 10:11, "I am the good shepherd. The good shepherd gives His life for the sheep."

God was very pleased with this sacrifice. The sacrifice that re-births humanity. It is the sacrifice that creates all over again. That is why it says…

"Therefore if anyone is in Christ he is a new creation, old things have passed away, behold, all things have become new" (2 Cor.5:17).

It is like beginning Eden all over again with Jesus as the second Adam. That is why the blessings came with Jesus and curses began with Adam. If you are still born of Adam, you have no dominion or power over anything that God has promised. You are still in bondage. If you are born again, you are entitled to all the dominion that Christ paid for. Children of God, stop settling for less, claim your glory and dominion back from the enemy in the name of Jesus.

"Therefore My Father loves Me, because I lay down My life that I may take it again. No one takes it from Me, but I lay it down of Myself. I have power to lay it down, and I have power to take it again. This command I have received from My Father" (John 10:17–18).

Jesus did it all out of love of His Father and of us. "If you keep My commandments, you will abide in My love, just as I have kept My Father's commandments and abide in His love" (John 15:10).

In other instances that reveal Jesus as a willing sacrificial Lamb, the prophet Isaiah said, "He was oppressed and He was afflicted, Yet He opened not His mouth; He was led as a lamb to the slaughter, And as a sheep before its shearers is silent, So He opened not His mouth" (Isa. 53:7).

Like a lamb to the slaughter, He spoke not a word. He never fought with those who came to hurt and kill Him. He had come for this very reason. Abel was not a lamb. He must have fought for his life, but Jesus knew that sacrificing His life was His Father's will.

> Yet it pleased Yahweh to bruise him. He has caused him to suffer. When you make his soul an offering for sin, he will see his offspring. He will prolong his days, and Yahweh's pleasure will prosper in his hand. After the suffering of his soul, he will see the light and be satisfied. My righteous servant will justify many by the knowledge of himself; and he will bear their iniquities. Therefore will I give him a portion with the great, and he will divide the plunder with the strong; because he poured out his soul to death, and was numbered with the transgressors; yet he bore the sin of many, and made intercession for the transgressors. (Isa. 53:10–12 WEB)

"For all the fullness was pleased to dwell in him; and through him to reconcile all things to himself, by him, whether things on the earth, or things in the heavens, having made peace through the blood of his cross." (Col. 1:19–20 WEB).

We see this fact demonstrated when the soldiers came for Jesus. His disciples pulled their swords, and Peter cut off one of the soldier's ears. Jesus stopped his disciples from fighting His enemies and then said to His enemies that He could easily call on His dad, who would give Him more than twelve legions of angels to wage war for Him.

"Or do you think that I cannot now pray to My Father, and He will provide Me with more than twelve legions of angels?" Matthew 26:53

In other words, He was letting them know that they had no power over Him, and that what was happening was all as planned. He was a willing sacrifice who would restore us back to God. His Kingdom was far greater, more powerful, and not of this world. He did not call on His Kingdom to fight in His place because if He did, then the scriptures would not have been fulfilled. The script written about Jesus would be messed up and would make God a liar and as a result, humanity would be destroyed forever. His GGT would be aborted because, the scriptures that say He should suffer also say that after the suffering He will be given the name that is above every other name.

Giving His life to us was His Father's will and Christ embraced it. When Jesus prayed in the garden of Gethsemane, He was in so much agony that His blood vessels burst, and He sweat blood, asking His Father to take the cup of suffering away from Him, yet He asked not His will but the will of the Father be done. If the Father took away the cup of suffering or that part of the script, He would have lied to so many generations, and the scripture that says He honors His Word over His name would be a lie. This would have allowed the enemy to win over humanity forever.

"For assuredly, I say to you that many prophets and righteous men desired to see what you see, and did not see it, and to hear what you hear, and did not hear it" (Matt. 13:17).

"Your father Abraham rejoiced to see My day, and he saw it and was glad" (John 8:56).

Therefore, if any part of scripture were removed, it would make God a liar. He would be worse than the devil, who is a liar and the father of lies because the devil lives up to his name and fame faithfully. Not only that, the scriptures that speak of the prize Jesus would receive would be removed, too, because only winners get the prize. Only those who run and finish the race in first place get the greatest prize.

"Do you not know that in a race all the runners run [their very best to win], but only one receives the prize? Run [your race] in such a way that you may seize the prize *and* make it yours!" (1 Cor. 9:24 AMP)

The prize for Christ was spoken of by the prophet Isaiah in Isaiah 53:12 and Philippians 2:5–11

Simply put, yes, the blood of Abel was not voluntary, so it cried for HELP! The blood of animals was not voluntary, either. The animals never wanted to die, but they had to.

Animals are lower in ranking than people, and so their blood cried for MERCY! Mercy is given to someone lower in rank than another, as a servant receives mercy from his master. Animal blood covered sin but couldn't take away sin. It is like owing someone $1000 and then paying back $10 and asking the person to forgive the debt because you could not pay the whole debt. You did not have enough to clear the debt, so you are always in debt to the one you owe and are under his or her mercy. The blood of Jesus was the only voluntary sacrifice for us that cried GRACE! Jesus Christ was higher in ranking than the fallen person, and so sacrificing His life was like us owing $1000, and paying back $999,000,000,000,000,000,000 and more. This not only clears the debt we owed, but it also pays FOREVER for anything we will ever owe! It gives us the power to rule over all our former creditors, and now they owe us. This is called GRACE which is God's power!

Sin has no more power over us. We do not owe the enemy anything. Instead, he owes us more than he can ever pay. He is at our mercy now and can never make us his slaves again as long as we are in Christ. This is the POWER we have in the blood of Jesus! The blood of Christ takes away all our sin, justifies us (just as if we never sinned), and clothes us with the righteousness of God. We no longer walk naked, the glory is restored, and now we are back to sitting on the throne with God Himself! This same blood does not stop there, but it continually speaks and intercedes for us. It does not cry HELP! It does not cry MERCY! It cries and continually speaks GRACE unto God for you and me if we are in Christ.

Grace is given to someone with the same standing as the other. Grace restores us back to the initial glory we had with the Father at creation when we named animals with Him as He created them. We were God's partner in creation. Grace gives us back our dominion and power over all and restores our relationship as children of God, co-heirs with Christ.

Thus the scripture that says that the blood of Jesus speaks better things than the blood of Abel in Hebrews 12:24. Another says, behold the Lamb of God, Jesus Christ, who takes away the sins of the world (John 1:29).

Prayer:

Thank You Father, for the perfect plan of salvation. Thank You Holy Spirit, for Your help in executing it. Thank You Jesus, for Your willingness to come down from Your throne and humble Yourself from Creator to the created to identify with us. Thank You for yielding to the Father and to the counsel of the Holy Spirit, for being faithful even unto death, death on the cross, to take our sin away by willingly shedding Your blood for us. We sprinkle this blood of Jesus in our lives today in Jesus's name. Amen!

Grace in the blood of Jesus gives us the same standing with God, it restores the glory we once had with the Father. It gives us back the dominion we once lost to sin and allows us to rule and reign with Christ.

Mercy was found in the Garden of Eden and in the Law of Moses. The blood of animals cried mercy, and that is why there was the mercy seat in the holy of holies. Grace came only with Jesus Christ! Are you under mercy or under grace?

Why the blood? Because life is in the blood. That is why the blood, not the mouth, speaks grace to God. No one can stand and sweet-talk God and plead his or her case for salvation, forgiveness, and life because life is not in your mouth or the eloquence of your words, but in the blood. That is why we stand before God only in Jesus's name, for He was the sacrifice for all humanity, and His blood is speaking grace for those who receive Him. If you come to God in your name or any other name, you will die. For there is no other name under heaven given to us by which we must be saved but the name of Jesus! (Acts 4:12)

Remember when Adam and Eve sinned? Who atoned for their sin? They tried to justify themselves with their mouths and made covering of their nakedness of sin with leaves. Justification of sin by mouth is like covering your nakedness with leaves. The leaves will dry out, fall off, and expose your nakedness. The leaves have no life in them when separated from the tree. The leaves cannot compare to people; they have no blood.

By Adam and Eve making a covering out of leaves, they were telling God that they were not even worth being human, but they were lower in ranking than the leaves on the tree. This was what the enemy lied to them. Satan stripped their value and self-esteem from them because of the sin they committed. Sin will cause guilt and shame and low value or self-worth. This mind-set was insulting to God, who created them in His image and likeness; it was a slave mentality. I believe that was why Cain's sacrifice was not accepted, because there was no life in his sacrifice, because life was in the blood and not in the leaves or vegetables. He should have bought a lamb with his produce from his brother so that he can give God an acceptable sacrifice to atone for his sin. He repeated the same mistake his parents did, using leaves for cover instead of animal sacrifice. He knew better and that is why God said to him if he did the right thing he would be accepted. His baby brother Abel did the right thing and Cain was jealous.

> And in the course of time Cain brought to the Lord an offering of the fruit of the ground. But Abel brought [an offering of] the [finest] firstborn of his flock and the fat portions. And the Lord had respect (regard) for Abel and for his offering; but for Cain and his offering He had no respect. So Cain became extremely angry (indignant), and he looked annoyed *and* hostile. And the Lord said to Cain, "Why are you so angry? And why do you look annoyed? If you do well [believing Me and doing what is acceptable and pleasing to Me], will you not be accepted? And if you do not do well [but ignore My instruction], sin crouches at

your door; its desire is for you [to overpower you], but you must master it." (Genesis 4:3-7 (AMP))

Our good works can never save us apart from the blood of Jesus. Remember the scriptures says that the payment for sin is death, but the gift of God is eternal life through Jesus Christ His Son. There was no death until sin came into the picture. Sacrifices and death came after sin.

God the Father made the *first* sacrifice ever out of His agape love for us, or else He could have killed humans right there in the garden. God had to kill an animal to cover Adam and Eve's nakedness from sin with the animal's skin, which was a temporary regimen. This opened the Old Testament sacrifices.

Out of God's agape love again, He made the *final* sacrifice for us. He sacrificed His only begotten Son, Jesus Christ, once and for all, and clothed us with the righteousness of Christ, covering our nakedness forever!

God made the first and last sacrifice for humanity. He truly loves us with everything He has—an everlasting love, agape love in action! He gave us all He had. He has nothing to hold back from us. He truly is the Alpha and Omega, beginning and the end.

"He who did not spare [even] His own Son, but gave Him up for us all, how will He not also, along with Him, graciously give us all things?" (Rom. 8:32 AMP)

God's Perfect Plan

Jesus's rebuke to Peter in Matthew 16:23, was not directed to Peter but to Satan, who spoke through Peter: "Jesus turned to Peter and said, 'Get away from me, Satan! You are a dangerous trap to me. You are seeing things merely from a human point of view, not from God's.'"

Here Jesus reveals the enemy's weakness—his sight is limited, and he is not aware nor does he understand the things of God. The devil was cut off from God and so he is never sensitive or in tune with God's plan and ways. If Satan had known, he would have never made Jesus suffer by wounding, bruising and crucifying Him on the cross, because that led to Satan's ultimate defeat and God's ultimate victory forever. The devil never understood how brutal death could lead to victory instead of defeat. That is why he still deceives many people with the same misconception he had.

Jesus revealed to us a very great secret that all Christians must know. Before Jesus died and rose again, when Satan still had dominion, he was a loser because he was blind from God's will. Satan was working against himself, and his central intelligence was very poor. When a kingdom has very poor central intelligence, the kingdom will be overthrown easily. If the United States has a poor CIA, the country is at stake. This was the case in Satan's kingdom. He thought that by killing Jesus he would have dominion over humanity forever; he had no idea that instead he would lose his dominion forever.

The enemy has no more power over those who are in Christ Jesus. He is like a fisherman with a hook and bait on it. The only way he can get you is if you take the bait. He cannot make you take it, but he will entice you. For instance, he will put the bait of offense in his deadly hook and have someone offend you to see if you will take the offense. If you do, then you are in his control, but you can repent and call to Jesus to deliver you from this hook. You will be wounded, because it is a sharp hook. But if you put on the full armor of God, submit all your will and feelings to God and obey His Word, you will be able to resist the devil, and he will flee from you (James 4:7), and the fisherman, the devil, will go home hungry and humiliated as a loser.

Remember, Jesus disarmed him: "He canceled the record of the charges against us and took it away by nailing it to the cross. In this way, he disarmed the spiritual rulers and authorities. He shamed them publicly by his victory over them on the cross" (Col. 2:14–15 NLT).

Someone explained it so well by the following metaphor: The devil is like a mouse with a microphone in a dark room, roaring like a lion, but when you turn on the light (the truth, the Word of God, Jesus Christ), you will only find a little mouse roaring like a lion on a microphone. The devil pretends to have authority over us but in reality he doesn't. People have a free will and can choose whom they will serve, whom they will be loyal to, and who will have authority over them by whomever they chose to obey.

The devil is just like a bad boss who got fired but still sneaks into the office sometimes to exercise his stolen or deceptive authority over those who do not know the truth that he was fired. But those who know the truth have dominion and authority over him to kick him out and expose him to more shame than he had before he was fired. Being fired by his boss, God, was more prestigious to the devil than being fired by the children of his boss, who now own the place he once ruled over. It is humiliating, degrading, and embarrassing to him that the people he once ruled over, those who used to be his subjects and objects of oppression, are now ruling over him with much greater power and authority. That is why he hates us with great passion, and we are at war with him daily because the devil wants to get this dominion back. The Kingdom of heaven suffers violence, but only the violent take it by force.

"And from the days of John the Baptist until now the kingdom of heaven suffers violence, and the violent take it by force" (Matt. 11:12).

The reason why God calls us more than conquerors is because Jesus conquered the enemy, and we now walk in the conquered and finished work of the cross and the power of Christ's Resurrection. The devil has no power or authority over you unless you are ignorant enough to give it to him. People of God perish for lack of KNOWLEDGE. What you are ignorant about will rule over you. If ignorance is no defense on earth, it is no defense in heaven. Just because you do not know the law of the land and you break it, doesn't exempt you from punishment. It is your responsibility to know the rules and laws of the country or kingdom you live in and represent.

The devil is a thief, and his kingdom thrives from ignorant and passive Christians. For him to have dominion, he must come into you, and the only way he can come into you after you accept Christ and are delivered, is through sin. Sin is an open door for him, so he makes sure he is sneaky about it so that you will open doors for him without your knowledge or out of ignorance. Jesus made it clear to us that we have dominion over the enemy when He commissioned His disciples:

"And Jesus came and spoke to them, saying, 'All authority has been given to Me in heaven and on earth. Go therefore and make disciples of all the nations, baptizing them in the name of the Father and of the Son and of the Holy Spirit, teaching them to observe all things that I have commanded you; and lo, I am with you always, even to the end of the age. Amen'" (Matt. 28:18–20).

"And then he told them, 'Go into all the world and preach the Good News to everyone. Anyone who believes and is baptized will be saved. But anyone who refuses to believe will be condemned. These miraculous signs will accompany those who believe: They will cast out demons in my name, and they will speak in new languages. They will be able to handle snakes with safety, and if they drink anything poisonous, it won't hurt them. They will be able to place their hands on the sick, and they will be healed'" (Mark 16:15–18 NLT).

No wonder the devil is angry. In Jesus's name we have the power to expel him and his demons and power to speak in a language he cannot understand, through the Holy Spirit. So he cannot attack our prayers because he does not know what we are saying, and in this language the Holy Spirit, through us, speaks directly to God. We have authority over the cunning snake; now it cannot harm us, and we cannot be cursed or bewitched or poisoned. We have authority over sickness to give it back to the devil so that we and others around us can live free of torment. All the enemy's authority has been stripped and destroyed by Christ. Like the Americans say, "There's a new sheriff in town." The enemy has been overthrown.

In Luke 24:44–49, Jesus told His disciples clearly and plainly as He opened their minds to understand that all He did and all He went through to the time of His ascension, was all written in the plan that

God the Father had laid out. This was revealed to Moses, King David in Psalms, Isaiah, and other prophets. What Jesus was saying to them was that the master planner or the vision bearer had the plan of His life on earth written out, and Jesus had a part to play, a part to act out in the script, and the movie of His life had to be acted out just as the script said.

Before a movie is made, a script is written and acted out. Before Jesus came to fulfill His GGT, a script was written. He calls it a scroll that was written for Him to follow that could not be altered. He played His part so successfully that His dad, the script writer and the producer, stopped in between scenes and applauded Him, and identified Himself with Him, when He said in Matthew 3:17, "And suddenly a voice came from heaven, saying, 'This is My beloved Son, in whom I am well pleased.'" And again in Matthew 17:5: "While he was still speaking, behold, a bright cloud overshadowed them; and suddenly a voice came out of the cloud, saying, 'This is My beloved Son, in whom I am well pleased. Hear Him!'"

Jesus taught His disciples many times and prepared them for His GGT so they would not despair.

"Then Jesus began to tell them that the Son of Man must suffer many terrible things and be rejected by the elders, the leading priests, and the teachers of religious law. He would be killed, but three days later he would rise from the dead" (Mark 8:31 NLT). Luke also reports this in Luke 9:22.

Jesus knew His GGT and what He should do, but it was never by His might or power. It was all done by the Spirit of the most high God, and that is why Jesus NEVER began His ministry before He was baptized and filled with the Holy Spirit. He told His disciples the same thing—not to begin the commission without the Helper, the Holy Spirit.

In the Last Supper, Jesus reveals His GGT again. Read Matthew 26:17–30, Mark 14:12–16, Luke 22:7–13, and John 13–14:7.

Beloved, your God-given task script was written long before the earth existed. Do you know it? Have you read it, and are you performing your God-given task with confidence like Christ? Jesus was rejected, ridiculed, and mocked. They wanted to stone him, yet he did not stop or give up healing their sick and raising their dead. He was ready to be alone if everyone deserted Him for obeying His Father, God. He knew who He was, where He came from, and where He was going, and He was determined to be profitable in God's Kingdom.

What about you? Do you like receiving praise from people over praise from God? Are you as shortsighted as the enemy is? Do you plan for eternity? Or you plan for your retirement on earth only and when you die you will leave others enjoying it while you suffer eternally in hell? Are you, like Christ, investing in the eternal Kingdom, where you came from? Do you understand that you were sent here on earth with and for a purpose? With God, NOTHING JUST HAPPENS! God has a reason for everything. He created you for a reason. Do you know your assignment? Are you offering your body daily for Christ to use to accomplish His work on earth? Do you know you belong to God and you are not of your own? Being a created being, you owe all you are to your creator and believe it or not, Your creator is Jehovah Elohim, The great I AM, Yahweh.

Portrait

> *Our God-given task is part of the God-planned portrait best seen*
> *From heaven...heaven's eye view, through the eyes of God.*

Once I read about an artist and his great work from the internet. (http://www.huffingtonpost.com/2013/10/21/jorge-rodriguez-gerada-girls-portrait-field_n_4136932.html.) *Wish*, in Titanic Belfast, by artist Jorge Rodríguez-Gerada, is a huge and very amazing eleven-acre land-art portrait of a six-year-old anonymous Belfast girl. This project is best seen from a high place, like from a helicopter, with a bird's-eye view. When seen from ground level, nothing of it makes sense. The portrait is nothing but lines of sand and soil, i.e., dirt! With nothing to attract you at all, it seems like a lot of materials have been wasted and a big piece of land has been used carelessly.

At the high point, however, the portrait comes alive, and it is breathtaking! A beautiful sight to behold! It is here where we get to see it through THE EYES OF THE ARTIST. The planning of this project took eighteen months, while its implementation took only one month—a ratio of 18:1. The materials used must have cost a lot and weighed a ton, and there may have been a lot of donations. There was a lot of manpower used to make the project a success and a reality. The artist said in the article, "*Wish* wasn't something that just got presented, it was a process," Rodriguez-Gerada told the Telegraph. "Getting to know the city on multiple trips and letting the creative flow helped bring the image to me of what I wanted to do."

"For *Wish*, Rodriguez-Gerada said he purposefully chose an anonymous child, spotted on a research trip to Belfast this summer." (See article source above)

There was only one master planner who incorporated all the different skills and talents to make his dream a reality. He saw the end from the beginning, even when no one did. He shared his vision with the workers and was with them on the ground, overseeing and working with them. He delegated different duties and made sure the workers were fully equipped to accomplish everything he desired to finish his work to perfection.

The workers never brought their own ideas into play, they never thought of the portrait or the materials, and they never worried about the cost of the project or the funding; all they did was work for the most famous and the greatest artist whom they believed in, and they delivered their services fully.

The artist is the mastermind; he thought of the project, planned it and got land, materials, and workers. He may have spent late nights working on the project and finding resources to make it happen, but the workers did not lose sleep over the project, as they were not the founders of the project. They worked with what the founder gave them to work with, which he supplied for his own project.

The project was not just another piece of art; the artist needed to know more about the city so as to present the city on the portrait. He invested his time, left his home, and went physically to the city. He did not Google the city to know about it on the Internet, in order to present the perfect piece of art that amazed the world! The artist took his time to prepare and get his inspiration for his project and to get the picture, the idea, the details, the land, the manpower, and the training for the crew as necessary for the task. Some people probably wondered why it was taking so long to start the project, but as with anything we know, preparation takes longer than the project itself. There was an appointed time for this project, and when the time was right, the task began and was finished on time.

In the same way, God is our maker and the master planner of our lives and destinies. He thought of our assignment here on earth before He created us. He saw the end from the beginning, and He knows the appointed time for us to start and finish our God-given task. We may not see the whole picture or the end result of this beautiful work of art right now, but as the apostle Paul said, we are a building whose builder is God. The cornerstone is Christ, and all of us have a part in it.

> For we are God's fellow workers. You are God's farming, God's building. According to the grace of God which was given to me, as a wise master builder I laid a foundation, and another builds on it. But let each man be careful how he builds on it. For no one can lay any other foundation than that which has been laid, which is Jesus Christ. But if anyone builds on the foundation with gold, silver, costly stones, wood, hay, or stubble; each man's work will be revealed. For the Day will declare it, because it is revealed in fire; and the fire itself will test what sort of work each man's work is. If any man's work remains which he built on it, he will receive a reward. If any man's work is burned, he will suffer loss, but he himself will be saved, but as through fire. (1 Cor. 3:9–15 WEB)

Jesus Christ is the foundation and cornerstone in God's Kingdom. We have God with us every step of the way providing us with all we need for our GGT, instructing us and coaching us as we build His Kingdom, through His Holy Spirit. We have on the ground with us God the Holy Spirit, whom Jesus spoke about saying, He will teach us ALL things and remind us of what Christ has spoken to us in His Word and in our spirits (John 14:26). He also reveals to us the deep things of God, the secret things so we can accomplish our GGT, which cannot be seen or approved by people from a satellite view. It only looks beautiful from heaven, from God's eye view.

The artist of our lives, our heavenly Father, is at the highest place and He planned out our task from up in heaven, the highest place. He then sent us to Earth with each person's task cut out to fulfill. As much as He has all power and authority, God never forces anyone to do anything; it is voluntary. A slave is someone who has been forced to work, but a free person goes to work out of his or her own free will. If you go to your workplace because you have to, then you are a slave, and it is not work; it is just a job. On the other hand, if you go to work and you feel privileged to get to do what you do, and you can do it without getting paid or without man's approval and still enjoy it, and in it you work as unto God and not man, then you are a free person, and you don't have a job; it is work. God never created jobs, He created work for us to do. Jobs are man-made out of rebellion from doing our GGT. As long as you have a job, you will be unhappy, always struggle and die poor spiritually. The opposite is true of work, you will be fulfilled and when you die, you will live eternally in wealth and prosperity that never ends.

When you find out your God-given task and do it, you will always find joy, because the joy of the LORD will be your strength. Not because you will not face challenges, but because even in the midst of all challenges, you have the full backing of God Himself. When we accept the ultimate sacrifice of Christ on the cross, we in turn give our lives to Him. We become His servants and He becomes our LORD. We accept our assignment even when it involves working in dirt, i.e., the dirt of offenses and ridicule, friends and family forsaking you or betraying you, your spouse abusing or leaving you, being abused and misunderstood by many, or your humility and trust in God being interpreted from the world's point of view as being prideful.

Caleb and Joshua were interpreted as being prideful when they believed in and stood on the promises of God and confessed that they were well able to defeat the giants in the Promised Land. To God, believing and trusting Him fully is perfect humility. However, instead of the Israelites believing and trusting God and taking Him at His Word, they trusted in themselves and in their strength, which was prideful in God's eyes. The Israelites saw Caleb and Joshua as being prideful and careless in their eyes and they reasoned that acting on God's Word would compromise their safety. They forgot that it was God who watched over them in the wilderness, helped them cross the Red Sea while their enemies were in pursuit, destroyed their strong enemies, protected them and led them this far.

But just as the Word of God says that God opposes the proud but gives grace to the humble (Prov. 3:34), God gave Caleb and Joshua the grace to inherit the Promised Land while He opposed the other children of Israel and did not let them inherit the Promised Land. They inherited the wilderness because that was what their own strength, faith and confession could give them, but those who trusted in God got what the strength of God could give them, the Promised Land.

Which side are you on? The proud, according to the world, but humble in God's sight? Or humble in the sight of the world yet prideful in God's sight? Our logic gets in the way and stops us from receiving from God, because God is a faith God and not a sight God. The devil is a sight devil, not a faith devil. Those who live by faith and by every word that comes from the mouth of God will lack no good thing. This is because God loves and cherishes those who fully trust and believe in Him. Without faith it is impossible to please God, and those who come to Him must believe that He exists and that He is a rewarder of those who diligently seek Him (Heb. 11:6). Fight the good fight of faith. God supplies according to His riches in glory (Phil 4:19). If you ask a low income person for financial assistance, you may not get it or if so, very little. But if you ask a billionaire for financial assistance, they may help more than you asked for. That is God. He gives us exceedingly, abundantly, above all we ask of or even imagine (Eph. 3:20).

When Peter, the disciple of Jesus, was in the boat and Jesus was walking on the stormy sea, Peter asked Jesus to call him to Himself so he could walk where everyone was afraid to walk; where it was dangerous and impossible for people to survive. Peter knew he could not do it in his own strength but had to accept his weakness and in humility fully trust in Christ's ability and step out in faith to walk on the water at Christ's word. As the other disciples watched him, they probably thought of him as being prideful and a show-off, but to Christ, Peter was humble enough to trust in Him and His word that invited him to walk on the stormy sea to rule over the storm with Christ, instead of the storm having power to rule over him.

Jesus had the power to calm the storm for Peter to walk on a calm sea, but He did not! He allowed the storm to continue and for it to beat even harder when Peter came out of the boat into the sea, because He wanted to teach Peter and all of us that we have authority over the storm, even the raging storms in our lives. As we walk on them, they do not drown us as long as our eyes and trust are fully on Jesus. Regardless of how strong and how loud the wind is, we have dominion over it! The storm never harmed Peter as long as he had His eyes on Jesus.

Peter began to sink when he got his trust off Jesus and he put it in the storm. He trusted in the storm's ability to destroy him, because he must have had first-hand experience of the harm that a stormy sea can do. Before he met Jesus, Peter was a fisherman by trade and must have witnessed many destructive storms, and he knew the raging storm was a great danger. He had probably seen people lose their lives and properties destroyed; he therefore allowed his experience to take the place of his faith, even though he had another experience where Jesus had calmed the sea when there was a great storm once before. Peter fell back on his familiar territory instead of his new-found faith in Christ, the ruler of the sea!

When Peter sowed the seed of doubt in God and placed his faith in the storm, the storm had dominion over him, and it began to destroy him. But Peter was also quick to realize his sin, the sin of taking his faith from Jesus who would keep him walking on the stormy sea, and placing his faith in the storm, believing in the ability of the storm to drown him. Peter, realizing he had misplaced his faith, cried to Jesus, and Jesus, being merciful, saw that Peter believed that He was his only hope in his fallen state. Jesus took Peter's hand and walked with Peter on the stormy sea and into the boat, and the wind stopped. The wind did this on purpose to scare Peter and to shift his faith from Christ to the storm. In the storm you may be facing, only you can give it power over you, or you can have power over it. The main thing is where you place your faith (Matt. 14:22–33).

When David the shepherd boy said he would kill Goliath by God's grace; his brothers called him prideful and a show-off instead of seeing his humility and trust in God Jehovah to defeat the enemy of God and His people. God worked through him and gave him victory, and through him the whole nation was set free from the enemy. Truly, we see God opposes the proud but gives GRACE to the humble. Because of your humility, nations can be delivered from the enemy's stronghold, be courageous and have faith in God's ability.

Daniel, in Daniel 6, refused to disobey God by refusing to pray to the king. He chose to disobey the king and he was seen as being prideful by people, but in God's eyes he was humble. He obeyed God and trusted fully in His ability to deliver him from the lion's den as he walked blamelessly before God. His faith was in God's ability to deliver him from the starving lions and not on the starving lion's ability to devour him, and God delivered him.

Shadrach, Meshach, and Abednego refused to bow down and worship an idol; they refused to compromise their faith for their life, they valued God more than life itself, and God showed up in the fire and saved them. They had faith in God's ability to save them from the fire and not in the fire's ability to consume them, and God won their battle.

These people's full trust in and fear of God was seen as humility by God from God's view, but the world saw it as rebellion and pride. Their faith in God and not in their situation saved them from destruction.

We should not give up or get weary of doing well because in due season we shall reap if we faint not (Gal. 6:9). Even if the work, our GGT, may be dirty, unappealing, or does not make sense to the world, we, like the workers in the *Wish* portrait, share the same vision as our artist. We know it looks amazing from God's view. We know He is smiling down and being proud of us as He was with His Son Jesus and kept applauding Him in the midst of many who loved Him and opposed Him.

Your GGT may look dirty from the earth's point of view, but it is a sight to behold from heaven's viewpoint. Jesus's death was dirty from here on earth but was a sight to behold from heaven. It was the perfect foundation of the GREATEST masterpiece ever created, A FOUNDATION OF RIGHTEOUSNESS, a reconciliation of God the Father to His long-lost children. God the Father shares with us His vision and the end result through His Holy Spirit and in His Word. We should not worry about where we should get the materials or the funding of our God-given task. Just like the workers in the *Wish* portrait, God the Father provides us with His own materials which He wants on His portrait.

God is wealthy enough to fund His own project. He is responsible for planning and increasing His portrait as He sees fit, and all He requires of us is to follow Christ in obedience to Him. We are to do just as Jesus did. Jesus is our perfect example. He left His home in glory and came to live as a human being with the human race that He created. The ratio of His assignment on earth was 30:3, which is the same as 10:1. For every ten years of preparation, there was one year to accomplish the work. He lived in preparation for thirty years for the task ahead and accomplished the task in three years. Preparation is the key to a successful end. If God's Son had to prepare for thirty years and live doing His assignment for three years, how much more us? We have a level of preparedness that we need to do in our lives to be successful in our God-given task, and without this, we would fail miserably. This implementation of our God-given task, after all the preparation has been made, is called THE APPOINTED TIME.

David was anointed as king when he was a shepherd boy, but he became king after many years of challenges and hardship in his destiny. Yet God was with him, taking him through each challenge and every step of the way, and this made him a great and humble king.

> Jesus answered them, "The time has come for the Son of Man to be glorified. Most certainly I tell you, unless a grain of wheat falls into the earth and dies, it remains by itself alone. But if it dies, it bears much fruit. He who loves his life will lose it. He who hates his life in this world will keep it to eternal life. If anyone serves me, let him follow me. Where I am, there will my servant also be. If anyone serves me, the Father will honor him. (John 12:23–26 WEB)

Jesus knew His part in the piece of art that God had planned out. He was the foundation and cornerstone; without Him, there would not be any portrait. He came to lay the foundation of it so that we would have a place in it. He also knew that it was never for His glory but for the Father's glory.

Without Jesus, the art would not exist. We therefore have a place in it, only in Christ Jesus as the foundation. If one is not in Christ Jesus, born again into God's family by accepting Jesus Christ as his or her LORD and Savior, then he or she has no part in the great art. This story's artist and author is God; He is the author and the finisher of our faith. It is all voluntary. No one "has" to do it; one only "gets" to do it and gets to partner with the Creator of the whole universe, the greatest artist of all and the work of art of all times that never fades but lives forever. This is the largest, most valuable piece of art that everyone in the whole world has a part to play, if they accept to be in Christ Jesus. It is best seen from

God's viewpoint. Remember, the wisdom of God is foolishness to them that are perishing, but unto us, it is eternal life in Christ Jesus. (Read 1 Cor. 1:18–31.)

Our God-given task is therefore only built on one foundation and one solid rock that can never be shaken or destroyed and lasts forever, Jesus Christ, the Son of the living God.

As a nursing-house supervisor, my work is to ensure the smooth running of the hospital, to give beds to patients in the hospital who are waiting for admission, or to the ones in the hospital who need transfers to a different units within and without the hospital. I solve the problems that arise in the hospital and ensure that all units in the hospital are fully staffed with licensed nurses and certified nursing assistants. I deal with the doctors and all other health care providers, housekeeping supervisors, case managers, social workers and management as a whole to ensure proper running of the hospital. This tells you that I see the big picture of the whole hospital while the different units and departments see only their individual units and departments.

When I do staffing, I staff the whole hospital with nurses and nursing assistants, but the individual units only see their unit staffing. When they are short of nurses, I can see the whole picture and decide where I can get a nurse from to go and assist them. When they are worried about this, they must consult with me and trust that I can help them to supply them with their needs for patient care. Sometimes I will close off rooms because of staffing needs, and before I do, I ask the units to call in extra nurses because I see the need for nurses in different units. Some charge nurses confidently say that they are OK in their units and do not need to call in nurses, but I let them know that I need nurses in other units. I also anticipate any call offs. Their vision is only limited to their unit staffing, but I have the big picture of what the whole hospital needs.

In the same way, the president takes care of the whole country, the senators and governors take care of the state and we take care of our own homes etc. The president sees the bigger picture, while we see the limited picture of our homes and neighborhoods. Likewise, God sees the whole world and our destinies and knows how to fix everything that concerns us. He will use people you never thought of or have never seen to fund His Kingdom. When we stop trusting in people and we consistently put all our trust in God, we will prosper in our God-given assignment. We must take off all the boundaries and limits we place on God and allow God to be God. Many times people have asked me how certain things happen in my life to my favor which is uncommon. They think it is because of someone I know in authority, and they are right. I do know someone in authority in heaven and earth and that is JESUS CHRIST! He knows everyone and He is the one who gives me favor before kings and others in authority. He gives me favor and influence for His glory, not mine. I love my Jesus!

CHAPTER 14

Whom Do You Live For?

And He died for all, that those who live
should no longer live for themselves
But for Him who died for them and was raised again.

THE GREATEST GIFT GIVEN TO us is the gift of everlasting life through Jesus Christ our Lord (John 3:16). God defeated sin and death through His Son Jesus Christ. He became sin who knew no sin that we may become His righteousness. They stripped off Jesus's robe of righteousness and clothed Him with shame and ridicule; they did to Him what one would do to a sinner. They condemned Him to die for what He did not do. They, through their eyes, judged their own Creator and didn't even know it! Their maker and life giver lived among them and came to give them eternal life, much more than they had known and what they did not deserve. He came to take back from the enemy what he had stolen from God's creation—power, dominion, authority over all creation, and direct fellowship with God—yet they perceived Him as their enemy. They, on the contrary, treated their enemy as their friend.

People were so blinded by the enemy and so accustomed to the enemy's way of life that they chose a thief who killed their loved ones, stole from them, and destroyed them and their property. They released Barnabas, who represented the devil and who was a murderer and a thief, and chose to destroy Jesus Christ, their life giver. They gladly chose death rather than life. Many people still do this today; they choose death rather than life. It is sad when one has to convince someone to choose Jesus rather than the devil. It is a no-brainer, but the Bible makes it clear that the prince of this world, the devil, has blinded them.

> Therefore, since God in his mercy has given us this new way, we never give up. We reject all shameful deeds and underhanded methods. We don't try to trick anyone or distort the word of God. We tell the truth before God, and all who are honest know this. If the Good News we preach is hidden behind a veil, it is hidden only from people who are perishing. Satan, who is the god of this world, has blinded the minds of those who don't believe. They are unable to see the glorious light of the Good News. They don't understand this message about the glory of Christ, who is the exact likeness of God. (2 Cor. 4:1–4 NLT)

One day I had taken a vacation and upon returning to work, the first thing I noticed when I entered the hospital unit was a strong, foul smell! I had never noticed the smell of the hospital while I worked day in and day out; it was normal for me. The mixture of all the smells was an awful stench that hurt my stomach, and I wanted to go back home. I wondered how I would make it through twelve hours. I called my husband and told him about it.

He said that is so much like life. When you are in a bad situation—for example, you are in debt or even living in sin—you get used to it, and it is part of your life. But when you get out of the situation awhile—you get out of debt or live in righteousness and taste the rewards thereof—you realize the filth and stench you had lived in and how much bondage you were in, that you would not want to get back into that lifestyle.

If a blind person got a new set of eyes, he or she would realize the deep darkness he or she had been living in, but until then, that person has no problem being blind because there has been no light to compare with the darkness. He or she does not know light. On the contrary, someone born with perfect eyesight, who then goes blind, would know darkness darker than the person born blind. That person would be more depressed, because he or she now knows both light and darkness.

Think about it—the first thing we do when we get into a dark room is look for the light switch! When the lights go out we look for flash lights, candles or some other light because no one enjoys living in darkness. Christ came to rescue us from the darkness in our spirits. We had been created in the light but Adam traded in our light for darkness. Jesus came to undo this by giving the darkness back to the devil and restoring our light which we had lost, that we may live forever as children of the light!

"If we are out of our minds, it is for God. If we have our right minds, it is for you. [For] The love of Christ controls [compels; drives] us, because we know [are convinced; have concluded] that One died for all, so all have died [we died spiritually with Christ, the penalty for our sins]. *Christ died for all so that those who live would ·not continue to [no longer] live for themselves, but for him who died for them and was raised from the dead.*" (2 Cor. 5:13–15 Expanded Bible (EXB); italics added).

As children of the light, we must lose our minds for the mind of Christ. We must not be conformed to this world, but we must be transformed by the renewal of our mind, and only with this renewed mind can we know what is the good and perfect will of God. Rom. 12:1–2.

Benefits of Living and Working for God

Reward for Good Works

> Be dressed for service and keep your lamps burning, as though you were waiting for your master to return from the wedding feast. Then you will be ready to open the door and let him in the moment he arrives and knocks. The servants who are ready and waiting for his return will be rewarded. I tell you the truth, he

himself will seat them, put on an apron, and serve them as they sit and eat! He may come in the middle of the night or just before dawn. But whenever he comes, he will reward the servants who are ready. Understand this: If a homeowner knew exactly when a burglar was coming, he would not permit his house to be broken into. You also must be ready all the time, for the Son of Man will come when least expected. (Luke 12:35–40 NLT)

Reward awaits those who do and finish their God-given task.

Revelation 22:12, "And behold, I am coming quickly, and My reward is with Me, to give to every one according to his work."

Jesus was no exception to the rules; He had to finish His God-given task to receive His full reward. Here is what He prayed:
"I brought glory to you here on earth by completing the work you gave me to do. Now, Father, bring me into the glory we shared before the world began" (John 17:4–5).

Paul, the apostle, wrote to Timothy as he was close to the end of his life and said:

> But you be sober in all things, suffer hardship, do the work of an evangelist, and fulfill your ministry. For I am already being offered, and the time of my departure has come. I have fought the good fight. I have finished the course. I have kept the faith. From now on, there is stored up for me the crown of righteousness, which the Lord, the righteous judge, will give to me on that day; and not to me only, but also to all those who have loved his appearing. (2 Tim. 4:5–8 WEB)

Paul also teaches us, saying that we ought to fight and run this race in order to win the prize.

"Don't you know that those who run in a race all run, but one receives the prize? Run like that, that you may win. Every man who strives in the games exercises self-control in all things. Now they do it to receive a corruptible crown, but we an incorruptible. I therefore run like that, as not uncertainly. I fight like that, as not beating the air, but I beat my body and bring it into submission, lest by any means, after I have preached to others, I myself should be rejected." (1 Cor. 9:24–27 WEB).

For the joy set before Him, Christ endured the cross.

"Therefore let us also, seeing we are surrounded by so great a cloud of witnesses, lay aside every weight and the sin which so easily entangles us, and let us run with patience the race that is set before us, looking to Jesus, the author and perfecter of faith, who for the joy that was set before him endured the cross, despising its shame, and has sat down at the right hand of the throne of God." (Heb. 12:1–2 WEB).

"For our light affliction, which is for the moment, works for us more and more exceedingly an eternal weight of glory; while we don't look at the things which are seen, but at the things which are not seen. For the things which are seen are temporal, but the things which are not seen are eternal." (2 Cor. 4:17–18 WEB).

God Fights for His Workers

When you work for God, He will protect you and fight those who fight you like Jesus did for the woman with the alabaster box. In Mark 14:3–9, Jesus knows when we do a good work for Him even if the world despises us. There will always be an excuse as to why we should not do the good work unto God but instead do good works unto people. The disciples knew the reward from God is far better and more significant than the reward from people. It is better to be wise in God's eyes than in the world's eyes. The wisdom of God is foolishness to them who are perishing, but unto God's children, His wisdom is eternal life (1 Cor. 1:18). Men and women, boys and girls, both young and old, we need to arise against all odds and decide to live like Jesus lived regardless of what people may think or say of us

The Bible tells us in John 2:24–25, "But Jesus did not commit Himself to them, because He knew all men, and had no need that anyone should testify of man, for He knew what was in man."

> Then six days before the Passover, Jesus came to Bethany, where Lazarus was, who had been dead, whom he raised from the dead. So they made him a supper there. Martha served, but Lazarus was one of those who sat at the table with him. Mary, therefore, took a pound of ointment of pure nard, very precious, and anointed the feet of Jesus, and wiped his feet with her hair. The house was filled with the fragrance of the ointment. Then Judas Iscariot, Simon's son, one of his disciples, who would betray him, said, "Why wasn't this ointment sold for three hundred denarii, and given to the poor?" Now he said this, not because he cared for the poor, but because he was a thief, and having the money box, used to steal what was put into it. But Jesus said, "Leave her alone. She has kept this for the day of my burial. For you always have the poor with you, but you don't always have me."." (John 12:1-8 WEB)

The disciple who rebuked the woman for breaking her alabaster box and pouring very expensive perfume on Jesus wanted the perfume sold so he can have more to steal. He did not value Christ. He was not sensitive to the things of the spirit but was sensitive to things of the flesh. The woman who walked in obedience to God was not even one of the twelve disciples. This goes to tell you that you do not have to be a preacher ordained by people or with a registered ministry to do a good WORK for God. Even the ones who are called fall short sometimes; to work for God means to obey God against all odds.

In the Jewish culture back then, the men dominated the women, and this was a very intimidating situation this woman found herself in.

She knew that women were not to speak in church but to be quiet. This woman had an idea of the ridicule she would face because she lived in this culture, yet she chose the ridicule of people over their praise. She chose to worship God with all she had, which was very costly worship, and others were jealous of her. Her actions were directed unto God, not people. She knew God's reward counted for much more than people's ridicule. She must have known the scripture in Romans 8:31 that said, "If God is for us, who can be against us?" She must have heard Jesus say in Matthew 10:28, "Do not to fear those who kill the body but cannot kill the soul." She also must have read Psalm 118:6: "The Lord is on my side; I will not fear. What can man do to me?" and Psalm 56:11 "In God I have put my trust; I will not be afraid. What can man do to me?"

This woman was Mary, Martha and Lazarus's sister. Remember Jesus, in Luke 10:38–42, went to Martha's house upon her invitation. Martha invited Jesus, but her sister Mary sat at Jesus's feet, and the Bible says that Mary heard His Word. Martha, on the other hand, went to prepare food and do a lot of work to entertain her guests and thought she was doing a good work for God, but Mary, sitting and listening to Jesus speak, was the one doing what God required her to do. To the world, Martha looked like she was doing a good work for God and Mary was lazing around.

This brings us to the next point we will see in our discussion of God's view vs people's or the world's view. Martha was so offended by Mary's behavior that she went to her Creator, Jesus, to report her. I'm assuming Martha hinted to Mary that she needed help, but Mary was too involved with listening to Jesus, sitting at His feet, taking in His counsel, and knowing Him that her ear was closed to all other voices around her. She was so consumed with knowing this God and learning His ways. She was spiritually right but physically wrong; Martha was physically right but spiritually wrong. Friendliness with the world is enmity with God, and friendliness with God is enmity with the world.

Martha got the response that she did not expect because she was blinded by the cares of this world. If she knew Jesus, she would have known like Mary did what He valued most. Eating and drinking was never a priority for Him, and He made this clear to His disciples when He was with the Samaritan woman at the well (John 4:31–34). When His disciples urged Him to eat, "But He said to them, "I have food to eat of which you do not know." Therefore the disciples said to one another, "Has anyone brought Him *anything* to eat?" Jesus said to them, *"My food is to do the will of Him who sent Me, and to finish His work."* (John 4:32-34; italics added).

Jesus knew and quoted Deuteronomy 8:3 in Matthew 4:4, saying, "Man shall not live by bread alone, but by every word that proceeds from the mouth of God."

Mary seemed to have known what God desired. She wanted to hear the words that proceeded from the mouth of God because she knew she could live on these rather than on all the delicacies in the world. Martha asked, "Lord, do you not care that my sister has left me to serve alone? Therefore tell her to help me." Jesus confirmed that Mary knew what God desired when He answered Martha, saying, *"Martha, Martha, you are worried and troubled about many things. But one thing is needed, and Mary has chosen that good part which will not be taken away from her"* (Luke 10:41–42; italics added).

This treasure that Mary found led her to intimacy with Christ so that she felt His need and ministered to Him at the right time regardless of what the crowd thought. She was sensitive and right on in the spirit about preparing Christ for burial. Although she knew the poor needed to be helped, too, God's desire and will came first. It was the right work to do, and since she was sensitive to want to know God and His will, God included her in His great work of salvation. Do you feel God's need to be loved and ministered to or are you too preoccupied with earthly things?

Even Jesus's own mother or brothers were not right on when it came to this. It took one who sat at the feet of Jesus to learn from Him and to do His will. It was not enough to share the same womb with Jesus or to carry Him in your womb, Jesus values obedience over these. Look at this incident,

"Someone told Jesus, "Your mother and your brothers are standing outside, and they want to see you." Jesus replied, "My mother and my brothers are all those who hear God's word and obey it."" (Luke 8:20-21 NLT)

About Mary, Jesus said in His Word, that whenever the Gospel is preached in the whole world, Mary's works will be told as a memorial to her (Matt. 26:6–13, Mark 14:3–9). She got rewarded here on earth, and in the life to come, she has a reward for participating in the perfect plan of redemption. She prepared God's only son for burial, which was beautiful in His sight and in the Father's sight. In these two circumstances, Mary did not have to fight or answer to anyone who accused or attacked her. Jesus fought for her, gave her the victory, and glorified her name before people.

God fights for His workers and rewards them handsomely if they do it unto Him and not unto people, allowing Him to fight their battles. Anyone who attacks God's workers attack Him directly, and that is why He steps in and fights. John also reveals to us that the disciple who betrayed Jesus was Mary's accuser and attacker. He had gone to the extent of valuing the perfume at three hundred denarii to be given to the poor, not because he cared for the poor, but because he was a thief and had the money box; he used to take what was put in it. He was a thief in God's Kingdom. He was so much a slave to money that he betrayed Jesus for thirty pieces of silver.

Remember when Jesus confronted Saul on his way to Damascus to persecute Christians? Jesus did not ask Saul why he was persecuting His followers or His people. Jesus was very clear in His statement because He was the one living in and through them. Therefore when Saul persecuted Christians, he persecuted Christ in them because if they did not have Christ, he would not persecute them.

"Then he fell to the ground, and heard a voice saying to him, "*Saul, Saul, why are you persecuting Me?*" And he said, "Who are You, Lord?" Then the Lord said, "I am Jesus, whom you are persecuting. It *is* hard for you to kick against the goads."" (Acts 9:4–5; italics added)

Kicking against the goads was an expression used in the past that referred to someone being stubborn and rebellious only to their own hurt or disadvantage. When the ox kicked against the goads, it only hurt itself more. The ox goad is a long stick that has a pointed piece of iron tied to one end. The master used this to guide the ox to plow in the desired direction, but when a stubborn ox attempted to rebel and kicked back against the goad, the ox would cause more pain to itself, driving the pointed end deeper into its flesh.

When people fight against Christians, they are fighting Christ Himself. It will only hurt them.

"For many are called, but few are chosen."
Matthew 22:14

God has invited all of us to His great work of building His Kingdom. Initially, only the Jews were given the invitation, but since they refused and made light of the invitation, God sent His servants. One of them was Paul, the one who was converted from persecuting Christians whose persecuting name was Saul but was renamed Paul after he became a Christian. He was sent to the Gentiles to invite them to the wedding feast because the children whom the feast was prepared, the Jews, refused to come. According to the parable that Jesus gave in Matthew 22, the ones for whom the feast was prepared refused the invitation, and "they made light of it and went their ways, one to his own farm, another to his business. And the rest seized his servants, treated them spitefully, and killed them."(Matthew 22:5-6)

To all who accept Christ's invitation and Lordship, He restores to them the glory we once lost when we sinned as romans 3:23 says "for all have sinned and fall short of the glory of God"

What is glory? In the English sense, as the *Merriam-Webster Dictionary* states, *glory* is public praise, honor, and fame. In Hebrew, glory is *kavod*, meaning heavy battle armaments, heavy weapons and defense in battle, unbeatable power and victory beyond human comprehension, supernatural victory in battle. We grow from glory to glory; that is God's way to promote us in ranking in the spirit. Just as you would be more intimidated by the strength and might of a grown lion than you would be by a little lion cub, the enemy is intimidated and defeated by high-ranking children of God.

Demons would cry out, submit to and worship Jesus because His glory or ranking was very high. Other apostles like Paul experienced this too.

> "One day we were going to the meeting place where people talked with God. We met a girl who had a bad spirit. She used to tell people what was going to happen. Her master received much money when she did this. This girl kept on following Paul and us. She was shouting, 'These men are servants of the High God. They are telling us how to be saved.' She did this for many days. This troubled Paul. He turned and said to the spirit in her, 'In the name of Jesus Christ, I say to you, come out of her!' And the spirit came out at once" (Acts 16:16–18 WE).

A security guard without a gun is not as intimidating to any bad person as a police officer with a loaded gun. A county police officer is not as intimidating as a state patrol. A state patrol is not as intimidating as the next high-ranking officer, and so on. The higher you go in rank, the tougher the training, the stricter the discipline, and the fewer the people in that rank. They get to deal with very high-intelligence assignments, which are done with so much skill and discretion that the enemy gets caught unaware, just like Christ caught the enemy of our souls unaware.

"However, we speak wisdom among those who are mature, yet not the wisdom of this age, nor of the rulers of this age, who are coming to nothing. *But we speak the wisdom of God in a mystery, the hidden wisdom which God ordained before the ages for our glory, which none of the rulers of this age knew; for had they known, they would not have crucified the Lord of glory"* (1 Cor. 2:6–8; italics added).

> To me, who am less than the least of all the saints, this grace was given, that I should preach among the Gentiles the unsearchable riches of Christ, and to make all see what is the fellowship of the mystery, which from the beginning of the ages has been hidden in God who created all things through Jesus Christ; *to the intent that now the manifold wisdom of God might be made known by the church to the principalities and powers in the heavenly places, according to the eternal purpose which He accomplished in Christ Jesus our Lord,* in whom we have boldness and access with confidence through faith in Him. (Eph. 3:8–12; italics added)

"But You, O Lord, are a shield for me, My glory and the One who lifts up my head" (Ps. 3:3).

God is our glory, our shield, our victory, and the lifter up of our heads; He gives us victory so we walk unashamed. Without His glory, we walk with our heads bowed in shame like we used to, before we accepted Jesus Christ as our Lord and Savior. He is our LORD when we give our all to Him in exchange for all of Him in us.

After Adam and Eve lost their glory, which was their defense, they immediately ran to hide because they were now in danger of being captured as slaves. They sold out the entire Kingdom because they disobeyed God. They believed the lie that Lucifer told; he magnified what they did not have and diminished the great wealth they had. He did this with his words. He pulled his great three temptations on the first day he tempted people; he did the same with Christ, who is the second Adam. He messed with their identity and then their material wealth, and then he made them worship him in disobedience. Know confidently who you are in Christ!

CHAPTER 15
The Enemy

The enemy comes to kill, steal, and destroy

IN OUR GGT WE HAVE an active enemy, the devil, who is determined to detour us from our assignment. He makes sure that most of us have our priorities all wrong which makes us too busy for our GGT. Your GGT is meant to build God's Kingdom and destroy Satan's kingdom that is why he never sleeps until he makes sure you are busy doing everything but your GGT. In the end this will bring you condemnation when you go back to God the Father to give account of all you have done with your GGT. Let us look at how he does this.

1. The devil plants doubt of God's word, magnifies the negative, and diminishes the positive.

"Has God indeed said, 'You shall not eat of every tree of the garden'? (Gen. 3:1)

The woman, Eve, knew the Word of God, His commands! She responded, 'God has said, "We may eat the fruit of the trees of the garden; but of the fruit of the tree which is in the midst of the garden, God has said, "You shall not eat it, nor shall you touch it, lest you die."'" (Gen. 3:2-3)

The devil magnified what they did not have and diminished what they had, even though what they had was so much more than what they didn't have; thousands of trees compared to one tree. The command from God was for their own good. They had access to the tree of life, where they would live forever like God, yet they chose to eat from the forbidden tree of knowledge of good and evil, which brought about death. God's command was for their good if they obeyed it. His commands lead to life, but the wages of sin is death.

"I don't speak on my own authority. The Father who sent me has commanded me what to say and how to say it. *And I know his commands lead to eternal life*; so I say whatever the Father tells me to say" (John 12:49–50 NLT; italics).

Don't let the enemy speak to your mind and magnify what you do not have to get your GGT done, rather look at what you can do now to get started with your GGT. Prayer, fasting and writing down what God has said to you is very important. Ask yourself 'what can I do now to get this assignment going?' Stop waiting for finances or till you get more time. These are some of the things the enemy will tell you so that you push your GGT to the side and get busy making a living instead of living the making. Start eating right and exercising, because your health determines whether you will get your GGT done or you will spend all your time and money on health issues. If you lack discipline and self-control in your daily life, it will reflect in your spiritual life. I noticed that if the devil does not get you to sin against God in any other way, he will get you to sin against God's temple by putting junk in it, because there is no man made law about it.

How many overweight Christians do you know? I used to be one of them until the Holy Spirit revealed this to me. Our bodies are not ours, but God's. He will be very limited with what He can do with a sick body due to poor choices and habits. Faith without works is dead, so you cannot live carelessly and expect God to step in and heal you so you can continue to abuse His temple. How much junk do you buy to put in your house? We buy the best furniture and spend money cleaning our homes, yards and cars, yet the house of the spirit is neglected. Let us resolve to build God's temple, our bodies and maintain them for His use and glory. Always incorporate the big three when you do this; prayer, eating right and exercise daily. 'Ask yourself in every situation, what would Jesus do?'

2. The devil contradicts God's Word.

Gen 3:4 "You will not surely die. For God knows that in the day you eat of it your eyes will be opened, and you will be like God, knowing good and evil."

The devil, being the father of lies, lied to Eve and twisted the truth. The truth was that it was the tree of knowledge of good and evil. The lie was that they would not die. The devil knew that they would have this knowledge of good and evil and they would die because of their disobedience.

3. The devil made Eve doubt her identity and made empty promises so that they would worship him.

"Your eyes will be opened, and you will be like God, knowing good and evil." (Gen 3:5)

Their eyes were already opened to see what God wanted them to see for their own good. They were already made in the image and likeness of God in Gen. 1:26–28.

Not only did God create Adam and Eve in His own image and likeness, He also gave them dominion over all creation. They were made as gods on earth. Guess who always wanted to be like God but was demoted instead? You are right! Satan. Then Satan saw God forming a human being out of the cheapest material ever—dust—and this human is actually made in the image and likeness of God and is given dominion over all of God's creation!

I can almost hear the devil say, "This should have been me as the ruler of all of creation, with power to multiply, fill the earth, and subdue it. Dominion of the earth should be mine! I am the most beautiful, elegant, and extravagantly created angel with all the precious jewels. I rule over a third of heaven's angels. Who is this creature of dust, who has no leadership experience, who is not as elegant as I am, who is made of the cheapest and dirtiest material—worthless dirt yet he has been created in God's likeness and image and given higher ranking than the angels and has been called god? He is even God's partner in creation. He has named all creatures and now has been given all dominion and power over all creation and wealth of the earth!"

"I must go take this power and dominion from this man and woman. I must get this glory that was bestowed on them and put it in my hands, where it belonged in the first place. But how can I do it? This man and woman are holy and righteous and extremely high ranking, next to God, so I cannot send my demons to do this work. This is my work and has to be made perfect, or we [the devil and his demons] have no place on earth. We have been kicked out of the third heaven in which we once lived and almost took over. Now we have to live in the second heaven and await judgment. We are on death row. Why not destroy what God, the Creator, is doing, by turning his own people whom He has given all dominion, against Him and causing them to disobey Him so He can curse them like He did us, and only then can we, evil, have the power and dominion. Then we can rule the earth!"

"They do not know, nor do they understand; they walk about in darkness; all the foundations of the earth are unstable. I said, 'You are gods, and all of you are children of the Most High. But you shall die like men, and fall like one of the princes'" (Ps. 82:5–7).

Here, God confirms He created humans as gods, never to die or fall, but their disobedience and rebellion leads to their deaths like mere humans and falling from the position of glory like one of the princes did, Lucifer.

See the temptation of Jesus in (Matt. 4:1–11 WEB)
Then the Spirit led Jesus into the desert. The devil tried to make Jesus do wrong.
Jesus did not eat anything for forty days and forty nights. Then he was very hungry. The one who tries to make people do wrong came and said to him, `If you are God's Son, tell these stones to be changed into bread.' But Jesus answered him, `The holy writings say, "Man cannot live on bread only. He needs to live by every word that God says." 'Then the devil took Jesus to the holy city. He put him on a high part of the temple. The devil said to him, 'If you are God's Son, jump own. The holy writings say, "God will tell his angels to take care of you. They will hold you up in their hands so that you will not knock your foot on a stone." '
Jesus answered him, `The holy writings say, "You must not test the Lord your God." 'The devil took Jesus to a very high hill. He showed him all the countries of the world and how great they were. He said to Jesus, `I will give you all these if you kneel down and worship me.' But Jesus answered him, `Get away, Satan. The holy writings say, "You must worship the Lord your God. And he is the only one you are to worship." Then the devil left Jesus. Angels came and took care of him. (Matt. 4:1–11WEB)

Jesus knew that the devil knew He was the Son of God. This is because there was no previous encounter where Jesus told the devil that He was God's Son, so where did the devil get this idea from unless he was convinced that Jesus was the Son of God?

Adam and Eve had been given God's defense and protection and ranked very high but they sinned and traded their high ranking for slavery. God looked for Adam in his rank but couldn't find him. God is not interested in your physical location, but in your spiritual position wherever you are. God asked Elijah, in 1 Kings 19:13–14 NLT:

"...And a voice said, "What are you doing here, Elijah?" He replied again, "I have zealously served the Lord God Almighty. But the people of Israel have broken their covenant with you, torn down your altars, and killed every one of your prophets. I am the only one left, and now they are trying to kill me, too."

God asked Elijah what he was doing there. In other words, Elijah and Adam were not occupying their positions of glory but had traded them away because of lack of consultation, full trust and faith in God. They both once ranked very high, but they both traded their ranks for worldly wisdom: one with the lust of the eyes and the pride of life; the other traded faith for fear. God in His wisdom made a way out for Adam and Eve. God always will make a way out. But the initial plan that God had for them that was so great had they trusted in God and consulted Him before accepting the lies from the enemy.

After the fall, curses of having to work hard, defend and provide for themselves came to pass. The devil knows he can beat you anytime if he gets you to sin and fall short of God's glory, away from protection, provision, victory, supernatural power, strength, and ability. The devil knows you are dust and very weak without God, but with God you are unbeatable. God stores His treasures in earthen vessels. In Jeremiah 32:14, God told Jeremiah to store his title deeds in earthen vessels so they would last many days. An earthen vessel is not the most prestigious vessel, but God puts His treasure in it so that the earthen vessel will not be seen as glorious, but the treasure and the owner of the treasure in the vessel will be seen, that he may receive all the glory, not the vessel.

"But we have this treasure in earthen vessels that the excellence of His power may be of God and not of us" (2 Cor. 4:7).

We therefore cannot receive any glory in the English sense as *Merriam-Webster* states that *glory* is "public praise, honor, and fame." We give it to God, and He glorifies us in turn.

Sin is serious—it will get you out of your GGT very easily. It is a matter of life and death, and that is why God was careful to make a distinction that it is not by works that you toil and labor for your sins to be forgiven but by the life that God provides that a human cannot provide by his own strength. The death of one brought life to another, because life is in the blood.

The devil cannot penetrate the glory of God. He wanted God's glory to begin with, and that led to his downfall. That is why he caused Adam and Eve to unclothe themselves because he saw that God had made humans from the dust, which has no value or glory of its own, and then clothed this dirt with the most precious thing in Heaven that causes the angels to stand in awe of God—His very own glory that He never clothed angels with. Only God is full of glory. That is why the angels cannot receive any glory and are our servants. Because angels cannot receive any glory, God uses us as His channel for Him to receive glory here on earth, because people are nothing without God's glory.

> When I consider your heavens, the work of your fingers, the moon and the stars, which you have ordained; what is man, that you think of him? What is the son of man, that you care for him? For you have made him a little lower than God, *and crowned him with glory and honor.* You make him ruler over the works of your hands. You have put all things under his feet: All sheep and cattle, yes, and the animals of the field, The birds of the sky, the fish of the sea, and whatever passes through the paths of the seas. Yahweh, our Lord, how majestic is your name in all the earth! (Ps. 8:3–9 WEB; italics added)

God crowned us with GLORY and HONOR. No angel has been crowned with these. Only God has GLORY and HONOR, which we give all unto Him. We are stewards of His glory and honor, not the angels. They make sure no human keeps it for himself but receives it and gives it to God, because God has entrusted us with His glory.

King Herod was struck by an angel when he refused to give God the glory but took it instead, after he gave a great speech where people said he spoke like a god.

"The assembled people kept shouting, "It is the voice of a god and not of a man!" And at once an angel of the Lord struck him down because he did not give God the glory [and instead permitted himself to be worshiped], and he was eaten by worms and died [five days later]." (Acts 12:22–23 AMP).

In Psalm 82:6-7 and John 10:34, God calls us gods, which in Hebrew is *Elohim*, which means "mighty ones, the judges." But He says since we do not take our positions to bring His Kingdom and righteousness on earth, we are living like mere mortals, claiming we are human, we will be weak and die as mere humans. Have you heard anyone justify their sin by saying, "I'm just human?" God does not see us as "just human." He calls us mighty ones, the judges, the gods on earth. In other words, He is the Supreme Court, and we are the other courts that enforce the laws of the Supreme Court everywhere we go. We are called judges, but the Supreme Court judge is greater. We do not judge in the form of creating laws; He judges, i.e., He creates the law, and we enforce it in our jurisdiction here on earth.

A child of a snake is a snake, no matter how big or small it is, or how strong or poisonous it is. A child of a monkey is a monkey, a child of a kangaroo is a kangaroo and a child of a lion is a lion: it cannot be anything else because it is called like its parent. Therefore, a child of God is god. Jesus taught us to know people by their actions, not by their words alone. Paul wrote clearly to the Romans and told them how to know mature sons of God in Romans 8. Jesus confirmed this when He said in John 10:22–39 that God called them gods, to whom the Word of God came, and the scripture cannot be broken. He went on to say He is the Son of God, and the proof is, in vs. 37 and 38, "If I do not do the works of my Father, do not believe Me; but if I do, though you do not believe Me, believe the works, that you may know and believe that the Father is in Me and I in Him."

Just like Christ, our works, what the Father does through us, should lead the world to know we are children of God and believe in Christ. It is hard to convince the world to follow Christ Jesus when our actions are not Christ-like. Just as we know who a person is by their actions more than just their words, the world also will know us by our actions and by how we carry ourselves. Our confessions and actions must match. Let us follow Christ's example and point the world to Him by our actions through the help of His Holy Spirit.

What happens when you are following God's will but the enemy is pursuing you? Do not be afraid, do not adjust God's instructions to accommodate the enemy; do not move from your position. Learn from the children of Israel in Exodus 14 when the Egyptians pursued them to enslave them…Trust that God's got your back and makes ways where it is humanly impossible. He is the God of all universe, everyone and everything is totally subject to Him including the devil himself. Keep working without being destructed, don't move, let God move on your behalf.

> The Lord will fight for you while you [only need to] keep silent and remain calm." The angel of God, who had been going in front of the camp of Israel, moved and went behind them. The pillar of the cloud moved from in front and stood behind them. So it came between the camp of Egypt and the camp of Israel. It was a cloud along with darkness [even by day to the Egyptians], but it gave light by night [to the Israelites]; so one [army] did not come near the other all night. Then Moses stretched out his hand over the sea; and the Lord swept the sea back by a strong east wind all that night and turned the seabed into dry land, and the waters were divided. The Israelites went into the middle of the sea on dry land, and the waters formed a wall to them on their right hand and on their left. The waters returned and covered the chariots and the charioteers, and all the army of Pharaoh that had gone into the sea after them; not even one of them survived. But the Israelites walked on dry land in the

middle of the sea, and the waters formed a wall to them on their right hand and on their left. (Exodus 14:14, 19-22, 28-29 AMP)

Provisions for Christ's Ambassadors

'God does not call the qualified but He qualifies the called,' is a true saying that I have heard many times. I believe that God qualifies us during creation. He then stirs up what He put in us and we carry it out by His grace, not by our human-learned ways. God told Gideon, a real coward who never thought he had what it took to be a leader of a great army and was currently hiding from his enemies, to go fight his enemies with the strength that he had. God never said with the strength He would give him; rather, He said that Gideon already had the strength needed to fight the enemy. He says the same to us today. Let us go and do our God-given task with the strength that God has already placed in us!

"Then the Lord turned to him and said, 'Go with the strength you have, and rescue Israel from the Midianites. I am sending you!'" (Judg. 6:14 NLT)

Today, Christ is sending us out as His ambassadors. We must go and represent Him everywhere we are stationed. Who is an ambassador and what does an ambassador do?

Ambassadors are the highest-ranking representatives of their country to a foreign nation. They protect and promote the interests of the country they represent. They are required to protect the legal interests of the citizens from their country who are traveling to the host country. Ambassadors have benefits like paid staffs, bodyguards, paid for housing, cars, drivers, and entertainment allowance. They also have military protection from their country of residence, and rescue from the enemy is readily available from the country they represent. They get paid with the currency from the country they represent.

How much more benefits and privileges do we have as ambassadors of Christ? We are representatives of heaven on earth. We actually own the earth because the King of heaven owns it. Therefore, unlike the earthly ambassador, we can override the world's legal systems and enforce the Kingdom of God on earth. We are entitled to benefits better than the earthly ambassadors, as Jesus said In Mark 10:28–30 WEB.

> "Peter began to tell him, "Behold, we have left all, and have followed you." Jesus said, "Most certainly I tell you, there is no one who has left house, or brothers, or sisters, or father, or mother, or wife, or children, or land, for my sake, and for the sake of the Good News, but he will receive one hundred times more now in this time, houses, brothers, sisters, mothers, children, and land, with persecutions; and in the age to come eternal life.'"

This is the benefit of being Christ's ambassador. So do not only accept persecution, also accept prosperity, and don't only accept prosperity, accept persecution, too. We are also entitled to angelic protection (Ps. 91). We enforce the Word of God on earth, and we cause His Kingdom to be manifested on earth. We are greatly rewarded, as God promised in Malachi 3:17–18 AMP

> "They will be Mine," says the Lord of hosts, "on that day when I publicly recognize them *and* openly declare them to be My own possession [that is, My very special treasure]. And I will have compassion on them *and* spare them as a man spares his own son who serves him." Then you will again distinguish between the righteous and the wicked, between the one who serves God and the one who does not serve Him."

Relationships in Your GGT

The devil is very cunning. He likes ignorant people, so he will allow you to be ignorant of the relationships you keep. Another area I will touch on briefly is how you got your name, how you name your children or the so called nicknames you get or you name others. Believe it or not, names are very important in fulfilling your GGT. Your name may delay or abort your GGT if you are ignorant of this.

You must know when it is time to cut off some relationship and move on to the next level. Jesus knew how to do this. He knew whom to take to the mountain with Him and who to leave out among His disciples. We must know this too. The Holy Spirit will guide you in this. God has taught me never to trust in people, but to trust Him to bring the right person for the work at any given time in my life. Divine connection. After all, it is His Kingdom, allow Him to choose His employees. For example, when I travel, there are those who see me off at home, those who come with me and see me off at the airport, and there are those who travel with me. When the plane lands, we all go to different destinations. There are those who pick me up from the airport to take me to my hotel or house.

All these people are very important, but at different levels, times and stages in life. If I insist on boarding with the ones who took me to the airport, they will delay my trip and I will miss my flight because they are not ready to fly. They may need to get a passport and pack clothes, or ask permission from their families, etc. If I insist on travelling with someone who was going a different way, I will miss my meeting and my trip will be in vain. We must let God pick our help at specific levels in life so we can be successful in our God given tasks. We must pray about ALL relationships.

Names are Very Important in Fulfilling Your GGT

All over the world, people have names. They are identified by their names. These names come from different sources. Some parents name their children traditionally according to the weather or the season in which the child was born, others name them after their family members, themselves, their friends or celebrities and others from a book, etc.

How did naming start? It started with God. How did God name people? If I ask for a spoon, the picture of a spoon comes to mind and people know what I want. They will not bring me a fork or knife or plate. Names are very important because they reveal the authority and jurisdiction of a person in the spiritual realm. They are meant to reveal God's will and purpose for your life. Just like titles on earth reveal your authority and jurisdiction. Names are very spiritual.

What you are called, you will become. If you are named after your family member, you will become like them. Many in the bible got a name change to promote them and reveal their assignments and jurisdiction in the spirit here on earth. A spoon is called a spoon and reveals its use and purpose. A cup is called a cup for what it was made for. A pen called a pen according to its purpose. What is your name? Is it God given or man given? A God given name will give you limitless benefits and favor from God, but a man given name will create bondage in your life because humans are limited.

Look at Nabal's name which he lived up to that he almost got his family destroyed. His destiny was cut short by his name which he lived up to. Be careful as your name can cause harm or blessings to those around you by living up to it.

"As soon as Abigail saw David, she got off her donkey and fell on her knees at his feet, her face to the ground in homage, saying, "My master, let me take the blame! Let me speak to you. Listen to what I have to say. Don't dwell on what that brute Nabal did. *He acts out the meaning of his name: Nabal, Fool. Foolishness oozes from him.*" (1 Samuel 25:23-25 MSG; italics added)

Curses and demons have legal right to a person through a name. Naming someone after another is called ancestral worship. That is idol worship.

When we disobey God knowingly or unknowingly, we suffer the consequences because ignorance is no defense. We perish for lack of knowledge. God never named anyone after another, or gave two people the same name. Where did we get the idea of naming people from if we are not following God's example?

Let us look at a few name changes by God. There is a reason why God changed people's names. If names were not important, God would never have changed people's names or even bother naming them.

ABRAM TO ABRAHAM:

"What's more, I am changing your name. It will no longer be Abram. *Instead, you will be called Abraham,* for you will be the father of many nations." (Genesis 17:5 NLT; italics added)

SARAI TO SARAH:

"Then God said to Abraham, "Regarding Sarai, your wife—her name will no longer be Sarai. From now on her name will be Sarah. And I will bless her and give you a son from her! Yes, I will bless her richly, and she will become the mother of many nations. Kings of nations will be among her descendants."" (Genesis 17:15-16 NLT; italics added)

JACOB TO ISRAEL:

"When the man saw that he would not win the match, he touched Jacob's hip and wrenched it out of its socket. Then the man said, "Let me go, for the dawn is breaking!" But Jacob said, *"I will not let you go unless you bless me."* "What is your name?" the man asked. He replied, "Jacob." *"Your name will no longer be Jacob,"* the man told him. *"From now on you will be called Israel*, because you have fought with God and with men and have won." (Genesis 32:25-28 NLT; italics added)

Solomon named Jedidiah:

"Then David comforted Bathsheba, his wife, and slept with her. She became pregnant and gave birth to a son, and David named him Solomon. *The Lord loved the child and sent word through Nathan the prophet that they should name him Jedidiah (which means "beloved of the Lord"), as the Lord had commanded.*" (2 Samuel 12:24-25 NLT; italics added)

Simon Bar-Jonah (Son of Jonah) named Peter:

"Then he asked them, "But who do you say I am?" Simon Peter answered, "You are the Messiah, the Son of the living God." Jesus replied, "You are blessed, Simon son of John, because my Father in heaven has revealed this to you. You did not learn this from any human being. *Now I say to you that you are Peter (which means 'rock')*, and upon this rock I will build my church, and all the powers of hell will not conquer it. And I will give you the keys of the Kingdom of Heaven. Whatever you forbid on earth will be forbidden in heaven, and whatever you permit on earth will be permitted in heaven." (Matthew 16:15-19 NLT; italics added)

Naming of Isaac:

But God replied, "No—Sarah, your wife, will give birth to a son for you. *You will name him Isaac*, and I will confirm my covenant with him and his descendants as an everlasting covenant. (Genesis 17:19; italics added)

Naming of John the Baptist:

Luke 1:11-20 The Message (MSG); italics added

> It so happened that as Zachariah was carrying out his priestly duties before God, working the shift assigned to his regiment, it came his one turn in life to enter the sanctuary of God and burn incense. The congregation was gathered and praying outside the Temple at the hour of the incense offering. Unannounced, an angel of God appeared just to the right of the altar of incense. Zachariah was paralyzed in fear. But the angel reassured him, "Don't fear, Zachariah. Your prayer has been heard. *Elizabeth, your wife, will bear a son by you. You are to name him John.* You're going to leap like a gazelle for joy, and not only you—many will delight in his birth. He'll achieve great stature with God. "He'll drink neither wine nor beer. He'll be filled with the Holy Spirit from the moment he leaves his mother's womb. He will turn many sons and daughters of Israel back to their God. He will herald God's arrival in the style and strength of Elijah, soften the hearts of parents to children, and kindle devout understanding among hardened skeptics—he'll get the people ready for God." Zachariah said to the angel, "Do you expect me to believe this? I'm an old man and my wife is an old woman." But the angel said, "I am Gabriel, the sentinel of God, sent especially to bring you this glad news. But because you won't believe me, you'll be unable to say a word until the day of your son's birth. *Every word I've spoken to you will come true on time—God's time.*"

Luke 1:59-66 (MSG); Italics added

> On the eighth day, they came to circumcise the child *and were calling him Zachariah after his father. But his mother intervened: "No. He is to be called John." "But," they said, "no one in your family*

is named that." They used sign language to ask Zachariah what he wanted him named. Asking for a tablet, Zachariah wrote, "His name is to be John." That took everyone by surprise. Surprise followed surprise—Zachariah's mouth was now open, his tongue loose, and he was talking, praising God! A deep, reverential fear settled over the neighborhood, and in all that Judean hill country people talked about nothing else. Everyone who heard about it took it to heart, wondering, "What will become of this child? Clearly, God has his hand in this."

Naming of Jesus Christ:

In the sixth month of Elizabeth's pregnancy, God sent the angel Gabriel to the Galilean village of Nazareth to a virgin engaged to be married to a man descended from David. His name was Joseph, and the virgin's name, Mary. Upon entering, Gabriel greeted her: Good morning! You're beautiful with God's beauty, Beautiful inside and out! God be with you. She was thoroughly shaken, wondering what was behind a greeting like that. But the angel assured her, "Mary, you have nothing to fear. God has a surprise for you: You will become pregnant and *give birth to a son and call his name Jesus. He will be great, be called 'Son of the Highest.'* The Lord God will give him the throne of his father David; He will rule Jacob's house forever—no end, ever, to his kingdom." (Luke 1:26-33 MSG; italics added)

Gideon:

'Then the angel of the Lord came and sat beneath the great tree at Ophrah, which belonged to Joash of the clan of Abiezer. Gideon son of Joash was threshing wheat at the bottom of a winepress to *hide* the grain from the Midianites. The angel of the Lord appeared to him and said, "*Mighty hero*, the Lord is with you!" (Judges 6:11-12 NLT; italics added)

How does a coward become a mighty man unless God steps in?

There is a name that God calls you, do you know it? When you find out you will live a victorious and productive life.

Jabez:

He was very wise. He asked for a name change from 'one who causes pain' to 'one who is blessed'. He must have been very unhappy with his life. He got in trouble and caused a lot of pain that he researched and looked back at what was causing so much grief in his life. After crossing all the T's and dotting all the i's, his name stood out as the enemy of his life. "JABEZ" meaning; sorrow, trouble or affliction.

"There was a man named Jabez who was more honorable than any of his brothers. *His mother named him Jabez because his birth had been so painful.* He was the one who prayed to the God of Israel, *"Oh, that you would bless me and expand my territory! Please be with me in all that I do, and keep me from all trouble and pain!" And God granted him his request."* (1 Chronicles 4:9-10 NLT; italics added)

After the blessing, the bible takes time to mention him and give the reason as to why he was "MORE HONORABLE THAN ANY OF HIS BROTHERS." Then they continue mentioning other people's names in the family of Judah without telling their story. He stood out in the family of the tribe of Judah. How about you? Do you stand out in your family?

You too can change your story and destiny with a single prayer to change your name from which man called or calls you to what God calls you. There is a reason why this story is told, every scripture is inspired by God through the Holy Spirit. The whole city must have witnessed this

Jabez and his deliverance from a trouble and pain causing man to the most honorable man in his family. That is why the writers took their time to tell his story. I am sure he never prayed out loud before men for a blessing from his name of sorrow but to God alone. When everyone saw the change in him and the blessings and honor bestowed upon him, they must have inquired of him and he told them his story which is now told throughout all generations. If you are wise, you will hear what the Spirit of God is teaching you right now.

In all these names, God named people according to their assignments and blessings. Adam was named by God, and Adam named Eve according to where she came from, from man.

"At last!" the man exclaimed. "This one is bone from my bone, and flesh from my flesh! She will be called 'woman,' because she was taken from 'man.'" (Genesis 2:23 NLT; italics added)

After the fall, Adam names her again, instead of asking God what her name was, or her assignment on earth, in (Genesis 3:20 NLT; italics added)

"He, man—Adam—named his wife Eve, because she would be the mother of all who live"

God gave Adam the authority of naming animals, God never cared about naming them, because they were not created in His image. We were created in God's image so God is the only one qualified to name us according to who He is in us. According to God's likeness and qualifications that He put in us. Adam didn't do this while naming the woman, rather he named her according to her origin which could have been reason for her not to believe that she was like God. Do not let anyone name you according to their understanding or wisdom. Ask God what He calls you and live in the freedom and victory of who God created you to be. You were called into greatness!

After the fall, Eve was named by Adam again instead of by God as one who will be the mother of all who live. That is why women have been despised over the years all over the world, and have been seen as child bearers only. Even today, although it is getting better, we see few women leaders or presidents than men.

People have a habit of naming their children without asking God first. Adam was awake and witnessed God creating the animals and so he knew what was put in the animals and was very qualified in naming them. On the other hand, Adam was in deep sleep when Eve was being created so he had no idea what God put in Eve therefore Adam should have asked God what God put in Eve and have God name her. I believe things would have been different if he did. I believe this was his first mistake because Eve did not believe she was like God. She believed she was just from man as her name 'woman' suggested. She didn't see that man was from God and she was in man because God had not separated male and female, they were both in Adam. So she too was from God. That was why the devil was able to convince her that if she ate the fruit she would be like God.

Do you know where your name came from? What does God call you? Are you still bound and can't progress or breakthrough because of your name? One time my mother, a deliverance minister, was praying for someone to be delivered from demons and the demons were very angry at my mother for changing my sister's name. They said through the person being delivered that; "You changed her name so we cannot locate her. We have been looking for her." My mother asked the demons which name they were looking for and very angry they replied, "But you burnt it!" You have the power to burn in the spirit the name man called you and ask God what He calls you.

MY STORY:

I am originally from East Africa, Kenya, a town called Kinoo. Yes for those who know this town it is always made fun of in Kenyan comedy. Someone would be justified to say, can anything good come out of Kinoo?' Just like Nathaniel said about Jesus, 'can anything good come from Nazareth?' According to the Kikuyu tribe and custom which I was born in, people are named after their family members. This ensures that the family member lives throughout many generations and never dies. This continues to this day even among Christians. It is a sin of ancestral worship, hidden in innocent traditions. In the culture, the first child would be named after the husband's parent.

If it's a boy, he would be named after his dad or if a girl, after his mum. Then if the second child is a boy, he would be named after the wife's father and if a girl the husband's side of the family is named first, so it would be his mother, and so on including naming them after the brothers and sisters. This tells you that when a child was born in my culture, people did not have to ask for the name of the child. All they did was ask for the gender of the child, and they automatically knew the name of the child. This was so bad that there would be favoritism because of who you are named after, or rejection depending on who you are named after and especially so, if you are named after a bad person. This is almost like the Jewish tradition of John the Baptist's parents.

My older son's name meant 'difficult to comprehend'. He struggled in school and could not comprehend even the simplest concepts. My husband and I were very frustrated and my son was always crying and frustrated. One day I found him in the bathroom as he had excused himself from his homework table because we were all frustrated thinking that he does not want to get it or he is just stupid. He was crying deeply in prayer pleading with God to help him comprehend and understand what he is being taught. He was only 7 or 8 years old at the time. His younger brother had no problem understanding his older brother's homework.

I was deeply moved and I knew that there was a force greater than stupidity working against my son. My husband and I prayed and changed our son's name, without care or worry of the consequences of tradition. We had to set our children free!

We repented, denounced their ancestral names and called them what God calls them and the change was instant. They broke out into a rush, both the first and second son. Because the baby was not named after anyone, we had become wiser and named him what God called him so he was not affected.

From that day on till now, our son is the head only and never the tail, above only and not beneath. He became the most popular kid in school for great achievements behaviorally, academically and sportsmanship. He made us famous in his school. All we had to say is we were his parents and everyone wanted to meet us and congratulate us on raising such a great son This went on all through middle school and now high school. He has become a great student and is always on honor roll.

My middle son's name meant a traditional dance. Yes my son was a dancer like no one else! In pre-school, all students and teachers would come to his class to watch him dance and a special CD was made for him with all the music he liked. The problem was he danced to every music even secular music which was not pleasing to God. Now the bondage was broken and he is not the addicted dancer he used to be.

My baby was not named after anyone, but when I almost lost him during pregnancy and my mother prayed, God spoke and said, "Peace is all well". My husband wanted to name him after himself and I refused and prayed for wisdom because I carried the children and had given him the privilege to name them. My husband was already struggling with who he was and whom he was named after and I did not want to put my child into more bondage. I prayed and God answered wonderfully. My husband came one day and said to me, "I have a name for our son, he shall be called 'Amani'". This is a Swahili name which means "Peace". A perfect confirmation of what God called our son. His exact Word to my mum was; "Peace is all well" and Peace was well. My baby was named by God as Peace and he was and still is the most peaceful boy I know.

As for me, I was named after my grand-mother, my father's mother named "Esther Warigia" because I was the first girl. My grandpa used to call me his wife. My mother could not discipline me in my grandmother's presence because my grandma would tell her to place my punishment on her instead because she took it very personal. It was so personal, that my mother would be scolded in public by my grandma because my grandma would say that my mother had something against her and was trying to take it out on me. I grew up being very proud like my grandma, had anger and held on to grudges from a little child just like she did. In most of my childhood pictures I was angry.

This was great bondage for me. My grandmother later had multiple strokes due to uncontrolled high blood pressure from stress and anger. She was non-verbal when she died. I had the spirit of pride and grudge keeping. I would not speak to my offender even if it was a family member for weeks and even months at my young age. One time at about three years of age my mother disciplined me and I got very angry at her. I told her that if she called me, I would not answer her and if she sends me I would not go. This happened in the morning and I sulked at her the whole day. In the evening she called me and I kept quiet. She called my name again and threatened to spank me and I looked at her sitting on the chair sucking my right thumb, then I took my thumb out of my mouth long enough to answer her. I said to her;

"What did I tell you after you spanked me? If you call me I will not answer, and if you send me I will not go!" I spoke this in Swahili language and went on sucking my thumb. She remembers to this day. Yes I was very bad. Thank God for her prayers and discipline. I brought this into my marriage and had a list of all wrongs ever done to me by my husband. What bondage and a slave I was to grudge keeping and pride. I had prayed for God to deliver me from these spirits, but there was a strong hold I had not pulled down, the roots were still there. I was in sin and didn't even know it.

One day as I walked to my car from my University class, I had a very bad headache on the left side of my brain, a stroke-like headache. I happened to looked at my watch and it was 3:30 p.m. I went home praying that the headache would leave; but it remained until later that evening. The following day after class again, the excruciating headache started. When I looked at the time, I don't know why I looked at the time then but I later knew that God was telling me something, it was 3:30 p.m.

again. Then I remembered that the devil will program things to happen to you at certain times because he cannot be in all places at the same time in order to destroy you. I immediately called my parents and told them what was going on and they both said, "Change your name!" They had known this was spiritual. I prayed and disowned my name and prayed against all curses and demonic activity programmed through that name on me to be destroyed in Jesus name.

The following day my mother and I decided that we would attack this evil headache spirit before it attacks again. The following day I had home health practical lesson and was out in the field with my preceptor. I grabbed a book that I had been given a while back by a couple who were teaching on deliverance. I had never had a chance to read it but for some reason the Holy Spirit led me to reading it.

This topic of deliverance was not well accepted in the church then, because Christians were ignorant of the fact that you can be born again but not delivered. In the book, the Holy Spirit led me to a place where it discussed ancestral worship. It explained that naming people after others is ancestral worship. God revealed to me this hidden sin which I did not know about. We had accepted the gospel of Jesus Christ as Africans who were idol worshipers, but our traditions remained in us so we never really left idol worship, we just incorporated it into Christianity. What deception, what bondage. We truly perish for lack of knowledge. Many still practice this today.

Like David prayed, I prayed...

"Who can understand his errors *or* omissions? Acquit me of hidden (unconscious, unintended) *faults*." Psalm 19:12 (AMP)

I repented as I rode in the car with my preceptor on our way to the patient's house. At three 3:20 p.m., as my preceptor was speaking with the patient, I laid my hand on my head and began praying against that ancestral spirit curse and the demons that came in me because of this sin. At 3:30 p.m., the headache never came. The curse was broken! I was excited and free! Glory to Jesus and the power of His Blood.

My mother told me that as she was praying, she experienced a very bad headache, she could hardly believe the pain I had experienced. She prayed and when the curse was broken, she knew it because the pain she experienced was gone. Sometimes God will allow you to experience someone else's pain as you pray for them so you can pray with deep intensity since you are in the same shoes. You know you have breakthrough when the pain leaves. This happens in the gift of word of knowledge. Christ became a curse so we could be blessed. Don't live in the curse anymore.

After this victory, I was nameless waiting for God to name me, and He did! One day, in my sleep, I saw my old full name written "Esther Warigia Nguru (Kibuiya)" and then crossed out and the name 'GIFT' was written. When I woke up, I was excited, I went to wake my sons up to go to school. On the way to school my older son said, "mum, when you woke us up, did you say 'good morning boys, I have a new name!?'" His brother laughed and said, "No! She said Good morning boys, it's time to wake up!" His brother was right. I then revealed to them the dream I had and how God gave me a new name. My son was used to confirm that it was real I had received a new name given by God the Father.

Earlier that week, my mother had a prophet visiting her church who did not know her. He was a guest speaker in her church through someone she knew. He prophesied to her and said, "You have a daughter in the United States, and she is in the medical field. God calls her Gift. Is her name Gift?"

I was nameless by then which he had no idea. When I called my parents, my mum answered the phone and said, "Hi Zawadi?" (Zawadi means Gift in Swahili) I was amazed at her greeting and she told me all that God said through His prophet. I love God because He confirms His word if you trust Him. I did not go to look for a name, or think of a name, I allowed Him to name me. I now go by my new name, Gift or Zawadi or both.

How about you? Who named you? Remember even nick-names are names. Do not let anyone or circumstance or trials in life name you, let God tell you what He calls you so you can live in His glory and power in Jesus name!

A lady from the Philippines once told me that in their culture they would change a child's name if the child often got ill. Once the name was changed, the child would experience better health. Don't give the enemy legal right to your life through a name. Don't perish for lack of knowledge, you have no excuse because now you know.

Even if you don't officially change your name on papers, you can still change it in the spirit. Let people call you by your new name. Remember Daniel, Hananiah and Mishael got a name change when they were captured by the enemy. The enemy cannot succeed by using God's names.

"Now among these were, of the children of Judah, Daniel, Hananiah, Mishael, and Azariah. The prince of the eunuchs gave names to them: to Daniel he gave the name Belteshazzar; and to Hananiah, Shadrach; and to Mishael, Meshach; and to Azariah, Abednego. But Daniel purposed in his heart that he would not defile himself with the king's dainties, nor with the wine which he drank: therefore he requested of the prince of the eunuchs that he might not defile himself." Daniel 1:6-8 (WEB)

One man who was named Moses, a Kenyan who was into devil worshiping, after deliverance as he was preaching he disclosed the secret behind names. He said that when he was being recruited into devil worship, they said they could not use his name 'Moses' because it belongs to the 'Very One' (God). They changed his name to 'Moroni'. Even the devil himself is smart enough to know the power in names. He cannot possess what belongs to God. If your name is put on something, it means that the item belongs to you. If God names you, it means you belong to Him. Who do you belong to? Who named you? Be wise!

Luke 16:8b (KJV) "for the children of this world are in their generation wiser than the children of light."

CHAPTER 16
How to Stay on Task

§

STARTING OUR GOD-GIVEN TASK IS one thing but staying on task is another. How many times have you or someone you know started on a project and not finished it? How do we stay on task as we fulfill our God given assignments? We must have THE map, light and lamp to light our way, and the sword of the Spirit, the Word of God, to destroy the enemy who comes our way. We MUST pray, fast and trust in God's ability. We must be humble and have proper goal setting.

THE WORD OF GOD

We stay on task by knowing and doing God's will. How do we know what His will is and what He requires of us? How do we listen to Him so we can please Him? How do we get to know His voice?

We know God's will by reading the bible, meditating and doing His Word. Before I read the bible, I ask the Holy Spirit to reveal to me what the scriptures mean and lead me to what God wants to teach me. I ask Him to open my mind, heart and spirit to understanding and receive all that God desires of me. I have found that when I do this, I get to know the heart of God and receive direction in every stage of my assignment.

Reading the word of God is as important as reading a will that someone left for you. Scripture was written from the Old Testament and the New Testament so that we may know God and understand who He is, what He desires and His will for our lives. If we get too busy to read and study the bible, God's WILL to us, we cannot know what He expects of us; therefore we cannot please Him. We will never know His promises and all He has given us to be successful in our assignments.

The Bible is a Will that God has left for us to know what He wants us to do with the property (our bodies and everything else that He has granted us) for His Kingdom and glory. It is a Will that tells us what God has for us. If we read and do what it says, we shall prosper.

Take for instance, you have written a will for your children and in the will, you left them a lot of land and finances enough to give them complete financial freedom. However, your children get too busy with their jobs, friends, and pleasures that they do not read your will. How much of the financial freedom will they have? They will struggle and not have enough time to spend with their families. They will continue to be in debt because they ignored the will. They will live in the same financial situation they were in before you left them the will.

They will not increase their wealth or their influence as long as they keep ignoring the will. What if they read some of it and ignore most of it? They will only possess what they know. But if they take the time to read the whole will and to do as it says, they will possess all that you had in store for them. In the same way, God has written all His desires and has given us a lot of promises in His Word that if we read it diligently, seek and obey Him, we will know what He desires and we will be able to possess that which He has promised.

That is why the enemy makes sure that you get to be too busy to read God's Word or bored and sleepy when you try to read it. It is amazing how many of us can read a secular book and stay up for hours to finish it, or watch a secular movie or news for hours, but cannot stay excited through a thirty minute sermon, or read a chapter in the bible with undivided attention.

Let us hunger and thirst for God's Word and eat it daily that we may never lose our way. That is why God led me to study and send scripture daily to the bible study He began through me to keep our paths lit. Just as we need the sun and food daily to be productive, God's Word, Jesus, is our spiritual light and daily bread which our spirits need to grow strong and operate daily in victory.

Prayer

We must constantly consult with Jesus Christ through His Holy Spirit.

Beloved, lack of daily and throughout the day consultation with God will lead to bondage and delay in your God-given task. What if Adam and Eve took a minute to tell the serpent, "Let me consult with God about this," don't you think the world would have been a different place and the devil would have been defeated forever? All we need is to pause and consult with God instead of making choices that seem right at the time but in the end destroy us. When you run alone, you ran a race which you can easily lose because your winning is dependent entirely on your own strength. On the other hand, when you run with God, your winning is sure because you are guaranteed God's grace. You run with His strength not yours.

How many times throughout the day do you inquire of God? We see in the scripture what happened when men and women relied on their own understanding instead of God's understanding. I am excited because I have a God who sees the end from the beginning. How great it is to have such intelligence as you live in this world full of uncertainties and competition. There is power in trusting God and in obeying His commands. God's plan doesn't needs a plan B because it is perfect. Whatever God does is perfect, and He does this so people will fear before Him. We must pray because prayer allows God to operate legally on earth. When we pray, we give God permission to fulfill His promises to us.

What is prayer? Who should pray? Why pray? When do we pray? How often? How do we pray? What are the different types of prayers? How do we pray effectively?

Prayer is communicating with God. Prayer is talking to God in the same manner you would hold a conversation with your friend. Imagine having a conversation with someone who reads out their speech to you or says the same thing over and over.

No wonder Jesus said in Matthew 6:7–8, "And when you pray, do not use vain repetitions as the heathen do. For they think that they will be heard for their many words. Therefore do not be like them. For your Father knows the things you have need of before you ask Him."

When we pray we must trust in God's ability to hear and answer our prayers in His wisdom, not according to our wisdom. In so doing we ask that His will for our lives should take preeminence. When we pray, we are having a conversation with God, our Creator, our Lord and Master, Savior, Father, Friend and Counselor. For a conversation to be effective, we must know the person we are addressing so as to address them correctly. We also must take time to listen to the person we are talking to. Prayer is not a monologue as many make it to be, but a dialogue between us and God. Imagine speaking with someone who just talks and doesn't give you a chance to talk or respond to them.

Do this exercise: breathe out and then hold your breath. How long can you stay without breathing in? If you don't breathe in, you will die because you will lack oxygen in you, which is a requirement for life. Receiving a response from God in prayer is the breathing in part. I did not ask you to breathe in but you did because your lungs required it and you could not hold your breath any longer. What makes you think you can live without God speaking to your spirit? You must breathe in His Word into your spirit which gives you life. Many people have a dead prayer life because they do not breathe in God's Word. His commands and Word give life. That is why Jesus quoted the scripture in Deut. 8:3 when He was being tempted by the devil in Matt.4:4 that man shall not live by bread alone, but by every Word that proceeds from the mouth of God. Prayer is not just talking to God, but most importantly, it is listening, waiting, and hearing from God.

Someone once asked me if there was any special ways of listening to God? There is no special way of listening to God, just as there is no special way of talking to Him. The main thing is to know His voice because Jesus says in John 10:27

"My sheep hear My voice, and I know them, and they follow Me."

Just as you know the voice of your parents or friends because you speak and listen to them often, in the same way, the more you talk to God and turn off the noises around you, the more you will hear His voice. Knowing His Word by reading the Bible is another key. This will help you to know if what you heard was His voice, according to His principles and promises in His Word. Every child knows what their parents would say or approve of, and when someone else tries to pretend to be their parent, the child will know it because he or she knows the parents' principles, rules and even their voice.

God speaks in our heart, sometimes audibly, in visions, dreams, or through revelation knowledge from His Word. So you can't just wake up and have a special microwave solution to hearing God; you MUST turn off all the other loud voices in your life and seek God, spend time with Him, and meditate on His Word, and you will know His voice. You will have to say NO to some friends who drive you from Him. Some phone calls you will ignore. You will pass on some party invitations to please God and stay in His presence so as to hear His voice.

Sin and compromise stops us from hearing God's voice. From my experience, when I asked to know God more and to hear Him, the first thing He did was reveal to me how busy my life was with many things and cares of this world. The voices in my life were so loud that every spare time I got I was on the phone talking with friends, or looking for somewhere to go and have fun. I was busy pleasing people and compromising my eternity. I had no time set apart daily with God, to spend time not just praying before food or at bedtime, but a time where I just turn off everything, and we talk.

When I obeyed and turned off all the noises in my life and I valued God higher than everyone or anything else; His voice became clearer and louder until it became the loudest voice in my life. I know that Jesus is with me always, so if I am invited somewhere or I am holding a conversation with anyone, I ask myself if Christ would go where I have been invited to go or if He would enjoy the conversation I am holding. If not, I will say NO! Because I live to please Him. I will not leave Christ behind so I may please or entertain man. I had rather be all alone with Jesus than with the whole world without Him.

There were times in my life when I slacked or compromised my walk with God to please man and I realized that other voices ruled over His. I had less peace and more stress. I then decided to dwell in His secret place, where there is peace, and I can hear Him in all situations and can boldly stand on His Word. All this was done in total submission and reliance on His Spirit and His grace. I now live my life stress free and worry free when in this zone, because with God nothing is impossible! What I don't know, He knows, what I can't fix, He can.

We pray to God not just because we need something and are asking for it, but because we were created and sent by God to do His will on earth. We must communicate with Him throughout the day so as to get instruction on how and what we should do to complete our God-given assignment successfully. How would you like it if someone only spoke to you when they needed your help or favor, but when they are happy and partying, you are the last person on their minds?

God has a need to be loved just like you and I. He desires a relationship of deep intimacy with His children; that is why He did not bail Jesus out from suffering and death when Jesus asked Him to. He loved Jesus but saw many sons and daughters that would love Him in the future. He loves to be loved and we show our love by obeying Him. When we put Him first, He rules our day; when we put Him last, the day rules us! Right priorities produce right and great results. Whoever is first in your life rules your life. If it is money, you will work for money; if it is your spouse, you will be their slave. If it is God, He has already paid for our freedom, and instead of being slaves to sin, we are slaves to righteousness and rulers and heirs with Christ Jesus! Christ must be the LORD of our lives at all times. He owns everything and it is an honor to be guided and led by Him.

Pray Without Ceasing

How often must we pray? Continually, without stopping.

"Rejoice always, pray without ceasing, in everything give thanks; for this is the will of God in Christ Jesus for you" (1 Thess. 5:16–18).

Who should pray? Everyone.

The old way of waiting for someone to pray for you, either a priest or pastor, is gone. You have direct access to God the Father through Jesus Christ. You may have people help you pray, but you must not rely on them to pray for you; you must pray for yourself! People who wait to go for confession to the priest, like most Catholics do, are in trouble if they die before they get to the priest because they will die in their sin.

Jesus came to eliminate these human-made limitations and the limitations of the law, so we can boldly enter His presence with His blood. This means that we must pray in His name only! He was the ultimate sacrifice for our justification and only by Him must we approach God. This means, we MUST not pray to or in the name of the dead or the people we call saints because this is idle worship. None of them died to pay for our sins; none of them rose from the dead for our redemption and forgiveness of sin. They are not God, so they cannot be in all places to hear all the prayers offered to them. They are not even aware that you are praying because they are also the redeemed and needed to be forgiven and redeemed by Christ. They cannot pray for you either because they are dead, out of this world. Only the Great High Priest Jesus Christ can pray for you.

Only the redeemer, Jesus Christ, the Son of the only living God, can hear and see all. Praying to or in the name of saints is people's idea, and it is religious deception. Only God is in ALL places at all times and hears all our prayers. He will not hear or answer any prayer not prayed in the name of His Son, Jesus Christ, who paid for our redemption. All prayer must be made in Jesus's name. Jesus never told anyone who came to him to pray for healing that they should pray to the saints or even to His mother, Mary, anywhere in the scripture. The Bible says that "Nor is there salvation in any other, for there is no other name under heaven given among men by which we must be saved" Acts 4:12. Jesus said to His disciples in John 14:13–14, "And whatever you ask in My name, that I will do, that the Father may be glorified in the Son. If you ask anything in My name, I will do it." In John 16:23–24, He said, "And in that day you will ask Me nothing. Most assuredly, I say to you, whatever you ask the Father in My name He will give you. Until now you have asked nothing in My name. Ask, and you will receive, that your joy may be full."

You see, our Lord Jesus never gave us any other name, and the Father will not hear or answer us if we go to Him in any other name! Jesus paid the price. His name is the only valid name to get to the Father. Jesus is the only password to the Father; otherwise, we have no access. If you pray or have prayed in any other name as many religions teach, you must repent and obey the teaching of Jesus on praying in His name only. Then your prayers will reach heaven, and the Father will answer, and He will be glorified.

When Jesus said in the scripture above that "...Whatever you ask in My name, that I will do..." He did not mean that we can pray and ask for anything we desire and it will be done. He means that whatever we ask for the sake of His name, to glorify His name and for His Kingdom, He will do it. We need to check our prayers and motives and see if it is for our glory or for His glory. If you pray for your glory He will not answer even if you use His name. We are to use His name for Kingdom purpose only and not selfishly.

"*And praying always with all prayer and supplication in the Spirit,* being watchful to this end with all perseverance and supplication for all the saints and for me, that utterance may be given to me, that I may open my mouth boldly to make known the mystery of the gospel, for which I am an ambassador in chains; that in it I may speak boldly, as I ought to speak" (Eph. 6:18–20; italics added).

We must pray all kinds of prayers in the spirit, be led by the Holy Spirit, and pray for one another that we may be bold and faithful to do what God created us to do—boldly in the fear of God and not in the fear of people, as we ought to. Pray this for yourself and all children of God in Jesus's name that we may live in obedience, boldness and the fear of God to fulfill, by His Spirit and grace, the work we were created to do. Amen!

In Matthew 6:9–15 NLT, Jesus taught us how to pray.

> Pray like this: Our Father in heaven, may your name be kept holy. May your Kingdom come soon. May your will be done on earth, as it is in heaven. Give us today the food we need, and forgive us our sins, as we have forgiven those who sin against us. And don't let us yield to temptation, but rescue us from the evil one. If you forgive those who sin against you, your heavenly Father will forgive you. But if you refuse to forgive others, your Father will not forgive your sins.

Beloved, prayer MUST have the following to be effective; forgiveness toward others for God to forgive you, you must believe and have faith in God's ability, you must be persistent, and you must be led by the Holy Spirit so as to ask according to God's will. We must petition heaven by praying God's Word. I find my prayers to be very effective when I pray with the knowledge of what God says about the situation, which can be found in the Bible or when He speaks to you.

"I tell you, you can pray for anything, and if you believe that you've received it, it will be yours. But when you are praying, first forgive anyone you are holding a grudge against, so that your Father in heaven will forgive your sins, too" (Mark 11:24–25 NLT).

"The disciples were amazed when they saw this and asked, 'How did the fig tree wither so quickly?' Then Jesus told them, 'I tell you the truth, if you have faith and don't doubt, you can do things like this and much more. You can even say to this mountain, "May you be lifted up and thrown into the sea," and it will happen. You can pray for anything, and if you have faith, you will receive it'" (Matt. 21:20–22 NLT).

We must pray without getting tired or getting discouraged even when the answer takes too long. One day Jesus told his disciples this story to show that they should always pray and never give up.

> "There was a judge in a certain city," He said, "who neither feared God nor cared about people. A widow of that city came to him repeatedly, saying, 'Give me justice in this dispute with my enemy.' The judge ignored her awhile, but finally he said to himself, 'I don't fear God or care about people, but this woman is driving me crazy. I'm going to see that she gets justice, because she is wearing me out with her constant requests!' Then the Lord said, "Learn a lesson from this unjust judge. Even he rendered a just decision in the end. So don't you think God will surely give justice to his chosen people who cry out to him day and night? Will he keep putting them off? I tell you, he will grant justice to them quickly! But when the Son of Man returns, how many will he find on the earth who have faith?" (Luke 18:1–8 NLT)

"Confess your sins to each other and pray for each other so that you may be healed. The earnest prayer of a righteous person has great power and produces wonderful results" (James 5:16 NLT).

Praying in Tongues

God also gives the gift of praying in tongues. Ask and it will be given unto you in Jesus's name. Praying in tongues is a gift and a sign that will follow those who believe in Jesus Christ.

"When the Day of Pentecost had fully come, they were all with one accord in one place. And suddenly there came a sound from heaven, as of a rushing mighty wind, and it filled the whole house where they were sitting. Then there appeared to them divided tongues, as of fire, and one sat upon each of them. *And they were all filled with the Holy Spirit and began to speak with other tongues, as the Spirit gave them utterance"* (Acts 2:1-4; italics added).

God started the first church with the POWER of the Holy Spirit from God, who came and gave them the gift of speaking in tongues, and three thousand people believed in Christ! What POWER! Let's review some scriptures on this.

"And these signs will follow those who believe: In My name they will cast out demons; *they will speak with new tongues*" (Mark 16:17; italics added).

"Even as Peter was saying these things, the Holy Spirit fell upon all who were listening to the message. The Jewish believers who came with Peter were amazed that the gift of the Holy Spirit had been poured out on the Gentiles, too. *For they heard them speaking in other tongues and praising God.* Then Peter asked, 'Can anyone object to their being baptized, now that they have received the Holy Spirit just as we did?'" (Acts 10:44–47 NLT; italics added)

The Holy Spirit was poured out to the Gentiles to fulfill the prophecy in Joel 2:28, that in the last days God will pour out His Spirit to ALL flesh!

> Now, it happened that while Apollos was away in Corinth, Paul made his way down through the mountains, came to Ephesus, and happened on some disciples there. The first thing he said was, "Did you receive the Holy Spirit when you believed? Did you take God into your mind only, or did you also embrace him with your heart? Did he get inside you?" "*We've never even heard of that—a Holy Spirit? God within us?*" "How were you baptized, then?" asked Paul. "In John's baptism." "That explains it," said Paul. "John preached a baptism of radical life-change so that people would be ready to receive the One coming after him, who turned out to be Jesus. If you've been baptized in John's baptism, you're ready now for the real thing, for Jesus." And they were. As soon as they heard of it, they were baptized in the

name of the Master Jesus. *Paul put his hands on their heads and the Holy Spirit entered them. From that moment on, they were praising God in tongues and talking about God's actions.* Altogether there were about twelve people there that day. (Acts 19:1–7 WEB; italics added)

The gift of the Holy Spirit and speaking in tongues is very powerful! This is because it is the Holy Spirit of God HIMSELF speaking through you! He speaks perfectly and on point. It is the only undefiled prayer with guaranteed results. It is one prayer that your mind cannot fight with. It bypasses the mind, the intellect, the heart, and the soul. It is fully Spirit-to-Spirit communion: Spirit of God in you speaking to God the Father. It is the perfect spirit connection.

If you do not have this gift, desire it and ask for it, so you may enjoy perfect fellowship and supernatural manifestation of God in your life. If you have the gift of tongues and haven't used it for a while, you will need to stir up the gift of God in you. God does not take back His gifts; it is still in you. You need to stir it up because it is inactive. Repent for neglecting to use it, stir it up, and use it in Jesus's name.

"Therefore I remind you to stir up the gift of God which is in you through the laying on of my hands" (2 Tim. 1:6).

"For the gifts and the calling of God are irrevocable" (Rom. 11:29).

"Pursue love, and desire spiritual gifts, but especially that you may prophesy. For he who speaks in a tongue does not speak to men but to God, for no one understands him; however, in the spirit he speaks mysteries" (1 Cor. 14:1–2).

Speaking in tongues is effective when speaking to God not men because the human mind does not and cannot comprehend the heavenly language.

"I thank my God I speak with tongues more than you all" (1 Cor. 14:18).

"Likewise the Spirit also helps in our weaknesses. For we do not know what we should pray for as we ought, but the Spirit Himself makes intercession for us with groanings which cannot be uttered. Now He who searches the hearts knows what the mind of the Spirit is, because He makes intercession for the saints according to the will of God" (Rom. 8:26–27).

When I pray in tongues, many mysteries are revealed to my spirit, and impossible situations give way! God's will is revealed in many situations and since the devil cannot understand it, he cannot fight the Holy Spirit praying through me. It is the perfect prayer because it by-passes the mind, so you get out of the way of God, and you are not in doubt of the prayer because you don't understand it. It is beyond what your mind can comprehend; it is faith undefiled. The devil will try to make you doubt it because one way to get your prayers not to be answered is through unbelief. He will give you the idea that it is a fake language, it sounds funny or that you are making it up, etc., but you must go beyond the lie of the enemy because he knows that when you pray in the spirit in tongues, he is in trouble with God Himself, and He will lose miserably because he doesn't understand the language and he cannot fight with the Holy Spirit.

Talking of speaking in tongues, when I was growing up, I used to hear my mum pray a lot in tongues and sing in tongues while she was in prayer. It sounded really interesting. I would stay outside her bedroom door or climb up the freezer on the hallway to peek inside her room through a window at the top of her bedroom door so I could see what she was doing in prayer. She was either kneeling or lying prostrate on the floor, praying. One day she was in the shower, and even there she used to sing and pray in tongues.

This particular day, she called me all of a sudden as she was getting out of the shower and told me to go tell Kamale, our watchman and yard helper, to get ready because God said thieves were planning to come and rob us that night. I was shocked at the news, but knowing my mum and her God, I never questioned. I went and told Kamale all mum told me, and he too was shocked. He acted as if I didn't know what I was talking about, so he went to confirm this with my mum.

My mum responded firmly and with authority, "It is exactly as you've heard. Get ready!" Later on she said that she had been told the same thing one time before we got robbed, but she didn't take it seriously, so this time she did not want to ignore or doubt what she heard. In the middle of the night, as sure as God said through my mother, the thieves came, but they were attacked before they broke in. Kamale had electrocuted the fence around the yard and was sitting at a high place with a bow and some poisonous arrows ready to wound them as he saw them coming in through the fence. I was woken up by the midnight commotion as my parents got out of the house when the thieves were attacked, and the thieves ran away. God will reveal mysteries and the enemy's secrets and plan to destroy you when you speak in tongues.

When I was growing up, my mother knew everything I did in secret because she was in close communion with God. It was so bad that I would pray and ask God not to report me to my mum. The most successful Christian is one who speaks in tongues because he or she releases God's power on earth. When we speak in tongues, we speak mysteries, and the supernatural is released into the natural. Another day, years ago, I had gone for praise and worship practice and as we practiced, I felt a great heaviness in the atmosphere. I stopped the practice, and instructed everyone to pray. Everyone prayed in their corner. I prayed in tongues with heavy groaning deep in my spirit until the heaviness was lifted, and then we all resumed to great praises with tremendous breakthrough.

As I went home that night with my two little boys in my big SUV, I had one lady from praise and worship follow me to my house for an overnight visit. While driving on the busy highway at about 70 MPH in the carpool or fast moving vehicle lane, my SUV got a tire burst. My friend said that she suddenly saw smoke on the road. I moved over four lanes to the right, and when I got to the side of the road, my SUV stopped and turned itself off. I couldn't start or steer it. It was dark, and we were about an hour's drive from home. Thank God we didn't roll over or hit any other cars, especially since my SUV tires were bigger than normal. My friend had AAA, so she called for help, and they came very fast and changed the tire. They too were shocked that the truck didn't roll over. We went home safely—glory to God—and the car was able to start with no problem after the tire was changed. God, through our intercessory prayer in tongues, stopped the destruction that had been planned by the enemy and gave us victory over him. Praying in tongues is extremely powerful!

When you speak in tongues, God will reveal mysteries to you to edify the church of Jesus Christ through revelation and prophecy. Speaking in tongues is very controversial in this day and age. The enemy doesn't want people to use this weapon against him. Do not be afraid to speak in tongues and prophesy as instructed by God. Deliver the prophetic message faithfully and rebuke the spirits of doubt and fear.

You may not be received very well as you prophesy or deliver God's message unless it suits the receiver. But look at it this way; the mail carrier delivers your mail to your mailbox without choosing the mail that will please you. When you open the mail, you don't address the mail carrier but you address the one who wrote you the mail. Likewise, prophets are God's mail carriers. They don't write the mail; they just deliver it. If people question you, tell them to seek God on the issue because He is the One who said it, not you.

One time God gave me messages for a particular church, and I would take them to the pastor and his wife. The pastor started to dislike me because he did not think God would speak through me, a common person and not a pastor or someone with a big title. But remember, God will use anyone yielded to Him. I was a student and home-maker then. God was warning them to turn back and obey Him as well as promising blessings if they obeyed Him. One day God told me to tell the pastor that he needed to go back to the place where God had called him first, because before he was called to be a pastor, God had called him first to Himself. The pastor was so busy with pastoring, that he had no time for God. Relying on intercessors isn't enough, preachers! You must seek God and be at His feet to receive from Him food for you and His people.

Because I knew that the pastor despised me and had called me demon possessed and had told it to other people in the church, I told God I would deliver the message faithfully, but this time the pastor had to come to me, rather than me going to him. That same evening, as we were having fellowship with some brethren at our home, there was a knock at the door. It was the pastor. I was not shocked, but I was amazed at God! The pastor tried to explain why he came unannounced by saying that he was just in the neighborhood, and he felt strongly that he must come to see us. I gave him his word in private; he wept, thanked me, and immediately left. I was grateful that I obeyed God. See Ezekiel 33:1–9.

Praying in tongues unleashes power. It empowers your spirit, which is the real you, and as you speak, it edifies you so you may edify others. It charges your spirit, gives you the boldness that you need to fulfill your God-given task, and reveals God's will and plan for your life so you may prosper in your destiny.

Paul spoke in tongues more than anyone else back then, and see how many churches and people he edified and how many books of the Bible he wrote—about thirteen books of deep revelation—more than all disciples who walked side by side with Christ in person! He edified and still edifies many to this day. He was able to know his end, as he was continually led by the Holy Spirit. As he said, he had run the race in 2 Timothy 4:6–8:

"For I am already being poured out as a drink offering, and the time of my departure is at hand. I have fought the good fight, I have finished the race, I have kept the faith. Finally, there is laid up for me the crown of righteousness, which the Lord, the righteous Judge, will give to me on that Day, and not to me only but also to all who have loved His appearing."

He finished his race on earth well, because he relied on the Holy Spirit to edify and guide him.

You cannot feed others if you are hungry; you cannot set others free when you are bound; you cannot give others what you do not have. You cannot fulfill your God-given task without God's supernatural power! Desire to speak in tongues that you may be edified and in turn edify others.

When I hear God's Word, I release the Word as soon as I get it in confidence because God is faithful and true to His Word. From my experiences, whoever rejected God's Word paid the price. People would call me Joseph the dreamer because God spoke to me a lot in dreams, in prayer, in worship and as I went about my day. Christ and I communicate continuously, and I don't stop having a conversation with God.

God speaks continually if you speak to Him and listen continually. He has a lot to say. See in the Bible how Jesus used to teach day and night for days? He has not stopped. Now we have God the Holy Spirit, who speaks all languages, and just as it is written in John 7:38, 'out of your belly shall flow rivers of living waters'. The Word of God is living water for the spirit, soul, and body. Those who live by bread alone, feeding their flesh only shall perish, but those who feed their spirits by obeying the Word of God shall live forever. When you dwell in God's presence, it will be normal to hear God's voice, since you will know His voice. Keep practicing the presence of God until it is your new normal.

Fasting

We must live a life full of prayer and fasting. Prayer and fasting are two very powerful weapons. One cannot have a powerful prayer life and results without fasting. When Jesus taught on fasting, He said WHEN you fast, not IF you fast in Matt 6:16-18. This is because fasting is a requirement for all Children of God.

The very first place the Holy Spirit led Jesus, (The Word), was in the Wilderness to FAST. It is important to see what God does first, as He has a reason for everything. Nothing just happens with God. We must see His wisdom in His choices and from this we will know what is important and well needed as a believer in Christ to be successful. The Holy Spirit showed us how important it is to crucify our flesh and offer our bodies as a living sacrifice, holy and pleasing to God for His use just like Jesus did. This was lesson number one for Jesus in succeeding with His GGT. In this, the Holy Spirit made it clear that without Fasting and praying, Jesus Christ would not have defeated the devil miserably like He did.

If Jesus, being the Son of God in human flesh, was taught on fasting as His first lesson before working of any supernatural miracles, how much more must we learn this lesson? It is impossible for us to fulfill our GGT successfully without fasting and prayer and reading God's Word as a lifestyle! This is because without this combination, the enemy will defeat us.

Jesus fasted as He was led by the Holy Spirit. Fasting is effective when it is led of the Holy Spirit. I have realized that every time the Holy Spirit leads me into a fast, He strengthens me supernaturally, gives me His grace and teaches me a lot. I do not fast because I need to or want to ask for a favor from God; rather I do so to walk closer with God. I have been led to forty-day fasts and had great communion with God, where He revealed His plan for my life. It could be any number of days, just follow the leading of God the Holy Spirit.

When you fast, you must, like Christ, be hidden in God's Word. His Word is sharper than a double-edged sword. Fasting is a place of testing, and the enemy will throw at you everything he can and twist the Word of God, but you must be led by the Holy Spirit to be reminded of the Word of God which you need to speak back to the enemy. Fasting feeds your spirit, it is the spiritual boot camp. When we fast, we must pray and read the scripture and wait to hear from God. If this combo is not there, then what we are doing is not fasting, but a dieting program.

Granted, fasting helps to detox your body, helps you to lose weight, and strengthens your spirit; making it more sensitive to God's voice. Fasting also helps our bodies to get rid of unhealthy behavior, which in turn benefits God's kingdom when we stay healthy. It benefits the temple of the Holy Spirit whose body you are. We are able to be used by God more when we are healthy than when we are sick (from abusing His temple). Some people use fasting as a bribery to get what they want while others as spiritual warfare to pray over stubborn problems, but I figure if I, like Christ, make my life a lifestyle of prayer and fasting, I don't have to struggle with the stubborn spirits like the disciples did in Matthew 17:18-21.

Deuteronomy 8:3 says that man SHALL NOT live by bread alone, but by every word that comes from the mouth of God.

If you are living by bread alone, you are disobedient to God. People were never created to live by bread alone. That was a lesson from the Old Testament in the wilderness. One time, the disciples of Jesus were not able to cast out some demons. They asked Jesus why it was so, and Jesus told them it was because those demons only responded to the authority that comes from prayer and fasting. Prayer and fasting give you greater authority in the spirit than someone who does not fast and pray.

To fulfill your God-given task successfully, your life must be one of prayer and fasting. It must be a lifestyle, as the Holy Spirit told me. Read, memorize, and claim the scripture because it is the authority of God on earth. God will confide in those who pray and fast and spend time with Him with no strings attached. Fast because you love Him and have a hunger to do His will. Just as you wouldn't reveal your secrets to just anyone but to your close friend, God will only reveal His secrets to His close friends. Dare to be one of them. Let God say of you what He said of Abraham; that He cannot destroy Sodom and Gomorrah before He tells His friend Abraham what He is planning to do.

Do you want to be in the same league with Abraham and even closer? Give up your all to Him, spend your life in His presence, dwell in the secret place of the most high God, and Psalm 91 will be your portion.

Every Word of God is a doing Word. He expects action when He speaks. Do God's Word, be faithful in obeying Him, and then He will dwell in you. You will be undefeated and unstoppable just like Him. If you are to succeed in your assignment, you MUST have these ingredients as a lifestyle: prayer, fasting, reading, memorizing, confessing, and doing the Word of God. When Joshua was going to succeed Moses in leading the children of God into the Promised Land, God instructed him in

Joshua 1:6–9 to be strong and very courageous, not to be afraid or discouraged, to obey God and he would succeed in his GGT.

"And when you fast, don't make it obvious, as the hypocrites do, for they try to look miserable and disheveled so people will admire them for their fasting. I tell you the truth, that is the only reward they will ever get. But when you fast, comb your hair and wash your face. Then no one will notice that you are fasting, except your Father, who knows what you do in private. And your Father, who sees everything, will reward you" (Matt. 6:16–18 NLT).

"One day the disciples of John the Baptist came to Jesus and asked him, 'Why don't your disciples fast like we do and the Pharisees do?' Jesus replied, 'Do wedding guests mourn while celebrating with the groom? Of course not. But someday the groom will be taken away from them, and then they will fast'" (Matt. 9:14–15 NLT).

> When they came to the multitude, a man came to him, kneeling down to him, saying, "Lord, have mercy on my son, for he is epileptic, and suffers grievously; for he often falls into the fire, and often into the water. So I brought him to your disciples, and they could not cure him." Jesus answered, "Faithless and perverse generation! How long will I be with you? How long will I bear with you? Bring him here to me." Jesus rebuked him, the demon went out of him, and the boy was cured from that hour. Then the disciples came to Jesus privately, and said, "Why weren't we able to cast it out?" He said to them, "Because of your unbelief. For most certainly I tell you, if you have faith as a grain of mustard seed, you will tell this mountain, 'Move from here to there,' and it will move; and nothing will be impossible for you. But this kind doesn't go out except by prayer and fasting." (Matt. 17:14–21 WEB)

Jesus showed us that fasting is not an option; it is a WHEN, not an IF. He says we will be rewarded in public if fasting and prayer is done right, discreetly, between you and God. He also said that when He goes back to heaven, the disciples will have to fast, so fasting is a must. If Jesus, the Son of the most High God, fasted while on earth, how much more must we fast?

Finally, Jesus reveals the weapon of our warfare against the stubborn demons which cannot be defeated except by prayer and fasting! If you want to be an unstoppable child of God, pray and fast often. Also, we find in Acts 13 prophets and teachers of the church fasted:

"While they were serving the Lord and fasting, the Holy Spirit said, 'Set apart for Me Barnabas and Saul (Paul) for the work to which I have called them.' Then after fasting and praying, they laid their hands on them [in approval and dedication] and sent them away [on their first journey]" (Acts 13:2–3 AMP; italics added).

God's plan is revealed to us when we pray and fast. God reveals to us the right people to have in our GGT when we pray and fast. Fasting is successful only when, like Christ, you are led by the Holy Spirit. It is not easily done on your own strength. The devil fights it because he knows its benefits to your spirit and God's Kingdom, and the defeat on his part and his kingdom. We have the Sword of the Spirit, which is the Word of God, to fight against all temptation. You may feel as if it's very hard to fast, or you may believe that you work so much that you cannot fast.

That is a lie from the enemy giving you excuses in order to stunt your spiritual growth and intimacy with God. When God the Holy Spirit leads me into a fast and I feel like my strength is gone and I am tempted to eat, I stand on God's Word in Matthew 4:4 (AMP; italics added)

"But Jesus told him, *"No! The Scriptures say, 'People do not live by bread alone, but by every word that comes from the mouth of God.'"*

I speak this to the enemy when he tries to tell me how hungry I am or how I am missing out on delicacies, or when he uses people who never offer me food to be more generous and offer me what I really like. I always ask God to give me His strength (GRACE) to fast, because mine is insufficient.

God is always faithful. He turns off my physical stomach literally and energizes me like never before. He reveals a ton of wisdom and heavenly secrets to me. My spirit grows as I feed from God's feast table. My children now know that Jesus is feeding me when I don't sit at the table to eat with them.

The main thing you must remember is that fasting must be accompanied with prayer and reading God's Word; otherwise, it is a starvation diet with no spiritual benefits. It MUST be between you and God alone.

When you combine fasting, prayer and the Word of God, the spirit person grows tremendously, and being more like Christ becomes a reality. However, if you feed your flesh more than your spirit, being like Christ will be just a wish, a dream that will never become a reality. Salvation must be *worked out* with fear and trembling. Fasting doesn't have to be done because you need something from God. Jesus didn't fast to get specific things from His dad but to grow in the knowledge of His dad and His will. We fast to love God and spend time with Him and as we do this, He reveals more of Himself to us! When you go to visit your friend, do you go because you want something from them? Or do you go to spend time with them and enjoy their fellowship? Likewise fast to hang out with God! Just for fellowship.

Jesus faced great challenges with people, but it was not impossible for Him because He often took time to feed and grow His Spirit in God. Jesus often withdrew Himself to pray. It was His lifestyle as we see in Luke 5:16 (NLT) "But Jesus often withdrew to the wilderness for prayer." And so must we so that we can do what He said we would do. We shall do greater things than He did if we believe in Him and follow His example.

"I tell you the truth, anyone who believes in me will do the same works I have done, and even greater works, because I am going to be with the Father" (John 14:12 NLT).

Let us seek God and FAST to fully equip our spirits to prosper in every good work set out for us to do in Christ Jesus. God ALWAYS answers prayers if you believe and remain steadfast in Him!

"Peter was therefore kept in prison, but *constant* prayer was offered to God for him by the church" (Acts 12:5; italics added).

God sent an angel to break Peter out of prison and save him from death. God answered the *constant prayers* of the church.

"Peter finally came to his senses. 'It's really true!' he said. 'The Lord has sent his angel and saved me from Herod and from what the Jewish leaders had planned to do to me!' When he realized this, he went to the home of Mary, the mother of John Mark, where many were gathered for prayer" (Acts 12:11–12 NLT).

"*Don't worry about anything; instead, pray about everything.* Tell God what you need, and thank him for all he has done. *Then you will experience God's peace, which exceeds anything we can understand.* His peace will guard your hearts and minds as you live in Christ Jesus" (Phil. 4:6–7 NLT: italics added).

The people praying for Peter were so shocked to see him knocking at the door that they thought it was his ghost. When we pray without ceasing, we unlock things in the spirit and set the captives free because God answers us in His wisdom and we stand amazed! Prayer releases angels to work on our behalf to fulfill kingdom purpose. Never stop praying. The prayer of faith is the power that moves God on our behalf. Someone came up with the meaning of PUSH—Pray Until Something Happens!

"Are any of you suffering hardships? You should pray. Are any of you happy? You should sing praises. Are any of you sick? You should call for the elders of the church to come and pray over you, anointing you with oil in the name of the Lord. Such a prayer offered in faith will heal the sick, and the Lord will make you well. And if you have committed any sins, you will be forgiven" (James 5:13–15 NLT).

James 5:17-18 (NLT) tell us, "Elijah was as human as we are, and yet when he prayed earnestly that no rain would fall, none fell for three and a half years! Then, when he prayed again, the sky sent down rain and the earth began to yield its crops."

"Now this is the confidence that we have in Him, *that if we ask anything according to His will*, He hears us and if we know that He hears us, whatever we ask, we know that we have the petitions that we have asked of Him" (1 John 5:14–15; italics added).

The most effective way to pray is praying the will of God. If you know what God says about a situation, you are 99.9 percent closer to your manifestation of the prayer. All you have to do is speak it! Repeat it, call Him to account, and it will be done. That's why it's important to have HIA (heaven's intelligence agent), God the Holy Spirit, to let you in on God's will. My children have me as their home intelligence agent in our home because I know what their father's will is for them. If I tell them to ask their dad for something, it is because it is according to his will for them. Their request is therefore guaranteed to be granted.

The Holy Spirit of God knows God and His will. To know God's will, you MUST read His Word which the Holy Spirit inspired, ask Him to teach you, reveal it to you, and give you an understanding of it. Spend time with Him, get to know Him, and you will have a great prayer life, like Jesus did. He fasted, prayed, and sought His dad's will and His prayers were all answered. He lived in the supernatural manifestation of God's power.

"Now then, we are ambassadors for Christ, as though God were pleading through us: we implore you on Christ's behalf, be reconciled to God" (2 Cor. 5:20).

We represent heaven, so our prayers must be for the interest of God's Kingdom. Just as the American ambassador represents the United States in whatever country he or she is in and whatever requests the ambassador makes must be beneficial to the country he or she represents and not just to himself or herself or another nation, God answers prayers that benefit His Kingdom.

> You lust, and don't have. You murder and covet, and can't obtain. You fight and make war. You don't have, because you don't

ask. You ask, and don't receive, because you ask with wrong motives, so that you may spend it for your pleasures. You adulterers and adulteresses, don't you know that friendship with the world is hostility toward God? Whoever therefore wants to be a friend of the world makes himself an enemy of God. (James 4:2–4 WEB)

Jesus Himself learned this and prayed in Luke 22:42; italics added; "Father, if it's Your will, take this cup away from Me; *nevertheless not My will, but Yours, be done.*"

Let's represent heaven well, as Jesus Christ did, and we shall live in the supernatural! Psalm 37:4 says, "Delight yourself also in the Lord, and He shall give you the desires of your heart."

Delighting yourself in God means that you want what He wants even when it hurts, even unto death. Like Jesus said to Paul, that Paul must suffer for the sake of the Gospel and Paul never bailed out. If Jesus suffered persecution, we will also suffer persecution because a servant is not greater than his master. Loving your enemies, forgiving them, doing good to those who persecute you is not pleasant or easy, but as you do this God puts His desires (what you should desire to fulfill your assignment on earth) in your heart.

The desires He puts in you are bigger than what you can fulfill with your might, therefore you must commit your life and all your ways to Him. Trust that He can do greater things with you in His hands than with you on your own. He will then fulfill all the GRAND desires He put in you that you would not have thought of or otherwise accomplished. He will show Himself strong through you, and you will shine as a light for Him that people will marvel, just as He did Christ.

"Commit your way to the LORD, Trust also in Him, And He shall bring it to pass. He shall bring forth your righteousness as the light, and your justice as the noonday" (Ps. 37:5–6).

Our desires may not be His desire. How true is that—because our spirits always war with our flesh. Jesus experienced this, when His desire was not to take the cup of suffering, but it was not God's desire.

God never granted His request, but when Jesus delighted Himself in the LORD GOD, and His desires lined up with God's desires, He fulfilled the greatest assignment ever done. The foundation of the Kingdom of God that was very deep and so strong that there is no limit to how high this building can go. The Bible said He descended and then ascended, which means He dug to the deepest place and rose the building to the highest place, so we must not let Him down.

Let us get busy and build upon this great foundation, Jesus Christ! Hallelujah to the glory of the most high God! He saved all humanity that WHOSOEVER accepts Him has everlasting life. He is now exalted high above all! Jesus said in Revelation 3:21,

"To him who overcomes I will grant to sit with Me on My throne, as I also overcame and sat down with My Father on His throne."

Beloved, the throne is not for easy sailors, but for overcomers.

"These things I have spoken to you, that in Me you may have peace. In the world you will have tribulation; but be of good cheer, I have overcome the world" John 16:33).

Paul walked closely with God the Holy Spirit, who warned him in Acts 20:23–24, "except that the Holy Spirit testifies in every city, saying that chains and tribulations await me. But none of these things move me; nor do I count my life dear to myself, so that I may finish my race with joy, and the ministry which I received from the Lord Jesus, to testify to the gospel of the grace of God."

Jesus said, in John 4:34 NLT; "My nourishment comes from doing the will of God, who sent me, and from finishing his work."

May we have the same attitude as Christ had in Jesus name! It is not according to our will, and that is why Paul said…

"And the Holy Spirit helps us in our weakness. For example, we don't know what God wants us to pray for. But the Holy Spirit prays for us with groanings that cannot be expressed in words. And the Father who knows all hearts knows what the Spirit is saying, for the Spirit pleads for us believers in harmony with God's own will." (Romans 8:26–27 NLT)

How perfect that we have the Holy Spirit as our intercessor. We have all we need. Let us lean not on our own understanding. Our desires can be right, but if the motive is wrong, then God cannot grant us our desires.

"When you ask, you do not receive, because you ask with wrong motives, that you may spend what you get on your pleasures" (James 4:3 NIV).

Our desires must be in line with God's desires always. We should not shy away from asking God what we need, just like children. He will always answer yes, no, or wait, just as we answer our children.

Also, one important thing I have learned when I pray is to report for duty. When you pray, release yourself to God, and let Him give you your day's assignment, not you giving Him His day's assignment. Many times people pray and tell God their plans and then ask God to come and do what they want Him to do. We are the created, not the Creator. We get our assignment from God; we do not give Him assignments. Like a student, you get homework and classwork from the instructor and not the other way around. We must know that this world is His, and we have been invited to rule and reign with Him. He is the Supreme Court, and we are the little courts on earth, enforcing what the Supreme Court wants!

Prayer is talking to God and yielding to His will as our Creator, Father, Lord, and Savior, knowing that it is not our will but His will be done on earth as it is in heaven. By the Holy Spirit, our prayers will be perfect and effective. Remember, the persistent prayers of a righteous person are powerful and effective. Righteousness is by faith through Christ. Abraham believed God and was credited to Him as righteousness. As we believe and trust in His perfect plan, we pray according to His will by His Spirit, and we are called the righteousness of God in Christ Jesus! Amen.

Jesus prayed often, and He prayed even more earnestly when He was in agony in Luke 22:39–46. Most of us are unable to pray in the hardest of times just like the disciples. Jesus also said to pray not to fall into temptation. We must pray to be victorious over all temptation even more at the most trying times, the most sorrowful times. Jesus had no one to help Him pray. He never had a high priest to help Him pray like we do. Glory to God that we have Jesus Christ praying for us even when no one else is praying for us. The disciples needed to pray—if not for Jesus, at least for themselves because temptation was coming. They needed to stand and not fall into it; this was, and still is, Jesus's instructions to all His disciples. Thank God for Jesus. God sent angels to strengthen Jesus, and angels are sent to our rescue when we pray. Angels of God are ministering spirits unto us who are in Christ.

"But to which of the angels has the Father ever said, 'Sit at My right hand [together with me in royal dignity], until I make your enemies A footstool for your feet [in triumphant conquest]'? Are not all the angels ministering spirits sent out [by God] to serve (accompany, protect) those who will inherit salvation? [Of course they are!]" (Heb. 1:13–14 AMP).

Thank God for Jesus and His angels. Psalm 34:7 says, "The angel of the Lord encamps all around those who fear Him, and delivers them."

Amen! Let us therefore pray and obey and keep the angels busy. They minister unto us as we submit our will to God's will. Angels came to Jesus as He prayed and submitted to the Father's will in the wilderness;

"Then the devil left Him; and angels came and ministered to Him [bringing Him food and serving Him]." (Matt 4:11 AMP)

And in the Garden of Gethsemane...

"Now an angel appeared to Him from heaven, strengthening Him. And being in agony [deeply distressed and anguished; almost to the point of death], He prayed more intently; and His sweat became like drops of blood, falling down on the ground." (Luke 22:43 AMP)

An angel came to Peter and broke Him out of prison as the church prayed…

> And behold, an angel of the Lord stood by him, and a light shone in the cell. He struck Peter on the side, and woke him up, saying, "Stand up quickly!" His chains fell off from his hands. The angel said to him, "Get dressed and put on your sandals." He did so. He said to him, "Put on your cloak, and follow me." And he went out and followed him. He didn't know that what was being done by the angel was real, but thought he saw a vision. When they were past the first and the second guard, they came to the iron gate that leads into the city, which opened to them by itself. They went out, and went down one street, and immediately the angel departed from him. (Acts 12:7-10 WEB)

An angel broke the Apostles out of prison so they can preach more of the good news of Jesus Christ that they were arrested for in the first place.

> But the high priest stood up, along with all his associates (that is, the sect of the Sadducees), and they were filled with jealousy *and* resentment. They arrested the apostles and put them in a public jail. But during the night an angel of the Lord opened the prison doors, and leading them out, he said, "Go, stand and *continue* to tell the people in the temple [courtyards] the whole message of this Life [the eternal life revealed by Christ and found through faith in Him]." When they heard this, they went into the temple [courtyards] about daybreak and *began* teaching. (Acts 5:17-21 AMP)

An angel came to Daniel with the answer to his prayer when he prayed and fasted for twenty-one days. Angel Gabriel was sent with the message to Daniel.

> Then he said to me, 'Don't be afraid, Daniel; for from the first day that you set your heart to understand, and to humble yourself before your God, your words were heard: and I have come for your words' sake. But the prince of the kingdom of Persia withstood me twenty-one days; but, behold, Michael, one of the chief princes, came to help me: and I remained there with the kings of Persia. (Daniel 10:12-13 WEB)

An angel came to the rescue and killed 185,000 mighty men of the great Assyrian army, who threatened to destroy the children of God when King Hezekiah prayed.

'That night the angel of the Lord went out to the Assyrian camp and killed 185,000 Assyrian soldiers. When the surviving Assyrians woke up the next morning, they found corpses everywhere." (2 Kings 19:35 NLT)

Our Heavenly Father is the King of kings, The God of angel armies and the angels are our servants in Christ.

As long as I am in Christ, I don't have to beg for God to send me angels, the angels of the LORD must encamp around me because I fear and trust in God in obedience to God's word in Psalm 34:7 AMP;

"The angel of the Lord encamps around those who fear Him [with awe-inspired reverence and worship Him with obedience], And He rescues [each of] them."

My Stories: Fasting and Prayer

One day, when I was led on a forty-day fast, I was all alone in the house, and I had about seven more days left. I felt very weak, and as I sat on the couch, I spoke to Jesus and said, "Jesus, the scriptures tell me that when you fasted and prayed, you had angels come to minister unto you and strengthen you. Now where is my help?"

I then went to bed. About thirty minutes into my sleep, I was laying on my back, and I had a dream that I was in a room with tinted glass walls all around. I lay weak in the bed, unable to move. As I looked out, I saw some men outside the room and I was hoping they wouldn't see me because if they did and came in, I would be in trouble because I was so weak and could not get out of bed. Immediately I looked in front of me through the thick glass wall and saw Jesus. He was dressed in full battle armor, coming into my room with so much authority and boldness. He made one step into the room through the thick glass wall, and the whole place shook heavily like a great earthquake. My stomach felt as if there was a huge fan inside, fanning it.

I woke up, sat up in bed immediately pressing down onto my stomach. I felt the same feeling in my stomach that I felt while in the dream. It was so real. I then said to Jesus as I sat on my bed, "Jesus, oh Jesus, come back again. I will hold my stomach this time so I can stand Your presence." Little did I know that was my strengthening that I asked for before I went to bed.

I went back to sleep and from that moment, I was extremely strengthened and felt so much energy, more than I have ever felt when eating food. I went through the rest of the week of fasting with the greatest energy ever, with joy and awe, knowing that God had heard and answered my prayer. Because I was obeying His Word that commanded me to fast, and I acknowledged the need of His strength and grace, Jesus Himself came to strengthen me. He did not send any angels, oh glory to God. Jesus is a present help in times of trouble! Hallelujah!

Another day as I was on another forty day fast, God literally turned off my stomach and I did not desire anything to eat but I was very strong! This was amazing! Working two jobs and raising a family and slacked in nothing. On one occasion I was lying in bed looking up and meditating upon the goodness of God when I heard Him say to me that I had been promoted in my workplace and He gave me the title of the position which I was promoted to. I did not know of any job opening because I was not even looking. God saw the position and told me about it.

I immediately went downstairs and told my husband what God said. I updated my résumé and took it to the office. They told me that if I had gone two weeks ago, the position would still have been open. They had already hired someone for the position. I did not lose hope because I knew that God did not speak two weeks earlier and He never lies. I also had acted quickly in Faith according to His Word and had not put it off, therefore I knew that the word which God spoke was still valid. I said to her, "OK. No problem. Keep my résumé and call me."

I went on praising God for the position, and started addressing myself using the new title in my heart and at home. I would speak it out until it manifested in the physical. I did not need to go back and pray about it because I already knew God's will. I kept it to myself and only revealed it to my husband, children and one person who stood with me in agreement with God's Word. You must be very careful who you reveal to what God has promised you so as not to abort the promise. The Holy Spirit will reveal to you whom you need to tell. I called those things that were not at the moment as though they were.

I even began shopping and bought my new attire, had it embroidered with my name and new title on it and prepared for the position. I met the lady who had been hired for the position, she came to where I was working and introduced herself to me. We had a great conversation and she said that people often asked her how she got such a high position and she would tell them that it was by God's grace. I congratulated her on her new position and I was genuinely happy for her. I wished her success and God's blessings.

About one to two months later, I received a phone call about the position and I accepted the offer. The position not only had the perfect hours giving me more time for my family, it also paid great! What a glorious and mighty God I serve. If you are faithful with little, God will entrust you with much. I was faithful in the assignment I had before God promoted me.

My standard is that everyone is Jesus to me. I was a witness of Christ to everyone around me; my co-workers, patients and their families. Christ said that whatever you do to the least of others, you do it unto Him (see Matthew 25:31-46). I told people about Jesus and His great sacrifice and promise of eternal life and led all who desired to Christ. I prayed for their healing and peace. Others refused Him even on their death beds, others accepted Him, and others did not want anything to do with Him. I respected their choices and showed the Love of God by how I cared for them.

I remember one prisoner whom I shared Christ with when he had been hospitalized, He accepted Jesus as his LORD and Savior, he asked for a bible and was reading scripture in the hospital. He was excited and enjoyed his new relationship with Christ. A few months later, He came back to the hospital, now a free man, to say thank you for leading him to Jesus and testified of how his life and his family, including marriage had been changed for the better.

By God's grace I started a few Bible studies where I text God's Word daily to many. I also began a women's fellowship where many marriages have been healed and many women strengthened to step into their rightful position of prayer in their homes. God can use you wherever you are if you allow Him to. When Christ's light in you shines big in the place you are in, He enlarges your territory so that you may shine His great light in an even bigger place.

Floodlights are found in the stadium, not in a small room. How big is your light? Are you ashamed of Christ or do you share His greatness and goodness wherever you go? If people do not mind offending you as they curse, and their words do not give life, why should you be afraid of offending them by being like Christ and speaking His Word that gives life? Do you take God at His Word and act on it? Or are you afraid of looking stupid? What if God spoke to me about the promotion and I just agreed and sat at home and prayed? Would I have received my promotion? Absolutely not!

We must receive God's Word, believe it and act it out for it to be fulfilled. Do all you can do to prepare and God will do His part. Remember, God releases His promises to us in the spiritual realm, but it is up to us to bring it out into the physical realm. I never thought I would do what He said I would, just like Gideon, but I knew He is my creator and He knows what strength He put in me when He created me so I believed Him.

One of the people confessed to me later that they never thought I would make it and were waiting for my downfall. They were not happy for me because it took them a longer time to get that position and they had worked for a long time in it too, double digit number of years while it took me a very short time. I encountered some animosity from some of them and other many challenges but I always reminded the devil what God said about me and who I was and because God said it, I was it. I had God's spoken Word to fall back on in the dark times. Remember not to doubt in the dark what God spoke to you in the light.

It is not going to be easy because the kingdom of heaven suffers violence, and only the violent take it by force. The devil was angry because I was going to displace him and pull down his stronghold in that place and he had to fight me but I know his face too well. I love my persecutors and my enemies because they are innocent victims of the devil. I do not fight them, rather I pray for them and fight their master, the devil, to set them (his captives) free. Beloved, God's favor is not fair! He doesn't look on the outside like man does, He looks on the inside. He is a rewarder of those who diligently seek Him. Are you diligently seeking Him? If yes, await your reward!

We need to realize that we are in a Kingdom, and in a kingdom, there is no democracy. You do not own anything in a kingdom because the King owns everything and He only allows you to be a steward of His Kingdom. Therefore, the more profit you bring to the Kingdom, the greater the authority you receive and territory you get to possess so that you can bring even greater profit to the Kingdom. It is very unfortunate that children of

God do not understand this. Because we live in a democracy, they believe that they need to vote on what God says or commands. There is no vote here! You have no say whatsoever on making laws in God's Kingdom. You are either for the Kingdom and obey the rules and laws, or you are against the Kingdom. We cannot compromise or allow the laws of people to supersede the laws of God. God will never be democratic. He will never ask for your input on His laws.

Even if God has called you and you serve Him, you are no exception if you break His commands. If you reject the Son of the King, who died to redeem you, you will be rejected by the King because as the King rules, so does His Son. Moses was chosen by God for the great task of rescuing the Israelites from bondage, but he was no exception to God's laws. God almost killed him before he began his task when he disobeyed God by forgetting to circumcise his son. Forgetting will not bail you out of punishment. His wife obeyed God fast enough to save her husband from God's wrath. God is no respecter of persons. He is a consuming fire and consumes sin regardless of who bears the sin. Even Jesus Christ, His only begotten son, couldn't escape the punishment for the sin He took for us. He had to die.

"On the way to Egypt, at a place where Moses and his family had stopped for the night, the Lord confronted him and was about to kill him. But Moses' wife, Zipporah, took a flint knife and circumcised her son. She touched his feet with the foreskin and said, "Now you are a bridegroom of blood to me." (When she said "a bridegroom of blood," she was referring to the circumcision.) After that, the Lord left him alone. (Exodus 4:24-26 NLT)

Trust in God, Not in Man or on Your Understanding

According to the *Oxford Dictionary*, *trust* means "firm belief in the reliability, truth, ability, or strength of someone or something."

> This is what the Lord says: "Cursed are those who put their trust in mere humans, who rely on human strength and turn their hearts away from the Lord." They are like stunted shrubs in the desert, with no hope for the future. They will live in the barren wilderness, in an uninhabited salty land. But blessed are those who trust in the Lord and have made the Lord their hope and confidence. They are like trees planted along a riverbank, with roots that reach deep into the water. Such trees are not bothered by the heat or worried by long months of drought. Their leaves stay green, and they never stop producing fruit." (Jer. 17:5–8 NLT)

"Trust in the Lord with all your heart; do not depend on your own understanding. Seek his will in all you do, and he will show you which path to take. Don't be impressed with your own wisdom. Instead, fear the Lord and turn away from evil. Then you will have healing for your body and strength for your bones" (Prov. 3:5–8 NLT).

"Some trust in chariots and some in horses, but we will remember and trust in the name of the Lord our God. They have bowed down and fallen, But we have risen and stood upright" (Ps. 20:7–8 AMP).

Are you walking under a curse or a blessing? Trusting in people or in God? God knows the hearts of people, so trust Him to pick and choose who will participate in your God-given assignment. Jesus did. He prayed and inquired of His Father God before choosing His twelve disciples. He was led by God through the Holy Spirit of God. We must follow His perfect example and consult God with our every move. Do not lean on your own understanding. Trust God with your life. He created you; He knows all He has in store for you. Don't disqualify yourself or allow people to disqualify you, because God has qualified you and that is all that matters! Like He told Jeremiah, He is saying this to you today.

> Now Yahweh's word came to me, saying, "Before I formed you in the womb, I knew you. Before you were born, I sanctified

you. I have appointed you a prophet to the nations." Then I said, "Ah, Lord Yahweh! Behold, I don't know how to speak; for I am a child." But Yahweh said to me, "Don't say, 'I am a child;' for you must go to whomever I send you, and you must say whatever I command you. Don't be afraid because of them, for I am with you to rescue you," says Yahweh. Then Yahweh stretched out his hand, and touched my mouth. Then Yahweh said to me, "Behold, I have put my words in your mouth. Behold, I have today set you over the nations and over the kingdoms, to uproot and to tear down, to destroy and to overthrow, to build and to plant." Moreover Yahweh's word came to me, saying, "Jeremiah, what do you see?" I said, "I see a branch of an almond tree." Then Yahweh said to me, "You have seen well; for I watch over my word to perform it." (Jer. 1:4–12 WEB; italics added)

God is watching over His word to fulfill it in your life.

"Those who trust in the Lord are as secure as Mount Zion; they will not be defeated but will endure forever" (Ps. 125:1 NLT).

"But those who trust in the Lord will find new strength. They will soar high on wings like eagles. They will run and not grow weary. They will walk and not faint" (Isa. 40:31 NLT).

Isaiah 50:10-11(AMP) italics added

"Who is among you who fears the LORD, Who obeys the voice of His Servant,

Yet who walks in darkness and has no light? *Let him trust and be confident in the name of the LORD and let him rely on his God.* Listen carefully, *all you who kindle your own fire [devising your own man-made plan of salvation], Who surround yourselves with torches, Walk by the light of your [self-made] fire And among the torches that you have set ablaze. But this you will have from My hand: You will lie down in [a place of] torment."*

Self-reliance, trust in other men and lack of trust in God will lead us to destruction. We were created to consult, rely and trust in God FULLY and in ALL things, even the ones that seem simple, for our assignments on earth to be fulfilled. Let us look at one other scripture of a king who died because of this.

> At that time Hanani the seer came to Asa king of Judah and said to him: "Because you relied on the king of Aram and not on the Lord your God, the army of the king of Aram has escaped from your hand. Were not the Cushites and Libyans a mighty army with great numbers of chariots and horsemen? Yet when you relied on the Lord, he delivered them into your hand. *For the eyes of the Lord range throughout the earth to strengthen those whose hearts are fully committed to him.* You have done a foolish thing, and from now on you will be at war." In the thirty-ninth year of his reign Asa was afflicted with a disease in his feet. Though his disease was severe, *even in his illness he did not seek help from the Lord, but only from the physicians.* Then in the forty-first year of his reign Asa died and rested with his ancestors. (2 Chronicles 16:7-9, 12-13 (NIV); italics added)

Did you know as a believer before you go to the doctors you must pray and rely on God to give them wisdom on how to treat you? If you haven't been doing this, you must repent for relying on human wisdom than on God. Pray as you go to the hospital for treatment. Consult and pray to our Great Physician, Jesus Christ because He has already paid for your healing if you believe. If it is an emergency, as soon as you can, pray and get Him on the medical board of directors as the Chief of all doctors and allow His healing power and love to flow through you to impact many you will encounter there.

HUMILITY

Humility is a MUST have for God to use you. God never associates Himself with the prideful. He actually fights against them.

According to the *Oxford Dictionary*, humility is "a modest or low view of one's own importance."

Someone once wrote that, "Humility is not thinking less of yourself, but it is thinking of yourself less."

I came across someone in the Bible who was said to be more humble than anyone on Earth at that time. This was Moses. Why was he humble? What made him humble?

In Numbers 12 God said this about him....

> Miriam and Aaron began to talk against Moses because of his Cushite wife, for he had married a Cushite. "Has the Lord spoken only through Moses?" they asked. "Hasn't he also spoken through us?" And the Lord heard this. (Now Moses was a very humble man, more humble than anyone else on the face of the earth.) At once the Lord said to Moses, Aaron and Miriam, "Come out to the tent of meeting, all three of you." So the three of them went out. Then the Lord came down in a pillar of cloud; he stood at the entrance to the tent and summoned Aaron and Miriam. When the two of them stepped forward, he said, "Listen to my words: "When there is a prophet among you, I, the Lord, reveal myself to them in visions, I speak to them in dreams. But this is not true of my servant Moses; he is faithful in all my house. With him I speak face to face, clearly and not in riddles; he sees the form of the Lord. Why then were you not afraid to speak against my servant Moses?" The anger of the Lord burned against them, and he left them. When the cloud lifted from above the tent, Miriam's skin was leprous—it became as white as snow. Aaron turned toward her and saw that she had a defiling skin disease. (Numbers 12:1-10 NIV)

God used to speak with Moses face to face and Moses never boasted or saw himself as superior. He was selfless and gave up his life to do

God's will. God fought Moses's own siblings for speaking against His HUMBLE servant. HUMILITY moves God to defend you, glorify you before your enemies and fight for you greatly!

"No, O people, the Lord has told you what is good, and this is what he requires of you: to do what is right, to love mercy, and to walk humbly with your God." Micah 6:8 NLT

Let's look at some scriptures that reveal the importance and benefits of humility.

Humility Attracts God's Mercy

"Then if my people who are called by my name will humble themselves and pray and seek my face and turn from their wicked ways, I will hear from heaven and will forgive their sins and restore their land" (2 Chron. 7:14).

"Do you see how Ahab has humbled himself before me? Because he has done this, I will not do what I promised during his lifetime. It will happen to his sons; I will destroy his dynasty" (1 Kings 21:29 NLT).

"Because Rehoboam humbled himself, the Lord's anger was turned away, and he did not destroy him completely. There were still some good things in the land of Judah" (2 Chron. 12:12 NLT).

"You rescue the humble, but you humiliate the proud" (Ps. 18:27 NLT).

"The sacrifice you desire is a broken spirit. You will not reject a broken and repentant heart, O God." (Ps. 51:17 NLT).

Humility Leads You into God's Ways

"He leads the humble in doing right, teaching them his way" (Ps. 25:9 NLT).

Humility Attracts God's Grace or power

"In the same way, you who are younger must accept the authority of the elders. And all of you, dress yourselves in humility as you relate to one another, for 'God opposes the proud but gives grace to the humble'" (1 Pet. 5:5).

Humility Marks God's Assignment in us

We are assigned to serve, not to be served.

"For even the Son of Man came not to be served but to serve others and to give his life as a ransom for many" (Mark 10:45).

"You must have the same attitude that Christ Jesus had. Though He was God, He did not think of equality with God as something to cling to. Instead, he gave up his divine privileges; He took the humble position of a slave and was born as a human being. When he appeared in human form, He humbled himself in obedience to God and died a criminal's death on a cross" (Phil. 2:5–8).

Humility Attracts God's Treasures and Blessings

"For the Lord delights in his people; he crowns the humble with victory" (Ps. 149:4).

"Pride leads to disgrace, but with humility comes wisdom" (Prov. 11:2).

""The reward of humility [that is, having a realistic view of one's importance] and the [reverent, worshipful] fear of the Lord is riches, honor, and life." (Proverbs 22:4 AMP)

"I will bless those who have humble and contrite hearts, who tremble at my word" (Isa. 66:2).

Humility Is a Requirement for Walking with God

"No, O people, the Lord has told you what is good, and this is what he requires of you: to do what is right, to love mercy, and to walk humbly with your God" (Mic. 6:8).

"The high and lofty one who lives in eternity, the Holy One, says this: 'I live in the high and holy place with those whose spirits are contrite and humble. I restore the crushed spirit of the humble and revive the courage of those with repentant hearts'" (Isa. 57:15).

Pride vs humility

Difference between the two Thieves on the Cross

"One of the criminals hanging beside him scoffed, 'So you're the Messiah, are you? Prove it by saving yourself—and us, too, while you're at it!' But the other criminal protested, *'Don't you fear God* even when you have been sentenced to die? *We deserve to die for our crimes*, but this man hasn't done anything wrong.' Then he said, *'Jesus, remember me when you come into your Kingdom.'* And Jesus replied, 'I assure you, today you will be with me in paradise'" (Luke 23:39–43 NLT; italics added).

How interesting and eye-opening this was to see practically the different results between humility and the fear of God in one criminal and pride and lack of fear of God in the other criminal. One acknowledged he was a sinner, feared God, acknowledged Christ's righteousness, and went on to believe that Christ is God and is king and would not remain dead. He believed that Christ's crucifixion was a transition into His Kingdom! This thief knew and believed more than the teachers of the law, the Disciples of Christ, or anyone else on earth at that time! The thief must have heard Jesus teach on the kingdom many times, He must have believed but still struggled with sin. He acknowledged that he was a sinner and that he deserved his punishment, and that Jesus was righteous and only He could save him from the death he was about to face eternally. This is what everyone must do to be saved, or born again.

The thief believed that eternal death had no victory over Jesus, so he connected himself with Christ that he may also live eternally. He asked

Jesus to remember him when He came into His Kingdom. That thief was the first to be enrolled into God's Kingdom in the new covenant because of his belief and faith in God and his humility and fear of God at the cross. He had more faith and revelation of Jesus than the disciples who had walked with Jesus daily for three years. He and Christ had a moment there, where the fresh hot blood of Christ, which remains the same for ANYONE who believes and asks for it even now, washed him clean and gave him a new title and a new-home guarantee when he left earth! He even became a witness of Christ while still in the pain he suffered on the cross to His fellow thief. He defended Jesus and his heart was truly changed. What a cleansing; what a fountain; what assurance! Glory to the most high God! Glory to God for JESUS!

GOAL SETTING

Set your goals according to God's plan not your convenience.

When we want to achieve certain goals, we set limits and plan according to the timing and wisdom of the world. However, we cannot do the same exact thing with God's assignment and succeed. We must move in faith according to God's ability and timing. We must rely on His grace, which is His strength and not ours. When God gives you an assignment, you must not sit on it. Instead, ask yourself what you can do now to move toward the end result. Remember a long journey begins with the first step. Because the GGT bigger than man, if you rely on man's wisdom you will never get to see it.

A great example is the children of Israel. They had a promise to go into the Promised Land and they started on their journey but got distracted by hardships along the way. They faced many obstacles that when they found a little comfort along the way, they would settle for that. When they were thirsty without water, they complained, but when they found water, they did not want to leave the place of comfort even though it was not the Promised Land. How many times like them do we settle for less than God promised us because of the obstacles and discouragements along the way? We must not settle. We must push on knowing that God ALWAYS keeps His promise. We must not doubt in the darkest situations what God told us in the light.

When I pray daily, I ask God to help me accomplish all He had planned for me to do each day before the foundation of the earth. I pray against the spirit of manipulation, disruption and confusion to be destroyed in Jesus name. I then take account of every minute I spend and make it count toward building God's Kingdom. How many hours have you put in towards eternity? Do you have any hours or no paycheck at all? Are you working overtime? There is a lot of overtime in God's Kingdom because many people are a no call no show. Many 'call in busy' with earthly and worldly cares. If a human being pays you overtime at two and a half times your pay, how much more does God pay His overtime workers? His Kingdom is so wealthy that His streets are made of pure Gold. I am always signed up for overtime in God's Kingdom and I tell God to give me His grace to fulfill this. I used to work lots of overtime in my two full-time jobs, I got the money but the tax was very high. God on the other hand does not need to tax you, it is overtime tax free pay because He owns everything and is sovereign.

Whatever you do, let those around you desire God. Make goals daily to give your time, money and effort towards pleasing God and growing your gifts and talents. If singing, make time to practice and get a vocal instructor if you can to keep training so that you can give God the best and grow His Kingdom. The children of the world spend a lot of time and money in growing their talent for their benefit, how much more should we children of God do it for the Kingdom? Wake up early, cut off the many idle times in your life, you don't have to pick up every phone call, that is why we have voice mail, you don't have to reply every text immediately, be selective and discreet, and silence the volumes around you so as to hear God. This will keep you from gossip and entertaining evil, it will get rid of idlers in your life because they will not use your ears as a trash can where they deposit every junk they hear or think of. You will avoid unnecessary gatherings which are time wasting and displeasing to God. Even if the gathering may not be ungodly, it could be a distraction from your GGT.

We must learn to say NO so we can stay on task and please God. Learn to cut off your internet, social media and T.V time that you use for pleasure. Instead of getting worked up or impatient when you must wait in line or when you are stuck in traffic, use this time to pray and seek God's will. Turn off the music in your car even if it is gospel music once in a while and talk to God. Just like you would lower the volume of the music in your car when having a conversation with someone so you can communicate. When you listen to music, be selective. Listen to music that will glorify God knowing He is always with you, music that He will enjoy listening to with you. Choose music that will build your spirit, don't listen to just any trash out there. When you read a book, read something that will grow your spirit. When you watch T.V, watch something that will build your spirit and increase your knowledge of God. Invest in the spirit and you will find it easy to obey God because your spirit will be stronger than the flesh.

When you exercise, be it walking or running, sometimes leave the music off and talk to God. I do this every time I exercise and I have had great conversations with God. These are many ways you can stay in constant communication and knowledge of what God expects of you and stay on task. You will find yourself being more productive and fulfilling your GGT in God's timing. You can also make a journal or log so you can keep track of your progress. God will not give you divine assistance if you are lazy because this is wickedness in His sight. He will give you favor, divine assistance and connection when you put Him first in your life. Set your goals in accordance to His goals and timing. May God prosper you as you do this in Jesus's name.

CHAPTER 17
Challenges

Your God-given task will be fought with.

HATERS

THE FIRST HATER OF YOUR GGT is Satan himself. He has had this hatred from the beginning of creation and he still has not changed and will not change. His first tactic is to present God to you in a negative way. He knows if he makes you doubt God, His Word and promises to you, you will be an easy target for him to prey on.

In the Garden of Eden, Adam and Eve were given all dominion, power, and right to all creation. God did all the work and gave it all to them to run. What a gift of no sweat. They did nothing to deserve it; it was all by God's grace. He made them equal partners, and all they had to do was live in obedience. Why did God put the tree of knowledge of good and evil in the garden instead of leaving it out since it was not meant for them? Why did he instruct them against that tree? God would have made it easy for them to live in obedience without the tree and the "do not" instruction would not have existed. The answer is very simple. It is found multiple times in the Word of God. God desires to be loved, and love for Him is obedience to Him. "If you love Me, obey my commands" (John 14:15).

By the way, if you haven't noticed by now, after his fall, Satan is extremely obedient to God. He must do the Word of God. He has never defied God after the fall and He is afraid of even greater punishment, yet he works so hard to get you to disobey God because he knows disobedience gives him the legal right into your heart and home. It takes God's protection away from you, exposing you to spiritual danger which is physically deadly. Disobedience leads to curses from God not from the devil, and when God curses you, the enemy has access to you but when God blesses you, no devil or person can curse you; your blessings are sure and they make you rich in the spirit, soul, and body. The blessings of the Lord make us rich and add no sorrow (Prov. 10:22). That is why when you obey God's Word, the devil cannot mess with you because the angels of God are encamped around you. As the Word of God says, the angels of the Lord surround and defend those who fear God (Ps. 34:7).

If you submit yourself and all you are and have to God and you resist the devil, he will flee from you (James 4:7). Satan will not disobey God, which is why before he tempts you he must ask for permission from God like he did with Job and Peter, the disciple of Jesus.

God will never allow you to be tempted beyond what you can bear. Any temptation you go through, God has already screened it and made sure that it is something you can overcome and be victorious over. The devil cannot change the rules as he goes. Remember Job's story? The devil had to ask for permission each time he thought of a new temptation for Job.

Do not worry because we are more than conquerors in Christ Jesus. Just as tests are formulated for the student's specific level of education and the university student cannot get first-grade exams and vice versa, you cannot be tested on what God has not taught or put in you. Even in the temptation, the answer book is always in front of you, the bible, and your Counselor and Instructor, the Holy Spirit, is ready to answer your questions, revealing and explaining the answers. It is an open-book test, and it is won on a kneeling position, with prayer, faith and trust in God's Word.

Some challenges we face in life lead us to take offense, lack forgiveness and love for others. We will take a look at offense, forgiveness and love; how to overcome offense, how to forgive and how to have love in abundance for all regardless of the trials we face in life.

OFFENSE

Your God-given task will offend many and many will offend you.

Because your GGT is intended to please God, God does not consult people when creating and assigning it to you. Many people will not understand you and will be offended by you because your GGT is beyond human comprehension. You cannot fulfill any supernatural task with your natural strength; you need God the Holy Spirit to fulfill it. Many people will come into your life for a season and a reason, and you must learn to consult God about every one of them. Some will come to help you get to the next level and to encourage you; some will come to test you, to pressure wash you, and some will come to detour you or to distract you from your GGT.

Only by the help of God the Holy Spirit will we know whom we need to cut off and at what time, whom to embrace and whom to be careful about. Christ, even with the knowledge that one of His chosen disciples was a devil, continued to walk with Judas Iscariot until the appointed time for separation. He was also ready to be denied by His friends and for them to leave and forsake Him. He never took offense or revenge, He never left them or hated them because He knew that there are specific people chosen and assigned to us at different stages of our GGT.

The person who owned the tomb that Jesus borrowed – Joseph of Arimathea - (He borrowed it because He knew He was going to give it back on the third day after His resurrection) and the person who helped Jesus carry His cross had not walked with Jesus; they were not among

His disciples. The man assigned to help Jesus carry the cross was going about his business, when he was chosen to be part of a great spiritual turnaround. He became one who will be known for all eternity, while all along he had never been in the picture or had not even been chosen or visited by Jesus as His disciple or friend. This man was part of the great salvation story. His name was Simon of Cyrene.

The person who gave Jesus the upper room for the last supper or the one who owned the donkey that Jesus borrowed on Palm Sunday were not among His disciples either, but God used them to help Jesus fulfill His GGT. Jesus did not have to know them or be their friends for God to use them. We must know that God will use anyone to accomplish His task. Any vessel available. Remember, He has the picture and resources of the whole world, while we are limited to only what we know. Once on Easter season someone sent me the following piece...

> Two donkeys were walking in Jerusalem
> When one donkey said to the other,
> 'Just yesterday I was here carrying Jesus
> And the people were singing and shouting
> And throwing down their clothes for me to walk on,
> And today they don't even recognize me.'
> The other donkey replied,
> 'That's how it is my friend,
> Without Jesus you are nothing!' (Author Unknown)

You may not be the one in the limelight or popular, or go to the most popular church. You may not even be a sight to behold; you may have gone through life the hard way, and all it seems like is that you exist to make other people's lives easy and comfortable while you work as their slaves. Don't think God has forgotten you. As you remain faithful, God is able to cause people to favor you and see you and get you to a place, not necessarily of comfort, but of influence, where you will be assigned the God-given assignment that will change the world and grow God's Kingdom.

These people who helped Jesus fulfill His GGT were assigned a task they otherwise would not have picked or chosen to do. The assignment was NOT comfortable, painless, easy, critic free, financially rewarding, or full of enticing worldly benefits. It was a Kingdom assignment with eternal reward in God's Kingdom, but in their faithfulness, they did it and changed the spiritual world forever, enriching God's Kingdom. These people were part of a great battle in which Jesus came to fight to take back what the devil had stolen, but they did not know it.

Jesus's assignment was not easy or comfortable; it was very challenging and it provoked hatred and anger toward Him and God. It was never critic free. It was lonely but God was always with Him. Christ never got monetary reward from His assignment, but was spiritually rewarded. He never charged anyone for a miracle, but He freely gave. He also commanded His disciples to do the same.

"Heal sick people. Bring dead people to life. Heal people who have leprosy. Drive bad spirits out of people you got it free, so give it free to others." (Matthew 10:8 Worldwide English (WE))

Jesus was not a celebrity; no one was attracted to His assignment, and His very own friends left Him at the most difficult time of His great assignment. His GGT was not popular; it was controversial. It provoked ridicule and abuse both physically, emotionally, and spiritually. He even felt forsaken by God, His dad, so that He cried and asked why God had forsaken Him. It was not fun or wise in the eyes of people to perform such an assignment, and go through such pain, but it was God's wisdom which is foolishness to the world.

Trust in God and put His agenda and will for your life first, because He is all wise and all knowing. Don't lean on the wisdom of people for anything because God's reward is greater than people's, and it lasts forever! Jesus is now exalted above all else, and His name, which was ridiculed on earth, is now the name that is above every name, so that at the name of Jesus EVERY knee shall BOW, and every tongue shall confess, "Jesus Christ is LORD!" to the glory of God the Father (Phil. 2:10–11).

Offense will come, but don't take it!

"Then He said to the disciples, "It is impossible that no offenses should come, but woe *to him* through whom they do come!" (Luke 17:1)

Forgiveness

Beloved, let's talk about forgiveness. This is one area that will lead many to destruction here on earth and in the life to come.

> Then Peter came and said to him, "Lord, how often shall my brother sin against me, and I forgive him? Until seven times?" Jesus said to him, "I don't tell you until seven times, but, until seventy times seven. Therefore the Kingdom of Heaven is like a certain king, who wanted to reconcile accounts with his servants. When he had begun to reconcile, one was brought to him who owed him ten thousand talents. But because he couldn't pay, his lord commanded him to be sold, with his wife, his children, and all that he had, and payment to be made. The servant therefore fell down and knelt before him, saying, 'Lord, have patience with me, and I will repay you all!' The lord of that servant, being moved with compassion, released him, and forgave him the debt. "But that servant went out, and found one of his fellow servants, who owed him one hundred denarii, and he grabbed him, and took him by the throat, saying, 'Pay me what you owe!' "So his fellow servant fell down at his feet and begged him, saying, 'Have patience with me, and I will repay you!' He would not, but went and cast him into prison, until he should pay back that which was due. So when his fellow servants saw

what was done, they were exceedingly sorry, and came and told to their lord all that was done. Then his lord called him in, and said to him, *'You wicked servant! I forgave you all that debt, because you begged me. Shouldn't you also have had mercy on your fellow servant, even as I had mercy on you?' His lord was angry, and delivered him to the tormentors, until he should pay all that was due to him. So my heavenly Father will also do to you, if you don't each forgive your brother from your hearts for his misdeeds."* (Matt. 18:21–35 WEB; italics added)

Forgiveness is a command, not a request. It is a must do, or it will not be done unto you. Also, forgiveness must be done FROM THE HEART—not the mouth—or else it is not forgiveness at all. Our Lord's Prayer confirms this as Jesus taught us to pray, "Forgive us our sin as we forgive those who sin against us." The big question is, would you like God to forgive you in the same way that you forgive others? Because that is exactly how we will be forgiven.

"And forgive us our debts, as we forgive our debtors." (Matt. 6:12)

"For if you forgive men their trespasses, your heavenly Father will also forgive you. But if you do not forgive men their trespasses, neither will your Father forgive your trespasses" (Matt. 6:14–15; italics added).

When you say you have forgiven someone, do you feel sick to your stomach when you see them? Or remember the wrong they did to you as soon as you see them? Or when their name is mentioned, do you associate them with the sin they did against you and cannot stand to be in their presence? If so, you have not forgiven them from your heart.

When you forgive, you are doing yourself a favor because un-forgiveness makes you bitter and resentful, yet most times the person who has wronged you does not even know it or realize it and if they do, most of them don't care. Do yourself a favor and forgive. Un-forgiveness is like drinking poison and expecting the other person to die. It is like a story once told where a person was walking minding his or her own business, when a bird flew by and pooped on the person. The person became angry and refused to wipe the poop until the bird came back to apologize to him or her.

If this is you, you will be waiting forever; you will ruin your outfit and get ridiculed. You will remain stagnant and never make progress and miss out on life and fun because you have taken offense and will not remove the dirty outfit. You will not move from the place where the bird pooped on you, hoping that the bird will come back and apologize. What a waste of time! Your taking offense will never stop the bird from flying or living life to its fullest, but it will stop you.

Forgiveness is a gift for you, not your offender. Un-forgiveness punishes you, not your offender. It leads to stress, sickness, heart disease like high blood pressure, depression, and anxiety, etc.

So how do you truly forgive from the heart? It is easier said than done. Is there anyone out there successful in forgiving like God forgives? How do we do this? Forgiveness sets the prisoner free, and that prisoner is the one offended. I learned how to forgive in a very, very low place. Un-forgiveness separates us from God. Because I value my relationship with God more than all else, I took Him at His Word because He honors His Word over His name. His Word says to love our enemies and pray for those who persecute us.

"But I say to you who hear [Me and pay attention to My words]: Love [that is, unselfishly seek the best or higher good for] your enemies, [make it a practice to] do good to those who hate you, bless *and* show kindness to those who curse you, pray for those who mistreat you." (Luke 6:27-28 AMP)

I told Him the plain truth that I couldn't forgive and love like He does in my strength and my forgiveness. I acknowledged my insufficiency and asked for His sufficiency in me, for He says His grace is sufficient for me and His strength is made perfect in weakness. So I prayed and said:

> "Father, in Jesus's name, give me Your strength and grace to forgive like You do. Put Your forgiveness in my heart that I may forgive this person with Your forgiveness, and give me the love that You have for that person that I may love them with Your perfect love in Jesus's name, amen!"

God ALWAYS does it! He always answers this prayer every time because it is His will that we love as He loves and forgive as He forgives. Forgiveness and love is divine. It comes from God, so stop struggling trying to love people with your love, which is conditional and your forgiveness which is insufficient. Ask, and it will be given; seek, and you will find; knock, and the door will be opened unto you.

> Jesus said to His disciples, "Stumbling blocks [temptations and traps set to lure one to sin] are sure to come, but woe (judgment is coming) to him through whom they come! It would be better for him if a millstone [as large as one turned by a donkey] were hung around his neck and he were hurled into the sea, than for him to cause one of these little ones to stumble [in sin and lose faith]. Pay attention *and* always be on guard [looking out for one another]! If your brother sins *and* disregards God's precepts, solemnly warn him; and if he repents *and* changes, forgive him. Even if he sins against you seven times a day, and returns to you seven times and says, 'I repent,' you must forgive him [that is, give up resentment and consider the offense recalled and annulled]." The apostles said to the Lord, "Increase our faith [our

ability to confidently trust in God and in His power]." (Luke 17:1–5 AMP)

Jesus doesn't excuse or justify the offender. He actually condemns the offense in the offender, as He puts it. Offense comes through people, but where does it come from before it enters the person who comes to offend you? From the enemy—that's why we should be diligent about guarding our hearts, for the heart is the wellspring of life. We mostly set ourselves up for offense by our expectations. If a stranger offends you, it is easier to let it go than when your own friend offends you, because you expect more from your friend than the stranger, even if the offense is one and the same in nature. If someone in the world offends you, you may take it better than someone in the church offending you. Our trust in people and expectations open doors for offense. CURSED is the person who trusts in people. (Jeremiah 17:5)

What if the person who offends you does not ask for forgiveness? Does God forgive those who do not ask for forgiveness? Why should we forgive those who do not ask for forgiveness, then?

Someone once asked this in our Bible study group, "But I also thought that God waits for us to ask Him for forgiveness, and we are made in His image. Can we betray the CROSS and God just forgives us without us repenting? I am bothered."

I will answer all these questions with a question. Why does God have vengeance, yet He does not allow us to have vengeance?

"Dear friends, never take revenge. Leave that to the righteous anger of God. For the Scriptures say, 'I will take revenge; I will pay them back,' says the Lord" (Rom. 12:19 NLT).

"Understand this, my dear brothers and sisters: You must all be quick to listen, slow to speak, and slow to get angry. Human anger does not produce the righteousness God desires" (James 1:19–20 NLT).

God has already paid for our forgiveness with the blood of Jesus, but it is up to us to apply it like we do soap for cleansing. Remember in Exodus chapter 12, when the Israelites in Egypt were instructed by God to sacrifice a lamb and apply it on the doorposts of their homes so that the angel of death would by-pass their homes when he came to kill the firstborn children of the Egyptians? The sacrificed lamb saved them only because the blood was applied on the door post. If they sacrificed the lamb and did not apply the blood on the doorposts, their first born would have been killed too. The power of the blood of Jesus works in the same way, only when applied; just like having soap will not make you clean, but using it will.

If God would have waited for us to ask for forgiveness before He sent His Son to die, we would all be destroyed. When we ask for forgiveness from God, we accept the sacrifice of Jesus on the cross. We must also remember we do not deserve forgiveness; it is by God's grace. The people you will need to forgive do not deserve to be forgiven, but in the same way you have been forgiven, you must forgive. When they ask for forgiveness, they are just receiving what you have already made available for them. We must give forgiveness before the offender asks so that when they come to ask, it is already available, just like God does.

If they come for the forgiveness you have for them, it sets them free, but you are already free when you forgave and prayed for them. If you don't forgive, when they come to ask for forgiveness, you will not have it and they will leave you bound to your offense and in disobedience to God. God will forgive them if they ask because God has forgiveness readily available, but you will not be forgiven because you refused to forgive.

Loving your enemies, and praying for those who persecute you is a command from Christ that is easier said than done. So how does this work? I asked this same question when I was very offended by some student doctors in their first and second year whom I worked with. I remember telling my husband about it and then I went to prayer and told God about it. These were on two different occasions. Most student doctors are so excited to be called 'doctor' that the spirit of pride and arrogance almost always kicks in. However, there are also some pleasant and humble doctors who were a pleasure to work with.

My Story:

In the first incident, a junior (first year) doctor came into my patient's room, and in the presence of the patient she started quarreling me and asking questions about a wound that even the wound-care specialist had tried to deal with but was still problematic. This was because the wound was so close to his colostomy and he had very bad diarrhea. No matter how many times we dressed the wound and changed the colostomy bag, it leaked beyond control. I tried to explain this to the doctor but to no avail because before I could answer her, she would intercept rudely with another question and another and scolding and was non-stop. I gave up trying to reason with her so I kept quiet and let her talk, then I asked her what her name was because at this time I was done! I was going to write her up on her extremely rude behavior and un-professionalism. I politely asked, "Doctor, what's your name?" She rudely responded, "Go find it in the chart where I have written some orders."

By this time my patient, whom I had led to Christ during my shift and had seen me work all night to care for him, looked at the doctor and sternly said to her, "Stop it! She is a great nurse!"

The doctor was shocked at his response to her behavior. She had been very kind to him but mean to me. I was shocked too but very glad he spoke. At least someone, the one I was serving and one who mattered most, saw and appreciated my care for him. The wound-care nurse who had come to dress the wound earlier in my shift was also very rude to me because she assumed that I was not going to help her with wound care. This was because when she came in the patient's room, I anticipated my patient would be in pain for the wound care so I went to get him some pain medication before wound care started so that he would not be in so much pain. I knew that the devil was angry because the patient had just received Christ. I expected the attack, so I took no offense from the wound-care nurse. She later eased up and was sorry for her behavior, and I forgave her.

I went home that morning and prayed, but before I did, I quoted a scripture back to God and said to Him, "You said to love my enemies and pray for those who persecute me; now this had better work for me now…"

> You have heard the law that says, "Love your neighbor" and hate your enemy. But I say, love your enemies! Pray for those who persecute you! In that way, you will be acting as true children of your Father in heaven. For he gives his sunlight to both the evil and the good, and he sends rain on the just and the unjust alike. If you love only those who love you, what reward is there for that? Even corrupt tax collectors do that much. If you are kind only to your friends, how are you different from anyone else? Even pagans do that. But you are to be perfect, even as your Father in heaven is perfect. (Matt. 5:43–48 NLT)

I prayed for God to forgive me for taking offense and to give me His forgiveness and love to forgive and love this doctor with. I felt His love and forgiveness all over me as I prayed and I said, "In Jesus's name, I forgive her with God's forgiveness and love her with God's love." Immediately I had a great release in my spirit. I began praying for her, her family, her school, and her prosperity, that she would know God and be all she was created to be. I prayed as if I was praying for myself. I had a great peace in me and was FREE! My relationship with God always means more than anything or anyone to me. I did not want to allow un-forgiveness and offense to come between God and I.

The following day at work, my assignment changed. I always asked God to make my assignment, and I believed He did. I never argued at all with the charge nurse about my assignment. I accepted it gladly because I worked for God and not people. I believed that where I was assigned was the very place God wanted to work through me. I accepted my assignment and worked it. I did not have my same patient from the day before. Only he had been taken out of the assignment while all the other patients were left on for no reason at all.

In the morning, the same doctor, in the presence and hearing of everyone in the workstation where other doctors and nurses were working on their computers, saw me passing by; she said sternly and with such authority, "Hi! Did you know that it is leaking again?"

I looked at her and said very gently with a smile, "Hi. No, I didn't know this because I am not his nurse today."

She was shocked and felt so embarrassed, and she looked down.

Then I went on and said to her, "See, it was not my nursing skills that had a problem. I tried to explain this yesterday, but you were very rude to me that my patient had to stand up for me."

She said humbly, "I am sorry. I did not mean that your nursing skills were a problem. I was just angry because it has happened over and over even before you were his nurse, and I was tired of it because I have a great passion for my patients."

By this time everyone was listening in to our conversation and looking at us, and I was hoping they would so that her fellow doctors would never treat nurses with such dishonor.

I replied, "You and I both. I am here because I have a great passion for what I do and for my patients, but that does not make me disrespect others. You have a license, and I have a license. You are a professional just as I am. You need to respect me, and I respect you as we work together to better our patient's outcome. If you had listened to me, maybe you would have known where the problem is and fixed it instead of blaming nurses who had nothing to do with the surgery."

She apologized, and I forgave her. From that day on, she knew my name, addressed me by my name respectfully, and used the words "please" and "thank you." We worked together very well after that. I am almost sure no other nurse will have to suffer humiliation from her again or from other doctors who listened to the conversation. God provided a great opportunity for reconciliation. I took Him at His Word, and it worked!

In the second incident, the doctor was a neurosurgeon senior. He was very rude to me on the phone and then he hung up on me. He called back after a few minutes but I refused to answer. I gave the charge nurse my phone to answer him. The charge RN gave the doctor the same answer I had given him, so he was not happy. He asked the charge RN for my name so he could write me up. I wrote up the incident and took it to the assistant manager. Apparently he had been written up before for the same behavior of insulting and being rude to nurses. The assistant manager that night said she was going to report it to his attending. I went home and did the same thing and prayed in the same way I had prayed in my first incident.

One day, about two weeks after the incident, I had a patient where he was the doctor. He needed to have a conference with some family members and he wanted the patient's nurse to witness the meeting. In the meeting, he was so kind to the family members, it was like day and night compared to his previous behavior on the phone. He did not know me but I knew him.

Doctors can pretend to be the best people in the presence of the patient's family members because the family members are the ones who can hire or fire them.

After all was said and done and the meeting was over, I felt the Holy Spirit say that this was my opportunity for reconciliation.

I asked the doctor to remain behind, which he gladly did. I started the conversation by telling him how I appreciated his work and how he handled the meeting very well. Then I reminded him of our incident over the phone. I told him I had forgiven him and had prayed for him and his family, his school, and all that concerns him. He said he remembered that day and he admitted that he was very rude, and apologized for his behavior. He said that he was also a Christian but he had failed and wished he was half the Christian I was. I knew that I was not good but Christ was good in me. I told him I didn't get there easily, I had to ask God for His grace to be a doer of the Word, not just a hearer because God's Word works! We shared God's Word and spoke about our families, and from that day, I have not heard of any more incidences reported on him.

Beloved, it is not foolish to make the first step toward reconciliation. God says that as long as it depends on you, live at peace with all people (see Rom 12:18-21) and that if you go to pray and remember that someone has something against you, stop praying, go and reconcile, and then come back to pray so that God may answer you (see Matt 5:23-24).

You see, God is not asking about your offender. He is concerned about your spiritual and physical health. Forgiveness and reconciliation sets you free and gives you great health both spiritually and physically. You cannot be used by God and fulfill your God-given task successfully with un-forgiveness.

Brethren, God's Word is proven to be true! You don't have to try it. Just do it because it has already been tried and proven, and God has guaranteed it and honored it over His name. It is forever settled in heaven.

"Every word of God proves true. He is a shield to all who come to him for protection" (Prov. 30:5 NLT).

"Your eternal word, O Lord, stands firm in heaven" (Ps. 119:89 NLT).

"The grass withers and the flowers fade, but the word of our God stands forever" (Isa. 40:8 NLT).

It works! I do this with all who offend me, and God opens up a door for reconciliation. Sometimes I used to get tired of being the first one to make peace, but God says, blessed are the peacemakers, for they shall be called the sons of God. Again He says as long as it is possible with me, not the other person. God is looking at me to be at peace with all people.

God knows that we cannot control what others do or say to us, but we can control how we react! We can choose to be bitter and take offense, which is the bait of Satan, or we can choose the way of agape love. Love our enemies, and pray for them. Jesus said it is impossible for offense not to come, but woe to him whom it comes through! Jesus is not excusing the offender, but He, God, is the One who can take revenge for us. He does not allow people to be vengeful. God is sovereign, He can refuse to forgive, and He will not suffer, but if we don't forgive, we open doors for torturers and demonic attack. We cannot compare ourselves with God because He is the parent, and we are the children. We cannot fight our brothers and sisters and expect Dad to smile.

How would you like it if your children are fighting or not forgiving or not talking to each other? I always tell my sons never to hit each other or refuse to forgive their brothers when they wrong them. Instead, they should report them to me because I am their parent, and I know how to discipline my children. All they need to do is to love each other and let me know when there is a problem. I will fix it. If they fight, they both will be in trouble because they are not disciplining each other but revenging. Vengeance from people seeks to destroy, not to discipline. When my sons refuse to fight but report the other to me, then I will discipline the one who was wrong and I will not feel bad because discipline is mine, the parent, not theirs.

Let God do the repaying. You guard your heart, for it is the wellspring of life. Forgive and love and pray for those who hurt you. Pray for them to prosper, to love and to know God that they may be all that God created them to be. Pray for them passionately like you would pray for yourself or a friend. Let go and let God discipline His own children.

When you fight your fellow man and not the devil in them, it is as if an enemy comes at you, riding on a horse and you kill the horse, but you let the enemy go. He will always come at you using a different horse, and you will be the loser because you will be helping the enemy to destroy the innocent. But if you are spiritually alert and mature, you will kill the enemy who is riding on the horse and rescue the horse. The horse only goes where it is led.

Sometimes we must stand in the gap and be the stronger person and make peace. It is not a weakness in God's eyes, but to people, who are foolish, it may seem weak. Ignore people and please God. Remember, we do not war against flesh and blood, but against principalities and powers of darkness in the heavenly places! Let's win the real war and rescue our brothers and sisters instead of helping the devil to destroy us in Jesus's name! Let us not go by feelings but by God's Word. It works!

Jesus revealed this at the cross. When He was at His end, they mocked and ridiculed Him and caused Him great pain, but no one asked for forgiveness from Him. Jesus knew if He didn't forgive, He would remain in hell and not rise from the dead because the enemy would have the dominion over Him. He knew He was fighting against the devil, not the people He came to save. So what did He do? He forgave them and then took the next step and acted as a High Priest and interceded for them to the Father in Luke 23:34 saying, "Father, forgive them, for they do not know what they are doing!" He did not wait for the pain to go away before He forgave them. Jesus forgave them at the peak of His pain and prayed for the Father to forgive them too. He showed a great example to His Word that we should love and pray for our enemies and persecutors.

The other person who did like Jesus did was Stephen, who was full of the Holy Spirit. He was stoned to death, and he forgave his killers and prayed that God would not hold this sin against them.

> Now when they heard these things, they were cut to the heart, and they gnashed at him with their teeth. But he, being full of the Holy Spirit, looked up steadfastly into heaven, and saw the glory of God, and Jesus standing on the right hand of God, and said, "Behold, I see the heavens opened, and the Son of Man standing at the right hand of God!" But they cried out with a loud voice, and stopped their ears, and rushed at him with one accord. They threw him out of the city, and stoned him. The witnesses placed their garments at the feet of a young man named Saul. They stoned Stephen as he called out, saying, "Lord Jesus, receive my spirit!" He kneeled down, and cried with a loud voice, "Lord, don't hold this sin against them!" When he had said this, he fell asleep. (Acts 7:54–60 WEB)

When I learned who and whose I am, that my dad is the King of kings and Lord of Lords, the Creator and owner of the whole universe and that I rank so high in the spirit, I now feel so sorry for those attacking me. They have no idea who I am, and they are being used by the enemy. For example, if you mess with the president's child, you are as good as dead. The only one who can get you off the hook is the child of the president, who is highly treasured, if he asks his dad to forgive you. In the same way, and even more, my dad can kill both body and soul, so I feel so sorry for my attackers because they have no idea what mess they are getting themselves into. I pray for them and ask my Father God to forgive them because they have no clue what they are doing! If I don't pray for them, then I have no love, and I do not know who I am or who God is.

"Dear friends, let us continue to love one another, for love comes from God. Anyone who loves is a child of God and knows God. But anyone who does not love does not know God, for God is love" (1 John 4:7–8 NLT).

I don't think there is someone who would hurt me so badly that I would wish them hell. I will not help the devil destroy children of God. Just as Jesus knew who He was and how high He ranked and was loved by the Father, I too, pray for my enemies. I feel so sorry for them because they are messing with the daughter of the King of the heavens and earth, and the sad thing is that they don't even know it! The secret for forgiveness and praying for their forgiveness is to know who you are in God, and it will be easy.

My dad (God) loves me so much; I am the apple of His eye. His thoughts of me are more than the sand in the ocean. He calls me His own, so messing with me is the same as sticking your finger in His eye, which is death. I therefore work overtime to pray for my enemies that they may come to the realization of what they are doing and get to know my dad, God! He is always proud of His children who practice this. Let us know whose we are and who God is, so we may help others who don't know Him, instead of destroying them.

It is similar to a situation in which a president's child travels undercover to another country where people attack the child not knowing whose child they are. Once the attackers are captured and are sentenced to death, the child pleads for their lives and asks his or her father to forgive the attackers. In the same way, we must realize that we are here on earth undercover on assignment just like Jesus was. If people knew who Jesus was, they would have never spoken an evil word against Him or killed Him. If they knew who you are, they would never attack you or speak against you.

If you know who and whose you are and who and how powerful your Dad (God) is,
You will forgive and intercede for your haters!

People who hate their enemies instead of loving and praying for them do not know what agape love is. They do not know God, because God is love (1 John 4:7-8). They also do not know who they are in Christ. If they knew, they would be gracious, merciful, and abounding in love just like their Father, God.

In the same way Christ suffered for us even while we were still sinners and did not wait for us to be good to die for us, we also ought to do the same to our fellow people.

"But He was wounded for our transgressions, He was bruised for our iniquities; the chastisement for our peace was upon Him, and by His stripes we are healed" (Isa. 53:5).

He forgave us, justified us, broke all curses, gave us perfect peace, healed all our diseases, and healed all the wounds in our hearts, souls, and minds. If you are in Christ and are obedient to Him, and this is not evident in your life, claim it because it is yours and is already paid for at such a costly price. Don't let the enemy steal it from you.

"We know what real love is because Jesus gave up his life for us. So we also ought to give up our lives for our brothers and sisters" (1 John 3:16 NLT).

We must be able to separate the offense from the offender, the sin from the sinner. We must hate the offense but love the offender. Hate the sin and love the sinner, just like God does.

"Whenever you stand praying, forgive, if you have anything against anyone; so that your Father, who is in heaven, may also forgive you your transgressions" (Mark 11:25 WEB).

Forgiveness was tough for Jesus, too, but He also had to forgive them in His life on earth for us to be saved. Many people struggle with forgiveness from the heart, which is the enemy's easiest tool to win people over to his side! May God unveil our eyes to know that forgiveness benefits us, not so much the other person. We owe God more than our lives. Nothing anyone on earth can ever do to us will outweigh the debt we owed God that Jesus paid for with His (God's) own life! So there is no excuse whatsoever for un-forgiveness.

Jesus forgave at the time they were wounding and killing Him. They were not even sorry; instead, they had fun while at it. Not only did Christ forgive them, He also did what He commanded us to do. He prayed for them while on the cross for the Father to forgive them. It is a command that we love our enemies and pray for those who persecute us. Are we doing this?

My advice to you on offense? Don't take it from anyone! No matter how it comes. Jesus said it is impossible for offense not to come, but how you deal with it matters! Let it go! Don't take it. It is too costly and energy consuming, and leads to great loss in the spirit and in the body. No one is worth you losing your soul forever for or destroying your health and losing your peace over.

Love and forgiveness are divine. By our strength, we can't love or forgive like God commands. Ask for the grace to love and forgive from God in prayer and He will gladly give you.

Prayer to forgive like Christ.

"Father, in Jesus's name, You command me to forgive from my heart, to love my enemies, and pray for those who persecute me. I can't do this with my strength

but by Your strength I can, so please put Your love for all humanity in me that I may love them the way You love them. Put Your perfect forgiveness in me that I may forgive them with it. I rebuke the spirit of offense and any negative spirit that was invited in by the offense I took in Jesus's name! I receive the spirit of love, the peace of God, and the grace of God in Jesus's name. I now forgive all my enemies with Your forgiveness and love them now with Your perfect love in Jesus's name. I receive forgiveness for all my sins in Jesus's name I pray, believe and receive with thanksgiving."

Now pray for your enemies, because God has put His love and His forgiveness in you immediately. Pray for them as if they were your friends. Pray in the same way you'd pray for yourself. In this way, the devil loses and the Kingdom of God wins! Our real enemy is in the spirit. We fight against principalities and powers of darkness. Don't be deceived into fighting each other and helping the enemy destroy both of you. Remember, perfect love and forgiveness come from our Father God.

My mother, Rev. Priscilla KJ of Judean Reconciliation Ministries, whom God uses to minister deliverance and reconcile people to God and people to people, shared this in our bible study,

"In spiritual warfare we discover a lot of sicknesses come as a result of un-forgiveness. One day I was praying for a lady, and the demons said, '*I am cancer. I caused her not to forgive her sister so I could come in and kill her. She will go to the theatre and will die there.*' Of course we dealt with the demon, and she is free from cancer. Why should we give the enemy a chance of torturing us? Brethren, choose to forgive."

Let us look at what Jesus said about this.

"Then the angry king sent the man *to prison to be tortured* until he had paid his entire debt. That's what my heavenly Father will do to you if you refuse to forgive your brothers and sisters from your heart" (Matt. 18:34–35; italics added).

Torturers are demons of sickness, depression, and suicide, etc. People of God perish for lack of knowledge because they have rejected knowledge; therefore, God will also reject them (Hosea 4). It is one thing to ignore what people say, but ignoring what Jesus said? There is no excuse! See Deuteronomy 28 for blessings of obedience and curses for disobedience.

> If you will not observe to do all the words of this law that are written in this book, that you may fear this glorious and fearful name, YAHWEH YOUR GOD; then Yahweh will make your plagues fearful, and the plagues of your offspring, even great plagues, and of long duration, and severe sicknesses, and of long duration. He will bring on you again all the diseases of Egypt, which you were afraid of; and they will cling to you. Also every sickness and every plague, which is not written in the book of this law, Yahweh will bring them on you, until you are destroyed. (Deut. 28:58-61 WEB)

Cancer, panic attacks, and mental disorders are curses mentioned in Deuteronomy 28:27–28 NLT: "The Lord will afflict you with the boils of Egypt and with tumors, scurvy, and the itch, from which you cannot be cured. The Lord will strike you with madness, blindness, and panic."

God has the power to curse and to bless us but the devil does not. Once we disobey, we subject ourselves to curses instead of blessings. Because the devil has no power to curse you and he knows that the only way to get you cursed is through disobedience, he will make you disobey God so that you can be cursed. Once you are under a curse, then he has the right to access you and mess around with you. Remember the story of Balak and Balaam in the Bible in Numbers 22–23? Balak wanted to curse the children of Israel but he could not and instead he blessed them because he said that no one can curse whom God has blessed.

> He returned to him, and behold, he was standing by his burnt offering, he, and all the princes of Moab. He took up his parable, and said, "From Aram has Balak brought me, the king of Moab

from the mountains of the East. Come, curse Jacob for me. Come, defy Israel. How shall I curse whom God has not cursed? How shall I defy whom Yahweh has not defied? (Num.23:6–8 WEB)

"Like a fluttering sparrow or a darting swallow, an undeserved curse will not land on its intended victim" (Prov. 26:2).

Because the Israelites were obedient to God, the curses from their enemies were turned to blessings. When you are in disobedience, you are under a curse but when you obey, God protects you and He curses those who curse you and blesses those who bless you. When you are in obedience, your enemies will spend money and time and work overtime to bless you.

The children of Israel had no idea that they were being plotted against to be cursed and destroyed. Their enemy hired a costly diviner, sacrificed many animals, used their resources, but it was all turned around to bless the ones they intended to curse. God knew their enemy's plan and fought them without the Israelites knowledge. God is doing so even today. He fights the enemies of those who dwell in His presence and are obedient to Him even without their knowledge. God will make a donkey talk before He allows anyone to curse His obedient children like Balaam's donkey. Read Psalm 91.

"For we do not wrestle against flesh and blood, but against principalities, against powers, against the rulers of the darkness of this age, against spiritual hosts of wickedness in the heavenly places" (Eph. 6:12).

If you have an enemy attacking you, and he comes at you vengefully, riding on a horse, what would you do? Would you kill the horse or kill the enemy? Of course, the enemy! The enemy uses the horse to his advantage, but the horse can follow you and be tamed. What if you kill the horse? The enemy will still fight you because he can get another horse to ride on. In this case, the devil is your enemy, and the horse is your brother or sister who is used of the devil to offend you. If you fight your brother, then you are short sighted and on the enemy's side since his desire is to destroy God's family. Instead of looking up and seeing your real enemy riding the horse, you assume that the horse came to fight you. As you fight and destroy your brother, the enemy will destroy you.

The horse is desperate and needs to be rescued from the enemy who is using it for his evil pleasures. Rescue your brothers and sisters from the enemy by praying for them and loving them into the Kingdom of God. Pray for them to be delivered from the grip of the enemy. We must put on the eyes of God and refuse to be shortsighted. Let us fight wisely, not as ones beating the air, but as ones fighting the real enemy –the devil-.

"Therefore I run thus: not with uncertainty. Thus I fight: not as one who beats the air" (1 Cor. 9:26).

A story is told of two giants, who were best friends walking in the woods, talking and laughing until a huge coconut hit one of them on the head really hard! The giant was very angry at his friend that they had a heated argument. The fellow giant tried to explain that he didn't hit him, but the first one responded, "There's only two of us here. Why are you lying? Are you taking me for a fool?" They continued to walk along silently, still feeling angry at each other when another coconut hit the other giant very hard on the head. This caused the giants to fight vigorously, blaming each other. They attacked each other and fought to their deaths.

While they were on the ground dying, they heard monkey noises coming from a tree. When the giants looked up, they saw a monkey up a coconut tree, jumping up and down and covering its mouth, almost falling down with laughter at what he had done. One little monkey had succeeded in killing the giants by making them fight each other. Had the giants looked up in the first place, they would have easily known their enemy and taken him out as a team. But because they looked at each other as enemies, they worked to the monkey's benefit, who couldn't kill the giants on his own. Ask yourself whom you are benefiting when you fight your brothers and sisters. By so doing, the enemy will be defeated, and you will save your brothers and sisters from the devil's grip. The devil is only as powerful as you allow him to be, just like the monkey.

What if you need forgiveness?

"If we confess our sins, He is faithful and just to forgive us our sins and to cleanse us from all unrighteousness" (1 John 1:9).

"'Come now, and let us reason together,' says the Lord. 'Though your sins are like scarlet, they shall be as white as snow; though they are red like crimson, they shall be as wool. If you are willing and obedient, you shall eat the good of the land; But if you refuse and rebel, you shall be devoured by the sword'; for the mouth of the LORD has spoken" (Isa. 1:18–20).

> Yahweh is merciful and gracious, slow to anger, and abundant in loving kindness. He will not always accuse; neither will he stay angry forever. He has not dealt with us according to our sins, nor repaid us for our iniquities. For as the heavens are high above the earth, so great is his loving kindness toward those who fear him. As far as the east is from the west, so far has he removed our transgressions from us. Like a father has compassion on his children, so Yahweh has compassion on those who fear him. For he knows how we are made. He remembers that we are dust. (Ps.103:8–14 WEB).

"So then, since we have a great High Priest who has entered heaven, Jesus the Son of God, let us hold firmly to what we believe. This High Priest of ours understands our weaknesses, for he faced all of the same testing we face, yet he did not sin. So let us come boldly to the throne of our gracious God. There we will receive his mercy, and we will find grace to help us when we need it most" (Heb. 4:14–16 NLT).

There is mercy and forgiveness if you go to God and confess what you did and sincerely repent. God will hear and forgive you. He cannot forgive what you don't confess. I know we sin sometimes without our knowledge, but even so, we must confess for sinning knowingly and unknowingly. Just like David prayed, I also pray in Jesus name and say;

"How can I know all the sins lurking in my heart? Cleanse me from these hidden faults. Keep your servant from deliberate sins! Don't let them control me. Then I will be free of guilt and innocent of great sin. May the words of my mouth and the meditation of my heart be pleasing to you, O Lord, my rock and my redeemer" (Ps. 19:12–14 NLT).

In 2 Chronicles 7:14, God said, "If My people who are called by My name will humble themselves, and pray and seek My face, and turn from their wicked ways, then I will hear from heaven, and will forgive their sin and heal their land."

Thanks be to God for his mercy, grace, and love.

"Don't be misled—you cannot mock the justice of God. You will always harvest what you plant. Those who live only to satisfy their own sinful nature will harvest decay and death from that sinful nature. But those who live to please the Spirit will harvest everlasting life from the Spirit. So let's not get tired of doing what is good. At just the right time we will reap a harvest of blessing if we don't give up" (Gal. 6:7–9 NLT).

If you sow un-forgiveness, you will reap un-forgiveness from God! Let us all invest in the eternal. Forgiveness doesn't excuse the offense; rather, it allows God to fight for you. He says, "Vengeance is mine, I will repay." Leave vengeance to God; otherwise, it will destroy you and your assignment on earth. Love the offender and hate the offense. Owe no person anything but love! (Rom. 13:8)

My older brother put it so well: "Humility and forgiveness are attributes of Christ we MUST emulate. If He was not humble, He would not have allowed Himself to die for humanity. If He did not forgive, He would have cursed humanity when on the cross."

How would you like it if God felt the same way you feel over your enemy whom you have not forgiven, or whom you say you have forgiven but can't stand their presence or the mention of their name? With the same measure you give to others, the same you will receive. Do not put this off any longer. Deal with un-forgiveness now, for no one is worth you going to hell for. No one is worth your relationship with God.

"Finally, all of you should be of one mind. Sympathize with each other. Love each other as brothers and sisters. Be tenderhearted, and keep a humble attitude. Don't repay evil for evil. Don't retaliate with insults when people insult you. Instead, pay them back with a blessing. That is what God has called you to do, and he will grant you his blessing" (1 Pet. 3:8–9 NLT).

What are the benefits of forgiving?

You will receive forgiveness from God, peace of mind, joy, no anxiety or stress, healthy heart, healthy blood pressure, healthy relationships, no depression, stronger immune system, higher self-esteem, and more resistance to disease. Forgiveness keeps the torturers out of your life and invites blessings from God. Forgiveness keeps your communication line with God open. Bottom line—forgiveness is for you; un-forgiveness is poisonous to you, not to your enemy. If you love yourself, you will forgive.

Does forgiveness guarantee reconciliation? What if the person I'm forgiving doesn't change?

Jesus loved the Pharisees, but He didn't hang out with them as He did His disciples. In Matthew 5:44, Jesus says … "love your enemies and bless those who persecute you…" Jesus never said to befriend your enemies and persecutors, because most times it is not possible. The love of God is not dependent on the other person but on you. It knows no bounds. It is constantly praying for the best for the other person, even when you are not in communication.

On the other hand, if you cut communication because you still feel angry and you cannot stand being around them, then you have un-forgiveness. But just like we said, we must be able to separate the sin from the sinner, love the sinner, and hate the sin. Love the terrorists, but hate terrorism. Love them by praying their souls into eternal life, that they may know God and the only Savior, Jesus Christ, who loved them and died for them, too. While we were yet sinners, Christ died for us.

You may have the gift of working miracles, but with un-forgiveness you will be destroyed. Forgiveness is something you give before it is asked of you. "Fore" means "placed in front (before)." "Give" means to "FREELY transfer something to someone." Forgiveness is free! No condition of payment.

Jesus on the cross knew that He had to forgive His persecutors before they even repented because He had to overcome death and the grave. If He went to hell with un-forgiveness in His heart, He would not have made it out. He had many chances to take offense, but He refused to take it. In this the enemy could not touch Him or defeat Him. He said in John 14:30 KJV;

"Hereafter I will not talk much with you: for the prince of this world cometh, and hath nothing in me."

Why? Because He kept His heart pure. He knew to guard his heart, for it is the wellspring of life. Forgiveness is for us. It is God's plan for our healing and great health. For some people to be healed, they just need to forgive.

> You have heard that it was said, 'You shall love your neighbor and hate your enemy.' But I tell you, love your enemies, bless those who curse you, do good to those who hate you, and pray for those who mistreat you and persecute you, that you may be children of your Father who is in heaven. For he makes his sun to rise on the evil and the good, and sends rain on the just and the unjust. For if you love those who love you, what reward do you have? Don't even the tax collectors do the same? If you only greet your friends, what more do you do than others? Don't even the tax collectors do the same? Therefore you shall be perfect, just as your Father in heaven is perfect. (Matt. 5:43–48)

Beloved, it is hard to forgive but God's grace is sufficient for us. An enemy may be someone you think is your friend but the real intentions of their heart is for your downfall. That is why you need to ask God to reveal to you the intentions of the heart of people around you. Jesus knew Judas was His enemy all along but treated him as a friend. It is very scary not to know your enemies. If Jesus being the Son of God had many enemies, how many more enemies do you think you have and will have? An enemy is not only the one you make, but it is one who makes themselves your enemy with or without your knowledge. God does not make enemies, instead, people make themselves enemies of God. You will be surprised to know that some of your so-called friends are your greatest enemies. Terrorists make themselves enemies and kill many people.

Once I prayed for God to expose all the unfriendly friends (hidden enemies) in my life and to my surprise, the very best of my friends were my greatest enemies. When you know your enemies, you will have the upper hand just like Jesus did because you will know how to handle them and what to reveal in their presence. You will not hate or excommunicate them; rather, you will be wise around them.

Love

Without love, we are nothing, and our assignment is all done in vain. Everything God does, He does it out of who He is—He is love. His Kingdom is built on love. No wonder the greatest law of the Kingdom is to love the Lord our God with all of our hearts, minds, souls, and strength and to love our neighbors (anyone around us) as we love ourselves (Mark 12:30-31).

When God revealed my assignment to me, He also led me to pray for His agape love in me that I may do my assignment in His love. He is very faithful. I am now able to love my enemies and pray for my persecutors. My drive is to do my assignment in humility, as I love God and all people. My heart's desire is to see all people come into the full knowledge of Christ and the sacrifice He made for us and the power we have in His Resurrection. In 1 Corinthians 13, the Bible speaks well of love. Love is not a feeling; it is a choice. That is why you can love your enemy—because you choose to do it.

The Word of God says that He who does not love does not know God because God is love; and because God is love, His agape (unconditional) love is divine. Only God can give you this kind of required love as a daily ingredient to our God-given task. Love never fails, and it never ends.

Let us look at the different kinds of love. AGAPE LOVE is divine love, unconditional, God's love, and is a MUST have, a COMMAND from God, and we are NOTHING without it.

Agape does not depend on emotions, rather it is a choice, regardless of the other person's behavior or receptiveness to it, to do things unselfishly with concern and for the benefit of another person. It is the willingness to seek the best for another rather than yourself. This love never fails or ends, and it lasts forever throughout all eternity. It was the reason for the earth being created and for human existence. It is the essence of God Himself. It is who God is.

Phileo love is brotherly love—the one you have for a friend or people you share common interests with. This kind of love is conditional love. It lasts for as long as you are friends or share common interests.

Eros love is the romantic love only meant for a husband and his wife. It is based purely on emotion. It is triggered by sight and feelings. It is selfish and can die very easily and quickly.

The greatest kind of love is AGAPE. Without agape, the other kinds of love would never survive. Without agape, God wouldn't have sent His Son to die for sinners. Jesus Christ would not have laid down His life freely even when He had the choice of calling legions of angels to destroy the people who wanted to kill Him. Instead, Christ gave up His rights and chose to die in our place while we were *still sinners*. Without this love, we would not have any hope or salvation. This is the John 3:16 love: "For God so loved the world that He gave His only begotten Son, that whoever believes in Him should not perish but have everlasting life."

God requires us to do the same in 1 John 3:16: "By this we know love, because He laid down His life for us and we also ought to lay down our lives for the brethren."

This is the greater love Jesus is talking about in John 15:12–13: "This is My commandment, that you love one another as I have loved you. Greater love has no one than this, than to lay down one's life for his friends."

Our works will be tested in the fire of love. Did we serve God and others in agape love or were we selfish and loved conditionally? Without this agape love, we are nothing, and all our works are useless. I prayed and asked God not to send me out into ministry without this love because it would cost the Kingdom. Jesus said that our mark as God's children is our love for one another and for others.

1 John 4:7-8 AMP says "Beloved, let us [unselfishly] love *and* seek the best for one another, for love is from God; and everyone who loves [others] is born of God and knows God [through personal experience]. The one who does not love has not become acquainted with God [does not and never did know Him], for God is love. [He is the originator of love, and it is an enduring attribute of His nature.]"

We MUST have this sacrificial and selfless love just as God has loved us. We can't achieve or pay for it and we can't have it unless we ask for it. Love is divine. We can't give what we don't have, so I advise you to ask God now for this agape love, believe that you have received it without a doubt and start operating in it daily.

Let us pray the same prayer that Paul prayed for the Ephesians.

May He grant you out of the riches of His glory, to be strengthened *and* spiritually energized with power through His Spirit in your inner self, [indwelling your innermost being and personality], so that Christ may dwell in your hearts through your faith. *And may you, having been [deeply] rooted and [securely] grounded in love, be fully capable of comprehending with all the saints (God's people) the width and length and height and depth of His love [fully experiencing that amazing, endless love]; and [that you may come] to know [practically, through personal experience] the love of Christ which far surpasses [mere] knowledge [without experience], that you may be filled up [throughout your being] to all the fullness of God [so that you may have the richest experience of God's presence in your lives, completely filled and flooded with God Himself].* (Ephesians 3:16-19 AMP; italics added)

Prayer to love like God does.

"Father, in Jesus's name, thank You for Your perfect love for us. Thank You for Jesus and the greatest sacrifice of love. Thank You for Your Holy Spirit. Forgive me all my sins and cleanse me from all unrighteousness, create in me Your heart and fill me with Your Holy Spirit. Father, I stand amazed at Your love. Who would give a rebel such a costly gift? Who would give a sinner such a holy and righteous gift? Who would give a stranger all that they adore? I've never heard of anyone and I cannot comprehend. But You gave Your only Son Oh so precious, and dear to You. He was holy and full of righteousness but became sin just for me that I may live eternally, a sinner saved by your great love, God YOU ARE LOVE! You gave Your Son to die for strangers (us) who may or may not accept Your adoption as sons and daughters. Strangers who hated You and did not regard You as God! You were willing to graft me in, You valued me over all else and gave me, Your BEST, Your ALL. This Amazing kind of love I cannot comprehend! This confirms that You truly are LOVE. You paid the most costly, non-refundable cost of adoption for strangers without the guarantee that they will accept adoption as Your Children. Abba Father, may You help me to comprehend this love, how deep, high, long and wide. May I have the same love for You and others in Jesus's name! Put in me Your divine agape love so that I may love You and others with. Open my spiritual eyes and heart to see and receive all You have commanded. Help me to understand this love by giving me a revelation of Your agape love for me so that I may share it with others. I receive Your agape love in me now with thanksgiving in Jesus's name, amen!"

Now, thank God for the agape love in you.

The greatest revelation we humans can ever have is the revelation of God's love for us! Do you just hear or read of God's love for you or do you really know and are convinced that God loves you? John, the disciple of Christ, knew without a shadow of a doubt that Jesus loved him and no wonder he spoke a lot on love. He was so confident of God's love for him that he addressed himself as 'the disciple whom Jesus loved'. How confident are you of God's love for you? No wonder John lived longer than all the other disciples and was given great revelations. He even wrote the powerful book of Revelation in the Bible. He was shown great and mighty things by God.

1 Corinthians 13:1-8, 13 is the description of Agape love. We can sacrifice our lives but if we have no agape, we are nothing. I never thought people can sacrifice a lot without the agape love but it is very clear in God's Word that it is possible. People sacrifice so much even their lives like the radical Islam do but it is not out of Agape, it is deception of religious royalty, the work of evil. What is Agape?

Agape love is patient and kind. Oh, for grace to obey God always! When I consciously practice agape, I realize how easy it is to not have it and how easy it is to be impatient and rude. The world has programmed us for disobedience, but we must practice obedience until it is the air we breathe and until it becomes our new normal. Thank God for agape.

Agape doesn't envy, doesn't boast, and isn't proud. Agape does not dishonor others; it isn't self-seeking. Show honor to all you meet and live with. Think of them and how you can serve them (the greatest in God's Kingdom is a servant of all). Seek their progress and success, not just your own. Assist where you can; be selfless.

Agape isn't easily angered; it keeps no record of wrongs. Don't be quick to anger.

Think of all the records you have kept of all the wrongs done against you. Bring them out and lay them at Jesus's feet. Pray for God to forgive you for keeping these records, because it is sin and ask Him to destroy those records forever in Jesus's name, so that when you think of the people who wronged you, you think of them in agape, not in the wrong they did.

Also ask God to destroy the records of wrongs you have done that have been kept by others and by Him, because you reap what you sow. If you sow a record of wrongs, you will reap a record of wrongs, too, from others and from God.

Agape doesn't delight in evil but rejoices with the truth. Instead of giving in to entice others or agreeing with them in wrongdoing, be bold to stand with the truth of God's Word and correct them in love. Don't delight in the evil done, but stand and rejoice in the truth. If you are afraid, that is not agape, because perfect love casts out fear. (1 John 4:18).

Rebuke the spirit of fear tormenting you, and operate in agape. It may hurt for you and others to hear the truth, but in the end you and others will be saved from destruction. It is not popular to say no or to tell someone to stop doing wrong. Even Jesus wasn't popular for this, but He pleased God, not people. In the end, He saved humanity! People need to hear what they don't want to hear for their own good. Speak the truth always in love!

Agape always protects, always trusts, and always hopes. Protect all from being destroyed by the enemy in prayer and physically where possible. Trust that God is able to perfect all that concerns you and everyone in their lives and relationships. Never lose hope; always hope for the best every day, no matter what the situation.

Put on Love as a spiritual armor and never take off any part of the full armor of AGAPE by God's grace. Agape never fails! It is greater than faith and hope. You can have the faith of Christ, but without agape, you are nothing. Agape is what tests our works on earth.

"Each one's work will become clear; for the Day will declare it, because it will be revealed by fire; and the fire will test each one's work, of what sort it is. If anyone's work which he has built on it endures, he will receive a reward" (1 Cor. 3:13–14).

God's love gave us His Son and His Spirit. Christ's agape gave us His life. Agape gives without a guaranteed return. It's for the other person's good. God would still have been God even if He chose to destroy the whole earth instead of sacrificing His Son. However, because of agape, He chose the tough, selfless act of agape, and we, too, MUST build on this foundation, or our works will be burned if they are not done in agape. Jesus is the foundation of the Kingdom we are building, and His foundation is love.

Whatever you do, do you do it in agape, or do you do it for money, self-gratification or to impress people? Husbands, do you think saying you are sorry to your wife is stooping too low, and you embrace the foolish pride, which God hates, saying "I'm a man?" The truth is, Christ went down for His bride; His bride submits to Him willingly out of this agape. Agape comes first before submission. It is easy to submit to someone who loves you. Test every action or work you do in agape. If we do this, the world will want this love. Christ showed us the example of love which we all must follow. True agape never ends! It is a choice—never a feeling.

"Let everything you do be done in love [motivated and inspired by God's love for us]" (1 Cor. 16:14 AMP).

God's love is unconditional. God has never placed any condition to His love, but His blessings, His extra blessings, are conditional. God gives blessings like life, air, sun, rain, etc., to both good and bad people, but special blessings like divine protection, favor, wisdom, peace, ability to be the head and not the tail, and above and not beneath, promotion and influence, glory, are extra blessings given to His obedient children. He does just like a good parent would.

A good parent loves his or her children unconditionally and gives them blessings like food, shelter, and clothing, education, the basic stuff, but has conditions set for children to get extra treats or rewards when they obey or do well in school. God loves all people, even the ones who are going to hell now as we speak and the ones who hate Him. He doesn't give them extra rewards as He would give to His obedient children. He still loves them as they make the wrong choices and corrects them over and over as a good parent would. God's love is a constant, but His extra blessings are not.

> Pay to all what is due: tax to whom tax *is due*, customs to whom customs, respect to whom respect, honor to whom honor. Owe nothing to anyone except to love *and* seek the best for one another; for he who [unselfishly] loves his neighbor has fulfilled the [essence of the] law [relating to one's fellowman]. The commandments, "You shall not commit adultery, you shall not murder, you shall not steal, you shall not covet," and any other commandment are summed up in this statement: "You shall love your neighbor as yourself." Love does no wrong to a neighbor [it never hurts anyone]. Therefore [unselfish] love is the fulfillment of the Law. (Rom. 13:7–10 AMP)

"Yet in all these things we are more than conquerors through him who loved us. For I am persuaded that neither death nor life nor angels nor principalities nor powers nor things present nor things to come, nor height nor depth nor any other created thing, shall be able to separate us from the love of God which is in Christ Jesus our Lord" (Rom. 8:37–39).

"Behold what manner of love the father has bestowed on us that we should be called children of God! Therefore the world does not know us, because it did not know Him" (1 John 3:1).

Love is the greatest commandment. No sacrifice is greater than love because the greatest sacrifice was Love.

> One of the scribes came, and heard them questioning together. Knowing that he had answered them well, asked him, "Which commandment is the greatest of all?" Jesus answered, "The greatest is, 'Hear, Israel, the Lord our God, the Lord is one: you shall love the Lord your God with all your heart, and with all

your soul, and with all your mind, and with all your strength.' This is the first commandment. The second is like this, 'You shall love your neighbor as yourself.' There is no other commandment greater than these." The scribe said to him, "Truly, teacher, you have said well that he is one, and there is none other but he, and to love him with all the heart, and with all the understanding, with all the soul, and with all the strength, and to love his neighbor as himself, is more important than all whole burnt offerings and sacrifices." When Jesus saw that he answered wisely, he said to him, "You are not far from God's Kingdom." No one dared ask him any question after that. (Mark 12:28–34 WEB)

By this the children of God and the children of the devil are clearly identified: anyone who does not practice righteousness [who does not seek God's will in thought, action, and purpose] is not of God, nor is the one who does not [unselfishly] love his [believing] brother. For this is the message which you [believers] have heard from the beginning [of your relationship with Christ], that we should [unselfishly] love *and* seek the best for one another. (1 John 3:10–11 AMP).

"A new commandment I give to you, that you love one another; as I have loved you, that you also love one another. By this all will know that you are My disciples, if you have love for one another" (John 13:34–35).

God-Given Task (Work)	VS People-Given Task (Job)
Eternal reward from God	Temporary reward from people
Pleases God	Pleases people
Eternity driven	Reward (monetary) and feelings driven
Permanent, cannot retire or be fired	Temporary, can retire or be fired
Controlled by God	Controlled by people
Lasts forever	Lasts a few years
Too big for people, need God to succeed	People can succeed by themselves.
It is perfect and cannot be corrected.	It is flawed and always needs improvement.
It draws people to God.	It draws people to people.
It gives God the glory.	It gives people the glory.
It requires persistent prayer and submission.	It only needs hard work and determination.
It is a battle won in the spirit, drawing people unto God.	It is a battle in the flesh: who will be better than the other or have a better title than the other.
It causes people to fear God and revere Him.	It causes people to fear and reverence people.
It does not make sense to people.	It makes perfect sense to people.

It causes people to ridicule you.	It causes people to admire you.
It increases the fear of God on earth.	It increases the fear of people on earth.
It has great opposition from people.	It has little or no opposition from people.
It requires total trust in God's résumé and title—who He is, not who you are.	It needs trust in the system and in people's résumé and titles of honor given by people.
You never clock in or out. It is a lifestyle.	You clock in and out. It is not a lifestyle, but a job.
Lonely, friends easily lost	Makes you popular with many "friends"
Puts God first and pleases God	Puts people first and pleases people
Your flawed history/background check Works for you not against you because the blood of Jesus makes it clean. It is used in the Kingdom to strengthen others.	Your flawed background check works against you and disqualifies you from hire because no one can take it away. It is never useful in the world system.

Looking at Ecclesiastes 3:9–15, we see these pointers of the God-given assignment:

- Must bring profit to the Kingdom of God (verse 9)
- Was assigned before creation of the earth (verse 10)
- There is an appointed time when God makes it beautiful (verse 11).
- It lasts throughout all eternity (verse 11).

- It is done with eternity in our hearts, not just in our mind (verse 11).
- It is not perceived by people, but it is revealed to us by God steps by step because God knows the end from the beginning (verse 11.)
- Requires holiness and living right with God, rejoicing always even in our trials and temptations and doing good in God's eyes (verse 12)
- God rewards us here on earth and eternally too; we must therefore enjoy the fruits of our labor because it is God's gift to us (verse 13).
- It lasts FOREVER; nothing can be added to it or taken away from it because God is perfect, and so is His assignment (verse 14).
- God perfects His assignment so that people can be drawn to Him in reverence and fear (verse 14).
- The assignment was there before creation; it has already been made manifest in the spirit even before we began doing it (verse 15).
- We shall answer to God about what we have done in the past according to the assignment He has given us. (Verse 15).

Not Knowing Your Assignment on Earth Is Ignorance

Just because you don't know what your assignment on earth is doesn't mean you will not give account for it. Even the law of the land does not excuse your ignorance of the law. Someone once said, "Ignorance is no defense."

Take the hypothetical example that you have been hired to work in a place, and you do not know which department you are to report to, or which hours you are scheduled to work because you were ignorant and did not ask. If you show up to any department and start working, even if you work overtime, in the end you will be counted absent and will not get paid. You will be termed as a no-call no-show and may be fired even though according to you, you were faithful in your work. In reality, you worked for nothing. Your work never counted because your scheduled assignment was left undone.

One time a caregiver in the hospital where I supervised clocked in and went to work on a unit she was not assigned to. The unit that she was supposed to report to was short of a caregiver. We saw that she had clocked in; but we just could not locate her because she did not report to her assigned area of duty. She was ignorant of her assignment, so I told the staffing person to give me her timesheet so that when she came to clock out, she would have to report to me so as to know where she had been all night.

When she came to clock out, I remembered seeing her working from my rounds in the units but did not know who she was. She said she was new and assumed that she had reported to the right unit because they accepted her and gave her an assignment. The unit charge RN was wrong; she should have called me to verify her assigned unit because she was never assigned to them in the first place. I told her that the only reason she was excused for now was because I saw her working and she was new; otherwise, next time she would get in trouble and would be considered a no-show.

On the other hand, in God's Kingdom, if you are busy doing an assignment that you were not assigned to do while your assignment is left undone, you will not be compensated or rewarded because your reward is attached to your assignment. Your reward in heaven and earth is wrapped in your God-given assignment. Some of us cry to God and pray for God to help us and provide for us, but God already has. The day He created you for your assignment, He provided you with all you need for life and godliness.

His Word says your gift will make room for you (Prov. 18:16), not your résumé or you knowing someone in a high position. His Word also says that a person who excels in his work will stand before kings, not mere people (Prov. 22:29). This is so true. No one can fire you from your GGT on earth. For example, you cannot fire a fish from swimming or a bird from flying or a lion from roaring. Your gift and talent is for the Kingdom, not for your use whenever you feel like it or you need it; it belongs to God. He is the King.

Another example is; if you did not see a stop sign and you drove right past it, does that mean that you will not get a ticket or cause an accident? Ofcourse not! Ignorance is no defense with people or with God. Remember, people of God perish or are destroyed for lack of knowledge because they have refused knowledge (Hosea 4:6). If you ask, you will know the right thing to do. God will reveal to you your assignment for every season in your life; from glory to glory. God can adjust your assignment anytime as He sees fit. We must therefore be willing and flexible with God. Constant inquiry of His will is a MUST for us to be successful in our GGT. Do not reject knowledge and perish. Ask God and He will gladly reveal your assignment to you. This is because He wants you to accomplish your assignment successfully for the sake of His Kingdom and for His glory.

When you do not step up to your assignment, you are holding up someone else. "How?" you ask. This is like building. The person installing windows cannot install them before the wall is built. If your task was building the wall, you are holding up the painter, the person installing the window, the roofer and the interior designer, etc. It is a chain reaction. Do not be the one holding up God's Kingdom; rather, be the one who gets done with your task, one who encourages and helps others to step up into their GGT. Be the one who is willing to take up extra task for the sake of the kingdom.

Kathryn Kuhlman, a great woman of God, said she was not the first choice for God in her ministry. She was put in place of other men who rejected the calling of God. God used her to work mighty signs and wonders because she said "YES" to Jesus, "YES", to His Spirit. If you don't step up, God will get another to take your place. You can never frustrate God's agenda.

CHAPTER 18
True Worship and Final Prayer

Offer your body to God daily as a true act of worship.

"THEREFORE I URGE YOU, BROTHERS and sisters, by the mercies of God, to present your bodies [dedicating all of yourselves, set apart] as a living sacrifice, holy and well-pleasing to God, which is your rational (logical, intelligent) act of worship" (Rom. 12:1 AMP).

True worship is giving yourself to God for His use. Waking up in the morning and reporting to duty, receiving your assignment from God and enthusiastically in love and selflessness carrying it out by His grace.

Because we do not belong to ourselves and we did not create ourselves, we need to know that we cannot do anything on earth without God's help. Also, God will not do anything on earth without us. He can, but He will not. God can stop all the evil on earth but He will not do it without us praying and standing in the gap. He controls heaven but the earth He has given the dominion to man. In this I mean that we are the legal passage for God on earth. Jesus said that a body was created for Him to do God's will. In the same way, a body was created for us to do God's will, not our own will. Jesus said that He came to fulfill what was written about Him. We also must fulfill what God wrote about us in the assignment He gave us. Remember, you are a spirit in a body, and that is why when your spirit is taken away, the body is useless. We therefore must feed the spirit that it may control fully the body it lives in. We cannot let the body dictate what we should do and feel.

We were not created to move by feelings but by our free will, our choices. That is why God does not excuse sin because most sin is out of feeling or lack of self-control rather than choice. This is as a result of not feeding the spirit, so the soul and emotion is in control of the person. If God was a "soulish" being, we would all be dead if He paid us back by the way we make Him feel. But because God is not driven by His emotions but by His choices, He chooses to be slow to anger, merciful, and abounding in love. He chose to give us His only begotten Son and allowed Him to die brutally without His feelings or emotions involved even when His only baby, Jesus Christ, cried out to Him, begging Him to let the cup of suffering pass. God was driven by the perfect profit and end result to restore all people to Him and to give His Son the greatest promotion and name.

The reason Jesus qualifies as the Great High Priest forever is because He was a MAN who walked where we walked, had feelings and emotions, and was tempted just as we are, yet was without sin. He is now able to sympathize with us and our weakness, and tell God about it from human perspective and His experience. God never chose angels to be high priests because they would not sympathize or relate with our struggles and feelings. You cannot be a good advocate for someone you cannot understand, relate to, or sympathize with. The reason Aaron was a perfect great high priest for the Israelites was because he had led people into idol worship, and he himself needed forgiveness, and he was forgiven. He had a history of making mistakes, and so he was not going to condemn or judge the people who came to him for prayer; rather, he would sympathize with them and genuinely with sincerity groan in prayer to God for their forgiveness.

For God to operate on earth, man must give Him permission. That is why it is written in Psalm 115:16 NLT, "The heavens belong to the Lord, but he has given the earth to all humanity."

That is where prayer comes in. Prayer is authorizing God to perform His Word on earth. Prayer is returning God's Word to Him for accomplishment. I tell my children that if they have a 4.0 GPA and above throughout the year, I will buy them whatever they ask for within reasonable limits. They always get 4.0 GPA and above by God's grace and all they do is speak back the word I spoke to them, bringing me to remembrance and it is done! They just need to hold me accountable to my word and say to me what I said to them in the beginning of the year. In the same way, if you want God to fulfill His Word to you, keep your end of the deal, and then bring Him to remembrance. Speak back His Word to Him, and He shall do it!

"*Put Me in remembrance*; Let us contend together; State your case, that you may be acquitted" (Isa. 43:26; italics added).

"For as the rain comes down, and the snow from heaven, And do not return there, But water the earth, And make it bring forth and bud, That it may give seed to the sower And bread to the eater, So shall My word be that goes forth from My mouth; It shall not return to Me void, But it shall accomplish what I please, And it shall prosper in the thing for which I sent it. God's word never fails, He honors His word over His name! He will not send the rain and not cause plants to grow, as sure as the rain does its work, so does God's word do its work" (Isa. 55:10–11 NLT).

Not my will but Your will be done.

When Jesus lived on earth, He operated on this one principle and statement: He made it clear over and over again that He was sent to do the will of His Father. He made it clear that He had no business looking for glory or a good name, but on glorifying God the Father and presenting His perfect love and plan, demonstrating His love to all humanity through His only begotten Son, Jesus Christ.

People sometimes say how unfair God is, which is true, because nowhere in the Bible do we read of God being or playing fair. He is "a just God"—not "a fair God." He was not fair when it came to His Son. He sacrificed His only Son for the sins of others. It would have been fair for us to pay for our own sins instead of one who never sinned to pay for our sins.

Fair, according to Merriam Webster dictionary means, "treating people in a way that does not favor some over others and agreeing with what is *thought to be right* or acceptable." while just means "treating people in a way that is considered *morally right* and agreeing with what is considered morally right or good"

'Fair' does not operate in righteousness but 'just' does, God is righteous and that is why He is not fair. He is a just God.

When Jesus Christ lived a holy and sacrificial life, He died to self and to His desires and was alive only to His Father's will. He desired to do many things just like we do, but He remembered that this was not His mission. He did not send Himself to earth, nor did He ask the Father to make a body for Him so He could come to do His own will on earth. Jesus acted purely out of total obedience to His Father's will and calling. He had a great passion for His assignment. He was out to please God, not people.

In John 2:13-22 we see that the great temple of God was being used for everything else but God's glory. The temple then was a building, which Jesus said He would destroy and build it again in three days. Jesus meant that His death and Resurrection would set us free from worshipping in a building; rather, we would be sanctified and reborn to house God in us as His original plan was. In other words, He changed the sacrifices from the copy to the real temple we were created to be, our bodies. Paul reminds us of this as he reminded the Corinthians.

1 Corinthians 6:19 AMP: "Do you not know that your body is a temple of the Holy Spirit who is within you, whom you have [received as a gift] from God, and that you are not your own [property]?"

The zeal to keep this temple holy must consume us like it did Christ in John 2:16–22. He protected the temple in public and cleaned it out and drove out those that came in to defile it. Whose temple are you? The Spirit of God or the spirit of the devil? Spirits only operate legally on earth through a body, a temple. Be God's temple. What do you eat, drink, and allow to come in your mind from what you see or hear? What do you allow on your body which is the temple of God? We will give account to God for what we did with the temple He created for us to do His will.

"Do not cut your bodies for the dead, and *do not mark your skin with tattoos*. I am the Lord. (Leviticus 19:28 NLT; italics added)

"For I have come down from heaven *to do the will of God who sent me, not to do my own will*. And this is the will of God, that I should not lose even one of all those he has given me, but that I should raise them up at the last day. For it is my Father's will that all who see his Son and believe in him should have eternal life. I will raise them up at the last day" (John 6:38–40 NLT; italics added).

"So Jesus said, 'When you have lifted up the Son of Man on the cross, then you will understand that I am he. *I do nothing on my own but say only what the Father taught me*. And the one who sent me is with me—he has not deserted me. For *I always do what pleases him*'" (John 8:28–29 NLT; italics added).

"Father, if you are willing, please take this cup of suffering away from me. *Yet I want your will to be done, not mine*" (Luke 22:42 NLT; italics added).

Narrow is the way.

Jesus said in Matthew 7:13–14, 21 NLT
"You can enter God's Kingdom only through the narrow gate. The highway to hell is broad, and its gate is wide for the many who choose that way. But the gateway to life is very narrow, and the road is difficult, and only a few ever find it. Not everyone who calls out to me, 'Lord! Lord!' will enter the Kingdom of heaven. Only those who actually do the will of my Father in heaven will enter."

There is a reward for those who do their God-given assignment, which is the will of God the Father. Jesus stuck to His assignment, and now He is exalted and given the name that is above every other name.

Did Jesus face challenges in His assignment? Did He walk alone most times? Was He rejected by people? Was He ridiculed and mocked? Was His own family against Him and embarrassed by Him? Did His own brothers not believe in Him? Did His close friend deny Him when He was in trouble? Did His friends not help Him to pray when He needed their prayers most? Did all His friends leave Him and forsake Him? Did His disciple, who followed Him closely, steal from Him and betray Him? Did the people for whom He raised their dead, healed their sick, and set them free from evil spirits crucify Him? Did the same people He fed and had more than enough to eat with left overs, the same ones who wanted to make Him their King turn against Him?

Was He lied to and cheated on? Was He accused falsely and punished for sin He never committed? Did He get in trouble for speaking the truth and people tried to stone Him? Was He called names? Was His road lonely? Was it full of sacrifice? Was it full of opposition? Was

He tempted and tried? Was He wrongly perceived? Was He wrongly judged by people? Did He forgive His haters and those who sinned or offended Him? Did He experience loss? Pain? Sorrow? Death of a loved one? Did He cry? Did He bleed? Did he feel betrayed, discouraged, and misunderstood? Did he feel like bailing out on His assignment when He asked His Father to take away the cup of suffering from Him? Did He not yield to the will of the Father when He said, "Not My will but Your will be done?" Did He leave His hometown and His family to do the will of God His Father? Did He overcome evil with good?

Yes! And not only did He leave His earthly family but His heavenly family and glory, and He chose His Father's will over His own will or anyone else's.

Did Jesus hit back, or repay the evil He got with evil? Did He let evil overcome Him? Did He fight against people? Did He let the bad done to Him affect His assignment? Did He take offense or harbor unforgiveness in His heart? Did he get distracted or diverted from His assignment? Did hate His haters? Did He bail out on His assignment? Did He enjoy suffering and His lonely life?

No! Jesus Christ endured all this to profit God's Kingdom.

It was not easy for Christ, but He chose to please the Father rather than Himself or people. He chose the lonely route rather than the popular route. Christ chose the will of the Father, which was complex and did not make sense to many. He was most of the time alone; even His own disciples left Him. He was surrounded by many people who wanted to criticize and destroy Him and some who only wanted something from Him. He was hardly ever served by anyone; He was a servant to all, even though in reality He was the master of all. He knew the power He had, and instead of using this power to protect his life, He chose to use His power to lay down His life for us, sinners, people who never deserved it. He used His power to protect us. What a great husband He is for His church. A great husband, a strong man, is one who uses his power and strength not to lord it over his wife and children, but to protect them.

The difference between a country that succeeds and thrives and one that doesn't is in its leaders. Those leaders who are there to be served destroy a country, but those who are there to serve, build a country. Which of these are you?

No wonder Jesus said in Luke 9:23 (AMP), "And He was saying to them all, 'If anyone wishes to follow Me [as My disciple], he must deny himself [set aside selfish interests], and take up his cross daily [expressing a willingness to endure whatever may come] and follow Me [believing in Me, conforming to My example in living and, if need be, suffering or perhaps dying because of faith in Me].'"

"Sitting down [to teach], He called the twelve [disciples] and said to them, 'If anyone wants to be first, he must be last of all [in importance] and a servant of all'" (Mark 9:35 AMP).

Solomon was rewarded greatly because He put God's Kingdom first instead of his own desires. After offering to God a great sacrifice....see what happened to him.

> Solomon went up there to the bronze altar before Yahweh, which was at the Tent of Meeting, and offered one thousand burnt offerings on it. In that night God appeared to Solomon, and said to him, "Ask what I shall give you." Solomon said to God, "You have shown great loving kindness to David my father, and have made me king in his place. Now, Yahweh God, let your promise to David my father be established; for you have made me king over a people like the dust of the earth in multitude. Now give me wisdom and knowledge, that I may go out and come in before this people; for who can judge this your people, that is so great?" God said to Solomon, "Because this was in your heart, and you have not asked riches, wealth, or honor, nor the life of those who hate you, neither yet have asked long life; but have asked wisdom and knowledge for yourself, that you may judge my people, over whom I have made you king: wisdom and knowledge is granted to you. I will give you riches, wealth, and honor, such as none

of the kings have had who have been before you; neither shall any after you have the like." (2 Chronicles 1:6-12 WEB; italics added)

King Solomon asked to be empowered to do His God-given task. He desired to please God and to succeed in his assignment from deep down his heart. What about you? What do you pray for and desire from your heart? Do you, like Solomon burn with the zeal to please God and give Him your very best? Or are you only interested in what you will gain from your GGT? Is it about your glory or is it about God's glory? Does a fire burn within you making you zealous to do what you were created to do in EXCELLENCE? What are you willing to give God as a sacrifice? He wants your all. If God asked you the same question He asked king Solomon, what would your answer be from your heart? Once you give God your all, He will say to you, "Ask what I shall give to you."

We all enjoy eating some good breakfast, at least I do. I heard someone explain the concept of dedication and sacrifice very well using breakfast. They asked, between a chicken and a pig, which animal is more dedicated to you for breakfast? Is it the chicken, who lays eggs and continues living its life or the pig who gives up its life for you to enjoy its bacon, sausage and ham? Of course the pig is more dedicated to you. It dies for you to be filled. The chicken offers its services but continues with its own life. We as followers of Christ either have chicken dedication, i.e. go to church, play religion, but our lives are our own, we live as we please but offer God sacrifices and service. Or pig dedication, die to self and live only for Christ. Those with pig-like dedication crucify their flesh and offer their bodies as a living sacrifice holy and pleasing to God. They fill God's appetite more than the chicken-like dedicated Christians do. They go all out for God like the pig does. When a pig gets dirty it rolls on the mud with all its strength, when it eats it goes all out, when it gives it gives its all, its life, to feed us a simple meal, breakfast.

When I think about it, a chicken may die for lunch or dinner, a cow too will give you milk for breakfast but the chicken and the cow may die for lunch or dinner, but not for breakfast. *A pig will die for you from breakfast, lunch and dinner, all day long.* Are we Christians who give ourselves fully to God at all times or do we only do it in public but our private lives are full of filth and lack of God's love? Do we imitate Christ only when others are looking or at all times? Or do we do it only when it is convenient or always? Even in the simplest act of showing love and respect in your own home and be Jesus to your spouse and Children? How much are you dedicated as Christ's disciple?

We must lose our lives to gain eternal life. We must fully dedicate all we are to God, and allow nothing or no one to come between us and God. We must declare like the apostle Paul did in Galatians 2:20 that I no longer live but Christ who lives in me! When we do that, then we will start living! That is when we fill God's appetite. Like Jesus was asking for water from the Samaritan woman at the well because He was thirsty; thirsty for true worship, for relationship, for people to submit to God and do His will. God is looking for worshippers, He is hungry and thirsty for true worshippers who will die to self and live only for Him ALL THE TIME.

Choose Your Friends

Who Do You Hang Out With?

Find someone who challenges you to be all that God created you to be.

Blessed [fortunate, prosperous, and favored by God] is the man who does not walk in the counsel of the wicked [following their advice and example], nor stand in the path of sinners, nor sit [down to rest] in the seat of scoffers (ridiculers). But his delight is in the law of the Lord, and on His law [His precepts and teachings] he [habitually] meditates day and night. And he will be like a tree *firmly* planted [and fed] by streams of water, Which yields its fruit in its season; Its leaf does not wither; And in whatever he does, he prospers [and comes to maturity]. The wicked [those who live in disobedience to God's law] are not so, But they are like the chaff [worthless and without substance] which the wind blows away. Therefore the wicked will not stand [unpunished] in the judgment, nor sinners in the assembly of the righteous. For the Lord knows *and* fully approves the way of the righteous, but the way of the wicked shall perish. (Ps. 1 AMP; italics added)

Allow God to pick your friends for you. Involve Him in your social life and you will succeed. Once a prophet said to me that God created me to be like a balloon that goes so high but there are many people around me who are holding me down. These people were my friends. He said that God was going to cut them out from my life to allow me to soar very high. It happened as he said. It was painful because I tried to keep them but because I wanted God more, I had to let go. When God tells you to get out and separate yourself for His sake, please obey Him without any hesitation. Do not hold on to your past and your friendships. If you try to keep your life you will lose it but if you lose your life for Christ's sake, meaning, letting go and trusting God, you will preserve it. Remember Lot's wife! Get out and don't look back, trust God He's right. He has your best interest at heart.

Luke 17:32-33 AMP

"Remember [what happened to] Lot's wife [when she looked back]! Whoever seeks to save his life will [eventually] lose it [through death], and whoever loses his life [in this world] will keep it [from the consequences of sin and separation from God]."

My Story:

One day my husband took me for a hike up some hills. As we climbed higher, it got harder and quieter. It was quiet because many people were left behind. The higher we went, the colder it became. The air was fresher the higher we got. I tried to quit and talk my husband into going back before we got to the top, but since he had gone there before, he knew how beautiful it was and wanted to share this experience with me. My husband encouraged me, and we went higher and higher as he held my hand.

When we got to the top, the view was extremely amazing! Breathe taking! We could see very far, the beautiful lake and the whole city was visible! It was a sight to behold. In the midst of the summer heat, there was a real cool breeze. The Holy Spirit told me that in the same way, the higher we go in God, the crowd will be left behind, and not many will be there to cheer you up. It sure gets lonely, but your sight gets clearer, and what a sight to behold of God's view! In this high place, you breathe better and it is much cooler in the midst of the heat of life. God's presence is made manifest and you see what others do not see. Eagles rise above the storm where not many birds get to go. Here, they experience peace and tranquility in the midst of the storm because they rise above the stormy clouds.

If my husband and I had decided to stay down, our sight would be limited to the things around us that create a lot of noise and pollution. Our sight would be blocked by many buildings and we would not have seen much. But because we decided to do the unpopular, we saw and experienced the uncommon. We saw a lot at once and appreciated the beauty of the city we lived in. Beloved, dare to go higher in Christ, dare to do the unpopular and the uncommon, dare to go through the hard and narrow way. God is there to cheer you and most times, He will send someone who has been there to encourage you to go higher. Dare to see through God's eyes!

Choose your friendships, and surround yourself with people who are God-task oriented, who know who they are in God and what they have been sent on earth to do, and who are actually doing it!

Choose your literature, your movies, your TV programs, your music, your social media, what you do daily, and allow them to counsel you, knowing they will affect your destiny. Psalm 1 includes all these, not just human friendships. Be careful to account for your life. Remember, we are here for a season, but eternity is forever. Don't fill your spare time with junk, fill it with things that feed and mature your spirit for your GGT.

We shall give account for all we do here on earth, including how we spend our time. Just as when you go to work you are held accountable for the hours you are there and your breaks are timed. The employer gets all they can get from you to run a successful business. God, too, is holding you accountable for your time, and you will be rewarded according to how you use it—to build the Kingdom, to destroy the Kingdom or to stagnate it. With your earthly employer, if you sleep on your job, you will be fired without question, what if you sleep on your GGT? If an ordinary man is serious about the tasks which they assign you, how much more is God serious about His tasks which He has assigned us to perform?

Just as we have yearly evaluations on our progress at work, what is your evaluation in heaven for your work? Have you been a no-call no-show? Late to work, early to leave, or giving an unsatisfactory performance? Sleeping on the job or just doing enough to get by? Or are you always on time and working overtime as needed? Do you go way above and beyond your call of duty even when it goes unnoticed? Do you arrive there early and leave later than everyone else? Are you the good and faithful servant? May God help us to number our days that we may gain a wise heart!

God has a complaint against this generation as He had in the past.

Has a nation [ever] changed gods Even though they were not gods [but merely man-made objects]? But My people have exchanged their Glory (the true God) for that [man-made idol] which does not benefit [them]. "Be appalled, O heavens, at this; be shocked and shudder with horror [at the behavior of the people]," says the Lord. "For My people have committed two evils: *They have abandoned (rejected) Me, The fountain of living water, and they have carved out their own cisterns, Broken cisterns that cannot hold water.* Is Israel a servant? Is he a slave by birth? Why has he become a captive and a prey?" (Jer. 2:11–14 AMP; italics added)

Most of us have become entangled with the cares of this world; we are more concerned with what we need rather than what the Kingdom of God needs. We take the assignments given to us by fellow people with more seriousness than what God has given us. We will never get to work late, and we work around our business and work schedules, but when it comes to doing our God-given tasks, we put it on hold until we make more money or until we get older or until we enjoy life more with our friends, and then if we have any time left, we do a little of our God-given task. We do not grow our spirits; we unwind with things that do not grow us. Instead, we feed the flesh more than the spirit with movies, phone calls, T.V. or radio shows that do not benefit us. I learned that I would rather sleep and rest my body than sit and give my two or three hours to a movie or TV show or telephone conversation that will not help me succeed in my God-given assignment.

Remember, we have angels taking account of what we do and how much we accomplish of our assignments. We must be heaven and eternity driven, not flesh and earthly driven. Jesus stayed on task, worked continually, often withdrew himself to pray, and He finished His assignment in three years! Now this is working and staying on task day and night: all He did and spoke was from God; nothing was written or spoken out of His own agenda or selfishness. He came to earth to work with and for His Father, not for Himself.

Likewise, we must wake up and realize we are here for our Father, not for us or other people. Imagine if every word you spoke and action you did, including those done behind closed doors, were written down—how would you like it if the whole world read it? Would you like people to follow your example? Jesus Christ gave us the example! Do only what you see God doing; say only what you hear God saying. How is this possible? How do you do what someone else is doing and speak what they are speaking? By spending a lot of time with them! Spend all of your time with God, dwell in His presence, and you will be successful like Christ! Let God dwell in you, and He will do His work through you, His faithful vessel.

"Jesus answered, 'If anyone [really] loves Me, he will keep My word (teaching); and My Father will love him, and We will come to him and make Our dwelling place with him. One who does not [really] love Me does not keep My words. And the word (teaching) which you hear is not Mine, but is the Father's who sent Me'" (John 14:23–24 AMP).

God wants us to house Him so He may accomplish His will on earth. When His Kingdom comes in us, His will, the will of our Lord, will be done on earth as it is in heaven. Remember Jesus said that the Kingdom of God is within us in Luke 17:20–21.

Judgment for Living Your Will and Not God's Will on Earth

> My hands have made both heaven and earth; they and everything in them are mine. I, the Lord, have spoken! I will bless those who have humble and contrite hearts, who tremble at my word. But those who choose their own ways—delighting in their detestable sins—will not have their offerings accepted. When such people sacrifice a bull, it is no more acceptable than a

human sacrifice. When they sacrifice a lamb, it's as though they had sacrificed a dog! When they bring an offering of grain, they might as well offer the blood of a pig. When they burn frankincense, it's as if they had blessed an idol. I will send them great trouble—all the things they feared. For when I called, they did not answer. When I spoke, they did not listen. They deliberately sinned before my very eyes and chose to do what they know I despise. (Isa. 66:2–4 NLT)

God has never been and will never be pleased with sacrifices without obedience. Some people think that if they give their money to the poor and widows and go to church religiously, they are keeping all religious laws. This does not please God if obedience to His will and assignment is not observed. The sacrifices are detestable to God as above. God is looking for people who will go where He sends them, who will do what He wants, and who obey Him and lay down their lives for Him. Sacrifices He did not desire, but He desires a body to do His will on earth! This is a living sacrifice, holy and pleasing to Him. This is real WORSHIP!

After This Life in Heaven...

"All humanity will come to worship me from week to week and from month to month. And as they go out, *they will see the dead bodies of those who have rebelled against me. For the worms that devour them will never die, and the fire that burns them will never go out.* All who pass by will view them with utter horror" (Isa. 66:23–24 NLT; italics added).

Disobedience and rebellion to God leads to eternal death, just as obedience and submission to God leads to eternal life. We have free will to choose what we want to do. To choose life or death. We saw earlier that we can never be unyoked, or free of leadership. We are either on the devil's side or we are on the Lord's side. There is no demilitarized zone in the spirit. You are either a slave to sin or a slave to righteousness, yoked to Christ or yoked to the devil. Which one do you choose? Each choice has consequences.

Come-Back Call

"What makes you think I want all your sacrifices?" says the Lord. "I am sick of your burnt offerings of rams and the fat of fattened cattle. I get no pleasure from the blood of bulls and lambs and goats. When you come to worship me, who asked you to parade through my courts with all your ceremony? Stop bringing me your meaningless gifts; the incense of your offerings disgusts me! As for your celebrations of the new moon and the Sabbath and your special days for fasting—they are all sinful and false. I want no more of your pious meetings. "I hate your new moon celebrations and your annual festivals. They are a burden to me. I cannot stand them! When you lift up your hands in prayer, I will not look. Though you offer many prayers, I will not listen, for your hands are covered with the blood of innocent victims. *Wash yourselves and be clean! Get your sins out of my sight. Give up your evil ways. Learn to do good. Seek justice. Help the oppressed. Defend the cause of orphans. Fight for the rights of widows.* "Come now, let's settle this," says the Lord. *"Though your sins are like scarlet, I will make them as white as snow. Though they are red like crimson, I will make them as white as wool. If you will only obey me, you will have plenty to eat. But if you turn away and refuse to listen, you will be devoured by the sword of your enemies. I, the Lord, have spoken!"* (Isa. 1:11–20 NLT; italics added).

God desires obedience more than sacrifice. He is ready and willing to make a fresh start with us if we turn away from wickedness and obey Him. We must return to the basics at the feet of Jesus, we must go back to the message of the cross. Go back to what we know is truth from the Word of God before we accepted all the man-made rules that defy the Word of God. The Word of God is never up for debate because the kingdom of God is not democratic. Kings make the laws and those working for the king enforce the laws in the land. We live in democratic countries on earth but we are from God's Kingdom and we must differentiate the two. We must not compromise, rather we must enforce the kingdom of God on earth as it is in heaven. We are God's signet ring on earth, we enforce the King's authority on earth confidently because we know whose we are and the kingdom we represent.

> Thus says the Lord, "Stand by the roads and look; ask for the ancient paths, Where the good way is; then walk in it, and you will find rest for your souls."
> But they said, "We will not walk in it!" "I have set watchmen (prophets) over you, Saying, 'Listen and pay attention to the [warning] sound of the trumpet!'" But they said, "We will not listen." "Therefore hear, O [Gentile] nations, and see, O congregation, what [vengeful act] is to be done to them. "Hear, O earth: behold, I am bringing disaster on this people, the fruit of their schemes, because they have not listened and paid attention to My words, And as for My law, they have rejected it also." (Jer. 6:16–19 AMP).

There are consequences for disobedience. Let us follow God's Word; it is for our benefit, not His benefit. God will always be God, regardless of whether we obey Him or not. His commands give us protection, great benefits and blessings.

Reward for Your Obedience Despite Rejection from People

> Hear this message from the Lord, all you who tremble at his words: *"Your own people hate you and throw you out for being loyal to*

my name." "Let the Lord be honored!" they scoff. "Be joyful in him!" But they will be put to shame. What is all the commotion in the city? What is that terrible noise from the Temple? It is the voice of the Lord taking vengeance against his enemies. *"Before the birth pains even begin, Jerusalem gives birth to a son. Who has ever seen anything as strange as this? Who ever heard of such a thing? Has a nation ever been born in a single day? Has a country ever come forth in a mere moment? But by the time Jerusalem's birth pains begin, her children will be born. Would I ever bring this nation to the point of birth and then not deliver it?" asks the Lord. "No! I would never keep this nation from being born,"* says your God. This is what the Lord says: "I will give Jerusalem a river of peace and prosperity. The wealth of the nations will flow to her. Her children will be nursed at her breasts, carried in her arms, and held on her lap. I will comfort you there in Jerusalem as a mother comforts her child." When you see these things, your heart will rejoice. You will flourish like the grass! Everyone will see the Lord's hand of blessing on his servants—and his anger against his enemies. "And I will appoint some of them to be my priests and Levites. I, the Lord, have spoken! As surely as my new heavens and earth will remain, so will you always be my people, with a name that will never disappear," says the Lord. (Isa. 66:5–9, 12–14, 21–22 NLT; italics added)

God will bless you beyond measure and human comprehension and against earthly laws. He will give you supernatural prosperity and make you His own. He will personally protect you against all your enemies. Don't be afraid of human rejection and ridicule.

"Nevertheless, the firm foundation of God [which He has laid] stands [sure and unshaken despite attacks], bearing this seal: "The Lord knows those who are His," and, "Let everyone who names the name of the

Lord stand apart from wickedness *and* withdraw from wrongdoing." 2 Timothy 2:19 (AMP)

Not doing your GGT is sin. Heaven calls it wickedness. Remember the story of the servant who hid his talent instead of using it to multiply his master's riches and he was called a wicked servant in Matthew 25:26? If you hide your talent, GGT, instead of using it for God's Kingdom and glory, you are a wicked servant. Let us turn away from wickedness into righteousness by getting busy with our GGT. We must be about our Father's business like Christ was.

Final Prayer

FATHER, IN JESUS'S NAME, *I come to You with Awe and wonder of who You are. You are exalted in the highest place, magnificent, holy, glorious, faithful, awesome, almighty, King of Kings, Lord of Lords, everlasting Father, Sovereign God, wonderful way maker, worthy of all praise, glory and honor, more beautiful than any words can describe, or mind comprehend, words can't do justice to Your greatness and Your worth! I thank You so much for Jesus. Thank You for the finished work of the cross. Thank You for the blood of Jesus and the power of His Resurrection. Thank You for the gift of the Holy Spirit. Thank You for Your great love and kindness toward all humanity. Thank You for being patient with me and for giving me the power to become Your child, as I believe in Your only begotten Son Jesus Christ and accept the sacrifice He made on the cross. I forgive all those who have sinned against me with Your forgiveness, and I love them and my enemies with Your perfect love. Thank You for You Grace.*

Father, I pray that You forgive all my sins, cleanse me from all unrighteousness, create in me Your heart, and renew a right and new Spirit within me. Wash me with the precious blood of Jesus. I am sorry for not taking my body seriously as Your temple and for not doing Your will from the time You sent me to earth. I am willing to give up everything now for You. I give up my will for Your will, my ways for Your ways, and my thoughts for Your thoughts. I want to do Your will only. By Your power, I crucify my flesh and offer my body daily as a living sacrifice, holy and pleasing to Your sight as the true act of worship.

Lord, fill me with Your Holy Spirit and with the knowledge of Your will through all spiritual wisdom and understanding. Holy Spirit, reveal my assignment to me and help me fulfill it according to the Father's standards in

Jesus's name. Father, use me for Your glory. I evict all evil spirits that may have come in me from any sin committed by me, my parents, or my ancestors in past generations in Jesus's name. I disconnect my spirit, soul and body from them, and I connect my spirit, soul and body to Jesus Christ my Lord*. I break every generational curse by the blood of Jesus on the cross, where He became a curse so I would be blessed. I receive only what is from Christ. Holy Spirit, make my heart Your home, clean Your house in me, and purify me for Your use. I receive all the promises of God in Christ now with thanksgiving in Jesus's name.*

Like Christ, I choose to live a life of 'not my will but Your will be done'. Father, give me Your humility, patience and courage, equip me to enter into my assignment with Your boldness. Give me Your Spirits of understanding, knowledge, counsel, power, might, and the fear of the Lord*. May I, like Christ, delight in the spirit of the fear of the* Lord*. Let me be Your outfit on earth, yielded only to You and Your will. May I grow big and strong in wisdom and spirit and in favor with both You and people. Hide me in your secret place away from the scornful tongue. Hide me in Your shelter away from the plots of people. How great is Your goodness stored up for me because I fear and trust in You in the presence of many people. No weapon formed against me and my destiny and all that concerns me shall prosper, and every tongue that rises against me I condemn it in Jesus's name! May Psalm 91 be my portion and Psalm 35 be upon the evil one in Jesus's name! I love You Father. I love You Jesus. I love You, Holy Spirit. Thank You for hearing and answering my prayer. Teach me ALL Your ways. Show me ALL Your paths. Show me great and mighty things which I do not know in Jesus's name. I believe and I receive all these with thanksgiving and praise in Jesus's name, amen!*

Go to Work

Your Great Commission

The foundation, Jesus Christ, is already laid, waiting for you to build upon it!

"For no one can lay any foundation other than the one we already have—Jesus Christ" (1 Cor. 3:11 NLT).

Beloved, Christ cannot build your part of the Kingdom. You must do your part; do not delay others any longer. Step up into your God-given task so we can finish the work our Father God sent us to do, which He began in our LORD Jesus Christ. If you are not born again, go to the prayer under the topic "Salvation" in this book, pray it sincerely, and give your life to Christ. Then you can be reunited with your Creator, receive the right to be His child, become an heir to God's Kingdom and start building your part of the Kingdom. This Kingdom is only built on one foundation, and that is Jesus Christ.

If you have accepted Jesus Christ as your Lord and Savior but have been busy with the cares of this world, or you do not even know what you were created to do, there is hope. Pray the prayer in chapter 10 "the prayer" and believe it. Repent and get back on task because many people are waiting for you to step up and get back on task so that they can work and finish building their parts in God's Kingdom. Do not be the one holding others back because the punishment for this is great. We shall give account of what we have been doing on earth when we go back to God and this body goes back to dirt. Remember, you are a spirit whom God created a body for you to do His will, not your will. He did it so He can operate legally through you on earth for His glory, not your glory. Do not die full of gifts and talents that you did not use. Don't make the grave rich as many people have and are still doing. No more excuses! We must die empty like Jesus and proclaim of our God-given assignments that; "it is finished!" just like He did.

"Pay careful attention to your own work, for then you will get the satisfaction of a job well done, and you won't need to compare yourself to anyone else." Galatians 6:4 NLT

For those who are on task, keep up, be encouraged, and walk in humility and the fear of the Lord that God may be glorified every step of the way. Like Christ, be obsessed with giving God all the credit and the glory, for it is His Kingdom, and He is the only King. As you do this, beloved brothers and sisters, may the grace of our Lord Jesus Christ and the Love of God and the fellowship of the Holy Spirit be with you now and forevermore, in Jesus's name, amen!

Agape…

Notes

Chapter 2
Who are we?

Online Merriam-Webster's Learner's Dictionary

Chapter 5
Message

Online Merriam-Webster's Learner's Dictionary

Chapter 13
Portrait

(http://www.huffingtonpost.com/2013/10/21/jorge-rodriguez-gerada-girls-portrait-field_n_4136932.html.)

Chapter 14
Whom do you live for?

Merriam-Webster's Learner's Dictionary

Chapter 16
How to Stay on Task

The *Oxford English Dictionary*

Chapter 18
True Worship and Final prayer

Merriam-Webster's Learner's Dictionary